Clinical Social Work Practice

An Integrated Approach

FOURTH EDITION

Marlene G. Cooper
Fordham University

Joan Granucci Lesser
Smith College

Allyn & Bacon
Boston · Columbus Indianapolis New York San Francisco Upper Saddle River
Amsterdam Cape Town Dubai London Madrid Milan Munich Paris Montreal Toronto
Delhi Mexico City Sao Paulo Sydney Hong Kong Seoul Singapore Taipei Tokyo

Executive Editor: *Ashley Dodge*
Editorial Product Manager: *Carly Czech*
Senior Marketing Manager: *Wendy Albert*
Marketing Assistant: *Patrick M. Walsh/Shauna Fishweicher*
Production Manager: *Meghan DeMaio*
Editorial Production and Composition Service: *Joseph Malcolm/PreMediaGlobal*
Cover Designer: *Suzanne Behnke*
Cover Design: *Jupiterimages/Getty Images*
Printer/Bindery/Cover Printer: *Courier Companies*

Library of Congress Cataloging-in-Publication Data
Cooper, Marlene G.
Clinical social work practice : an integrated approach/Marlene G. Cooper, Joan Granucci Lesser.—4th ed.
p. cm.
Includes bibliographical references and index.
ISBN-13: 978-0-205-78728-9
ISBN-10: 0-205-78728-2
1. Psychiatric social work. I. Lesser, Joan Granucci, 1952- II. Title.
HV689.C65 2011
361.3'2—dc22

2010032943

10 9 8 7 6 5 4 3 2 1 CRS 14 13 12 11 10

Allyn & Bacon
is an imprint of

www.pearsonhighered.com

ISBN-10: 0-205-78728-2
ISBN-13: 978-0-205-78728-9

Contents

Preface ix

Acknowledgments xiii

1 ***An Integrated Approach to Clinical Practice*** ***1***

Theoretical Base for Clinical Social Work Practice ***1***

The Integrative Model ***2***

The Practice Class as Laboratory: Learning to Integrate 2
The Integrative Journal 2
Clinical Supervision: The Learning Alliance 8
Faculty Field Advisement 10
Practice Evaluation and Research 10

2 ***Key Issues in Clinical Practice*** ***12***

Brief Treatment ***12***

Research Perspectives 12
Models of Brief Treatment 13
The First Meeting 13
The Working Relationship 14
Mindfulness in the Therapeutic Relationship 14
Selection Criteria 15

Ethics and Boundaries ***15***

Sexual Relationships with Clients 15
Other Dual Relationships 16

The Suicidal Client ***17***

Guidelines for Assessing Suicide 17
Providing Safety 18
Child and Adolescent Suicide 20

Managed Care ***20***

Ethical Dilemmas under Managed Care 20

Opportunities under Managed Care 22
Coaching and Social Work 22
Confidentiality and Technology: HIPAA 23
Fee for Service 24
The Client in a System of Care 24
Spirituality and Religion 25
Social Work in a Global Economy 25

Therapist Self-Care and Self-Compassion 25

3 *The Clinical Interview: The Process of Assessment 28*

Beginning, Middle, and End Stages of Treatment 28
The First Meeting 28
Self-Awareness 29
Introductions 29
Why Is the Client Here? 30
Confidentiality 30
Answering Personal Questions 30

The Therapeutic Relationship 31
Transference and Countertransference 32
The Real Relationship and the Working Alliance 33
Resistance 33
Using These Concepts in Practice 34

Transtheoretical Model: The Stages of Change 34

The Middle Stage of Treatment—Moving to Contemplation, Preparation, and Action 39

The Ending Phase of Treatment 42

4 *The Psychosocial Study: The Product of Assessment 45*

Preparing the Psychosocial Study 45
A Human Rights Perspective 45
A Psychosocial Model Outline 46

5 *Multicultural Practice 65*

Cultural Competence 66

Multicultural Clinical Practice 67
Cultural Trauma 68
Roles for Cross-Cultural Therapists 69

Theoretical Models of Treatment 70
Therapy with Transnational Immigrants 71

Example of Culturally Competent Practice **72**

Example of Culturally Specific Practice: Research across Cultures **78**
Skilled Dialog 78
The Research 80

6 *Object Relations Theory: A Relational Psychodynamic Model* **82**

The Work of Melanie Klein **82**
The Internal Object: The Subjective Experience 82
Splitting and Projective Identification 83
The Internal Object and Child Abuse 83
The Internal Object and Internalized Oppression 83

The Work of Ronald Fairbairn **84**
The Internalized Bad Object: The Environmental Influence 84
Introjection and Self-Blame 84
Trauma Bonding 84

The Work of Harry Guntrip **85**
The Internalized Good Object 85
Object Loss and Ego Weakness 85

The Work of Donald Winnicott **85**
The Internal Object(s) and Interpersonal Relationships 85
The Transitional Object 86

The Interpersonal School **86**
The Significance of the Therapeutic Relationship 86

Eight Stages in Object Relations Theory and Practice **87**

Object Relations Theory and Brief Treatment **88**
Cyclical Maladaptive Pattern 89
Multicultural Considerations 90

Research Perspectives **98**

7 *Self-Psychology: A Relational Psychodynamic Model* **99**

Self-Psychology as a Theoretical Framework **99**
Empathy 100
The Role of the Therapist in Self-Psychology 100
Self-Psychology and the Treatment of Children and Adolescents 101

Self-Psychology and Learning Disorders in Children and Adolescents 102
Self-Psychology and Self-Harm in Adolescents 103
Self-Psychology and the Elderly 104
Self-Psychology and Brief Treatment 104

***Brief Psychotherapy with Women* 110**

8 *Relational Theory* 115

***The Therapeutic Relationship* 115**
Transference, Countertransference, and Intersubjectivity 115
Relational Theory and the Third Space 116
Relational Mindfulness 117
Self-in-Relation Theory or Cultural Relational Theory 122
Cultural Relational Theory and Women's Groups 123

9 *Cognitive Theory: A Structural Approach* 129

***History and Definition* 129**

***The Therapeutic Relationship* 129**
Research Perspective 130
Client Characteristics 130
A Structured Approach 130

***Rational Emotive Therapy* 131**
The ABCs of RET 132
Frequent Disturbances in Thinking 132

***Constructive Perspective* 134**

***Beck's Model of Cognitive Therapy* 136**
Testing of Automatic Thoughts 138

***Schema Therapy* 138**

***Cognitive Processing Therapy* 142**
Positive Psychology 142

10 *Behavior Therapy: A Structural Approach* 152

***The Three Generations or Three Waves* 152**
Traditional Behavior Therapy 152

***Behavioral Assessment* 154**
Cognitive Behavior Therapy 154
The Third Generation of Behavior Therapy 159

The Therapeutic Relationship 160

Research Perspectives 160
Empirical Evidence 164

11 *Narrative Therapy* ***166***

A Postmodern Approach 166

The Language of Narrative 167

The Structure of Narrative: Narrative as Metaphor 167

The Deconstruction of Narrative 168
Externalizing Conversations 169
Therapeutic Strategies 171
Reauthoring 171
Positions 172
Definitional Ceremony 173
Therapeutic Documents 174

Cross-Cultural Counseling 174

Collective Narrative Practice 182

Narrative Theater 182

Research Perspectives 183

12 *Solution-Focused Therapy* ***184***

A Postmodern Approach 184

The Editorial Reflection 186

Postassessment Session and Self-Reflection 187

Solution-Oriented Family Assessment 187
Interdisciplinary Collaboration 189
Solution-Focused Strategies 189

Crisis Intervention 196

Research Perspectives 196

13 *Clinical Practice with Children and Adolescents* ***198***

Developmental Assessment 198

Child Psychopathology 199

The Clinical Interview **200**

With the Parent(s) 200

With the Child or Adolescent 203

Confidentiality 203

Learning Disturbances **204**

Play Therapy **204**

Behavioral Therapy **208**

14 *Integrating Research and Practice* *214*

Evidence-Based Practice **214**

Research Methods for Clinical Practitioners **217**

Single-System Design Methodology 217

Qualitative Research **222**

How Knowledge Is Constructed 223

The Researcher as Instrument 223

Data Collection and Data Analysis 223

Discussion and Implications **230**

Mixed-Methods Research **230**

References 236

Index 249

Preface

This book grows out of our experiences as practitioners and as clinical faculty at our respective schools of graduate social work. Both of us have taught clinical practice to students over the years and have struggled with ways to build on the foundation level curriculum so that the advanced year could become a meaningful expansion of both knowledge and skill. The mandate of the social work profession is ever growing, as is the two-year MSW curriculum. We have the challenge of teaching—and the students have the challenge of learning—multiple theoretical practice models. What has been increasingly obvious to us in our teaching of clinical practice is that this focus on breadth, while appropriately inclusive of the wide range of thinking in the field, contributes to problems with depth. It is indeed a challenge to help students understand the constructs of a theory and also help them use that theory to guide assessment, establish goals, and plan interventions. This process is multidimensional and involves integration on many levels. Students must integrate respect for client self-determination with professional expertise; social work values and ethics with the constraints of a managed health/mental health care environment; a strengths perspective with attention to clients' symptoms; and the use of self with theory and practice.

We chose the term *clinical social work practice* over the more generic term *social work*. There is tension within the profession whether the mission of practitioners is social change, or individual and family change. We believe that the overall commitment of the profession is to facilitate social change so that individuals have fewer problems resulting from conditions of poverty and oppression. We also strongly believe that clinical social workers have a professional and ethical responsibility to work therapeutically with those individuals and families whose lives have been profoundly affected by these larger social issues.

There has been conflict, over the years, as to the language used to describe the clinical social worker and the client. In the Freudian model, the client was referred to as a patient, and the therapist, as a doctor. Some social workers today are referred to as therapists; others are called practitioners, clinicians, consultants, trainers, teachers, providers, and even conductors. In some settings, clients are called members; in others, they are referred to as consumers. The language that describes the participants in the therapeutic relationship is often a reflection of the theoretical perspective being used. Different theories use different language, and there is room for all of these terms.

We are aware that social work education today is quite broad. However, we are firmly committed to teaching clinical knowledge and skills, for it is these components that enable our students to evolve into true professionals. Our book, therefore, has taken on that charge. We have included an array of theories that are psychodynamic, transtheoretical, relational, cognitive, behavioral, and postmodern. Despite their differences, the theories included in this book all view the therapeutic process as being created by the therapist and client in an atmosphere of mutuality and collaboration.

The theoretical chapters of *Clinical Social Work Practice* are "student friendly," illustrating technique with dialogue from actual work with clients. Our clients reflect the larger social issues of our times: They are survivors of child abuse and neglect, domestic violence, discrimination, racism, and mental illness. The case discussions show both clients' and social workers' struggles with change and the therapeutic process. We include process recordings that reflect our work with individuals, families, and groups of different cultural, racial, ethnic, and religious backgrounds. The clinical work is presented authentically, describing our successes as well as our mistakes.

The book is divided into 14 chapters. In the first chapter, we present our model for integrating theory and practice, using the core practice class as a laboratory for knowledge building, skill development, evidence-based practice, and the acquisition of a professional self. A process recording from an interview with a Latina woman struggling in her role as wife and daughter describes the integration in detail. In Chapter 2, we discuss some key issues in clinical practice: brief treatment, ethical and boundary concerns, suicide, the complexities of clinical practice in a technological, managed care environment, fee for service work, the client in a system of care, spirituality and religion, therapist self-care and self-compassion, mindfulness in the therapeutic relationship, and the issues involved in addressing social work from a global or international frame of reference. In Chapter 3, we move into the clinical interview and the processes that evolve during the beginning, middle, and end stages of treatment. Discussion and case material focus on several meetings with a teenage boy diagnosed with a conduct disorder. The transtheoretical model, the stages of change, frames the clinical interviews. In Chapter 4, the psychosocial study, we discuss the preparation of the psychosocial summary on an advanced level. We present a clinical example of a 7-year-old African American boy who was placed in a residential treatment facility. This material serves as a model for teaching the conceptualization of a theoretical formulation and a diagnostic impression based on the *DSM-IV* and the mental status exam.

Chapter 5 discusses multicultural practice. It is our belief that sensitive, skilled clinicians can meet the challenge of working effectively with clients of different cultural backgrounds. We include content on intersectionality—socially constructed categories or social locations of oppression and privilege—and cultural trauma. We include two examples—a Vietnamese adolescent with substance abuse problems and cross-cultural research between two U.S. investigators who collaborated with Jamaican social workers in studying the effects of violence on children and families in an urban community in Kingston, Jamaica, West Indies. These cases illustrate practice that is culturally sensitive and culturally competent.

Chapters 6 through 12 present clinical illustrations through the lenses of specific theoretical models. Each of these chapters includes a detailed discussion of a theory, assessment, and treatment. Dialog is used to illustrate how theory guides practice. We have selected theories that offer insight into clinical social work practice with individuals, families, and groups whose lives have been profoundly affected by social, cultural, political, sexist, racist, and emotional forces.

In Chapter 6, we present object relations, a psychodynamic theory, and its relevance to contemporary social work practice with vulnerable client populations. Clinical intervention with a female survivor of severe childhood abuse illustrates this concept. Chapter 7 presents the theory of self-psychology and its application to brief treatment. The theory is illustrated in interviews with an elderly woman seeking counseling to understand why her son has undergone a sex change and how she can relate to him now that he has become her daughter. This case further shows the complexity of doing clinical social work practice against the backdrop of social stigma. Also in this chapter is a discussion of the application of self-psychology to brief group therapy with heterosexual women who have experienced domestic violence. We introduce relational theory in Chapter 8. Attention is given to contemporary psychoanalytic relational theory as well as cultural relational theory, which evolved from the earlier feminist model of "self-in-relation" theory. Group treatment with women who are learning to assert themselves in their work and family relationships demonstrates this model.

In Chapters 9 and 10, we discuss cognitive and behavioral social work practice, respectively. We illustrate cognitive theory with the treatment of a client suffering from anxiety and depression in Chapter 9. Behavioral theory is explicated in Chapter 10 in the case discussion of the brief treatment of a woman who suffers from obsessive-compulsive disorder.

Chapters 11 and 12 illustrate two postmodern theories—narrative and solution-focused therapies, respectively. Both chapters also demonstrate family treatment. Treatment of a Puerto Rican family grappling with intergenerational differences as they attempt to acculturate to U.S. society illustrates the narrative model, which is presented in Chapter 11. A group of children diagnosed with ADHD illustrates the use of externalizing conversations in narrative therapy. The application of a solution-focused approach to family treatment with a child who is lying is presented in Chapter 12.

Chapter 13 addresses clinical practice with children and adolescents. It includes developmental assessment, childhood psychopathology, play therapy, learning disturbances, and the clinical interview with a child or adolescent and the parent(s). Our case material describes play therapy with a 10-year-old Latina girl suffering from selective mutism, behavioral therapy with the parent of a 4-year-old child with temper tantrums, and behavioral treatment of a 12-year-old African American boy diagnosed with ADHD and ODD.

Chapter 14 addresses research and evaluation in social work practice. We begin with evidence-based practice and empirical research, highlighting how different theories may lend themselves to different evaluation approaches. Single-subject design methodology provides a model for accountable practice and is graphically illustrated. The subject of this research is the client suffering from obsessive-compulsive disorder. Qualitative inquiry is also detailed and illustrated by interviews with focus-group participants from Kingston, Jamaica, West Indies, who participated in a cross-cultural international study of violence against Jamaican children. Mixed-methods research is addressed and illustrated with an example of a research study of depression in Chinese elders located in the United States and mainland China.

We hope that this book will provide students and mental health professionals with the knowledge and skills that are required to practice on an advanced clinical level and that they will learn as much by reading it as we have by writing it.

Acknowledgments

We acknowledge with gratitude all those whose contributions have made this book a reality. Our thanks and praise go to Steven Bogatz for his technical support and research assistance, and our gratitude to Ann Bernales, Catherine Boyer, Constance Crain, Laurie Engstrand, Heide Eriksen, Farnsworth Lobenstein, Janice Malin, Jennifer Cass Markens, Alina Patton, Ariel Perry, Carol Rayl, Karen Seltzer, and Helen Solomon for case material. We thank Yunena Morales, former President of the Jamaica Association of Social Workers, and the Executive Board for their generous research collaboration; Fanteema Barnes and Lisa deCarolis for their research assistance; and Nicole Kutcher and Michele Bala for their administrative support. We would also like to thank Professor Ann Roy, Springfield College School for Social Work; Florence Loh, doctoral candidate at Smith College School for Social Work; Yu Cheng, Sun Yat-sen Center for Migrant Health Policy, Guangzhou, China; and Li Han and the social work students at South China Agricultural University for their generous research collaboration. A special thank you to Mary Fong who traveled with us to China and provided translation as well as numerous other supports.

A very special thanks to Dr. Carolyn Jacobs, Dean of Smith College School for Social Work; the late Dr. Mary Ann Quaranta, former Dean of Fordham University Graduate School of Social Service; and Dr. Peter Vaughan, Dean of Fordham University Graduate School of Social Service for their support and guidance. We also gratefully acknowledge the Brown Foundation, Inc., the Smith College School for Social Work Clinical Research Institute, Fordham University Graduate School of Social Service Research and Development Fund, and the Fordham University Office of Research and Sponsored Programs for their financial support.

Joan gives special thanks to her husband, Martin, for his heartfelt emotional support; to her children, Eric, Rebecca, and Julia, for providing joy and inspiration; to her mother for her standards of excellence; and to her father, who would have been so proud. Joan also thanks her sister Patricia for modeling an enduring spirit, her brother Philip for his kindness and integrity, Marlene and Alex for being in her life, and Pauline and Laura, who will always be remembered for their many gifts of friendship and collegiality.

Marlene dedicates this book in memory of her parents, Thelma and Daniel Cooper, and gives special thanks to her son Alex, who has become an adult during the several revisions of this text, and to Joan, her wonderful collaborator and dear friend.

In addition, we would like to thank the following reviewers whose comments contributed to the book's development through several editions: Marilyn A. Biggerstaff,

Virginia Commonwealth University; Daniel Coleman, Portland State University; Jill Davis, University of Central Florida; Elizabeth Dungee-Anderson, Virginia Commonwealth University; Carol P. Kaplan, Fordham University; Robert H. Keefe, Syracuse University; Alice Leiberman, University of Kansas; Mary Katherine Rodwell, Virginia Commonwealth University; Maureen Braun Scalera, Rutgers University; Carole A. Winston, University of North Carolina at Charlotte; and Jan Wrenn, St. Andrews University.

1

An Integrated Approach to Clinical Practice

Theoretical Base for Clinical Social Work Practice

Clinical social work must be guided by theory as well as principles. Harry Guntrip (1969), a noted object relational theorist, considered all theories of human nature to be influenced by the cultural era, the prevailing intellectual climate, and the dominant ideas of their time. Francis Turner (1996, p. 12), writing in contemporary times, echoes Guntrip's earlier observations about theories: "Each is recognized and prized to differing degrees, at different times, in different parts of the profession, and at different stages in the lives of colleagues."

Clearly, social work educators today face many challenges. Students need to learn how to practice from a theoretical base; examine these theories as applied to social work practice with diverse clients in their field work settings; develop a professional, ethical, and creative use of self in clinical practice (Gomory, 2001; Munro, 2002; Thyer, 2001); and find the best evidence for selecting their interventions and the means to evaluate the effectiveness of their work.

In this chapter, we offer an integrative model for clinical social work practice. The integrative model has five components: (1) practice class as laboratory, (2) the integrative journal, (3) clinical supervision, (4) faculty field advisement, and (5) practice evaluation and research. This model is not linear—it is reflexive. There is a back-and-forth sharing among its parts. For example, sections of the integrative practice journal that contain process records are shared with the clinical supervisor and faculty advisor, and evidence-based practice occurs in both class and field. For purposes of clarity, we discuss the components in discrete sections. However, the reader should bear in mind that the overarching component of this model is the practice class as laboratory.

The Integrative Model

The Practice Class as Laboratory: Learning to Integrate

The practice class is the forum for integrating the various components of the model. When designed as a laboratory, the students are given both the conceptual framework for practice and the opportunity to try out various aspects of their learning in class and field.

The Integrative Journal

The basic linking tool for class and field is the integrative journal. Journaling is a highly effective learning tool; it helps students deconstruct and demystify theory, look at things from different perspectives, and move closer to the actual experience (Godwin, 1996). Writing about their understanding of different theories, testing the application of theory to clinical material, planning interventions and evaluative measures, and seeking best practice evidence give students the opportunity to reflect on their use of self, their personal style, their emerging self-awareness as practitioners, their understanding of difficult concepts, and their ability to listen to what clients have to say on multiple levels.

The journal is a window into the unique way in which each student is absorbing the material. For the instructor, the journal is a tool that helps her attend to each student's learning style and needs. The instructor's written comments throughout the student's journal entries offer support, guidance, clarification, and constructive criticism. Student feedback to the instructor allows for modification and adjustment of course content. Journaling operationalizes the collaborative learning process that takes place in the classroom.

The instructor is very active during classroom exercises where journals are shared, meeting with each individual group to listen, clarify, and participate in the process of explicating themes from the students' case material and drawing on specific theoretical concepts from the literature that would be helpful in determining treatment goals and/or guiding treatment interventions. The students then practice these interventions by doing role-plays in small group settings. Following the small group exercise, the students convene as a whole, and each group has an opportunity to discuss its process and role-play with the entire class as an audience. At this juncture, the classroom instructor invites other students to expand the role-play by considering additional clinical themes and/or introducing other theoretical models that may also be relevant. Students could also conduct their role-plays on the telephone. Another options might include videotaping role-plays between two or more students done within the classroom on a CD and having them available for viewing by the students (Siebert & Spaulding-Givens, 2006). Process recordings can include discussion of these role-plays as the basis for self-reflection and integration of theory.

In this technological age, student journaling and the responses of practice instructors can be done through web-based educational systems such as Moodle and Blackboard, offering additional learning opportunities (Siebert & Spaulding-Givens, 2006).

Instructors can also use the "chat" mechanism of Blackboard and Moodle to conduct role-plays in real time using text messages. Students can share their journaling with each other and their supervisors on discussion boards, and the supervisor can facilitate the group conversation. We do not believe that online journaling and communication should replace classroom journal sharing if the opportunity for the latter exists. The relationship between students and their clients is the heart of social work practice, and social work teaching models the helping relationship and there are obstacles to modeling relationship building in web-based instruction. Siebert and Spaulding-Givens write: "Discussion in face to face classes can be multi-faceted and instructors can take advantage of student comments to guide the discussion in ways that meet the students' needs and cover the required materials as well." Online discussion format not are asynchronous, and discussions take place in a linear, bulletin-board format. Although participants can organize their discussions by topic, the result is generally a long list of individually posted messages. The volume of the reading can also pose problems in response time, making it difficult for the instructor to guide the discussion. Several authors (Harris & Parrish, 2006; Ko & Rosen, 2001; Schoech & Helton, 2003) feel that the primary difference between online teaching and classroom teaching is the way in which the instructor communicates with the student. Smith and Wingerson (2006) offer several suggestions to model effective helping relationships and for creating an atmosphere conducive for students to build good relationships with each other in a virtual classroom (p. 31). First, orientations and faculty training can be implemented to alert participants to potential obstacles to relationship building–such as visual and auditory clues, so important when working with students from different cultures. Forms of verbal clarifying such as questioning, particularly when emotional responses are unclear, can help to assess whether silence indicates discomfort with the content under discussion. The instructor should make special efforts to model awareness of the effects of oppression and discrimination (Smith & Wingerson, 2006, pp. 31–35).

Process Recording. Process recording, a time-honored tradition in clinical social work practice, has gone in and out of favor over the years and has often been considered outdated. Nonetheless, when sitting alone, painstakingly trying to remember what transpired in the counseling session, the student learns about himself as well as his client.

Students are asked to include sections of process recording in their journals. The recordings selected should reflect the students' attempts to talk with clients within the framework of different theoretical models. Students can use their journals initially to reflect on their understanding of the theory. They can then use their process recording to see what their interaction with clients has been, and then try to apply theoretical concepts to their work with clients.

Technology has made writing process recording somewhat easier, and supervisors may be able to make comments by using the Track Changes feature in Microsoft Word. Process recordings can become more interactive: for example, with the student posting a recording, the supervisor making comments and/or asking questions, the student answering, and the dialog continuing with subsequent process recordings. Again, this is not intended to take the place of valuable face-to-face discussion on process recordings.

Dialog	Studzent's Self-Reflection	Student's Application of Theory

FIGURE 1.1 *Three-Column Model for Process Recording*

Example of Student Process Recording. The student, a male graduate intern, attempts to use self-psychology in his work with a 38-year-old Dominican woman who is experiencing depression. The theory he selects—self-psychology—is described in detail in this book. The student struggles with the concept of mirroring (Kohut, 1971, 1977). This concept relates to a mother's ability to recognize and reflect to the developing child an appreciation of his capabilities and talents. The mother acts as a self-object—a person who is experienced intrapsychically as providing an enduring sense of availability, which fosters the developing self. When the child does not have this experience, the internalization of psychic structures cannot occur and shame and humiliation result. This section of process recording demonstrates the student's use of the three-column approach as he attempts to understand the theory of self-psychology in his work with his client (see Figure 1.2).

The student writes: "Mrs. Diaz came to the session with her 3-year-old daughter. I asked a case aide if she could watch the child while the mother and I talked. The aide initiated an argument with me in front of Mrs. Diaz. The process picks up after the case aide leaves me in the interview room with Mrs. Diaz and her daughter."

Dialog	Student's Self-Reflection	Student's Application of Theory
Intern: Don't worry Mrs. Diaz. The two of us will clear things up later. It is her job to supervise children while parents are in session. Can I comment on something that I have noticed?	She's always feeling responsible for other people. Now she feels responsible for me (would Kohut see this as Mrs. Diaz being the self-object for others?)	I am trying to be the *self-object* for Mrs. Diaz.
Mrs. Diaz: Yeah, sure.		
Intern: You had nothing to do with the situation with the aide, and yet you felt really guilty about what had happened.		Offering *reassurance* and *interpretation* but I think I need to be more empathic—maybe say "You really feel responsible for many things. . . ."
Mrs. Diaz: I don't know . . . I just feel responsible somehow. I feel responsible for my husband's depression, my sister's unhappiness, and my mother's too.	She takes on a lot.	*Listening* and *exploring*

Dialog	Student's Self-Reflection	Student's Application of Theory
Intern: Wow, you are responsible for a lot of people—your daughter, your husband, mother, sisters, etc.	Mrs. Diaz nods with a forced smile. I must have hit on something here. In the past, Mrs. Diaz told me that she was reared to be the caregiver for the younger children in the family, and that this role was typical in Latin-Caribbean cultures. Her situation was compounded by the sense of abandonment she felt when her mother left for New York without her. She was deprived of the chance of having a mutually empathic relationship with her mother, and may have begun to feel unworthy. This client is not able to achieve warm and fulfilling relationships with others because of the lack of foundation set by the mother.	I am trying to use *mirroring* but I don't think I really understand how to do this.
Intern: When you were trying to separate from Mr. Diaz, who supported you during that time?		I think I move away from theory here. I have to try harder to stay with Mrs. Diaz's experience.
Mrs. Diaz: No one at that time—even my mother came and put a guilt trip on me so I would stay with him.	She's so alone. Her own mother wouldn't take her side.	
Intern: That must have been really hard on you.		I attempt another self-psychology intervention here, providing *empathy*—a *mirroring* response—I think. Am I using mirroring correctly now?
Mrs. Diaz: Yes it was. No one ever supports me, not even my friends.		
Intern: What are your friendships like?	I wonder why I was questioning this here.	*Exploration*—but maybe I should have continued *mirroring.*
Mrs. Diaz: Well, my friends are like my sisters. They all have these problems with their husbands and their children—they all need help too.	She seems sad.	

(continued)

FIGURE 1.2 *Continued*

Dialog	Student's Self-Reflection	Student's Application of Theory
Intern: It sounds as if you are more overburdened being a mother to everyone. I can understand how you feel; actually I can feel the heaviness when you walk into the office.		I am using *empathy* here.
Mrs. Diaz: I am a mother to everyone.	I made a good comment here. She seems to be *reflecting* on what I said.	
Intern: No one deserves to feel that way, especially when you have so many positives going for you.	I'm feeling sad for her. I want to raise her self-esteem.	I am trying to continue offering *support*—being *empathic*—offering myself as a *self-object.*
Mrs. Diaz: I don't feel like I have any positives.		
Intern: You said that your mother is always yelling for you to clean your apartment even more than you do— right? Your apartment looks beautiful.	Her apartment is always immaculate. She doesn't see her own worth.	I am helping to *build her self-esteem* by *providing support.*
Mrs. Diaz: Yes, she wants me to be the perfect Dominican housewife, while my husband stares at the wall doing nothing.	She seems angry. He sounds like a real loser.	Perhaps I should ask something about Dominican culture? Is this the norm for all marriages? Or is this another example of how her mother can't put her first?
Intern: So you are expected to do everything for your family while your husband sits and rests all day.	How can she stay with him?	
Mrs. Diaz: Yes I am not going to have it.	Good. She's sounding stronger.	*Empowering*
Intern: I think we are getting somewhere today.		I use the "we"— a self-psychological concept called *twinship.* I will try to show her that I am allied in the work with her.
Mrs. Diaz: (crying) No one is there for me.	I wish I could take away her sadness.	

Dialog	Student's Self-Reflection	Student's Application of Theory
Intern: I can see how this must have been very upsetting to you. You love your mother, yet she wasn't always there when you needed her.		*Validating* and *mirroring*
Mrs. Diaz: No, she wasn't at all. She left my sisters and me with our cousin while she went to New York to follow her dreams.		
Intern: So as a mother, would you say she was excellent, very good, good, or poor?		*Scaling*
Mrs. Diaz: I love my mother, she is not a bad person. She just. . . well she was not very good . . . she always sent money and we had food and clothing, but she wasn't there when I needed her.		
Intern: That must make you angry.	Mrs. Diaz has been socially conditioned to show empathy for others in her roles as caregiver, mother, and wife. She often feels guilty when she does something for herself. She's beginning to show anger at others—her husband and, mother—who do not show empathy toward her. I view her anger as a strength because it shows that she has not been taken over by oppressive forces or social conditioning.	My goal is to provide her with an *empathic relationship*. That is different from what she has experienced. I am again using *mirroring*.
Intern (continuing): This must be a really difficult situation for you. Instead of concentrating solely on getting child care and job training over the next couple of weeks, could we talk about how your relationship with your parents has impacted all of your other relationships?	I want to continue exploring the past and how it relates to her present situation. I am trying to be empathic, but this is becoming challenging. I'm afraid of overstepping my boundaries by talking about "we" and "us."	*Empathy.* I use the concept of *twinship* here when I talk about the "we." This is the *partnering self-object*—I show her that we're in this together.

FIGURE 1.2 ***Example of Student Process Recording***

If the student shares this process recording in class, he will benefit from the feedback. Most certainly, the practice instructor and the field supervisor should read the journal entry and make comments on the process record, and it should travel with the student to his next supervisory conference, providing linkage between the classroom and the field.

Clinical Supervision: The Learning Alliance

Supervision is a contractual learning process that begins with an agreement between the supervisor and the supervisee (student) on what is to be learned and how the learning will take place. The supervisor must be selective and goal oriented, focusing on the process recording, the student's comments and use of theory, and, above all, the client. Too much focus on the student's feelings makes the client an involuntary co-participant in the supervisee's therapy (Burns & Holloway, 1990). Although the examination of countertransference issues should, when appropriate, be part of the supervisory process, giving primacy to student self-reflection over the development of skill, particularly at this early stage of clinical education and experience, often leaves students practicing from instinct or intuition, rather than a sound knowledge base. It is also important for the supervisor to be mindful that students should reflect on feelings that may have influenced certain choices within the context of the client's needs. This distinguishes supervision from therapy and keeps the professional boundaries intact (Congress, 2001). Ganzer and Ornstein (2004), writing from a relational approach to supervision (see Chapter 8), suggest that the boundaries and limits of the supervision be negotiated by the participants and that investigating transactions in the supervisory relationship should not be an end in itself but be used to further the treatment of the client (p. 439). Kron and Yerushalmi (2000) offer a view of supervision as an intersubjective process that transpires between supervisor and supervisee (p. 99) that parallels the intersubjective perspective in clinical practice. For example, rather than focusing on freeing the supervisee of countertransference responses, the supervisor now works with the supervisee to develop the capacity to use countertransferential responses to understand what is happening in the therapy.

Supervision, too often, is removed from the learning going on in the classroom. Many supervisors do not communicate with practice instructors (or vice versa) unless those teachers are advisors to their students (Fortune, McCarthy, & Abramson, 2001). In the integrative model, the supervisor reads the student's process recording with a focus on the development of knowledge and skill. The supervisor should be clear about the importance and use of this teaching tool and that the student has presented this dialog to her practice class. This allows input from two sources and enables the student to have time to think critically about her intervention.

The Clinical Agenda. The clinical agenda is a working document that provides the beginning clinician with a tool to improve practice skills and develop professional awareness. The agenda brings focus to the supervisory conference as both the supervisor and the student prepare for the meeting by writing an agenda of clinical issues that they each would like to discuss. The supervisee is responsible for preparing agenda items that reflect his view of clinical practice with clients, considering emerging themes that suggest areas of struggle or concern. This agenda should be given to the supervisor in advance of the conference. The supervisor's agenda, written after a careful review of the supervisee's process recording, should include observations and comments about the student's process record that will help the student translate the theory into dialog. The student should have this before he meets with his supervisor.

The classroom dialog and exercises provide a direct link to supervision because students' participation in the practice laboratory (class) helps them develop a clinical agenda based on their own unique learning needs. Through this process, the classroom instructor and the student make the field supervisor aware of what is occurring in the practice class. In turn, the supervisor contributes to students' development in the field by providing important feedback that they can integrate into process records, journals, and classroom discussion and exercises.

Following are two examples of clinical agendas. The first was written by the student intern following his interview with Mrs. Diaz. The second is the supervisor's clinical agenda, written after reviewing the same process recording.

Example of Student's Clinical Agenda

1. I think I felt embarrassed that the case aide and I had an argument in front of Mrs. Diaz. It threw me and I forgot for the moment that I was using the self-psychology model with Mrs. Diaz. How should I have handled it within the framework of self-psychology?
2. I'm worried about how Mrs. Diaz sees me. I am a male intern with white privilege, and she is an immigrant Latina woman living in poverty. She has problems with her husband, whom she claims is abusive. Should I address the gender and cultural issues with her? Would I be able to do that within the self-psychology model? Or am I coming from my own anxieties instead of focusing on being more empathic with Mrs. Diaz?
3. Mrs. Diaz was traumatized by her mother's early migration and what she perceived as abandonment. I, too, have some early abandonment issues. I feel very close to Mrs. Diaz when she talks about this. I'm afraid of overstepping my boundary because I identify closely with her struggle. What do you think? How do you think I can guard against this?
4. I struggled with the concept of mirroring—I would like to review the places in the process recording where I attempted to use it.

Example of Supervisor's Clinical Agenda

1. Self-psychology is an excellent model to use because it demonstrates the use of empathy. Did you select this theory intuitively, or did you find some evidence that this was the model of choice?
2. You are highly empathic during most of the interview. Can you recognize the times during the interview when you move from the empathic response to another intervention? Do you know what you were thinking or feeling during those times? How could you continue to be empathic and what would you say?

3. What was your practice evidence for using a scaling intervention during the interview? What theoretical model were you incorporating into your work? What were you feeling at that time?
4. In the interview you speak about raising Mrs. Diaz's self-esteem. Can you think about how this would be accomplished within a self-psychological framework?
5. How would raising the gender and cultural issues help your client? What do you think about her marital expectations within the context of her culture?
6. Let's talk more about your concerns re: boundary issues.
7. How might you begin to think about evaluating your practice interventions?

Faculty Field Advisement

The role of the faculty field advisor is a critical one. It provides linkage between the field and the classroom curriculum. It is ideal, but not always possible, to have faculty advisors serve as practice instructors. It is most difficult in large schools where students have different specializations, and practice classes house too many students for one advisor to manage. However, we feel strongly that faculty advisors and supervisors should be oriented to the practice curriculum, to the three-column method of process recording described, and to the integrative model. Students should be able to remove process recordings from their journals to ensure confidentiality. The practice instructor should be the only person to have access to the entire integrative journal, as this allows the student to struggle freely with complex material without fear of repercussions from the fieldwork faculty. Faculty advisors who are not practice teachers should attend training workshops, as should field supervisors, so that they will be familiar with the theoretical models taught in the curriculum. We suggest that they receive continuing education credits for their participation and that distance learning also be incorporated into the curriculum. Finally, guidelines and models for all these materials—the integrative journal, the process record, the clinical agenda, and the supervisory conference—should be included in the fieldwork manual and in the student manual, so that all students, supervisors, and advisors are clear about the guidelines and requirements.

Practice Evaluation and Research

The Council on Social Work Education (CSWE, 2008) mandates the use of scientific inquiry throughout the social work curriculum, and most social work students will enter a field where both public and private funding sources will insist on results-oriented outcomes to ensure high-quality service (Rock & Cooper, 2000) and where practice evaluation will be a professional necessity. Addis and Waltz (2002) point out that, although the different rationales for psychotherapy dissemination research have been well articulated, the most effective means for bringing research products to clinical practice have yet to be determined, and there is a lack of research on training in the integration of science and practice at the undergraduate, graduate, and postgraduate levels. In the integrative model, students are asked to seek the best evidence for their choice of theoretical approach in their work with clients. They are required to search the literature for support for the efficacy of using their interventions, and also to provide a plan—and sometimes a product—evaluating the effectiveness of their work. Ideally, the practice class and the research class would be linked so that students would learn practice evaluation and theory application simultaneously during a semester.

Summary

Social work has evolved over the years, taking on the challenges of the times. The profession now espouses a breadth of theoretical approaches and treatment modalities, a commitment to diversity and social justice, and a trend toward empirical evaluation of practice. Graduate social work education is, for many, the first step to becoming a skilled clinician. Schools of social work have the challenge of integrating classroom learning with clinical practice. In the integrative model illustrated in this chapter, we have presented a guide that students and instructors can use to ensure that students will truly know how to bring their knowledge of theory into the interview and counseling meetings with their clients. We hope this model will be used by students in the practice class, field supervisors, and faculty advisors so that an integrative learning experience will take place.

2

Key Issues in Clinical Practice

In this chapter, we will discuss those key issues that require special consideration. We include content on brief treatment, ethics and boundaries, suicide, managed care, and therapist's self-care.

Brief Treatment

Research Perspectives

Currently, brief treatment perspectives are influencing social work practice. The value of brief treatment for a variety of conditions has been recently documented by Dewan, Steenbarger, and Greenberg (2008) and Greenberg and Dewan (2009). Brief treatment is considered one of the primary strategies for managing third-party costs for outpatient mental health services.

However, brief treatment has become the treatment of choice for reasons other than just cost containment. Outcome studies in which clients were randomly assigned to either time-limited or time-unlimited treatment showed no difference in the effectiveness between these two treatment modalities regardless of diagnosis (Corwin, 2002). In studies of the effectiveness of a variety of brief treatment perspectives with no-treatment control groups, Pekarik (1996) found that those persons who received brief treatment functioned more effectively than control group members. In well-designed psychotherapy studies, with experienced therapists, clinically representative clients, and appropriate controls and follow-up, Koss and Butcher (1986) demonstrated that brief therapy was as effective as longer courses of treatment. Large numbers of clinical studies determined that even when clinicians decided on the need for long-term treatment, in actual practice, most treatment was unplanned brief treatment, with the average number of sessions being between six and eight (Koss & Butcher, 1986; Smyrnios & Kirby, 1993). Howard, Kopta, Krause, and Orlinsky (1986) found that clients make their greatest improvements in functioning in the early sessions of therapy. Garfield (1994) studied the expectations of therapy of 70 clients in an outpatient clinic and found that over one-third thought that therapy sessions would last a half hour or less, 73 percent anticipated some improvement by the fifth session, and 70 percent expected treatment to last 10 sessions or less.

Models of Brief Treatment

Koss and Butcher (1986) identified 53 models of brief treatment in the literature. Since that study was published, new models have appeared. Epstein and Brown (2002), trying to minimize the difference among the models, break the classifications into three categories: psychodynamic, problem solving, and mixed eclectic. Psychodynamic brief treatment makes use of psychoanalytic principles such as uncovering, working through repressed material, analysis of defenses, transference, countertransference, and resistance. The goals are fairly flexible, and analysis of conflict is supplemented by environmental management. Problem-solving models focus on target problems, selection of mutual goals, teaching of problem-solving strategies such as skill acquisition, and discussion of alternatives and obstacles. Cognitive behavioral treatment would fall into this category. The mixed-eclectic approach is composed of a diverse selection of the psychodynamic and problem-solving components plus additions and rearrangements constructed by particular theorists (for a review of the literature on this approach, see Budman & Gurman, 1988; Cummings, 1990; Parad & Parad, 1990; Strupp & Binder, 1984).

The First Meeting

The initial contracts in brief therapy can be reviewed and renegotiated, but it is essential to establish the parameters of the treatment. The theoretical model or framework of the therapy generally defines the responsibilities of the patient and the therapist. Generally speaking, detailed information about the presenting problem is rapidly obtained, and the clinician moves quickly from general, open-ended questions to more specific questions as the interview proceeds (Kadushin, 1997). Time must be used flexibly. Budman and Gurman (1988) suggest that some clients may benefit from more intensive meetings at the beginning of therapy and less frequent meetings as the therapy progresses. Budman, Hoyt, and Friedman (1992) consider the first session to be critical in brief treatment. They delineate 11 tasks that need to be accomplished in the first meeting: (1) establishing rapport; (2) orienting and instructing the patient on how to use therapy; (3) establishing an opportunity for the patient to express his or her thoughts and feelings; (4) assessing the patient's strengths, motivations, expectations, and goals; (5) evaluating possible psychiatric complaints such as biological factors, suicide/homicide risk, and substance abuse; (6) mutually formulating a treatment focus; (7) making initial treatment interventions and assessing their effects; (8) suggesting homework tasks; (9) defining the treatment parameters; (10) scheduling future appointments; and (11) handling issues such as confidentiality, fees, insurance, or releases, as indicated. Single-session solutions (Hoyt, 1995) may be appropriate for patients who come to solve a specific problem for which a solution is in their control, for patients who essentially need reassurance, and for patients who come for evaluation and need a referral for medical and/or other nonpsychotherapy services.

The Working Relationship

Research shows that psychotherapy works best when there is a good working alliance between patient and therapist (Martin, Garske, and Davis, 2000). This is supported by recent technological developments in neuroscience that highlight the importance of developing and maintaining a therapeutic relationship through activation of areas of the brain related to the attachment system (Fonagy, 2006). The clinician must develop an immediate positive working relationship in brief treatment. A high level of activity is demanded of the therapist, as well as a collaborative mindset and an ability to stay focused and intensely alert throughout the course of treatment. Within the context of this positive relationship, the therapist and client agree on goals and objectives and contract for the number of sessions needed to achieve these. Goals are focused and reflect those issues that are most compelling to the client (Corwin, 2002). Problems in the therapeutic alliance are dealt with in the here and now, and signs of resistance are handled in the moment so that the therapist and client can work toward a better therapeutic relationship.

In the middle phase of brief treatment, the client and worker maintain the focus and make progress toward the stated treatment goals. In some brief treatment models, such as cognitive and behavioral therapies, homework assignments keep the therapy moving between sessions and help the client progress more rapidly.

Termination is built into brief treatment, beginning with contracting the number of sessions and followed by end-of-session reviews that summarize the meeting and the progress made toward goal attainment. Feelings of loss are not ignored, but there is less exploration of these issues. It is expected that clients may return to the therapist in the future if problems recur. Because the relationship in brief treatment is less intense than in open-ended therapy and centered on client strengths, there is less dependence on the therapist (Corwin, 2002).

Greenberg and Dewan (2009) describe the phases of brief treatment as engagement, discrepancy, and consolidation, which are similar to all brief psychotherapy models. Engagement sets the collaborative atmosphere and fosters alliance. In the discrepancy phase, there is heightened emotion, and new learning and mastery of new behavior patterns takes place. In the consolidation phase, the goal is to strengthen the changes made by the client, urging the continued testing for new behaviors.

Mindfulness in the Therapeutic Relationship

Hick (2008) and Lambert and Simon (2008) discuss the role of mindfulness in cultivating therapeutic relationships, which they agree is "central and essential in psychotherapy outcome" and which may be of even greater significance in brief treatment. Mindfulness has been described in the literature as a nonelaborative, nonjudgmental, present-centered awareness in which each thought, feeling, or sensation that arises in the attentional field is acknowledged and accepted as it is. Within the context of the therapeutic relationship, mindfulness is a way of paying attention with empathy, presence, and deep listening that can be cultivated, sustained, and integrated into our work through the ongoing discipline of meditation practice. Although most of the research on mindfulness has been related to models of practice and therapeutic interventions, several authors promote attention to the attitudes and behaviors that a therapist demonstrates. This includes self-observation, self-care, and cultivating presence and listening within the client–therapist relationship (Bien, 2006; Bishop et al., 2004; Hick, 2008). Practice that facilitates self-awareness and presence provide a path toward empathy that includes recognizing the biases through which the therapist attempts to understand the client (Walsh, 2008).

Selection Criteria

Brief treatment can utilize broad or narrow selection criteria in determining appropriate candidates. Contraindications for brief treatment models that utilize narrow selection criteria include patients who do not give the impression they can develop a working alliance with the therapist, patients who have not had at least one significant relationship in their lives, and patients who do not seem motivated to change. Additional contraindications for brief treatment may include patients with serious depression who are unable to form a rapid therapeutic alliance, patients with acute psychosis, patients with severe narcissistic disturbances, and patients with a history of severe trauma. Schizoid patients and patients unable to identify a central focus are also not considered appropriate (Bloom, 1997; Clarkin & Frances, 1982).

One of the prime considerations for brief treatment is whether the client's problems are long-standing or of recent occurrence. Short-term approaches may be contraindicated if the patient's issues are so severe that they are unlikely to be able to actively engage in treatment (Greenberg and Dewan, 2009).

Ethics and Boundaries

Sexual Relationships with Clients

The National Association of Social Workers (NASW) *Code of Ethics* (2008) states that "social workers should under no circumstances engage in sexual activities or sexual contact with current clients, whether such contact is consensual or forced." The code further admonishes against sexual contact with clients' relatives or other individuals with whom clients maintain close personal relationships when there is a risk of exploitation or potential harm to the client. Engaging "in sexual activities or sexual contact with former clients because of the potential for harm to the client" is also prohibited.

In spite of these warnings, sexual contact between social workers and clients does occur. A study of 300 closed adjudication cases for the years 1982 to 1992 on record at the NASW national offices found that sexual activity with a client accounted for 29.2 percent of the 72 substantiated complaints against social workers, almost double the next most common complaint of having dual or multiple relationships with clients or former clients in which there is a risk of exploitation of or potential harm to the client (NASW, 1995, cited in Berkman, Turner, Cooper, Polnerow, & Swartz, 2000). Reamer (1995) found that between 1969 and 1990, sexual impropriety was the second most common malpractice claim (18.5 percent) filed against social workers. In a study of 144 social workers by Mittendorf and Schroder (2005), 54 percent reported having seen a client who had sexual contact with a previous therapist—for a total of 245 clients who reported having sex with their previous therapist. The authors conclude that although one must exercise caution when relying on second-hand self-reports from clients, these allegations are disturbing. We believe that there is never a circumstance that would justify sexual relations between worker and client. And we further caution social workers not to engage in sexual relations with former clients or friends or relatives of a client. We say this without equivocation. It is never in the client's interests and can only serve to harm. The therapeutic relationship involves client vulnerability and practitioner influence (Kagle & Giebelhausen, 1994). The repercussions for the client are just too severe and the damage too extensive to ever warrant an exception to the rule: Never engage in sexual relationships with clients. Entering into a sexual relationship with a client after termination can still be exploitative. The client has shared her intimacies with you, and by doing so, has been made vulnerable to you. The therapeutic relationship is, by its very nature, a relationship that is unequal, and sexual relationships between practitioner and client always carry the potential for harm.

Other Dual Relationships

Unfortunately, far less information is available on nonsexual dual relationships, but such relationships can be exploitative, pose risks to clients, and lead to sexual intimacy between practitioners and clients (Pope & Bouhoutsos, 1986, cited in Berkman et al., 2000). But what about former clients or friends or relatives of clients? Again, as stated by the NASW *Code of Ethics,* the rule is *no.* Clients, former clients, and friends or relatives of clients should not become part of your personal life. There is always the potential for betrayal of past confidences or the stirring up of rivalries. It places a burden on your client, who may receive knowledge of you that she doesn't need to know. It may prevent her from seeking your help again in the future. It may cause her to doubt the help that you provided in the past. Keep your personal and professional lives separate.

Of course, there are times and places (particularly small towns) where clients' and social workers' lives *do* overlap. They may belong to the same religious organizations, be parents of children in the same schools, and appear at the same community functions. We have known students who live and work in the African American community and who attend the same churches as their clients. In the lesbian community, a complete separation between personal and professional contact may be impossible because there are aspects of the therapists' and clients' lives that will intersect, even when the therapist exerts great effort to avoid dual roles (Eldridge, Mencher, & Slater, 1993; Galambos, Watt, Anderson, and Danis, 2005).

Some practitioners have adopted feminist and other empowerment models that seek to redress the power imbalance between clinician and client (Kagle & Giebelhausen, 1994). Feminist writers suggest recognizing and validating the existence of overlapping relationships, because they may be unavoidable, and asking the therapist to accept responsibility for monitoring such relationships to prevent potential abuse of or harm to the client. They suggest making ethics a relational process: consulting, questioning, discussing, disagreeing, and clarifying—these relational processes help heighten one's awareness and capacity to create a living ethics for relational psychotherapy.

The Suicidal Client

Perhaps one of the most heart-wrenching and troubling issues in clinical practice is the threat of a client's suicide. The importance of the relationship between the interviewer and the client cannot be overestimated when working with the suicidal client. Trust is paramount when making an assessment, and the interviewer must be as tenacious as a detective in her inquiries. Remember, patients who are experiencing suicidal ideation (thoughts) may be reluctant to talk about it for a variety of reasons. They may feel ashamed or frightened that they will be hospitalized against their will. They may also want to die and not want to share that with anyone who they think will try to stop them. Whenever possible, the interviewer should check with corroborative sources to determine whether they have noticed any behaviors that might be of concern. Talking to others who have a relationship with the patient also provides the opportunity to determine what the specific stressors and/or supports are in the patient's life.

Those who write about suicide from a self-in-relation perspective (see, for example, Kaplan & Klein, 1990) emphasize the importance of the clinical relationship in work with potentially suicidal female clients. Their understanding can be extended to work with all suicidal clients, regardless of gender. They have identified three main relational functions for the therapist: (1) to monitor suicide and make contractual agreements; (2) to create a supportive, life-affirming, patient–therapist connection; and (3) to foster the client's connection to a sustaining support system. The suicidal client despairs of her capacity to maintain connection and finds safety within a process that awakens within her the possibility of finding connections. Citing Miller (1986), Kaplan and Klein point out that the sense of being deeply understood within the therapeutic relationship legitimates and validates the feelings that the suicidal client is trying to communicate and propels her toward further awareness of her relational potential and further confirmation of her right to life. The sense of being understood is life affirming. The therapist needs to engage the suicidal client with empathy, care, and concern, and to lend her own optimism that, even in the darkest of times, there are viable alternatives to taking one's life.

Guidelines for Assessing Suicide

There are some very clear general guidelines that therapists can use in assessing for suicide. Shea (1998, 2002) notes that the interviewer must be concerned with (1) the frequency of the patient's suicidal ideation, (2) the duration of ideation (how long does it last?), (3) the concreteness of the suicidal plan, and (4) the extent of action taken with regard to the plan. Having a specific plan and a lethal means available are clear indicators of imminent suicide (Bednar, Bednar, Lambert, & Waite, 1991, p. 115). A person who makes a suicide attempt at a time and a place where there is a good possibility of being discovered by someone does not represent the same risk as an attempt made where/when the possibility of discovery by another person is low (this is known as the risk/rescue ratio).

The Chronological Assessment of Suicide (C.A.S.E.) is a useful tool with a patient who has made a suicidal attempt or when suicidal ideation is intense (Shea, 1998). In step 1 of the C.A.S.E., the interviewer explores presenting suicidal events. She asks questions such as "How did the patient try to kill herself?" "How serious was the action taken with this method?" "To what degree did the patient intend to die?" "How does the patient feel about the fact that she did not successfully kill herself?" "Did alcohol or drugs play a part in the attempt?" In step 2, the interviewer asks about recent suicidal events by gathering information on any suicidal thoughts and actions the patient may have had during the previous six to eight weeks, questioning what plans have been considered, how far the patient took actions on those plans, and how much of the patient's time was spent on these plans. Step 3 involves exploration of past suicidal events that inform the practitioner about the patient's safety—for example, "What was the most serious suicide attempt?" and "When was the most recent attempt?" In step 4, the interviewer obtains information about the immediate suicidal events, any suicidal ideation the patient may be having during the interview, and the patient's prediction of future thoughts of suicide. The clinician might ask, "What would you do later tonight or tomorrow if you began to have suicidal thoughts again?" or "Right now, are you having any thoughts about killing yourself?"

Rudd, Joiner, and Rajab (2001, pp. 132–134) offer eight "essential components of a clinical risk assessment interview":

1. Predisposition to suicidal behavior
2. Precipitants or stressors (triggers)
3. Symptomatic presentation (affective system)
4. Presence of hopelessness (cognitive system, suicidal belief system)
5. The nature of suicidal thinking (cognitive system, suicidal belief system)
6. Previous suicidal behavior, preparatory behaviors (behavior system)
7. Impulsivity and self-control (behavioral system)
8. Protective factors

See Rudd et al. (2001) for further elaboration.

Providing Safety

A referral for a psychiatric evaluation is always required when a patient is suicidal. A psychiatrist's knowledge and expertise in this area supports our own, and many psychotropic medications that only psychiatrists can prescribe help stem the depressive course. If, in conjunction with the psychiatrist, it is determined that the patient presents a suicidal risk,

TABLE 2.1 *Suicide Risk Categories*

Risk Category	Criteria
I. Baseline	Absence of an acute (i.e., crisis) overlay, no significant stressors nor prominent symptomatology. Only appropriate for ideators and single attempters.
II. Acute	Presence of acute (i.e., crisis) overlay, significant stressor(s), and/or prominent symptomatology. Only appropriate for ideators and single attempters.
III. Chronic high risk	Baseline risk for multiple attempters. Absence of an acute (i.e., crisis) overlay, no significant stressors nor prominent symptomatology.
IV. Chronic high risk with acute exacerbation	Acute risk category for multiple attempters. Presence of acute (i.e., crisis) overlay, significant stressor(s), and/or prominent symptomatology.

Source: M. D. Rudd, T. Joiner, & M. H. Rajab, *Treating suicidal behavior: An effective, time-limited approach* (New York: Guilford Press, 2001). Reprinted by permission.

immediate hospitalization or another form of protection is required. In Table 2.1, Rudd et al. (2001, p. 137) delineate four categories to consider when making a risk assessment for suicide.

Whenever possible, try to encourage the patient to agree to a voluntary hospitalization if your assessment of his risk for suicide warrants inpatient care. Remember that if the patient is suicidal, you must breach confidentiality and take the necessary steps, which might include contacting family members, a crisis center, or the police. This is a difficult time for the interviewer because the patient may be angry, feel betrayed, and, at times, may verbally or physically lash out. Interviewers may understandably feel conflicted about pursuing a course of action that is against the patient's wishes. A discussion of whether suicide can ever be justified as being within the bounds of client self-determination is beyond the scope of this chapter. You need to remember that failure to properly assess for and/or take the proper steps to prevent a suicide can be construed as professional negligence. It is also important that you clearly document your assessment of suicide risk and the steps you took to try to prevent a suicide from occurring.

If a decision is made not to hospitalize, then family members or friends, if available, must be involved in monitoring the patient, calling for emergency help, or getting the patient to the hospital if there is an imminent threat of danger. They must be informed as to what constitutes suicidality in a patient and that it is important that they not leave the patient alone, even for a few minutes. It is important for the interviewer to establish a safety plan with the patient and to involve appropriate family members or friends whenever possible. Safety contracts can provide important insights for the interview into the patient's thinking about suicide. A patient may, for example, be reluctant to sign a safety contract (Shea, 1998). Remember also that, although safety contracts can be important deterrents, they offer no guarantee that a patient will not commit suicide. Additionally, the patient should be instructed to call the primary therapist at any time, even late evenings, and the therapist must be available to receive such calls. Home phone numbers should not be given. We recommend that all clinicians who practice outside of agencies have their own emergency paging systems so that patients can have immediate access in crisis. Agencies should also have 24-hour coverage.

Child and Adolescent Suicide

Children and adolescents must be directly questioned about suicide because, as Kaplan, Sadock, and Grebb (1994) point out, parents are frequently unaware of such ideas in their children. They must be specifically questioned about their fantasies, as teenagers often glorify suicide, viewing those who do end their lives as heroes and heroines. Fantasies of an afterlife among departed relatives and loved ones are common among depressed adolescents. Because adolescents are impulsive, they may see suicide as an immediate solution without thinking about consequences or alternatives. And, because adolescents operate in the here and now without a long view of the future, their despair is all the more compelling.

Because peer group identification and acceptance are so important during the development stage of adolescence, those who live on the margin are particularly vulnerable to suicide. Hispanic females have a 21 percent rate of suicide attempts, in part owing to the demands on these adolescents to balance traditional and acculturated roles (Zayas, Kaplan, Turner, Romano, & Gonzalez-Ramos, 2000). African American and non-Hispanic white female adolescents have rates of 10.8 percent and 10.4 percent, respectively. Adolescent males overall have lower rates of suicide attempts than their female counterparts (Zayas et al., 2000, citing a 1996 report from the Centers for Disease Control and Prevention). Gay youth have been found to attempt suicide at a rate two to three times higher than other adolescents (Kulkin, Chauvin, & Percle, 2000; Morrison & L'Heureux, 2001). Therapy is critical for these at-risk adolescents as it gives them the opportunity to discuss their feelings and fantasies in an atmosphere of confidentiality, with an empathic therapist who provides a safety net and a reality check, offering a way out of isolation and disconnection.

Managed Care

The management of client care is designed to meet two major goals: controlling costs while ensuring the quality of care (Corcoran & Vandiver, 1996). The oversight of health and mental health services is done by a third party, and need, duration, and continuation of these services and their rate for service reimbursement are predetermined by the payer. The notion is that by limiting unnecessary services, financial costs will be kept down.

Ethical Dilemmas under Managed Care

Of great concern to social workers are the ethical dilemmas created by the advent of managed care—in particular, the limits and scope of confidentiality. The therapeutic relationship between the therapist and the client now includes a third party.

Although reimbursement by third-party insurers always involved reporting on diagnosis and treatment sessions, detailed documentation is often required under managed care. Clinicians are required to report on a client's symptoms, diagnosis, goals and objectives, modalities, and length of time needed to obtain results. Most often, continued care is authorized only when need can be justified, such as a *DSM-IV* diagnosis of Major Depression or Bipolar disorder, both considered medical conditions. A global assessment of functioning (GAF) scale, which ranges from 0 to 100, often must show a score in the fifties for continued outpatient treatment. Clients who require help with problems of living (legitimate *DSM-IV* diagnosis such as adjustment disorders) receive limited services. The authorization process under managed care is often cumbersome, requiring copious paperwork and numerous telephone calls.

Managed care regulations often compromise the integrity of the therapeutic relationship. Situations can occur when clients may need to change insurance plans. Managed care companies have not consistently honored the relationship between client and therapist, suggesting that clients choose a therapist on their provider panel if they want continued reimbursement for their therapy. This is in spite of empirical research (Lambert, 1992; Luborsky, Crits-Cristoph, Mintz, & Auerback, 1988; Najavits & Strupp, 1994; Strupp, 1995) attesting to the importance of the therapist–patient relationship on treatment outcome. Managed care companies also encourage therapists to rely on therapies that have been empirically tested, such as cognitive and behavioral, as opposed to narrative and psychodynamic models that may be less amenable to quantifiable measurement (Chambliss, 2000). This occurs in spite of knowledge that good practice requires that an intervention be chosen on the basis of psychosocial assessment, not the preference of a managed care company.

Furman and Langer (2006) address the ethical dilemmas inherent in the managed care system that, they state, is driven by corporate dictates rather than emotional and spiritual health. Citing Furman (2001), they state that managed care is turning clinical social work into another medical intervention, at risk of losing its focus on the human spirit and the soul. An example may be moving too quickly toward medication management rather than conducting the comprehensive psychosocial assessment that should be at the forefront of clinical social work practice. The managed care patient, they believe, is not seen as a whole person, with a life's mission and goals, but as a broken machine needing to be fixed as quickly as possible. And often-persistent emotional and behavioral problems do not lend themselves to the quick fix. They also worry that under managed care, therapists, now taught by schools to provide symptom-related treatment, are becoming alienated from their clients and their profession. They call for social workers to challenge the hegemony of managed mental health care, by effecting policy and practice changes through consumer advocacy.

Reamer (1997, 2001, 2003) cautions that social workers who practice in managed care programs must be careful to avoid practices that constitute ethical violations. They need to be sure that utilization-review decisions that are contrary to their professional judgment are protested; that clients are adequately informed about the risks associated with short-term or limited intervention; that clients are assessed thoroughly for risks of self-injurious behaviors, including suicide and the potential to harm others; that other professionals are consulted when social workers believe they do not have the requisite expertise or resources to provide clients with the care they need in the time allotted; and that if they have supervisory responsibilities, they monitor supervisees carefully and conscientiously. Reamer offers some guidelines for ethical practice. First and foremost, the clinician must disclose to clients how delivery of services may be influenced by managed care policies and restrictions. Clients need to be fully informed of the pre- and current authorization process, their right to appeal a utilization decision, the potential invasion of their privacy by the review process, and other options available to meet their needs (Sabin, 1994a, 1994b). Reamer (2005) cautions that the ethics and risk management issues inherent in practice with children and adolescents may pose additional challenges (e.g., the social worker may owe a duty to her client—the child or adolescent—as well as to the parents of her client). Reamer recommends that social workers become familiar with standards in the NASW *Code of Ethics* pertaining to private, confidential, and privileged information. In addition, social workers should consult relevant state and federal laws pertaining to confidentiality and informed consent. Reamer concludes that social workers who are concerned about their ability, under managed care, to meet the needs of vulnerable clients, must organize clients and colleagues to inform key participants in managed care of the risks that managed care generates, the severity of mental health problems left that are not addressed, and the benefits of high-quality services.

Opportunities under Managed Care

Managed care presents benefits as well as disadvantages. Many marginalized clients who would otherwise be confined to the use of clinic settings with long waiting periods for services, overburdened practitioners, and overcrowded working conditions now have access to the private sector. They have a choice of providers (within the limits of their plans) with various specializations and levels of expertise (psychiatric, psychological, or social work). These clients have opportunities that were previously afforded only to the middle and upper class. This has brought equity into the health care arena and diversity into the sphere of private practice (Rock, 2001).

Coaching and Social Work

Coaching has been broadly defined to describe a goal-focused process of assisting individuals and companies to improve personal and professional achievement. Its practice focus includes personal, life, executive, career, corporate, professional performance, family, ADHD, and parenting (Caspi, 2005). Coaching can be an alternative or adjunct to clinical social work, and many clinicians are looking to coaching to diversify their practice. It can be done on the phone, in the client's home, and at the workplace. Like social work, it involves helping that focuses on self-understanding and self-discipline to change behavior (Caspi and Caspi, 2003). However, unlike social work, coaching is less concerned with avoiding dual relationships and practitioner self-disclosure. There are concerns though that directly impact social workers. Coaching does not require a license, and so, how are best practices ensured? Does coaching violate the code of ethics? How does one determine if coaching is the intervention of choice? Caspi (2005) suggests that social workers should explore ways to enage in coaching, test coaching interventions empirically, and organize state task forces to work with NASW chapters and state licensure boards to develop practice guidelines and regulatory standards to protect clients from coaches with no mental health training and to protect social workers' practice domain.

Confidentiality and Technology: HIPAA

"Confidentiality is a professional duty to refrain from speaking about certain matters; it is an ethic that protects a client from unauthorized disclosures of information" (Linzer, 1999, p. 51). Social work agencies are moving toward electronic records. We are using more electronic technology in teaching and research. Managed care relies heavily on technology for immediate transmission of information. Telephone reviews, facsimile transmissions, voice-mail reports, and computerized databases used by managed care companies as well as agencies seriously compromise the guarantee of confidentiality (Davidson & Davidson, 1996, cited in Rock & Congress, 1999). Today, most computers are networked both within and between agencies. This means there is no longer one case record, but in reality the case record sits on every worker's desk (Rock & Congress, 1999). Workers should recall the distinction between security and privacy: "Security refers to the protection of hardware, software, file tapes, and so on. Privacy refers to the protection of information in the system" (Linzer, 1999, p. 53).

The Health Insurance Portability and Accountability Act (HIPAA) of 1996, Public Law 104-191, which became effective on April 24, 2001, set national standards for the protection of health information, as applied to health plans, health care clearinghouses, and health care providers who conduct transactions electronically. Covered entities must implement standards to protect and guard against the misuse of identifiable health information. Failure to comply in a timely manner can result in civil or criminal penalties. The privacy rule established, for the first time, a foundation of federal protections to protect health information. Currently, all health and mental health care patients must sign forms signifying that they have agreed to allow their providers to transmit confidential information electronically. This is an expansion of the concept of "informed consent" that refers "to the use of clear and understandable language to tell clients about the purpose, risks, and limits of the service, relevant costs, reasonable alternatives, their right to ask questions and to refuse or withdraw consent to the service or treatment and the time frame covered by the consent" (NASW, 1996, cited in Linzer, 1999, p. 51). The rule does not replace federal, state, or other laws in effect that grant even greater privacy protections, and covered entities are free to adopt even more protective policies or practices. For a general overview of standards for privacy of individually identifiable health information, refer to the government website (www.hhs.gov/ocr/hipaa/guidelines/overview.pdf) (Reamer, 2001, 2003; Madden, 2003).

In spite of protective legislation, breaches of confidentiality should be expected to take place in electronic media, and confidentiality cannot be guaranteed. Social workers are therefore cautioned that information that is potentially life-threatening may be too risky to be stored electronically and should be secured in other ways.

Fee for Service

Some outpatient mental health agencies have shifted from hiring clinical social workers on a salaried line to a fee-for-service payment structure. Fee for service is similar to a private practice model that compensates the clinician based on the number of patient hours billed. In an agency fee-for-service model, policy decisions about cancellations, client populations serviced, outreach, and case management are controlled by the agency. Most agencies bill only for services rendered, thereby providing no compensation to social workers for missed client appointments. Additionally, many clinicians provide outreach services that require home visits. If the client is not home, the fee-for-service social worker not only loses out on compensation for the visit but may also have to pay for her own travel expenses.

Some agencies provide health insurance to full-time fee-for-service clinicians if certain productivity requirements are consistently met. Other agencies offer "vacation" privileges, but expect productivity to be "made up" within a subsequent period of time. The social work profession has always been committed to agency-based practice to serve those clients in the community who are the most vulnerable. However, vulnerable clients suffer numerous difficulties that render it unlikely that they can consistently fit into an agency appointment structure. They often need to appear at welfare centers and clinics and are subject to long waits for service. They may not come to their social work appointments because they simply are called elsewhere. Fee-for-service arrangements that meet agency needs must also begin to recognize social workers' needs. Professional organizations and educators must begin to monitor employment practices, advocating for those practices that are fair and reasonable and that support just compensation for fee-for-service social work practice.

The Client in a System of Care

Contemporary social work practice is reemphasizing a community-based model that is the bedrock of the profession, and that gained strength in the 1960s but went out of favor as psychoanalytic thinking and an emphasis on individual internal processes gained momentum (see, for example, Lightburn & Sessions, 2005). This model of community-based practice, the person-in-environment perspective, emphasizes all that is unique in the professional identity of social workers, and that differentiates the discipline from every other field of mental health. The environment, or systems of care, includes the community composed of family, friends, community-based health and mental health services, schools, religious affiliations, neighborhood houses, and home-based mental health treatment. The system of care model stresses programs of prevention and early intervention, and an interdisciplinary approach. It calls on the social worker to partner with multiple service agencies in the client's environment to form "communities of concern."

The clients social workers serve are the most vulnerable members of society. They are often isolated from social networks, and, when they do experience support, it is often fragmented and inadequate. We urge clinical social workers to view their clients holistically and to form multidisciplinary collaborations with the network of service providers in the clients' lives. This will not only improve clients' health but also lead to innovation in service delivery and bring new alternatives to existing approaches.

Spirituality and Religion

A recent issue of prominence in social work practice is that of spirituality and religion (Linzer, 1999). (Please refer to Chapter 4, "The Psychosocial Study," for a detailed explanation of these two concepts.) Jacobs (2010, citing Hodge, 2004, p. 40) writes about "spiritual competence in social work practice." This competence requires respect for a client's spiritual autonomy, curiosity about a client's worldview, sensitivity to people's different faiths, and monitoring one's own "religious countertransference." Social workers must identify with the values of the profession in the area of spirituality and religion as in all other areas of practice and not impose their own spiritual views on their clients, or make judgments that stem from their personal perspectives. Social work values always take precedence over personal values. The NASW *Code of Ethics* provides clear guidelines for ethical practice and should be referred to whenever a conflict of values may arise.

Social Work in a Global Economy

A great deal of contemporary dialog is focused on the definition and nature of international social work. Some of the issues raised include the process of globalization versus the development of locally based solutions to problems, the relevance of Western social work to developing countries, and concern as to whether the values of the social work profession may conflict with those of more traditional countries (Gray & Fook, 2004, p. 627). Gray and Fook caution against schools of social work—and the international social work agenda—becoming another form of cultural imperialism by generalizing about social work across international contexts (p. 638). Another issue is the possibility that focusing resources internationally may detract from working with poor communities in the United States, particularly as social work students seek field internships and experiences in other countries. Rosenthal (1991) notes that what happens in the rest of the world has a direct impact on what happens at home. Social welfare issues in Africa, Latin America, Southeast Asia, the Caribbean, Mexico, and the Middle East (to name only a few of the countries) affect the influx of refugees who migrate to the United States to seek a better life. This migration affects social workers, whose work, especially in urban centers, is largely dominated by the social problems of new immigrants.

It seems that, at a minimum, social workers across the globe can be united in the goals of social justice and human rights, sharing common missions and common values. All social workers believe in the worth of the individual and the right of clients to self-determination and self-respect. A genuine cross-cultural exchange of ideas and knowledge enables all practitioners to learn from one another and gain a real appreciation of their differences as well as similarities.

Therapist Self-Care and Self-Compassion

We conclude this chapter with the very important topic of therapist self-care. Using oneself authentically with a wide range of clients on a daily basis is emotionally demanding. It involves ongoing self-reflection and self-monitoring to ensure that the clinician responds professionally and empathically. Germer (2005, pp. 11–12) writes: "The therapy office can be like a meditation room in which we invite our moment to moment experience to become known to us, openly and wholeheartedly." Working with the most underprivileged members of society within the context of shrinking resources places social workers at risk for burnout (Ying, 2009), leading to high job-turnover and premature departure from depression (Maslach, Schaufeli, & Leiter, 2001). Hiratsuku (1991, cited in Pieper, 1999) coined the term *compassion fatigue* to describe what could happen when the clinical social worker feels stuck with unrewarding clinical experiences. When this occurs, the therapist might find herself disclosing more of her personal life than is appropriate, raising topics that the client has not expressed an interest in discussing, and, in general, gratifying her own needs and becoming less emotionally available. To protect oneself, a therapist must strive to achieve a sense of balance in her life. Therapist self-care protects from burnout by defining the balance between the therapist's caring for self and caring for others. The concept of self-care also reduces risk factors that are associated with ethical violations. Self-care enhances therapy by promoting and modeling growth and well-being (Porter, 1995, p. 250). A new term, *self-compassion*, has been defined by Neff (2003, p. 87) as being touched by and open to one's suffering, understanding and openness to one's pain, inadequacies, and failures, and viewing one's experience as part of the larger human experience. Self-compassion is a self-orientation with the components of mindful awareness, belief in common humanity, and self-kindness (Ying, 2009). Mindful awareness allows social workers to face their difficulties with equanimity instead of reacting emotionally, and protects against unethical practices such as acting out countertransference reactions (Ying, 2009). Self-compassion appears to be an emotional regulation strategy that transforms negative thoughts and emotions into self-acceptance, thereby enhancing effective coping (Gilbert & Proctor, 2006; Neff, 2003; Neff, Kirkpatrick, & Rude, 2007).

Fraunce (1990), writing from a feminist perspective, sees a connection in how the therapist behaves toward herself and her clients, as well as how clients behave toward themselves. She discusses the importance of the therapist's role-modeling effective self-care strategies, often something clients themselves struggle with in their own lives.

What tools can clinical social workers use to balance their own needs and the clients' well-being? We believe this begins in graduate education where the seeds for a professional clinical social work career are planted. Graduate schools of social work face a dilemma in contemporary times. There is an absolute need for flexible programs to make the profession available to those who may be economically challenged, to people of color who traditionally have been unable to pursue higher education, to those with family responsibilities and experience who may be returning to school, and to a host of others. However, a graduate program in social work is a challenging endeavor that requires time and commitment—intellectually and emotionally. This is difficult to handle when trying to balance other social and economic roles, contributing to role strain. Students are further burdened and stressed by the demands of their clients, often because they have not yet learned the importance of maintaining flexible but clear boundaries. In addition, students often have their own histories of trauma or loss that can easily be triggered in the social work practice setting. Balancing the rigors of graduate education with self-care is important because this is the time one begins to lay the foundation for professional practice. Schools of social work need to examine this issue carefully and find ways to make graduate education available and challenging while encouraging self-care.

We encourage faculty to space exams and papers so that students can have time to reflect and reconstitute their energies, rather than having to produce for all courses at the same time. We suggest more informal gatherings (such as lunchtime seminars) where students and faculty can engage in stimulating conversations and exchange new ideas. It is important for students to realistically assess their work, school, and family commitments, adjusting schedules to ensure some time to rest and refuel. In today's fast-paced world, students and faculty alike need opportunities to slow down, think, process, and nourish their minds as well as their selves. As Eldridge and colleagues (1993, p. 5) point out, "Therapist self-care is an ethical imperative. If we are not fairly consistent in caring for our changing personal needs, it will be very difficult to prevent us from meeting those needs in our therapeutic relationships."

We conclude this segment with a cautionary note. The movement toward community-based practice poses new challenges to social workers and students who may be visiting homes and working in agencies in impoverished neighborhoods that are no strangers to crime and violence. Schools of social work must require that outreach agencies take safety precautions with students, and students should assert themselves and insist on protection if they are at all uncomfortable in their surroundings.

The NASW recommends a multilevel approach to increased safety for the profession. It stresses that each agency and private practitioner should develop safety policies and procedures that address prevention, intervention, and aftermath strategies. There are extensive safety guidelines available through NASW that were drafted by the NASW Committee for the Study and Prevention of Violence Against Social Workers (see, for example, www.NASWMA.org).

We urge students to leave office doors open when interviewing violence-prone clients and to request that a security guard be placed nearby. Have an exit strategy. Request that agency personnel escort you to homes in areas where crime is rampant, and provide agency vehicles for travel whenever possible. Don't leave your belongings unattended (especially handbags and cell phones), and lock your office door when you are not inside. The field is constantly changing, as are the client populations. Therapist self-care reduces risk factors for clients—it should also reduce risk factors for those who serve them.

Summary

We encourage our students to continue discussing the important issues that have been highlighted in this chapter. Open speech in classes and supervision of potential ethical and boundary violations will help prevent clinicians from acting on unconscious feelings that might lead to behavior that is injurious to both the client and the therapeutic relationship. Clients at risk for suicide must be carefully assessed, and steps must be taken immediately to provide safety and care. It seems likely that managed care policies will continue to affect social work practice. Knowledge of brief treatment is essential if social workers are to provide quality service within the constraints of time. And finally, we stress the importance of therapist self-care. Working with clients is demanding and not always gratifying. Clinicians need to find ways to nurture themselves so that they can continue to be empathic, nonjudgmental, self-aware, and able to act in the best interests of those they serve.

3

The Clinical Interview: The Process of Assessment

Beginning, Middle, and End Stages of Treatment

In this chapter, we discuss the clinical interview in the beginning, middle, and end phases of treatment. Brief therapy with an adolescent boy diagnosed with a conduct disorder illustrates both the client's and the worker's responses to the various clinical issues that emerge at each stage. A transtheoretical model of treatment, the stages of change model, frames the case example of a teenage boy diagnosed with a conduct disorder.

The First Meeting

The initial clinical interviews are the process by which data collection takes place. The psychosocial summary, which is described in detail in Chapter 4, is the product of that therapeutic process. Initially, the worker needs to gather the information that forms the basis of the psychosocial assessment. She also begins to establish the working alliance.

Who should attend the first meeting? When a parent calls about help for a child, will the entire family attend? When you first see a new client, what do you observe? Sometimes it is how she sits in the waiting room. Is she reading, sleeping, pacing? Does she seem eager to respond to your greeting or anxious about entering your office? What and whom has she brought to the interview? How is she dressed? Seasoned practitioners seem to take in this information through their bones; inexperienced workers, however, will need to be very conscious and use all their powers of observation when meeting a client for the first time.

A question that frequently comes up with regard to the first meeting concerns theoretical framework. This is a tricky issue, and clinicians who work from a particular theoretical lens may conduct their entire diagnostic assessment within a particular framework. This may be based on the clinician's theoretical orientation, but it may also be based on the context of practice. Clinical program administrators may limit options to those that are favored by managed care companies (previously discussed in Chapter 2). These tend to be evidence-based models such as Cognitive and Behavioral Therapy that have a good degree of merit with certain conditions such as mood disorders, fears, and phobias. However, we recommend an initial interview that uses many open-ended questions and allows the client to tell her story as this is the best way to gather information, even when completing a more structured psychosocial study (see Chapter 4). Beginning interviewers as well as seasoned clinicians must also be self-aware or mindful of what makes for a good therapeutic relationship.

Self-Awareness

Self-awareness is an umbrella term. Within the context of the clinical interview, we relate self-awareness to an understanding of the multiple dimensions of the worker's identity and how that interacts with the multiple dimensions of the client's identity. This includes attention to race, gender, sexual orientation, spirituality, and social class. Sommers-Flanagan and Sommers-Flanagan (2009) propose an exercise to initiate the process of self-awareness: People sit in pairs and ask each other the same question a number of times; the same answer cannot be used twice. The questions they ask each other (changing roles) are "Who are you?" and "Who do you see?" (p. 13). Of course for beginning interviewers, this process of reflection on self and other may have to take place retrospectively. With time and experience, it will begin to happen within the interview.

Introductions

When you introduce yourself to a new client, use your full name. Then ask the client how he or she would like to be addressed. You may call a client by a first name if so directed; otherwise, using a title and surname is more respectful. This may be particularly significant when meeting older clients and clients from minority cultural groups. Obviously, there may be individuals and settings where this general rule can be relaxed, such as when meeting young children or adolescents for the first time (see Chapter 13, "Clinical Practice with Children and Adolescents," for further discussion).

Be on time for your first meeting with a client (and all subsequent meetings). If a client is late for the meeting, it is important to ask about this in a nonthreatening manner. Talk to your client about this openly and collaboratively establish the guidelines for subsequent meetings. This should include a discussion of when to call if an appointment needs to be cancelled. Remember, this first meeting often sets the stage for what is to follow.

It is important to pay attention to the seating in your office. You should avoid sitting behind a desk when you are interviewing a client, because this may introduce a power imbalance in the relationship. Clients who come from cultures where the "doctor" is expected to be an authority may relate to you more formally than someone who is born and raised in the dominant culture. Take your cues from the client's behavior. Remember, the client is assessing you while you are assessing her. Keep pictures of your partner, children, and pets at home; displaying personal items is inappropriate. If your client is struggling with finding a mate, she doesn't need to see you as part of a happy family. It may stir up envy and add to the client's burden.

Why Is the Client Here?

The best way to begin the initial interview is by learning why the client has come to see you. Questions such as "What brings you here today?" or "What is on your mind today?" are helpful in getting started. Frequently, clients are flooded in the beginning, often too overwhelmed to give much information. It's important to have a tissue box close to the seating arrangement—many clients cry as soon as they hear the comforting voice of a person whom they believe will be able to help them find a way out of their pain.

It is helpful to provide structure initially and to educate your client about what is going to take place in the interview, including what kinds of questions you will be asking and why. Try to present yourself as an interested, empathic, helpful person, and not an investigator or interrogator. Make sure that you have acquainted yourself with the questions on the intake form ahead of time so that you can move smoothly into new subject areas as you collect information. Open-ended questions are best to use at this time to give the client an opportunity to tell her story. If you are unclear about something, a gentle interruption, such as, "What you are saying seems very important—I'd like to ask you a little more about that," may be used. Listen for clinical themes such as substance use, mood disturbance, anxiety behaviors, physical complaints, social and personality problems, difficulty thinking, and psychosis (Morrison, 1995). This will help you question about specific symptoms, which may be diagnostically helpful as well as determine your theoretical frame of reference. It is also important to obtain information about the client's resources and coping capacities. Be mindful that the client needs some protection in the beginning—too quick a revelation of all her struggles and defeats may leave her feeling vulnerable and fearful of returning. Try to keep the interview moving. Long silences can create anxiety.

Confidentiality

Let the client know that you need to have some specific information that may be difficult to remember, such as demographic data or dates of certain events, and that you may have to write these things down. Explain what you are writing and get the client's permission before moving ahead. It is not helpful to have a completed intake form only to lose your client because she perceived you as insensitive or preoccupied with note-taking. It is also important to let the client know the parameters of the clinical relationship and what material will and will not be kept confidential. Clients should be informed of what types of information can be shared with third parties, and under what circumstances, and asked to sign service agreements that clearly address these issues. (See the section "Confidentiality and Technology" in Chapter 2 and Chapter 13 for further discussion.)

Answering Personal Questions

Clients may sometimes ask you personal questions in an initial interview. Different theoretical models understand and address this important issue in varying ways. In general, it is important to understand the meaning that such questions have to the client and, whenever you are unsure of the meaning, to feel comfortable asking. This is not to be confused with feeling threatened by a client's asking a personal question and reacting with a response such as "Why do you ask?" which can feel disrespectful or embarrassing to the client.

In most cases, clients ask personal questions because they want to know what kind of life experiences the clinician has had and whether she will be able to understand what the client is talking about. This issue has particular significance in cross-cultural work, especially when the therapist may be from the dominant culture and the client may be from a minority background. As greater numbers of minorities enter the helping professions, they may also find themselves working with clients from the dominant culture who may be questioning whether the minority therapist can understand their difficulties. Many years ago, a young African American female student was taken aback when a young white female client asked her how she felt about white people, since they were often mean to black people. White therapists have been asked many times when working with African American clients how they feel about black people. These are difficult and complex issues for which no simple answer is available.

The key is to understand the significance to the client and to always put her best interests first. The clinician may be uncomfortable about sharing personal information even when it might be helpful to the client; in these instances, the clinician needs to acknowledge his understanding of what the client is looking for and honestly share feelings of discomfort. For example, one might say, "I'm sorry. I'm not comfortable talking about my personal life with you. I can understand this may be disappointing to you, but I hope we will be able to work together in spite of my decision" or "I'm not comfortable talking about my personal life with you, but I'd like to understand what asking that question means to you or whether you feel I can help you without answering personal questions."

It is important to differentiate between questions the client may be asking about your personal life from those he or she may be asking about how your training, credentials, or personal values that could compromise your ability to be of assistance. You have an ethical responsibility to answer questions that will enable the client to make an informed decision about whether to engage in treatment with you. For example, you might be asked by a client if you are a "Christian therapist," and, upon hearing that you are not, the client might ask if you feel you could work with him and help with his problems even though you have different religious beliefs. You must also tell the client if you are a student or a clinical trainee, regardless of whether the client asks about your credentials. After stating your name, simply state, "I am a student (or an intern) training to be a social worker. I will be working at this agency until May. My work with you will be supervised by a licensed social worker. If you have any questions about this, I would be happy to discuss them." By inviting the client to talk about any concerns she may have, you convey a willingness to be of help, which the client will appreciate.

The Therapeutic Relationship

The concept of the therapeutic relationship has its origins in the psychoanalytic literature. Freud (1912) was the first to speak of the patient as an active collaborator in the treatment process. He introduced several theoretical concepts—transference, countertransference, the real relationship, the working alliance, and resistance—that have survived and, with revision, have continued to influence the theoretical relationship in clinical social work practice. In fact, every psychotherapeutic model that followed Freud (including psychoanalytic, cognitive, behavioral, and postmodern theories) has considered at least one or more of these constructs either within the context of the theoretical formulation or as a basis for departure (see, for example, DeLaCour, 1998; Greenberg & Mitchell, 1983; Jordan, Kaplan, Miller, Stiver, & Surrey, 1991; Monk, Winslade, Crocket, & Epston, 1997; Safran & Segal, 1996). Since these concepts form the core of understanding the therapeutic relationship, their original definitions and an understanding of their usage in current practice models will follow.

Transference and Countertransference

Transference, as originally introduced by Freud, is the "experiencing of feelings, drives, attitudes, fantasies and defenses toward a person in the present which are inappropriate to that person and are a repetition, a displacement of reactions, originating with significant persons of early childhood." Transference is based on a relationship in the past (Greenson, 1967, p. 33). Relational psychoanalytic theories place the concept of transference into the therapeutic dyad and consider that a client's transferential responses may be evoked by the therapist.

Countertransference is a controversial subject in contemporary times. It was originally defined as "a transference reaction of an analyst to a patient . . . when the analyst reacts to his patient as though the patient were a significant person in the analyst's early history" (Greenson, 1967, p. 348). Initially confined to the therapist's personal feelings, countertransference, like transference, has become more relational in scope. This concept is now considered to be both the result of the therapist's own unconscious processes and an appropriate reaction by the therapist to the patient—an important indicator of the patient's relational style. This reciprocal influence of the conscious and unconscious subjectivities of two people in the therapeutic relationship is called *intersubjectivity*. This concept expands the earlier definitions of transference and countertransference by suggesting that the therapist and the patient not only bring their own separate lives to the therapeutic encounter but also understand and change each other during this process (Natterson & Friedman, 1995).

Cultural Countertransference. Perez-Foster (1998, p. 42) describes *cultural countertransference* as a "complex and interacting set of culturally derived personal life values; academically based theoretical/practice beliefs; emotionally driven biases about ethnic groups; and feelings about their own ethnic self identity." Clinicians have an ethical obligation to be mindful of cultural countertransference especially in cross-cultural therapeutic relationships. Also attend to self-awareness and identity development multicultural competence and a respectful "not knowing stance" (Basham, 2004, p. 299) during the interview. Lesser and Pope (2010) remind us that clinicians from a background similar to their clients must also be aware of cultural countertransference because their assessment could be biased by subjectivity. Germer (2009) suggests using phrases such as "May you and I be free from the pain of prejudice." And "May we all be free from the pain of ignorance" can be helpful to the therapist struggling with cultural countertransference or when the therapist is faced with statements of bigotry from the client.

The Real Relationship and the Working Alliance

The *real relationship* is the "realistic and genuine relationship between analyst and patient in the here and now" (Greenson, 1967, p. 217). The concept of the real relationship is imbedded not only in psychoanalytic theories but also in the cognitive, behavioral, cross-cultural, and postmodern models presented in this book. In many ways, the real relationship between the therapist and the patient is the precursor to the concept of the *working alliance*—the rapport that develops between the therapist and the patient that makes it possible to work purposefully in therapy. Bordin (1979, p. 252) concurred with Freud's view that the alliance between the therapist and the client is "one of the keys, if not the key, to the change process." He elaborated on the importance of the working alliance across theoretical models by pointing out that all models include working alliances.

The effectiveness of therapy depends to a great extent on the strength of the working alliance. The strength of the alliance is determined by the "closeness of fit" (Bordin, 1979, p. 253) between the demands of the particular kind of alliance and the personal characteristics of client and therapist. The patient experiences insight, emotional growth, and increased problem-solving capabilities as a result of the therapist's understanding and contributions to this process. Saari (1986, p. 49) refers to this as the "therapeutic culture" created mutually by the client and the therapist during their interactions with each other.

Resistance

Greenson (1967, p. 60) presents the original psychoanalytic definition of *resistance* as "a counterforce in the patient, operating against the progress of the analysis, the analyst, and the analytic procedures and processes." He quotes Freud (1912, p. 103), who states: "The resistance accompanies the treatment step by step. Every single association, every act of the person under treatment must reckon with the resistance and represents a compromise between the forces that are striving towards recovery and the opposing ones." The concept of resistance has also undergone revision in psychoanalytic thinking. Originally considered an obstacle to the therapeutic work, resistances came to be understood as the source of important information regarding the patient's ego functions. Wachtel (1982, 2009) writing from a contemporary relational psychodynamic perspective (see Chapter 8, "Relational Theory") equates resistance with patient conflicts about changing. Beginning therapists, in particular, often view resistance as something that has to be overcome. Wachtel suggests instead that therapists view resistance as the way in which the patient is trying to communicate to the therapist at a particular point in the therapy. Behaviors that are considered "resistant" by the therapist may serve as adaptive functions for the patient and may protect the patient from experiencing pain, anger, shame, anxiety, or many other uncomfortable feelings. This is much more in line with postmodern theories that do not adhere to the concept of resistance and the cognitive and behavioral theories that view resistance as obstacles to the change process.

Using These Concepts in Practice

As you listen to the client's story, pay attention to the feelings that are stirred up in you. Often the best aid to forming a diagnosis comes from your own felt responses to the client and to the material that the client presents. A cautionary word is important here so that you do not confuse feelings that may be aroused in you by the client with acting on those feelings in an inappropriate manner. You have a responsibility to differentiate between countertransference feelings that may be aroused as a result of your own history and countertransference feelings that may be elicited by the client. No matter the source of the countertransference, you must always act in a professional manner and in the best interests of the client. Although this may seem obvious, when feelings in the therapist are stirred, it is easy to forget that this is a therapeutic relationship, not a personal one.

Transtheoretical Model: The Stages of Change

The stages of change model, developed by James Prochaska and colleagues in 1977, uses interventions from several theoretical models and is therefore called *transtheoretical.* (For a complete description of this model, see, for example, Prochaska, Norcross, & DiClements, 1994; Prochaska & DiClemnti, 2005; Prochaska & Norcross, 2010.) We include a discussion of it here, as it frames the case study provided in this chapter. We also believe the model can be used to guide the clinical interview, as it enables the worker to conceptualize the movement of a case from beginning to end.

This model has undergone several changes over the years, but the core stages of this model are described as follows:

1. *Precontemplation.* In this stage, the client is not considering change. Denial and rationalization are prominent defenses. The therapist, in this stage, validates the client's lack of readiness but encourages reevaluation, consciousness raising, and self-exploration. These techniques are borrowed from psychoanalytic theory.
2. *Contemplation.* In this phase, the client is considering change, but is perhaps ambivalent. Clarification, reflection, empathy, and warmth are the techniques borrowed from humanistic/existential theory and are important to use during this stage.
3. *Preparation.* In this stage, the client is trying to change, perhaps planning action with a month. Problem-solving techniques, borrowed from cognitive behavioral theory, help identify obstacles to progress, and an action plan (behavioral) with small initial steps are encouraged.
4. *Action.* In this phase, the client overtly modifies behaviors. This stage is behavioral, although the client can also change levels of awareness, emotions, self-image, and thinking. The therapist promotes the client's self-efficacy and focuses on social support.

5. ***Maintenance.*** In this stage, there is a continued commitment to new behaviors, and rewards are supported and reinforced. Coping with relapse is discussed. Humanistic/existential techniques such as empathy and warmth and behavioral techniques such as positive reinforcement are used.
6. ***Termination.*** In this stage, self-efficacy has been achieved.

As can be noted, some stages call for a combination of techniques from different theoretical approaches, and these approaches can be found in several of the chapters of this book.

The Case of Dan: An Example of the Stages of Change The Beginning

The Referral

Dan, a 16-yea r-old boy, was referred for treatment by the assistant principal at his school. She mandated that he attend therapy after he received 21 suspensions—all for being disrespectful to his teachers. Dan was described as a charismatic leader who was very angry. A board of education psychiatrist who saw the boy for an emergency consultation diagnosed him as having a "severe conduct disorder." The family agreed to treatment as an alternative to placement in a special school for children with disciplinary problems.

Reading and hearing this referral material would have placed the therapist on guard had she not already been experienced both in the public school system and with boys diagnosed with "conduct disorder." Many of those children so diagnosed had turned out to be deprived of nurture and eager to seek approval from delinquent peer groups. And frequently the school system had been too quick to pin a label on a nonconforming child.

Dan Tells His Story

Dan came to the first interview accompanied by his father. Dan was dressed in the baggy shorts and loose T-shirt typical of teenage boys today. What was notable was the baseball cap pulled down over his forehead, the scowl on his face, and his clenched hands. This boy was obviously tense and angry. His father, who was sitting in the waiting room with him, reading, looked perfectly pleasant, with a nice smile on his face and an anxious but warm greeting. Dan entered the office and took the far chair, displaying his desire to maintain distance by sitting far away from the therapist. With encouragement, he spoke readily but with anger about why he was here. According to him, he'd been in continual trouble in school because the teachers were all "idiots," and he backed this up with some credible examples. He spoke of how he had challenged their intellects as well as their authority. He had earned a reputation as a troublemaker, and no matter who was misbehaving in class, he felt that he was always singled out as the one to blame and given harsher and more frequent punishments than his peers. This had been a problem since elementary school. Dan also shared that he had lived with his mother after his parents divorced, between the ages of 6 and 13, that he "hated" his mother for physically and emotionally abusing him, that his father had tried for custody of him and his sister over the years but had not succeeded in court, and that, finally, his mother "disappeared" after some criminal activity and was last heard from two years ago on his birthday. He described her in profane terms and also said she was known to be "mentally ill." This was a lot of information to get from a teenager in an initial interview. The therapist commented to Dan that he was a good provider of information. He answered that he'd seen

(continued)

The Case of Dan Continued

shrinks before, told his story before, and that it hadn't helped. The therapist was interested in why and whether Dan had any hopes that this therapy might be helpful. He said that all the therapists did was listen but nothing ever changed in his life. He was just doing this so that he could get back into school.

The Therapist's Response

During his retelling of why he had been mandated to come to counseling, the therapist remained empathic, supportive, and inquisitive, letting Dan know that she was glad he was here, whatever the reasons, by simply telling him so. She could see that Dan was in the precontemplation stage of change. He was not ready to accept ownership of any of the difficulties he was encountering. The therapist explained that she didn't yet know what was the reality, but she accepted his story as his experience of what had happened to him. She mentally noted that she, like Dan, had encountered many incompetent professionals in her life, and she was sure that teachers as well as therapists could be included in that list. The therapist was interested to see if Dan had empathy for anyone, because without that quality, the prognosis would indeed be grim. He did say, when asked, that he had a lot of friends—a good sign—and that he cared about his dad. He seemed quite intelligent, and it was apparent that his cognitive abilities had not been impaired by the abuse he had suffered.

Although he was angry and challenging, the therapist felt for him, thinking how hard it must be to be raised without a mother's love. His father, when learning that the referral had been made to a woman, commented, "I hope she is smart." Would Dan test the therapist? Would his father? Would Dan be more comfortable seeing a man? The gender of the therapist can sometimes be of significance to certain clients, and he had been abused and traumatized by a woman. It was critical that the therapist be as kind and caring as possible, so as to provide a different relational experience for this very wounded child.

The therapist told Dan that she agreed that there were incompetent mental health professionals as well as doctors, lawyers, teachers, politicians, and so forth, but that since therapy seemed inevitable, she would like to try to help him out of the trouble he was in so that he could be successful at school. In spite of his protests and responses about "not caring," the therapist sensed that Dan cared very deeply about what people thought of him, that he had a wish to do well, and told him so. She spoke to Dan about confidentiality and explained that she would only reveal what he shared if she thought he was at risk of hurting himself or others. He had heard this before—from his previous therapists, and they were all idiots too. The therapist acknowledged that it can be hard to hear things repeated since he had been in therapy before, but that she felt it was important for her to understand how he was feeling this time around. She told Dan that she could understand that he might not be ready for change and that was not uncommon when someone was mandated for treatment and not there on their own volition.

When Dan was asked if there were any times when he was feeling bad enough to want to hurt himself in any way, he responded, "No, not now, I just feel angry now . . . there were times in the past when I wished I could disappear, though." The therapist said that it sounded like he may have been very discouraged at those times. "Did you ever think about ways that you might make yourself disappear?" Dan avoided eye contact at this point and said that there were times that he thought he might take some pills, but he didn't want to hurt his father. The therapist replied by saying, "Thanks for telling me about that, Dan. It isn't always easy to talk about these things."

The Case of Dan Continued

After they had finished talking, the therapist spoke with Dan and his father for 10 minutes together. An adolescent boy in treatment needs to feel separate from his family as he deals with adolescent issues of autonomy and independence. However, it is also important to establish an alliance with Dan's father, although he seemed nervous and not really interested in being part of the therapy. Often, parents feel discouraged and hopeless when they have a child in constant difficulty. The father seemed more than willing to have the professional handle things and wanted to be left alone. Nonetheless, it was important for Dan to hear his father's reasons for bringing him to therapy and equally important for Dan's father to hear Dan's view of the situation. Seeing father and son together would also establish a framework for future joint sessions, if deemed appropriate. Weingarten (1997, p. 311) discusses the importance of seeing adolescents with their parents: "A parent and adolescent can benefit from hearing each other's stories, and that each may be a resource for change for the other."

The Therapist's Conceptualization

Dan showed many of the characteristics of a precontemplator. He was rationalizing his problems, perceiving them as rooted in the lack of expertise of his teachers, and their scapegoating of him. He denied his own part in these troublesome interactions, projecting blame onto others who he saw as ineffectual and unhelpful. It was clear that Dan would need a great deal of understanding and encouragement to motivate him to move toward contemplating change.

It was important not to challenge Dan's perceptions, as confrontation in this precontemplation stage would not have helped him to engage. Dan needed to establish trust so that he could begin to think about what he might do to change. To engage Dan, she had made a conscious decision to be as nurturing as possible and began in a very concrete way—providing, in subsequent sessions, donuts and a drink. Dan ate and drank easily and was appreciative and polite. He had good manners—a sign that he could be respectful. As an eclectic practitioner, the therapist conceptualized her assessment in psychodynamic, object relational terms, thinking about some cognitive and behavioral interventions as well, all of which are elaborated on in other sections of this book. The cognitive and behavioral approaches were important because the client and practitioner had to make quick progress—the school needed results and Dan needed to feel a sense of mastery. She had a tentative working hypothesis: As Dan's story unfolded, she saw a boy who was now so vulnerable to criticism after his long history of abuse that he misperceived any adult slight as a dismissal and invalidation of his very being. When wounded, he felt wounded to the core and was very quick to retaliate the only way he knew how—by using his intelligence to plan and strategize a way to get back, usually by humiliating the perceived perpetrator. The therapist would need to be very careful not to hurt him by invalidating his experience in any way. She'd also have to help him learn better coping strategies, because eventually she or someone else would give an invalidating response, and Dan would have to learn to better manage his anger so as to have a more trouble-free existence in the real world.

Follow-Up to the Initial Interview

After the initial interview, an earlier school psychological report was requested by the therapist. This would provide important information and should always be part of the record when working with a child who has had previous evaluations. If there were no prior school reports,

(continued)

The Case of Dan Continued

the therapist might have talked with him and his father about having an evaluation done by the school-based support team or an outside evaluator. This would help her rule out any learning or attentional issues as well as give a basic understanding of Dan's intellectual capabilities. She was pleased to see that the impressions by the evaluator had matched her own. The psychological report spoke of a boy with "superior intelligence, who was intense, easily upset, moody and highly defensive. He appears to misinterpret the intentions of others and sees them as being hostile and threatening. He then responds with anger and hostility that he feels is reasonable and justified. He has particular difficulty with direction/criticism/correction when given by a female teacher."

During these first visits, the practitioner was also in contact with the assistant principal at Dan's school. She had made the referral and seemed to view him negatively. It was important to make an ally of this woman, and so, with Dan's (and his father's) permission, the therapist shared some of her initial impressions. This school-based intervention was an important one in which the therapist tried to clarify the relationship between Dan's emotional state and his behavior in the classroom. The assistant principal softened when she learned of the abuse and began to want to work with him. She became a great resource for Dan and, ultimately, his advocate at the school.

The therapist now had an initial picture of Dan from listening to his story and reading his evaluations. Equally important was her own response. Sensing a vulnerable child under his aggressive demeanor, she wanted to reach him and wanted him to trust her to do so. She shared the information in the psychological report with him. This was strategic—Dan wanted to know if he was "mentally ill" like his mother, and the report reassured him that he wasn't. It was important for Dan to know what the evaluator saw as his issues and not to paint a rosy picture. The practitioner shared her diagnostic formulation and told Dan that she saw it that way, too. She told him that she had some goals for him, and that one was to help him learn what his triggers were so that he could manage his anger. She told Dan that she would give him strategies for this—since he had a good strategic mind. The therapist would appeal to Dan's logic, which was his strength, by using a direct, truthful, and reality-oriented approach. This wasn't a child to talk with about feelings—not yet, at least. The practitioner would appeal to his strong mind and motivation to do well (yes, he did want to go to college, if only to be able to choose his own teachers and subjects so he could avoid the "idiots" he was so accustomed to).

Intervention Planning

The most important piece of history that informed the assessment and treatment planning was the knowledge that Dan had been mistreated. This fact influenced the therapist's choice of an object relations perspective to use within the stages of change model of conceptualization to understand Dan, particularly as it related to childhood abuse. Mistreated children often have an unconscious need to replicate the original trauma. They are hyperalert to signals of possible abuse, often misperceiving and thinking it is there when it may not be, and can provoke it out of an unconscious desire for mastery (James, 1994). This framework helped shape the practitioner's working hypothesis—that Dan was trying to master the abuse he had experienced at his mother's hand by provoking those in authority who appeared dismissive or critical of him in the hopes that he would hurt them and so be empowered and triumph.

The Middle Stage of Treatment—Moving to Contemplation, Preparation, and Action

Once the initial impressions have been formulated and the treatment plan selected, the worker has the task of moving the therapeutic process ahead to meet certain goals and objectives. The middle stage of treatment is where that process takes place. It is often referred to as the *working-through stage*. In the stages of change model, it is where contemplation begins, and preparation and action follow. Before the advent of brief treatment modalities—and more recently, managed care—the worker had seemingly endless time to engage in this phase of the therapeutic process. Clients spent years in therapy gaining insight and greater understanding, and some made major personality changes. But whether treatment is long term or short term, in the middle phase of treatment there are some predictable occurrences that must be addressed.

There are many reasons why therapy can get "stuck" in the middle phase. It is important to remember that it is normal for clients to be fearful of the unknown. Contemplation can be threatening, as the client faces painful emotions connected to events past and present. Change often threatens the stability of the client's situation, even when that stability is unpleasant. Couples may fight and appear to be unhappy in their marriages, but if change implies that the partnership will end, they may find ways to stay where they are. Resistance, or obstacles to progress as referred to in cognitive and behavioral models, takes many forms. Sometimes a missed session might indicate that the client is struggling with the therapeutic work. Arriving late or arriving early to a session might signal anxiety. Talking about the trivial, rather than the important events in a client's life, can indicate some fears about making changes. It is important that the worker appreciate that there are very real factors that can also present obstacles in the treatment relationship. Many clients lead chaotic or disorganized lives. A single mother may have to take a child to a clinic appointment and wait in line for many hours, missing her therapy hour. Clients are often called unexpectedly to their children's schools or to job interviews. Be mindful of the stresses in your client's life before labeling some behaviors as fears or anxiety about change.

When there appears to be an obstacle to progress in the middle stage of treatment, such as a missed session, a worker can address this by simply saying, "I missed seeing you last week. Did anything happen?" If the client answers vaguely, or indicates that she didn't feel like coming, gently ask if anything happened in the previous session that upset her. What has she been thinking about the therapy? What has she been thinking about your working together? That last question will bring you to issues of transference, which are important to air in the middle stage of treatment. Examine for yourself if you have said or done anything that might have offended or hurt your client. Were you too quick to make an interpretation, too confronting, too unempathic? If you cannot come up with the answer yourself, ask the client or your supervisor. Workers aren't perfect: They make mistakes. But transference reactions occur in spite of what practitioners do. Perhaps you begin to remind your client of a significant person who was critical or judgmental. You can get at this material by asking, "Did I say or do something to remind you of someone in your past—someone in your family or a friend? What was that person like?" It is very important to distinguish transference reactions from reality. Exploring the transference will often help the client make significant progress in present relationships. This is most obvious in couples therapy, when both partners begin to recognize that their strong reactions to spousal behaviors are often based on past anger or annoyances with parents.

Exploring the reality—the real relationship—will help the worker adjust to client needs. A client may be justifiably angry at a worker for numerous reasons. Perhaps she was inattentive, unempathic, or preoccupied. Something as seemingly slight as answering the phone during a client's session may feel like a drop in empathy and produce a strong reaction. You may not hear the reaction right away, but subsequent sessions will provide clues. The skilled worker pays sharp attention during the middle phase to the client's verbal and nonverbal behaviors. It is completely appropriate to mention, for example, that the client seems less talkative, or more edgy, or that something seems different. This is not to be confused with confrontation. Direct confrontation can be offensive and angering to a client, with the exception of those who have or are participating in recovery programs where confrontation is the norm. It is much better to gently comment that it seems hard for the client to talk about something, or to respond to your words, than to rush headlong with an interpretation such as "You are angry that I'm talking about your past." Interpretations often feel like wounds, especially if they are made too early in the work. And they can often be incorrect. It is more appropriate to explore and let the client come up with the meaning for herself. It is important to remember that what is crucial during this stage of therapy is that the client experience safety within the therapeutic relationship so as to be able to overcome the anxiety associated with change and take the necessary steps toward mastery (Wachtel, 1993).

The Case of Dan: Middle Phase Moving to Contemplation, Preparation, and Action

The practitioner's initial sense was that Dan needed a new relational experience—insight into how his past was impacting his current life and the tools to facilitate change. He complained of insomnia. Relaxation training seemed a good method to help him relieve stress. In their fifth session, she taught him a relaxation technique and put this on a tape that he played before bed. Also included on the tape were suggestions as to how he could manage stress. Dan played the tape religiously—it put him to sleep at night. The therapist shared with him her knowledge of what his trigger was, his vulnerability, his Achilles' heel. She did this within the context of her ever-present and conscious decision to make sure that Dan felt safe, respected, and nurtured in their relationship. She used those techniques critical to the contemplation stage of change—warmth, empathy, and clarification. Once trust was established, she could repeatedly, and gently, remind Dan that he overreacts when he feels criticized, humiliated, or dismissed by someone in authority. These interpretations enabled Dan to begin to consider that he had a part in his difficulties and that he could change his behavior. The therapist conveyed empathy and understanding by letting him know that his unsafe feelings originated very early, with his mother, and that was why his reaction was so powerful. In the beginning middle phase of treatment, the therapist made these interpretations rather than use exploration to help him gain this understanding for

The Case of Dan Continued

himself because his extreme behaviors were getting him in trouble in his school. Dan began to listen, and to consider what was being said.

The therapist also allowed Dan to ventilate, a technique that enables the expression of feelings and reactions, and he did this quite frequently. Mostly, Dan ventilated his anger. Using a behavioral intervention, the therapist taught Dan some self-statements that he could use when he felt criticized or dismissed. Instead of telling himself things that fueled his anger as he had been doing (e.g., this idiot is out to humiliate me), he was taught to use statements such as "This isn't personal. The teacher doesn't know me, he's not trying to hurt me. I'm reacting because of my past. I need to stay focused on my goals. I want to succeed. If I get through this I can go to college and be on my own. I need to keep myself cool, reacting with anger only gets me in trouble." Dan memorized these and added a few of his own that were positive in nature. Dan's acceptance of this behavioral technique demonstrated to the therapist that he was moving into the state of preparation. Dan was preparing to change his behavior, and the therapist was helping to give him the small steps required to do so.

Another technique employed was advocacy. The practitioner intervened in the environment, a concept basic to social work practice that is often critical in working with adolescents whose behavioral problems can be misunderstood by people in authority who react punitively, unwittingly replicating past traumatic experiences. She wanted to minimize the opportunity for Dan to become stressed in school. Talks with the assistant principal about Dan's needs resulted in her handpicking Dan's teachers for his fall semester, selecting teachers with experience who had good classroom management skills and nurturing styles. The therapist told Dan that this wouldn't happen throughout his lifetime, and he had the responsibility, ultimately, of managing his emotions, but that, for now, he needed a chance to be successful and have a positive school experience. His job was to stay cool, get good grades, and prove that he was not a troublemaker. Dan was now looking to the therapist as a source of support. Interestingly enough, he had started to decline the snacks that she brought for him. Psychologically, he didn't need my concrete demonstrations of feeding any more. He was being fed in other ways.

In continuing middle phase sessions, the therapist reinforced Dan's impulse control by appealing to his intellectual strengths. Recognizing and acknowledging his strengths helped shore up his adaptive capacities. Using the positive relationship, conversations began to focus on his mother more frequently. Dan began to talk about his memories of his mother's abuse, and the practitioner shared her assessment of the origin of some of his difficulties with anger—how his traumatic past has affected his relationships with authority in the present. "You know, Dan, I think some of the anger you have now may have started when you were a younger boy and you felt confused and upset over how your mother was treating you. . . . What do you think?" About five months into the treatment, Dan's mother called after a three-year hiatus. His initial reaction was rage—he wanted to meet her in person and ventilate his stored-up anger—to abuse her as she had abused him. Dan and the therapist discussed what he would need from her to let her back into his life. He was clear. He wanted an apology and some understanding as to why she had behaved so cruelly to him. And he wanted evidence that he could trust her—that she would be available to him on a consistent basis. The therapist supported him in this, noting how logical and correct he was. Dan and his mother began to correspond by email, and she kept up her part of the bargain by writing

(continued)

The Case of Dan **Continued**

every day. Dan had clearly moved into the action stage—he was changing, and his new behavior was having an impact on significant people in his life. The therapist continued to promote Dan's appropriate self-assertion and continued to use empathy and encouragement to help him negotiate this new relationship.

Simultaneously, Dan began to reduce his sessions to bimonthly. The practitioner speculated that Dan was getting closer to his mother and hence more fearful—something he did not want to think or talk about. Knowing his impulsivity, the therapist felt worried. She stayed in contact with his school and learned that he was becoming more explosive again, picking fights with students and teachers. Clearly, he was under stress. In exploring the reduced sessions with Dan, the therapist learned that his father was feeling the burden financially and that their insurance company was limiting his benefits. This was a reality that could not be ignored. The fact that Dan needed the help, and needed it on a consistent basis, could also not be ignored. (Biweekly sessions are useful for problem-solving therapies, but this client and therapist were now doing more in-depth work, and losing continuity.) The practitioner decided to use email to communicate with Dan between sessions and be available to him via computer from her home to his. She also provided concrete help by asking his insurance company to consider reinstating his benefits. She also spoke with Dan's mother by phone, because Dan was hopeful that, with the therapist's assistance, the mother would shed some light on the past abuse experience. It was the therapist's intention to help the mother convince Dan that he was not to blame. The therapist also referred Dan to a group for children of divorced families that was forming at his high school. This was done so that he could have the social support so necessary in the action stage of change.

Dan and the therapist did not talk about transference issues in the middle stage of treatment. The therapist was working with the positive relationship—quite deliberately—and wanted to keep it so. Negative transferential reactions (i.e., Dan's anger at the therapist) might have caused a rift in their relationship and that would not have been helpful. Dan needed to see the therapist as his ally and supporter—and she could only provide that within a framework of trust and security.

The Ending Phase of Treatment

In long-term treatment, termination is not necessarily agreed on beforehand but is an outgrowth of the therapeutic process that has reached an end. In today's managed care environment, endings may be influenced by insurance carriers who allow a limited number of sessions to reduce symptomatology and achieve clearly delineated objectives.

In these instances, workers generally contract for a definitive number of sessions and collaborate on identifying achievable goals. Often, sessions end before all goals are met. In those cases, the worker might try to make a community referral for continued care or help the client take credit for the progress that has been made and extend advice as to how he or she might continue to work on his or her own. Sometimes the client's goals have not been met because of limited internal and/or external resources, and treatment has not been successful. If the client has not been able to change the exterior of his or her life because of inadequate resources, it is important to empathize with the client's sadness and to validate his or her reality. If progress has not been made because of some inner problems, the worker needs to gently point out that perhaps the client wasn't ready to take on the necessary changes, and to share what internal roadblocks have made change difficult.

Termination can be planned or unplanned. Some clients leave unexpectedly, before the completion of the work. Often this can be due to the disorganization and chaos of the clients' lives. Other times, it may be because of a dissatisfaction in the treatment that did not get addressed. If an unplanned termination occurs, it is helpful to reach out to the client and let her know that the door is always open. If the client cannot be reached by phone, the worker should write a note to that effect and also express well wishes. Clients need to feel that they will not be punished for premature endings and that their actions will be understood within the context of their lives. Even the best planned termination can be fraught with difficulties. The end of a relationship with the worker is a loss, and often brings with it feelings of abandonment for clients, particularly if they have suffered other significant losses in their lives. Clients may react with anger, with sadness, or with little reaction at all. As a worker, it is important to be able to listen, explore, and empathize, but not to personalize. At times it will appear that there is a resurgence of problems when one is trying to end treatment. Or a new crisis may occur. This may present an opportunity for the client to continue the work through referral to someone else—but this is not a reason to hang on.

Workers need to let go when there are clear parameters to the treatment. If a referral needs to be made, it is important for the client to meet the new worker before you leave. When possible, try to facilitate the introduction. If the client comes back to you and reports that she doesn't like the new worker, that she's not as nice as you, be sympathetic but help the client see that there might be a period of adjustment. You need to appear confident in the new worker's abilities to help the client with the transition. In the ending phase, clients might ask for your home phone number or if they can continue to contact you. This is against ethical practice, and it makes it harder for the client to let go. The best way to be of help is to review with the client the progress that has been made, crediting her with her capacity to be effective, and to remain hopeful about the future. Point out next steps—be they continued psychosocial intervention or concrete service needs. Final good-byes can be ritualized by sharing a review of progress with the adult client, making a memory book with a child, or giving small gifts that are appropriate to the work accomplished (e.g., a small book of poems). And although therapists are cautioned not to accept gifts from clients, it is important to be culturally sensitive. For example, many Latina mothers like to express their appreciation of the help you extended to their children with a departing gift. Some cross-cultural students like to bring foods from their countries to the final practice classes. Types of gifts are opportunities to give back and should be accepted in the spirit in which they are presented.

The Case of Dan: Ending Phase of Treatment

Dan and the practitioner did not have an ideal ending. His father pulled him out of treatment prematurely, claiming that the insurance benefits had run out. This became one more abrupt termination for Dan in his lifetime. The court took him away from his mother after he made numerous complaints of child abuse. While he was ostensibly happy to be removed from that traumatic situation, there can be ambivalence toward perpetrators in the traumatized child. And although Dan claims to have been angry at his mother all these years, he readily accepted her efforts to come back into his life. The therapist was concerned that Dan would experience the termination of therapy as an abandonment, no matter how carefully planned. She also knew that Dan might leave therapy in anger. Or there would be denial of the therapist's importance, so as to keep his powerful feelings of loss at bay. They were left with only one session to terminate. During that brief time, the practitioner pointed out the positive steps Dan had taken, the management of his anger, and his ability to use his intellect to see his situation clearly, when not clouded by issues of loss, abandonment, and humiliation. She acknowledged that he might need to feel angry at her, because letting go in anger was easier than ending when you are really feeling good about someone. Dan said little. He kept reiterating that he didn't care, that he only came to therapy because he was forced by the school. The therapist used the transference and interpreted that it would be difficult for him to recognize her as an important person and to leave at the same time. Using the real relationship, she again stated that she was his ally, that she did care about him, and that she would be there for him if he needed her. The therapist felt sad losing Dan and she worried about him. But sometimes the most one can do is to leave the door open and hope that the strength of the relationship will carry the client back to you in the future.

Summary

As our case material has illustrated, clients do not always move smoothly through the stages of treatment. Each phase presents a significant challenge. Beginnings are critical because they provide a model for what will follow, whereas middle-stage issues present a different type of challenge because it is during that time that the treatment may appear to be stagnated, without goals or focus. The worker and client may seem to be covering the same ground again and again, and the same difficulties may be occurring. Eventually, perhaps when least expected, progress will occur, some goals will be achieved, and others will be abandoned in light of new and changing realities. Termination can be unpredictable and more often than not, terminations are difficult for student interns, who can experience the loss as sharply as does the client and can have difficulty letting go. On a final note, we want our students to understand that clinical competence requires continued learning, self-examination, and a willingness to take risks. One becomes a skilled practitioner with increased experience. By remaining open to learning from your clients, your mentors, and your mistakes, you will achieve this in time.

4

The Psychosocial Study: The Product of Assessment

Preparing the Psychosocial Study

In this chapter, we will discuss the psychosocial study. This assessment method consists of the following: (1) the data that have been gathered from the client and other relevant people and sources, (2) an assessment of the client's mental status and current level of functioning—including ego and environmental strengths, (3) the establishment of diagnostic criteria (*DSM-IV-TR*), (4) a theoretical framework that helps practitioners understand the collected data, (5) treatment goals, and (6) a method to evaluate the effectiveness of practice. Each of these components will be further explained in the following model. A sample psychosocial study of a child in a residential treatment center will illustrate this assessment method.

A Human Rights Perspective

The United Nations (UN) established in 1948 a Human Rights Commission and the "Universal Declaration of Human Rights," which were meant to protect vulnerable and oppressed populations and posited the ideas that all humans have worth, are equal in dignity and rights, and entitled to all fundamental freedoms without distinctions, accorded without regard to race, ethnicity, color, culture, country, religion, geography, economic environment, gender, language, opinion, origin, property, birth, demographic characteristic, or any other aspect of human diversity or social status (Hunt, 2007; Reichert, 2003; UN, 1948, in Poindexter, 2008).

The concept of universal human rights contains three intertwined vital principles: rights are (1) inherent, (2) universal, and (3) indivisible (Hunt, 2007, in Poindexter, 2008). First, human rights are by definition present at birth and transcend the biases or discriminations of cultures, religions, governments, and professions (Baxi, 2006, in Poindexter, 2008). Second, universality of rights means that all humans are equally and unconditionally entitled to all these rights and there should be equal access to equal rights (Ife, 2001; Reichert, 2003, in Poindexter, 2008). Third, all human rights are equal to each other, indivisible from each other, unable to be placed in a hierarchy. In sum, all human rights exist for every human unconditionally and are equally applicable to all humans.

Taking a human rights approach means that we must confront and deal with any form of oppression and encompasses a concern with all types of discrimination. In this way, human rights encompass the rights of women, children, elders, gays, transgender persons, sex workers, prisoners, indigenous people, people with disabilities and illnesses, drug users, poor people, dark-skinned people, refugees and immigrants with or without legal documents, and people of all faiths.

From a human rights perspective, assessments of individuals and families should include their awareness of their basic human rights, the effects of environmental gaps and social oppressions, and their links, stressors, and roles regarding social and economic institutions. Assessments should be expanded past the presenting problem into the realm of shelter, information, food, employment, legal, community, medical, cultural, and political realities in their lives. Mutually developed action plans should stem from this expanded assessment, so that interventions would include working toward the elimination of social and economic injustices, including partnering with service applicants and recipients to demand their rights (Rock & Perez-Koenig, 2002).

The paradigm of intersectionality considers how different identities constitute locations of oppression and privilege that simultaneously interact to create unique life experiences and relative amounts of privilege and oppression(Hulkok, 2009). It is a useful model when assessing from a human rights and social justice framework, as it includes both the client's perspective on all types of discrimination and the worker's self-reflection on experiences of oppression and privilege or domination both in her personal life and in the therapeutic relationship.

A Psychosocial Model Outline

Identifying Information. The leading paragraph in this section of the psychosocial study provides a general statement about who the client is. This requires a great deal of sensitivity in handling information about the client's age, gender, race, ethnicity, religion, marital status, employment, resources (family, friends, finances, household members), immigration status, and developmental and physical disabilities. For example, many gay, lesbian, bisexual, and transgendered individuals may not disclose these identity issues initially. They may not see them as being relevant to their presenting problems. It is important to use descriptive language that does not indicate the assumption of heterosexuality or gender (Sommers-Flanagan & Sommers-Flanagan, 2009). Describe the client's appearance, noting dress and grooming, able-bodiedness, and the quality of speech (hesitant, spontaneous, disconnected, pressured). The client's attitude toward the interviewer is also important—does she appear anxious, relaxed, angry, impatient, negativistic, cooperative, unfocused, or comfortable? Consider that this aspect of the assessment is linked to the interviewer's emotional subjectivity, including personal bias (Sommers-Flanagan & Sommers-Flanagan, 2009).

Referral Source. Who is the referring source? What does the referring source say about the client's problem? Is the client seeking treatment voluntarily or involuntarily? Does the client understand the reason for the referral?

Presenting Problem. This critical paragraph requires a statement of the present problems that have led to the referral. It is the reason that the client has come to see you. You may want to include a statement incorporating the client's exact words in presenting her problem. This may be especially significant when the client's presenting problem differs from the referral source's interpretation of the client's presenting problem.

History of the Problem. This section should tell the reader how the problem developed. Did the situation have a rapid onset, or is it chronic in nature? Describe the precipitating events, the course of the symptoms, and any previous attempts to solve the problem. If the client has had previous treatment for the problem, what was the length and frequency of that treatment, and what was its outcome? What was the client's response to the treatment? How did she feel about the therapeutic relationship? What are the circumstances under which the problem is currently manifested (home, school, employment)?

Human Rights and Social Justice. Ask about individual, community, and societal well-being. Is the client aware of her rights and are they being met? Elicit information about the protection of children, elders, women, and families. Inquire about oppression, stigma, and other abuses or violations of human rights. These areas are included here, however, a human rights, social justice, and well-being perspective should frame the entire psychosocial summary.

Previous Counseling Experience. Discuss any previous counseling attempts and their outcomes. It is helpful for the interviewer to have a complete record of the client's experiences with counselors as well as the client's perception of whether the counseling was helpful. Was the client an active participant in the counseling, treated with dignity and respect?

Family Background. Both the facts about the socioeconomic, educational, and occupational background of the family and some conceptualization of how the family members interacted should be included here. How does the client view her family, and how is she viewed by them? The genogram (McGoldrick & Gerson, 1985; McGoldrick, Gerson, & Shellenberger, 1999), a diagram of all members of the nuclear and extended family, can be a useful assessment tool in gathering this data. Genograms can be used in a variety of ways—for example, to illustrate a family structure, record relevant family information, or delineate significant family relationships. Akinyela (2002b) acknowledges the usefulness of the genogram in clinical practice but suggests a broader use by New Afrikan therapists. She suggests locating the family members' lives in the broader social and political context. For example, she writes "in telling the story of a black family in the south, in tracing the generations, it becomes critical to talk about the social, political and economic conditions that those ancestors were living in, and to be curious about how they survived those conditions of life" (p. 45). Other authors (Sommers-Flanagan & Sommers-Flanagan, 2009) remind us that the concept of family may be broader within different cultural contexts, not defined strictly along biological lines, such as families that may include gay, lesbian, bisexual, or transgendered parents; families formed through surrogate mothers, sperm donor fathers, and open adoptions that include the biological mother (or father) of adopted children; and families of adopted children whose ancestry may be unknown. Another useful assessment tool is the ecomap (Hartman, 1978), which offers a visual representation of the family's connections with their environment. Models for a genogram and an ecomap are presented in Chapter 11.

Personal History. This section may include a developmental history (with a child client) and information about prenatal care, birth, achievement of milestones (such as feeding, toileting, language, and motor development), and whether these milestones were achieved within normal time limits. Were there any complications? If assessing a child, include information about school and peer functioning, levels of achievement, and learning differences. (For a thorough developmental history outline in assessing a child, see Webb, 1996, p. 76.) The client's previous attempts to cope with problems should also be discussed. A vocational history should be noted, including adaptation to jobs, bosses, and coworkers, as well as recreational activities and special interests. Is there current and/or past use of substances such as alcohol and drugs, including prescription medication? It is also important to have the client's sexual history (where appropriate) as well as information about any past physical, sexual, or emotional trauma.

Medical History. A medical history helps to rule out the possibility of medical problems and/or organic factors that may be contributing to psychosocial difficulties and also focuses the client's attention on medical needs that may have been overlooked. It is essential that the client has had a recent medical examination. Were the client's rights to access to care upheld?

Educational/Learning History. It is very important to get as detailed information as possible on a client's educational and learning history (whatever the age) to consider whether there may be an undiagnosed learning disorder that needs to be addressed. These may include various learning disabilities such as dyslexia or central auditory processing problems, attention deficit/hyperactivity disorder (ADHD), or problems such as Asperger's. Although emotional problems may impact the ability to learn, it is important to remember that learning difficulties can also cause emotional problems. It is important to get any recent evaluations when working with children and to make appropriate referrals for neuropsychological and educational evaluations when working with children and adolescents, but also with adults, as appropriate. Immigrants and refugees or persons with limited fluency in the language in which the interview is being conducted may appear to lack intelligence or communication abilities; assumptions should not be made until a fuller assessment can be made. Is the client's right to a free and appropriate education being honored and upheld?

Social Class. Consider the socioeconomic history and current situation. For example, whether one comes from a lower socioeconomic class and now lives a middle-class lifestyle may cause a clash in values between parents and their children. Couples who come from different class backgrounds may also experience stress. The impact of social class may also affect the therapeutic relationship if the client comes from a lower—or a higher—socioeconomic class than the therapist. Have issues of social class resulted in stigma and oppression?

Cultural History. It is important to understand the presenting problem within the context of a relevant cultural framework. This would include issues of bicultural identity, generational differences in cultural identification, and degree of acculturation to U.S. society. Is the client able to enjoy his cultural rights? The culturagram (Congress, 1994) is a useful tool that addresses the family's reasons for immigration; their length of time in the community; their immigration status (legal or undocumented); the ages of family members at the time of immigration; language(s) spoken; contact with cultural institutions; health beliefs; holidays and special events; family, education, and work values; and traumatic stressors and crisis events. A model culturagram appears in Chapter 5.

Spirituality/Religion. Included in this section should be some discussion about the client's current or past religious affiliations or spiritual beliefs. It is important to differentiate between religion and spirituality. Spirituality is a personal sense of meaning or belief about one's life and the world. Religion is the way in which those beliefs are formalized, generally within a community context such as participation in a religious organization (Joseph, 1998). How do these factors help practitioners understand the client's perception of the events in her life, and how will this affect the counseling process? Griffith and Griffith (2002) raise the ambivalence the mental health profession has held with regard to spirituality and religion as a source of conversation with clients. We suggest that the clinician explore their own views about this complex topic and then move into inquiry regarding the impact spirituality and religion may have on the client's life. It is also important to remember to initially be open to the client's beliefs in any connection between religion, spirituality, and the sources of their distress (e.g., a punishment from God) as this may be embedded in a larger cultural system that needs to be appreciated (Sommers-Flanagan & Sommers-Flanagan, 2009). Puchalsi and Romer (2000, p. 131) consider spirituality as a potentially important aspect of every client's mental health as well as his or her physical well-being. They offer a spiritual assessment tool that uses the acronym FICA to explore relevant areas of inquiry.

F: Faith or Beliefs. What is your faith or belief? Do you consider yourself spiritual or religious? What things do you believe that give meaning to your life?

I: Importance and Influence. Is it important in your life? What influences does it have on how you take care of yourself? How have your beliefs influenced your behavior during this illness? What role do your beliefs play in regaining your health?

C: Community. Are you part of a spiritual or religious community? Is this of support to you and how? Is there a person or group of people you really love or who are really important to you?

A: Address. How would you like me, your health care provider, to address these issues in your health care?

Mental Status and Current Functioning. The concept of ego functioning is critical to social work assessment. (For an excellent social work text on this theory, see Goldstein, 1995.) Ego psychology is ideally suited to social work practice because of its emphasis on the environment, life roles, and developmental tasks, as well as on a person's inner capacities (Schamess, 1996). In the section on mental status and current functioning, the worker should include a discussion of the characteristic ego functions, mechanisms of defense, and any particular strengths or limitations—social, psychological, physical, or environmental. Also evaluate the client's motivation, ability to be consistent, degree of self-awareness, capacity for insight into her situation, and ability to follow through with treatment recommendations. The functions of the ego and their major components, according to Bellack and colleagues (1973), are briefly listed in Table 4.1. Table 4.2 shows a list of defense mechanisms.

TABLE 4.1 ***Ego Functions***

Ego Function	Components
1. Reality testing	Distinction between inner and outer stimuli. Accuracy of perception of external events and inner reality testing.
2. Judgment	Anticipation of consequences of behavior. Extent to which a manifest behavior reflects an awareness of its probable consequences. Appropriateness of behavior.
3. Sense of reality	Extent of derealization or depersonalization. Self-identity and self-esteem. Clarity of boundaries between self and the world.
4. Regulation and control of drives, affects, and impulses	Directness of impulse expression. Effectiveness of delay and control and the degree of frustration tolerance.
5. Object relations	Degree and kind of relatedness to others. The extent to which present relationships are adaptively or maladaptively influenced by or patterned on older ones and serve present mature aims rather than past immature ones.
6. Thought processes	Memory, concentration, and attention. Ability to conceptualize. Extent to which thinking is unrealistic or illogical.
7. ARISE	Adaptive regression in the service of the ego. Relaxation of perceptual and conceptual acuity (and other ego controls).
8. Defensive functioning*	Extent to which defenses adaptively affect ideation and behavior. Success and failure of defenses.
9. Stimulus barrier	Threshold for stimuli. Effectiveness of management of excessive stimulus input.

TABLE 4.1 *Continued*

10. Autonomous functioning**	Degree of freedom from impairment of primary autonomy apparatuses (e.g.. sight, hearing, intention, language, memory, learning, motor function, intelligence). Degree of freedom from impairment of secondary autonomy (e.g., habits, complex learned skills, work routines, hobbies, interests).
11. Synthetic-integrative functioning	Degree of reconciliation or integration of incongruities. Degree of active relating together of psychic and behavioral events, whether contradictory or not.
12. Mastery-competence***	How competent or effective one feels in mastering the environment.

TABLE 4.2 *Mechanisms of Defense*

Defense	Description
1. Introjection	Also known as incorporation, it literally means a taking in whole (with a secondary consequence of destroying the object).
2. Identification	A general process in which one takes over elements of another.
3. Denial	A negation or lack of acceptance of important aspects of reality.
4. Repression	More complicated than denial-it is when one excludes an unwanted memory, feeling, or thought from one's consciousness.
5. Projection	A mechanism whereby consciously disowned aspects of the self are rejected and put outward and attributed to others.
6. Displacement	A mechanism by which feelings or conflicts about one person or situation are shifted onto another.
7. Reaction formation	Similar to repression-it involves keeping certain impulses from awareness. The mechanism involves replacing the impulse in consciousness with its opposite.
8. Rationalization	The use of convincing reasons to justify certain feelings or actions so as to avoid recognizing their underlying unacceptable motive.
9. Intellectualization	Warding off unacceptable impulses and affects by thinking about them in a cerebral way, rather than feeling them directly.

The Mental Status Exam. The mental status exam is a way of organizing and recording information about the mental state of the client, according to guidelines established by medical schools in the United States (Jordan & Franklin, 1995; Othmer & Othmer, 2002; Paniagua, 2001; Robinson, 2001; Sommers-Flanagan & Sommers-Flanagan, 2009; Taylor, 1981). A mental status exam helps the social worker assess the quality and range of perception, thought, feelings, and psychomotor activity of a client so as to better understand how the client's behavior may be symptomatic of a mental disorder. It leads to establishing a diagnosis according to the criteria set forth in the *Diagnostic and Statistical Manual of Mental Disorders* (text revision) (American Psychiatric Association,

2000), a classification system that divides mental disorders into categories with defining features (Jordan & Franklin, 1995). The following are the broad categories that are considered in the mental status exam:

1. *Appearance.* Is the client well groomed or disheveled? Is his manner of dress appropriate for the occasion of the interview? Is he flamboyant or bizarre?
2. *Attitude.* Is the client cooperative? Guarded? Suspicious? Aggressive or belligerent?
3. *Motor Activity.* Is the client calm or agitated? Does he have tremors, tics, or muscle spasms? Is he hyperactive?
4. *Affect.* Is the client's tone appropriate to the conversation? Is he, for example, talking about a sad event and smiling? Is his affect flat or blunted, apathetic, or labile—rapidly switching up and down. Is he expansive or constricted? A *flat affect* is a term used to describe clients who seem unable to relate emotionally to other people. *Blunted affect* describes a client who has a restricted, minimal emotional response (Sommers-Flanagan & Sommers-Flanagan, 2009, p. 221).
5. *Mood.* What does the client report? How does the client seem? Is the client depressed or anxious? Is there variability in his mood? Mood tends to be longer than affect and changes less spontaneously than affect.
6. *Speech.* Is the client's tone of voice loud or soft, whiny or high pitched? Are there any unusual characteristics or affectations (such as an accent or a halting manner)? Is the speech rapid or pressured? Does he stutter?
7. *Thought Processes.* Do the client's thoughts flow logically? Are the thoughts organized or disorganized? Is the client coherent? Are there perseverations (repetitions of thoughts as if the client were stuck)? Does the client experience thought blocking (thought stopping or interfering thoughts) or loose associations (not following logically from one thought to another)?
8. *Thought Content.* Are hallucinations or delusions present? Does the client speak of being controlled by external sources? Is the content of his thoughts grandiose or bizarre? Is suicidal ideation present? Is the content circumstantial (the client demonstrates the loss of capacity for goal-directed thinking) or tangential (the client loses the main idea of the conversation and is unable to return to it)?
9. *Perception.* Is the client's view of reality correct, or are there distortions in his thinking? Is there evidence of depersonalization or derealization?
10. *Orientation.* Is the client oriented to time, place, and person? How is his memory for present as well as past events? (Does he forget what he ate for breakfast but recall childhood events?) How are his concentration level and attention span? Is anxiety, a mood disturbance, or a learning disability responsible for the difficulty in focusing?
11. *Cognitive Function.* What is the client's general fund of knowledge? Is it intact? (This function can be tested by asking the client to count backward serially by sevens.) It is important to consider the client's intellectual level when assessing cognitive function, as his IQ may impact his ability to perform this as well as other cognitive functions, including the ability to be abstract or problem solve.
12. *Abstraction.* Is the client an abstract or concrete thinker? (To help you assess this function, ask him to interpret a proverb.)

13. *Judgment.* Are there any disturbances in judgment? Does the client understand the consequences of his behaviors, and to what degree?

14. *Insight.* Does the client have insight into his difficulties, or are there impairments (minimal, moderate, or severe) that lead him to deny them? Is the insight intellectual or does he have an awareness of motives and feelings on an emotional level?

Establishing the Diagnosis According to DSM-IV-TR. Now that the clinician has a clear picture of the client from the mental status evaluation, she is ready to establish a multiaxial diagnosis using the categories and codes described in the *Diagnostic and Statistical Manual of Mental Disorders* (text revision) (American Psychiatric Association, 2000). Formerly, *DSM-IV-TR* was in the province reserved for psychiatrists. Now, most agency social workers and other mental health professionals need to use the criteria set forth in the *DSM-IV-TR* to diagnose their clients' symptoms. The *DSM-IV-TR* is based on a medical model and is symptom driven. Some social workers object to its use because they believe it is not congruent with the strengths perspective of social work. However, there are times when it is necessary to have a clear picture of a client's symptoms. This information may help reveal whether a client is suffering from a mood disorder and whether depression or anxiety is interfering with a client's functioning. The clinician may then elect to refer the client to a psychiatrist for a medication evaluation or recommendation for hospitalization.

These data guide the choice of theory, which, in turn, guides the treatment plan. For example, depressed clients may benefit more from a cognitive approach than from a psychodynamic model. An anxious client might need stress-management techniques framed within the context of behavior theory. Information about a client's mental state can also inform the worker if psychotic processes are involved, if suicidal thoughts prevail, or if the client is a danger to others. And, as more social work comes under the umbrella of managed care, practitioners are required to diagnose from a medical model and then to alleviate symptoms in order for agencies to receive financial reimbursement. However, the major purpose of the *DSM-IV-TR* is not for insurance reimbursement. It is to enable the practitioner to "come closer to fostering a connection between an accurate diagnosis and an effective treatment" (Abramovitz & Williams, 1992, p. 340; Sommers-Flanagan & Sommers-Flanagan, 2009, pp. 427–428). It is important, however, to consider that our current diagnostic system is culturally influenced. Symptoms may be similar across cultures, but causes may be viewed differently (e.g., in some cultures, depression may be viewed as stemming from some "badness" in the person's actions). Although the causes of certain problems may be viewed similarly across cultures (e.g., grief as the result of a death in the family), the disturbance may produce vastly different symptoms. There have been five components added to the *DSM-IV* and the *DSM-IV-TR* that address cultural concerns. They are (1) specific culture, age, and gender features, which are included under some diagnoses; (2) a revised and expanded Axis IV: psychosocial and environmental problems, which includes problems such as discrimination, acculturation difficulties, homelessness, and war; (3) three V codes—identity problem, religious or spiritual problem, and acculturation problem; (4) an outline for cultural formulation that includes general questions related to culture; and (5) a glossary of culture-bound syndromes that provides descriptions of 25 such syndromes (Hayes, 2008, p. 155).

The Multiaxial Diagnosis. The multiaxial diagnosis consists of five axes.

Axis I. Here, the clinician will place the principal diagnosis—the clinical disorder or other condition that may be the focus of attention—and its corresponding code. There can be more than one diagnosis noted on Axis I as well as a principal diagnosis and a second diagnosis that may eventually be ruled out (R/O).

Axis II. Personality disorders and mental retardation, and the corresponding codes are found on Axis II.

Axis III. Axis III explains any physical disorders or general medical conditions that are present in addition to a mental disorder. Included in this category are learning disorders such as expressive language disability (see the case example on Vincent in this chapter).

Axis IV. Here, the clinician lists psychosocial and environmental problems that contribute to the exasperation of the current disorder. The stressors can be positive (job promotion) or negative (job loss).

Axis V. On this final axis, the worker places a score according to a global assessment of functioning (GAF) scale, which ranges from 0 to 100. This scale is a composite of social, occupational, and psychological functioning. The higher levels of functioning prior to illness have a better prognosis. Enter the number indicating the client's highest level of functioning for at least a few months during the past year. Also indicate the severity of the disorder—mild, moderate, severe, in partial remission (full criteria for disorder were previously met but currently only some of the symptoms remain), or in full remission (no longer any symptoms but it is clinically relevant to note the disorder). Sometimes clinicians are asked to separate scores for the client's past, present, and future functioning (level to be achieved in order for treatment to terminate).

Summary. The summary section is the most difficult part of the psychosocial study to write, as it requires a high degree of conceptualization. All the information that has been gathered is now pulled together within the context of a theoretical framework that helps workers understand the data and establish treatment goals. Theories can be value and culture driven (Turner, 1996, p. 12) and are harmful when used to label pathology, since they compromise the practitioner's commitment to empathy. Although they often resonate with the therapist's sense and use of self (Greenberg & Mitchell, 1983), we do not think theoretical models that guide practice should be selected on the basis of subjective appeal. The advanced practitioner draws on a wide range of theoretical constructs to understand the client's story. He also uses empirical research findings to select the best model of treatment, and his own research design to test the effectiveness of the treatment as he undertakes the therapeutic work.

Recommendations and Goals for Treatment. In this section, the worker elaborates on the treatment goals that flow from the psychosocial summary and indicates the specific ways in which the theoretical model selected will be used to guide the treatment. It is also necessary to include the client's response to treatment recommendations (motivated, reluctant, needs to think about it, etc.) and whether alternative models (perhaps models not provided by the worker's agency) would also meet the client's needs. The duration and frequency of the treatment should be specified, as well as the treatment modality or modalities (e.g., individual treatment once a week combined with family sessions to be held on a monthly basis). The client should participate in this process, advancing her goals for treatment, and should also be informed of her rights to services at this practice location and other appropriate social services.

Plans to Evaluate. Evaluation should be built into the treatment plan. Reimbursement guidelines often dictate that treatment goals and objectives be written in behavioral terms that can be measured quantitatively. It is also important to remember that some theoretical models and treatment goals may be less amenable to quantitative description. Qualitative evaluation methods can be substituted when appropriate and/or used in conjunction with the more traditional quantitative methods that may not be able to totally reflect a treatment goal(s) (see Chapter 14, "Integrating Research and Practice").

Intersection of the Client/Worker Relationship in Developing the Psychosocial Summary. Discuss how the issues of power, privilege, and oppression were manifested during the data collection process. How did the client's identity, race, gender, sexual orientation, age, disability, faith, or social class intersect with the client's problems in living or in the development of the psychosocial summary? Propose any action plans that the worker and client may undertake to ensure that the client's dignity, self-worth, and human rights are being safeguarded.

The following case provides a model for the psychosocial study. It includes a mental status exam and a diagnosis according to *DSM-IV-TR*.

A Sample Psychosocial Study: The Case of Vincent, Age 7, a Traumatized Child

Identifying Information

Vincent W., age 7, is a small, active, alert, well-groomed, verbal, intelligent, and engaging African American Protestant child who has been in residential placement for one month. His mother voluntarily placed him in residential treatment following unsuccessful outpatient treatment in the community.

Referral Source

Vincent was referred by the Child Development Center at St. Mary's Hospital—which had been acquainted with Vincent and his family for the previous 18 months. Vincent was initially referred to the Center because of poor school adjustment and problems in academic achievement. The sources of information used in this report came from the records of St. Mary's Hospital and from Vincent's mother and are believed to be fairly reliable.

Presenting Problem

Vincent was admitted to residential treatment from his mother's home because of behavioral problems at home and in school. Vincent was manifesting severe anxiety, hyperactivity,

(continued)

A Sample Psychosocial Study Continued

aggressiveness, and a low tolerance for frustration. He would hit, punch, and kick other children in his classroom, rip up his work when he became frustrated, and have frequent temper tantrums. Vincent also demonstrated this behavior with his mother, but not with his mother's boyfriend, who seemed to have better control over him. Vincent's mother was using physical punishment to contain him, and his aggressive behavior was escalating. She feared that if she did not have him leave the home, she "would lose control and hurt him." Community supports did not appear strong enough to help her parent Vincent appropriately given his high level of difficulty.

History of the Problem

Vincent's emotional and behavioral difficulties had a gradual onset. At age 4, when Vincent entered daycare, he was seen as very demanding, whining, and pouting when his needs were not immediately met. At age 5, in kindergarten, Vincent was unable to sit still and was disruptive in the large group. He often had to be taken out of the classroom and restrained to prevent him from hitting another child or destroying things. Vincent went to after-school daycare, and on weekends he was cared for by a sitter while his mother worked. There is no information regarding his adjustment in those settings.

Vincent had difficulty entering first grade and was unable to function well within the large classroom setting. Vincent's mother was frequently called to take him home when he became defiant and destructive. The school, recognizing Vincent's difficulties, referred the family to St. Mary's Child Development Center for an evaluation. The Center gave Vincent a complete medical, neurological, psychiatric, and psychological evaluation. Their diagnostic impression was "normal intelligence with a childhood behavior disorder." The mental status report stated,

> Vincent appeared to be a well-dressed, 6-and-a-half-year-old black male who was immediately sociable. He was trying to be a clown, and seemed to have a short attention span. His mood seemed mildly sad and his affect appropriate. He showed considerable anxiety—which was manifested physically—when asked to perform. There seemed to be a moderate usage of denial and avoidance with other regressive adaptations at resolution. Vincent evidenced guilt over his "badness" and tried to seek disapproval and limit setting. His fantasies revolved around not talking about things so as to avoid getting hurt. There were recurrent signs of an early depression. He perceives his family as fragile and is looking for a male role model with whom to identify. Vincent blocked most material that tended toward the negative feelings he has toward his mother.

The medical report from St. Mary's noted no neurological abnormalities, and all findings were within the normal range. Some graphomotor difficulties were noted, and, academically, Vincent was behind the normal level for his age group in reading, spelling, and math. An expressive language difficulty was also noted.

A case conference was held at the school, and Mrs. W. participated in the evaluation process and was in agreement with the recommendations for academic remediation. She was given a copy of the statement on parental rights to special education.

A Sample Psychosocial Study Continued

Family Background

Mother. Mrs. W. is a 22-year-old woman who is herself the product of a traumatic background. She is the older of two children, whose father died when she was quite young. She was raised by a strict and aloof mother who administered severe beatings and punishments. At age 15, she became pregnant with Vincent and was pressured to marry Clark W., a violent man, who was three years older than she. They moved to a northern city so that he could find work. Mrs. W.'s preoccupation with Vincent's care after the birth allegedly infuriated her husband, and he became increasingly abusive toward her. Mrs. W. became pregnant with her second child when Vincent was 1½ years old, and Mr. W.'s subsequent abuse toward her accelerated. When Vincent was 3 years old, Mrs. W.'s daughter died at the age of 18 months. The exact circumstances surrounding the death are unknown, but Mrs. W. holds her husband responsible. According to her account, their daughter ingested some bleach, whereupon Mr. W. beat the child for misbehaving. Mrs. W. was severely beaten when she attempted to take the child to the hospital. Vincent was a witness to all this. The baby was eventually taken to the hospital but was not admitted. A question remains as to whether Mrs. W's rights to medical care were upheld. The child died the next morning. The couple separated one year later, and Vincent has refused to see his father since that time.

Father. Clark W. is described as abusive and volatile. He currently resides with his girlfriend and their 2-year-old child. He abused Mrs. W, but she did not seek protection as a battered woman, which was her right. He is said to be involved in criminal or sublegal activities and does not pay child support. Vincent expresses no interest in seeing his father.

Boyfriend. John S. has resided in the home for several years. He plans to marry Mrs. W. He is soft-spoken and articulate and appears to provide care and support to Vincent. Vincent is very attached to him and refers to him as his father. Although Mr. S. seems to care for Vincent, he was not opposed to residential placement, and, when Vincent was at home, Mr. S. was unable to help to contain him.

Personal History

Vincent was an unplanned and unwanted child, born into an arranged marriage. There were no medical complications during Mrs. W.'s pregnancy, but she remembers labor as having been long, arduous, and extremely painful. Vincent weighed 8 pounds at birth, and Mrs. W. remembers that her first feeling about him was that she wanted him to "grow up." Developmental milestones were achieved within normal limits, with no unusual occurrences noted, except for delayed speech. Vincent has had numerous separations and losses during his first 7 years of life. At 6 months of age, Vincent was sent to live with his maternal grandmother in the south for approximately one year, and then returned to his mother for a brief period of time. After his sister's death, he was again placed in his grandmother's care. When he returned at 4 years of age, Mrs. W. was working long hours and asked a friend, described as an alcoholic who had difficulty managing her affect, to look after Vincent. At age 4½, Vincent entered daycare. His mother dates her difficulties with him to the death of his sister, but acknowledges that she was too distraught over her loss to do much about Vincent's poor behavior.

(continued)

A Sample Psychosocial Study Continued

Medical History

Vincent's general health has been good and there have been no hospitalizations. His last complete physical examination was conducted at St. Mary's Hospital, prior to placement.

Educational/Learning History

Vincent is in the second grade in special education. His academic schoolwork is on grade level.

Social Class

This is a lower-middle-class family that has worked its way out of poverty.

Cultural History

Vincent is an African American child born to a teenage mother who was forced into an arranged marriage with the 18-year-old father of her child. The couple left their familiar southern town and extended families to seek work in a northern city. One can assume that as a young African American family with few familial or economic resources, Vincent and his parents faced hardships that may have strained their personal resources. She did acknowledge incidences of racial oppression in her childhood and feels that problems in finding better employment may be because of racial bias.

Religion/Spirituality

The family is Protestant, and Mrs. W. was an active member of the church in her southern community. She regrets having lost this affiliation when she moved to New York and aspires to become a more involved member of her congregation when time permits. Currently, she attends church only on holidays and special occasions. Although not a highly religious person, she does believe in a higher power and finds comfort in prayer. There were no incidences of religious oppression in her background.

Mental Status and Current Functioning

(To best illustrate how the mental status exam is used in practice, we have incorporated the mental status indicators in bold type within the text.)

At the residential treatment center, Vincent remains anxious **(mood)**, active **(motor activity)**, and somewhat depressed **(mood)**. He seeks support from his social worker and reassurance from the other adults in his environment **(attitude)**. He comes to sessions well groomed and takes pride in his appearance **(appearance)**. His speech is clear but there is some difficulty with expressive language **(speech)**. In sessions he is variable **(affect)**, and a wide range of functioning and unevenness of development do exist. There are frequent shifts between age-appropriate behavior and more regressed and infantile behaviors. In play, Vincent is creative, imaginative, and purposeful **(orientation)**, and underlying themes of inadequacy and badness and fears of abandonment are repeatedly played out. With family dolls, he repeatedly submerges the girl doll in water and then brings her up to the surface of the sink. This repetitive play occurs in each session. He can be demanding,

A Sample Psychosocial Study Continued

provocative, and at times genuinely obnoxious. His distractibility **(thought processes)**, emotional liability **(affect)**, and hyperactivity **(motor activity)** can generate considerable frustration in those who deal with him, and it is not always easy to avoid engaging in a power struggle with him. His reality testing is basically intact **(perception)**, as is his judgment **(judgment)**. Thinking is concrete **(abstraction)** and appropriate for his age. He seems to have some awareness of his provocative behavior **(insight)**, but an underlying sense of "badness," a need for punishment, impulsivity, and lack of control **(motor activity)** intrude on his conscious efforts to be more conforming. His good intellect, creativity, and artistic sense **(cognitive function)** are strengths. He is an emotionally vulnerable child who is fearful of abandonment **(thought content)**. Vincent's regressive and maladaptive defenses do not seem adequate to ward off his instinctual impulses, and it seems that he is in a perpetual state of anxiety **(mood)**. Vincent refuses to talk about his sister's death and avoids the worker's attempts to bring the subject up in therapy. He accomplishes this by changing the subject or running around the room **(motor activity)**. When asked by the psychiatrist what he would like to be when he grows up, he remarked, "I'm not going to grow up—I'll probably die soon anyway." Although Vincent cannot cope with his many internal conflicts, he does have a number of strengths. He is a likable child with a good intellect **(cognitive function)**. Vincent is warm and enthusiastic and has the ability to form relationships **(attitude)**.

Establishing the Diagnosis According to *DSM-IV-TR*

Axis I	309.81 Post-traumatic stress disorder 314.01 Attention deficit disorder/hyperactive-impulsive
Axis II	V71.09 No diagnosis
Axis III	Expressive language difficulty
Axis IV	Removal from home—Severe parent–child conflict Domestic violence (suspected abuse by father) Death of sister (circumstances unclear)
Axis V	(current) GAF 35

Discussion of *DSM-IV-TR* Diagnosis. (Although this would not need to appear in a psychosocial study, we include it here to help you understand the rationale for the worker's multiaxial diagnosis.)

Vincent is a traumatized child who meets the diagnostic criteria for post-traumatic stress disorder (PTSD). Diagnostic code: 309.81. The criteria for PTSD, according to the *DSM-IV* (1994), are as follows:

A. The person has been exposed to a traumatic event in which both of the following were present: (1) The person experienced, witnessed, or was confronted with an event or events that involved actual or threatened death or serious injury, or a threat to the physical integrity of self or others. (2) The person's response involved intense fear, helplessness, or horror. Note: In children, this may be expressed instead by disorganized or agitated behavior.

(continued)

A Sample Psychosocial Study Continued

B. The traumatic event is persistently reexperienced in one (or more) of the following ways: (1) Recurrent and intrusive distressing recollections of the event, including images, thoughts, or perceptions. *Note:* In young children, repetitive play may occur in which themes or aspects of the trauma are expressed. (2) Recurrent distressing dreams of the event. *Note:* In children, there may be frightening dreams without recognizable content. (3) Acting or feeling as if the traumatic event were recurring (includes a sense of reliving the experience, illusions, hallucinations, and dissociative flashback episodes, including those that occur on awakening or when intoxicated). *Note:* In young children, trauma-specific reenactment may occur. (4) Intense psychological distress at exposure to internal or external cues that symbolize or resemble an aspect of the traumatic event. (5) Physiological reactivity on exposure to internal or external cues that symbolize or resemble an aspect of the traumatic event.

C. Persistent avoidance of stimuli associated with the trauma and numbing of general responsiveness (not present before the trauma) as indicated by three or more of the following: (1) efforts to avoid thoughts, feelings, or conversations associated with the trauma; (2) efforts to avoid activities, places, or people that arouse recollections of the trauma; (3) inability to recall an important aspect of the trauma; (4) markedly diminished interest or participation in significant activities; (5) feeling of detachment or estrangement from others; (6) restricted range of affect; (7) sense of a foreshortened future (e.g., does not expect to have a career, marriage, children, or a normal life span).

D. Persistent symptoms of increased arousal (not present before the trauma) as indicated by two or more of the following: (1) difficulty falling or staying asleep; (2) irritability or outbursts of anger; (3) difficulty concentrating; (4) hypervigilance; (5) exaggerated startle response.

E. Duration of the disturbance (symptoms in Criteria V, C, and D) is more than one month.

F. The disturbance causes clinically significant distress or impairment in social, occupational, or other important areas of functioning.

Specify if acute (duration of symptoms is less than three months) or chronic (duration of symptoms is three months or more).

Specify (delayed onset) if at least six months have passed between the traumatic event and the onset of the symptoms.

Diagnostic Rationale. Vincent has witnessed physical abuse and the death of his sister within the context of domestic violence. He seems to be specifically reenacting his sister's death in traumatic play (Gil, 1991) as he repetitively drowns the girl doll in the sink and tries to rescue her by bringing her to the surface of the water. This qualifies him for a PTSD diagnosis based on Criteria A and B. For Criteria C, Vincent shows persistent avoidance of stimuli associated with the trauma by (1) refusal to have conversations about it, (3) inability to recall aspects of it, and (7) sense of foreshortened future (he doesn't think he will live to grow up). To further make a case for PTSD as a principal diagnosis based on the final criteria, for Category D it could be said that Vincent displays both irritability and outbursts of anger and difficulty concentrating. The duration of Vincent's symptoms has been several years, indicating that there is chronicity involved. This would rule out considering a diagnosis of

A Sample Psychosocial Study Continued

adjustment disorder with mixed anxiety and depressed mood (309.28), despite his two outstanding symptoms of anxiety and depression.

The second Axis I diagnosis of attention deficit disorder/hyperactive-impulsive (314.01) accurately describes Vincent's current behavior and is based on Vincent's meeting the minimum criteria of at least six symptoms for the disorder in the area of hyperactivity and impulsivity (American Psychiatric Association, 1994). These symptoms are as follows:

A. (1) Hyperactivity
   - (a) often fidgets with hands or feet or squirms in seat
   - (b) often leaves seat in classroom when remaining seated is expected behavior
   - (c) often has difficulty playing or engaging in leisure activities quietly
   - (d) often is "on the go" and acts as if driven by a motor

   (2) Impulsivity
   - (a) often has difficulty awaiting turn
   - (b) often interrupts or intrudes on others

B. Some hyperactivity-impulsivity or inattentive symptoms that caused impairment were present before age 7

C. Some impairment present in two or more settings (home and school)

D. There must be clear evidence of clinically significant impairment in social, academic, or occupational functioning (American Psychiatric Association, 1994)

Vincent has lived in a very uncertain environment for many years, with multiple losses and multiple changes. Young children lack the ability to verbalize what they are feeling; Vincent may be expressing anxiety through motoric behavior, thus giving the appearance of ADHD. Vincent should have the opportunity to be observed over time in his new setting, to see if his impulsivity and hyperactivity abate once he feels more tranquil and less overwhelmed.

On Axis II, Vincent was not given a diagnosis. As Axis II is reserved for mental retardation (Vincent is not retarded) and personality disorders (not used with children under age 12), the worker correctly entered "no diagnosis" on Axis II. She used the V 71.09 code because the absence of a code might indicate that the worker neglected to make a diagnosis.

On Axis III, there is noted an expressive language difficulty. This information was part of Vincent's referral material from St. Mary's Hospital.

On Axis IV, the worker has noted removal from home, severe parent–child conflict, domestic violence, and the death of his sister as psychological stressors for Vincent. His current GAF score is 35 on a scale ranging from 0 to 100, which gives him a low rating for overall functioning. Persons falling between 31 and 40 show either some impairment in reality testing or communication or major impairment in several areas, such as work or school, family relations, judgment, thinking, or mood. For Vincent, it would seem that the severe impairment in school and family relations justifies this low GAF score. The social worker has not been asked to predict a GAF score needed for discontinuation of placement, but Vincent would probably need to be functioning in a range above 50, showing moderate to mild symptoms, before discharge to outpatient treatment could take place.

(continued)

A Sample Psychosocial Study Continued

Summary

Vincent's past and current functioning can be best understood within a multidimensional framework that combines treatment principles from object relations and cognitive and behavioral theories (see relevant chapters in this text). From a psychodynamic perspective, Vincent's history suggests the coexistence of both trauma and attachment disturbances. Within a human rights perspective, Vincent's family seems to have experienced some racial injustice, and he and his mother, living in an abusive household, were not afforded their right to protection and freedom from harm.

Vincent had multiple caretakers from the age of 6 months when he was sent to live with his maternal grandmother in the south. He was returned to his mother at age 18 months, placed with questionable babysitters (one suspected of alcoholism), and finally placed in daycare. These events can be understood within the cultural context of the African American family where kinship care is customary when parents are working to support the family. They may also be seen as an accommodation to his mother's needs: She was attempting to separate from an abusive husband (Vincent's father) and find active employment, all the while grieving the death of her daughter. Vincent witnessed the physical abuse directed at his mother and his sister. We might speculate that he was also the victim of physical abuse, although we have no corroborating evidence.

Cognitive mechanisms such as Vincent's self-blame are often correlates of depression and low self-esteem, illustrating how the cognitive and affective consequences of trauma reinforce one another (James, 1989). Vincent also evidences destructiveness, identification with the aggressor, and feelings of loss and betrayal characteristic of children who have experienced trauma at an early age. There are developmental deficits as well. These include difficulties with trust, an inability to curb his aggression, lack of more mature defenses, and signal anxiety. Vincent's behavior therefore needs to be understood within the context of his attempts to deal with trauma that he is unable to cognitively or affectively process. This dramatically affects Vincent's ability to cope and master new experiences and expectations. Vincent's repetitive drowning and rescuing of the doll is of serious concern as it represents post-traumatic play (Gil, 1991). Vincent's unsuccessful attempt at mastery of his sister's death leaves him feeling vulnerable and helpless and clearly signals that attention must be focused on this particular trauma. In addition, Vincent worries that his mother will not take him home and that she will disappear from his life altogether. (She threw out his bedroom furniture once he left home, claiming that she needed the room for her study.)

Recommendations and Goals for Treatment

The goal of residential treatment is to bring Vincent's behavior under control so that he will be able to return home and attend school in his community. This will be accomplished through psychodynamic, cognitive, and behavioral therapy (which will help Vincent begin to address and work through his past traumas), while helping him develop the social skills and behavioral controls that will aid his adjustment at home and in school. The treatment

A Sample Psychosocial Study Continued

plan for Vincent and his family was determined with Mrs. W. as a full participant, and includes the following:

1. Providing a safe, supportive context to live and to grieve the death of his sister.
2. Using play therapy (as opposed to talk therapy) to help Vincent work out his feelings about the death of his sister. Vincent's traumatic play must be carefully interpreted so that he can experience some resolution to this conflict. The worker should talk to Vincent about what the "dolls" are feeling and thinking when he attempts to drown them in the sink. Working in this off-target way helps children gain some safe distance from highly charged material.
3. Addressing Vincent's internalized self-blame (his inner sense of badness) by clarifying the circumstances of his sister's death and the reasons for his separation(s) from his mother (family), to change the cognitive distortions associated with these events.
4. Working with Vincent on behavioral strategies to cope with his anxiety and fear.
5. Educating staff and primary caregivers in behavior management techniques that recognize Vincent's behaviors as manifestations of his past trauma. This would include structure, support, and firm, but empathic, limit setting.
6. Giving Vincent the opportunity to form relationships with positive male role models, particularly an African American male(s), with whom he can identify.
7. Providing a highly structured classroom setting where there are opportunities for Vincent to feel empowered. He also needs outlets for his creativity and physical energy and an accepting noncritical approach to learning.
8. Outreach and involvement with his mother and her boyfriend that is educational and supportive, so that his mother and her boyfriend can be a resource for Vincent when he leaves the residential treatment center. Informing Mrs. W. of her rights while Vincent is in care and giving her a copy of these rights. She will also be supported in advocating for herself and her family so that her rights for individual, community, and societal well-being are being addressed.
9. Placement not to exceed one year, with plans to transfer him to home and a community school, with parental permission.

Plans to Evaluate

1. A behavioral token economy should be set up with the teacher and with Vincent's cottage parents. The social worker will show them how to implement this. Vincent will earn points for good behavior that can be cashed in for privileges at the end of each week. Vincent and the staff will develop a list of these privileges. The staff will monitor his response by tracking three target behaviors—hitting other children, following commands, and temper tantrums. The monitoring of these three target behaviors will begin immediately, and the intervention will take place after one week.
2. The social worker will request feedback about Vincent's behavior from Vincent's mother following each home visit. This feedback will be documented in her record.

(continued)

A Sample Psychosocial Study Continued

The worker will specifically ask about Vincent's adjustment in behavioral and attitudinal terms.

3. The social worker will collect feedback on the above indicators from the cottage parents and the school following each home visit.
4. The social worker will interrupt Vincent's post-traumatic play through direct interventions that will allow him to consider other options in his play. For example, the social worker can comment on the child's play, take a particular role in the play, or get involved in the play. This intervention should begin immediately, and its effectiveness should be evaluated after each play therapy session to determine the extent to which Vincent has moved away from his post-traumatic play.
5. A follow-up meeting will be held in three months to discuss the results of the intervention plan.

Intersection of the Client/Worker Relationship in Developing the Psychosocial Summary

Mrs. W. has clearly been affected by her experiences of migration to the north, living in poverty, and marriage to an abusive spouse. Her submissive yet distrustful presentation during the interviews may be caused by her experiences as a black woman in a dominant white society. It will be important for the worker to explore, in supervision, her own reflections on experiences of oppression and privilege and to talk about these issues as they emerge in the therapeutic relationship.

Source: Case material supplied by Helen Solomon.

5

Multicultural Practice

The Association of Multicultural Counseling and Development (AMCD) asserts that multiculturalism recognizes multiple identifications such as age, culture, gender, language, physicality, race, sexual orientation, social class, educational background, geographic location, relationship status, religion, work experience, and recreational interests (Arrendondo & Toporek, 2004, p. 47).

These categories are dependent on both time and context; for example, a younger heterosexual woman may hold less privilege within the social construct of age as she gets older given the tendency toward ageism in our society (Hulko, 2009, p. 44; McCall, 2005; Murphy, Hunt, Zajicek, Norris, & Hamilton, 2009). Anderson (2005) notes that despite their intersectionality, social identity categories are not all equal. Racial identity, for example, has been used to deny voting rights, to organize the division of labor, to deny citizenship, or to define formal and legal personhood. Clearly, in the hierarchary of oppression, this must be placed at the summit.

Multicultural counseling requires an understanding of the value systems of other cultures and how those values influence the behavior of those with whom practitioners work. *Culture* is defined by Barrera and Corso (2002, p. 104) as "a pervasive and dynamic process that influences every aspect of how we perceive and interact with others." It includes the beliefs, language, and behaviors valued in a community, and is an important lens through which one can look to explain behavior. Akinyela (2002a), writing from a critical African-centered theoretical framework, offers another view of culture. She writes "culture is constructed as the more powerful and the less powerful segments of society contend for positions of power and privilege between themselves. This means that any given culture is actually a complex of contentious and complimentary interactions between asymmetrical class, gender, religious, language, sexual and other social groups . . . making it a constant dialectical process of construction and reconstruction . . . culture is constructed in a process of dynamic change" (p. 34). We therefore believe that cultural reference groups related to all the identities mentioned "exert a powerful influence over us and our worldviews" (Sue & Sue, 2003, p. 7). The 2005 Social Work World Congress identified the need to "address the impact of racism, other forms of oppression, social injustice, and other human rights violations through social work education and practice" (National Association of Social Workers [NASW], 2005, cited in Murphy et al., 2009, p. 41). Although we feel strongly about the need to acknowledge the existence of all group identities, such a discussion is beyond the scope of this chapter and we refer our reader to other sources (see, for example, Lesser & Pope, 2011) for further explanations. This chapter focuses on the powerful impact of race and ethnicity, the clinical competencies required for work with diverse populations, and several modes of intervention. A case example illustrates the knowledge and skills needed for work with clients of different cultural and ethnic backgrounds. Collaborative research across cultures is illustrated in a qualitative study that appears at the end of the chapter.

Cultural Competence

Cultural competence is the term used to describe the knowledge and skills necessary to facilitate communication and skill acquisition across cultures (Barrera & Corso, 2002). The NASW's recent standards for cultural competence in social work practice recognize the importance of cultural literacy, cross-cultural knowledge and skill in direct practice, and the social worker's awareness of her cultural limitations. Tseng and Streltzer (1997) disagree with the cultural literacy approach, as it assumes the practitioner is the "expert" who utilizes cultural-specific techniques, asserting that this approach can lead to stereotypes and generalizations. Ayonrinde (2003) also cautions against the danger of stereotyping people, especially in unfamiliar or challenging situations when cultural differences are emphasized. Dean (2001), drawing on a postmodern perspective, suggests that clinicians who practice cross-culturally need to operate from a position of "not knowing," with the client as the expert and the practitioner as the learner.

Three important components of cultural competence are put forth by Sue and Sue (2003): (1) therapists' awareness of their own personal biases, assumptions, values, and beliefs; (2) understanding the worldview of culturally diverse clients; and (3) developing appropriate intervention strategies and skills. *Worldview* is defined as "how a person perceives his or her relationship to the world (nature, institutions, and other people)" (p. 267).

Sue (2004, p. 764) cautions against *ethnocentric monoculturalism,* a term used to describe "the psychological dynamics related to the denial of differences—that is, equating it with normalcy and not understanding how it intrudes on the life experiences of those who do not share its worldview." Murphy et al. (2009) and Heron (2005) add another component to acquiring cultural competence: self-awareness through intersectionality. This includes evaluating the expressions of power the clinician may exert, consciously and unconsciously, based on her own social identity locations as well as the status of being the "professional" in the therapeutic dyad. A culturally competent assessment therefore requires that the client be understood according to the norms of the client's culture. In addition to confronting racial and cultural bias, therapists need to have knowledge about the client's cultural group, including what is normative and what is deviant (Eidelson & Eidelson, 2003; Hanna, Talley, & Guindon, 2000). Given the sheer numbers and diversity of cultures represented in today's society, particularly in urban

America, this is a daunting task. Obviously, clinicians will not be experts or equally well informed on every race and culture. What is important is the worker's willingness to learn. Although there is a fairly comprehensive body of literature that one can draw information from, listening to the client's experience in an open and nonjudgmental way and naming and engaging in discussion about social injustice may be the best way to learn.

Multicultural Clinical Practice

Multicultural therapy is unique in the way that the dynamics of power and powerlessness and those of cultural identity or ethnicity transact and profoundly affect the course of treatment (Carter, 1995; Pinderhuges, 1984). Comprehending and clarifying the client's worldview is essential if the social worker is to be effective practicing across cultures. Gonzalez (2002), like Sue and Sue (2003), writes about the necessity of understanding the client's worldview and offers the following four distinct worldviews:

1. *Native Oriented/Traditional*—reflects patterns of culture rooted in past familiar and cultural experiences.
2. *Bicultural/Multicultural*—results from the client's life experiences of two different ways of life—his or her own tradition versus that of the mainstream culture.
3. *Acculturated/Assimilated*—refers to the acquisition of the beliefs and values and behaviors of a group of which one is not a natural member. Assimilation is the end state of this process.
4. *Transactional/Marginal*—held by persons suspended between two cultures—their ethnic identity and mainstream culture—and who do not have strong identification with either group.

Locke (1992) introduced 10 significant cultural elements that need to be considered in multicultural clinical practice. The degree of a client's acculturation—the extent to which a racial/ethnic minority group has adopted the beliefs, values, customs, and institutions of the dominant culture—is primary. The other important factors are poverty, history of oppression, language and the arts, racism and prejudice, sociopolitical factors, child-rearing practices, religious practices, family structure, and values and attitudes. Therapists also need to assess whether a client's problems stem from internal or external dynamics, particularly since oppression and racism are so predominant in society; otherwise, therapists may be engaged in what Neville, Worthington, and Spanierman (2001) call *cultural oppression*—that is, imposing the worldview of the dominant culture on nondominant groups of people.

Lum (1997) focuses on four areas of skill required for multicultural practice: cultural awareness, knowledge acquisition, skill development, and direct ongoing learning (cited in Fong, 2001, p. 5). Fong extends Lum's model to include inductive learning—the social worker's continued quest to seek solutions, which includes finding other indigenous interventions and matching cultural values to Western interventions. Delgado, Jones, and Rohani (2005) add several specific challenges for work with immigrants and refugees, or newcomer populations. They discuss the dangers of "cultural encapsulation"—when the counselor has limited cross-cultural experience and exists in a cocoon of stereotypes. They further refer to "sociocultural dissonance," cautioning clinicians to be aware of the degree to which a client's cultural values and norms are consonant or dissonant with so-called mainstream values. The greater the degree of dissonance, the harder a client's adaptation process will be. Maki (1997, p. 3) writes, "Cultural identity that is formed out of a group's ethnic experience is not simply an integration of the original and new cultures. The cultural identity is a product that has been forged in the context of the group's collective successes, failure, obstacles, and advantages as well as physical visibility and institutionalized prejudice both in the United States and globally." Finally, a history of cultural trauma may greatly impact clients who are seen in clinical practice.

Cultural Trauma

Cultural trauma occurs when an entire culture experiences a historical, geographical event caused by the same persons or events (Jenkins, 1996). Refugees who have been oppressed in their countries of origin, who have experienced war, slavery, racism, and even cultural genocide, may carry the legacy of past trauma, and also pass it down to their children. Even under the most favorable of circumstances, immigration involves loss of country, home, family, friends, and, for many, occupation. Lesser and Pope (2011) write, "Strong attachments to people and lifestyles can lead to a deep sense of loss when the life of the culture is disrupted." Several authors (Alexander, 2004; Eisenbruch, 1991; Tseng & Streltzer, 1997) describe the impact of cultural factors on mental heath as being a disruption in collective—as well as individual—identity. Bass (2002), Saville (2003), and Eyerman (2003) talk about transmission of cultural and racial trauma from generation to generation, giving the example of how slavery affected the African American community psychologically, economically, and physically. Eyerman refers to this form of remembrance as "collective memory . . . that grounded the identity formation of a people" (p. 60). Reid, Mims, and Higginbottom (2005) introduce the term *post-traumatic slavery disorder* (PTSlaveryD) to describe the economic, cultural, political, and psychological impact slavery has had on Nubian people. Akinyela (2002a) also emphasizes how African American people have been blamed for the conditions resulting in continuance of racism as well as internalized racism that some black people experience. She writes "acknowledging the true effects of the past is a crucial first step in any process of reparation . . . there has never been a formal acknowledgement or any kind of any apology for what happened in this land to New Afrikan people" (p. 46). Akinyela offers a postcolonial worldview in talking specifically about the experiences of African American people in the United States. "Black people have been active subjects in the process of Africanizing the European culture that they encountered, and reshaping their own African culture in relationship to the new cultural practices they found themselves relating to" (p. 34). This has resulted in a "new collective ethos" or worldview that includes an understanding of history before enslavement, resistance and survival of the transatlantic slave trade, Jim Crow and racism, and the creation of "liberated cultural spaces" (p. 41), where clients can make sense of their relationships and their lives free from the interpretations and judgments of dominant Eurocentric culture (p. 41).

Miliora (2000) emphasizes the importance of understanding the impact of discrimination on clients and coined the term *depression of disenfranchisement* to describe the effects of cultural racism on self-esteem, confidence, and ambition (Lesser & Pope, 2010, 2011). Lifton (1979) writes about Jewish survivors of the Nazi holocaust who have a strong need to give testimony about what they endured in concentration camps. Calling this *symbolic immortality*, he reminds us that such legacies may be tributes to family members who perished and should not be pathologized out of a broad context of cultural understanding. Many authors (Alexander, 2004; Allen, 2001; deVries, 1996; Kaslow, 1999; Eyerman, 2003) caution against using ethnocentric diagnostic systems that erroneously label individuals as having psychiatric disorders when their symptoms may reflect a culturally determined suffering.

Roles for Cross-Cultural Therapists

Atkinson, Thompson, and Grant (1993) delineate seven important roles for cross-cultural therapists (see Figure 5.1). First, the therapist acts as an adviser to clients regarding potential problems they may encounter as members of a minority group. Second, the therapist must be an advocate who works on behalf of clients who are having problems related to oppression and discrimination. Third, the therapist must have knowledge of clients' indigenous support systems and be able to facilitate the development of new ones in the clients' present cultural environments. This includes the consideration of indigenous healing methods that may be important adjuncts to the help being offered by the therapist. Fourth, the therapist acts as a consultant—helping clients (and others in their lives) find ways to reduce discriminatory practices in the community. Fifth, the therapist as a change agent tries to effect changes in those conditions in the social environment

1. Adviser to clients regarding potential problems they may encounter as minority immigrants.
2. Advocate who works on behalf of clients who are having problems related to oppression and discrimination.
3. Must have a knowledge of the client's indigenous support systems and be able to facilitate the development of them in the client's new culture.
4. Consultant-helping clients (and others in their life) find ways to work toward reducing discriminatory practices in the community.
5. Change agent in which the therapist tries to affect changes in those conditions in the social environment that contribute to social injustice.
6. Counselor aimed toward preventing intrapsychic problems from occurring.
7. Psychotherapist aimed at treating intrapsycic problems.

FIGURE 5.1 ***Seven Important Roles for Cross-Cultural Therapists***

Source: Atkinson, Thompson, and Grant (1993).

that contribute to social injustice. Sixth, the therapist as a counselor aims toward preventing intrapsychic problems from occurring, and seventh, as a psychotherapist, aims at treating intrapsychic problems.

Theoretical Models of Treatment

There are several recommendations in the literature regarding which psychotherapies are effective in multicultural practice. Opinions on what is therapeutic range from psychotherapies that focus on intrapsychic change, the abandonment of therapy in favor of social action to promote change, and approaches that would include attention to both oppressive external environments and destructive personal behavior (Atkinson et al., 1993; Ivey, Ivey, & Simek-Morgan, 2007; Sue & Sue, 2003). Psychoanalytic therapy has traditionally been considered inappropriate for African American clients and clients of lower socioeconomic status (Helms & Cook, 1999), a view that could be interpreted as biased (Perez-Foster, 1999).

Mattei (1999) writes about the relationship between the client and the therapist in the here and now as being a context in which authentic dialog about the impact of the client's and the therapist's racial and cultural identity occurs. Contemporary psychoanalytic theorists (see, for example, Leary, 2000; McRae, 2000; Suchet, 2004) feel that psychoanalytic relational models of practice provide frameworks for such authentic dialogs. McClure and Teyber (1996, p. 5) propose a multicultural relational model for work with children and adolescents that emphasizes the therapist's ability to "articulate and enter the child's subjective worldview." This model encourages the therapist to be self-aware and recognize the subjectivity of her perceptions.

Asante (1987) and Akinyela (2002a) present an Afrocentric perspective for working with African American clients. This view claims that no group can claim centrality over the exclusion of any other—each group has a center of its own. Self-esteem building and skills are necessary to resist negative cultural images and validate the position of African American centrism. One therapeutic model, cognitive behavioral therapy, has been recommended for all clients regardless of racial, cultural, or socioeconomic condition because it emphasizes structure. Narrative therapy has also been recommended for all clients but for different reasons. Narrative therapy relies on storytelling—and culture is part of one's life story. Client-centered therapy has been advocated for traditional Japanese clients because the interventions are indirect (Hayashi, Kuno, Osawa, & Shimizu, 1992). However, client-centered therapy is not recommended for Latino clients (Ruiz, 1995; Velasquez, 1997) because of its indirectness.

McRae (2000) and Mattei (1999) talk about the importance of authenticity in the therapeutic relationship and the need for therapists to understand the client's racial or cultural identity development, as well as their own. They focus on the relationship between the client and the therapist in the here and now and believe the cross-cultural relationship is the context—or "metaframe"—for any theoretical approach (Mattei, 1999, p. 256). Another model that highlights the relevance of context is multicultural theory, described by Sue, Ivey, and Pederson (2004, pp. 11–12) as a "metatheoretical framework" concerned with helping clients within their own cultural frameworks and with respect for others. This includes attention to both universal and culture-specific strategies. Browne and Mills (2000) suggest social workers adapt empowerment theory and the strengths perspective, building on the ecological model for understanding multicultural individual, family, and community behavior. These broad-based perspectives consider the whole change system, rather than focusing solely on the individual. Devore and Schlesinger (1996) advocate an ethnic-sensitive framework, integrating the concepts of ethnicity, social class, and oppression in multicultural practice. Lum (1997) formulated a process stage model for generalist social work practice that affirms the similarities of Native, African, Latino, and Asian Americans while recognizing the differences among these groups as well.

Also emerging in practice is the community-based model, with a social justice perspective (Delgado et al., 2005), emphasizing capacity building, the strengths perspective, collaborative work with the community, and supplementing traditional office visits by more informal, community-based services (Berger, cited in Lightburn & Sessions, 2005). Lum (1997) has suggested that program services be integrated into ethnic group support systems such as indigenous religious and medical services. And finally, a model put forth by Ornstein and Ganzer (2000) integrates the strengths perspective and relational psychoanalytic theory, highlighting therapeutic communication and use of language.

Other authors (Portes & Rumbaut, 2001; Rigazio-DiGilio, Ivey, Kunkler-Peck, & Grady, 2005; Rosenberg, Gonzalez, & Rosenberg, 2005) suggest an ethnographic multicultural approach, particularly suited to work with immigrants and refugees. Their model is based on a comprehensive understanding of clients' lives in their countries of origin, their premigration stressors, their journeys to the United States, and their initial experiences of immigration. These clients are therefore the "cultural guides" who lead the way into experiences unknown by the practitioner. The culturagram (Congress, 1994) is a powerful tool that depicts the importance of events such as reasons for immigration; time in the community; legal status; age of family members at the time of immigration; languages spoken at home and in the community; health beliefs; holidays and special events; the impact of any past crisis; family, education, and work values; and contact with any cultural institution.

Therapy with Transnational Immigrants

Falicov (2007, p. 169) considers therapy with "transnational immigrants," those who maintain intense connections with the countries and their extended families. He suggests the importance of three contexts for work with immigrants: the relational, the community, and the cultural-sociopolitical. The relational context includes new definitions of family life in transnational contexts, transnational relational stresses such as separations and reunions, and acculturative stress in gender and generational relationships. Lesser (2011) writes about the relational experiences of first-generation Caucasian and Latina teenage girls whose parents emigrated from another country and continue frequent contacts and visits with relatives who remained behind. These girls faced a variety of internal conflicts related to beliefs about identity, guilt, betrayal of their parent's culture, and isolation when perceiving they did not fit into either culture. The parents are often challenged to reexamine the importance and validity of their cultural values and beliefs in the new country.

The community context for work with transnational immigrants includes the importance of contemporary virtual transnational communities, rebuilding ethnic networks and using community organizations such as English and citizenship classes), empowering experienced immigrants to orient newer ones, and engaging in collective expressions of art, music, and story circles.

The sociocultural and sociopolitical, or social justice, contexts for work with transnational immigrants include cultural diversity challenges such as honoring cultural differences, questioning value-based theoretical models of practice, and engaging in culturally competent service provision. Sociopolitical approaches focus on resisting oppression by combating the effects of power differences, racism, and differential access to resources based on immigrant or minority status.

Culturally competent therapists must remain aware that transnationals balance two countries and this needs to be explored. Working in a group with the parents of the girls described earlier, Lesser (2011) talks with them about how they, as transnational immigrants, balance two countries: "I can see what a struggle this is for you as parents, and for your daughters also. You grew up in one world. They are growing up in another world. I am wondering if we can figure out a way that you can all talk with your daughters about what life is like for them . . . as teenagers here in America . . . with parents who did not grow up in America? And perhaps you can share what life was like for you where you grew up? What do you think? It doesn't mean you have to change your values or the way you parent, but maybe it will help you understand each other a little better."

In general, therapists' training experiences, as well as their racial and cultural perspectives and personal identity development, shape their thinking about what approaches work best with different racial and cultural groups. We believe that postmodern thinking has contributed an intersubjective, relational focus that is well suited to multicultural practice. However, we also believe that all the major theoretical models of clinical practice can be adapted to work with clients of various racial and cultural groups. It is not the therapist's theoretical orientation, per se, but his cultural and racial sensitivity, his ability to set goals commensurate with the client's level of acculturation, his selection of a modality that is tailored to the client's needs, and his willingness to examine issues of values, power, and privilege that makes for effective multicultural practice.

Example of Culturally Competent Practice

The following example of social work with a Vietnamese adolescent is based on a constructivist framework (see Chapter 11, "Narrative Therapy"). It illustrates both the application of theory to work with a client from a different race and culture and a culturally competent practice based on an open examination of the therapist's cultural assumptions as well as those of the client. Lam (2005) offers several constructs—in addition to the social, political, family, and individual factors essential for any understanding of psychological distress—that he feels are salient to Vietnamese American populations: ethnic enclave, refugee experiences, and mental health beliefs. He also highlights the influence of refugee parents who left their homeland without adequate time or assistance to prepare for the cultural changes they would encounter in the United States (p. 90). A culturagram (Congress, 1994), previously discussed, is included in Figure 5.2.

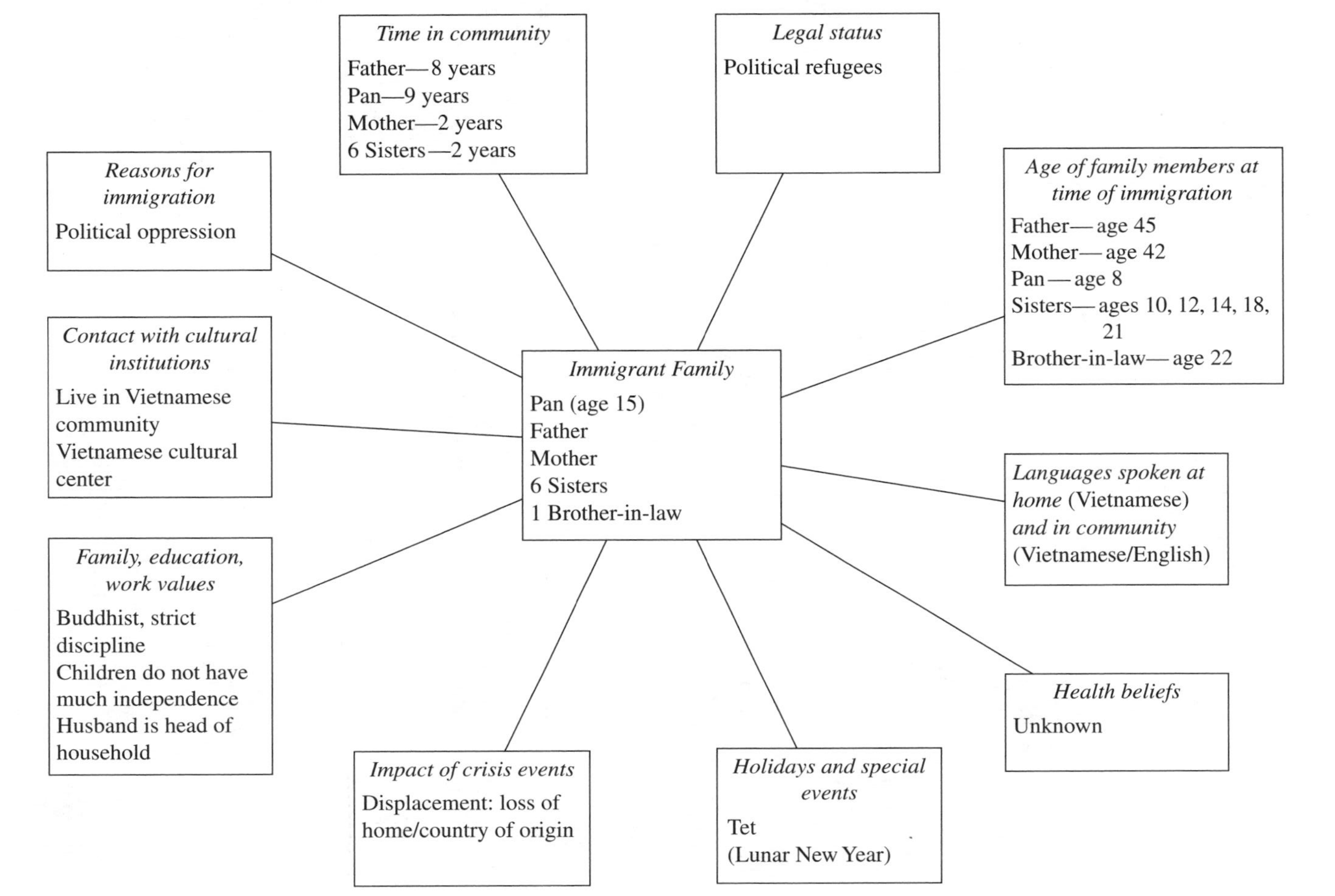

FIGURE 5.2 *Culturagram*

Case Study: Pan

Pan, a 17-year-old Vietnamese adolescent, was referred to a residential treatment facility by the Department of Youth Services. Pan had been committed to the Department of Youth Services on several charges, including two counts of possession of a firearm, possession of heroin and marijuana with intent to distribute, and larceny of a motor vehicle. The social work student, a white woman from a middle-class background, understood that for she and Pan to be an effective cross-cultural team, it was necessary to pay attention to what was important to him and to listen carefully so as to learn what was considered normative or deviant in his culture. Having no firsthand experience with people from the Vietnamese culture, the worker turned to the literature and learned that a constructivist perspective was considered well suited for work with Asian clients. This approach enables the therapist to "identify idiosyncratic variations within a culture as well as those culturally embedded behaviors presented by clients of diverse ethnoracial backgrounds" (Lee, 1996, p. 190).

Constructivism is a conceptual framework, and a basic tenet of treatment from this perspective is the use of narratives or stories. Narratives are reformulations of memories in a client's life that change over time and that are shared through dialog with the therapist, who balances questions with attempts at clarification as the client tells his or her story. A complete discussion of narrative therapy is presented in Chapter 11. Briefly stated, narrative therapy emphasizes the need to learn as much as possible about the client's problem within the context of the social and environmental forces surrounding it. In this way, clients are presented with the opportunity to explore various aspects of the presenting problem(s). Narrative therapy also helps reveal any cultural assumptions that may have contributed to the definition of the problem (Morgan, 2000; White, 1991; White & Epston, 1990).

Case History

Pan was born in a poor, primitive village outside Saigon three years after the end of the war in Vietnam. He was the youngest of eight children and the only male. Pan's father left for the United States when Pan was 7 years old. Pan, a married sister and her husband, and the youngest sister left to join their father the following year, leaving their mother and the others behind. The journey from Vietnam was treacherous, and the overcrowded boat nearly capsized several times. Before permanently relocating to a northern city, Pan and his family lived in refugee camps for two years where only Vietnamese was spoken. When at last he joined his father, Pan began to attend a public school and was exposed to a life very different from that of his cultural origins. At home, Vietnamese continued to be spoken; the family associated only with other Vietnamese families and insisted that Pan do the same. By the time he was a teenager, his mother and other sisters had joined him in his new homeland, making it even more difficult for the family to assimilate since his mother and other sisters had no knowledge of English, and his father, hard at work, was rarely at home. Falicov (2007) writes about how "despite many valiant attempts to keep relationships alive the meeting of children and parents separated by migration is more a meeting of strangers than a true family reunion" (p. 162). Torn between love for his family and conflict with their old-world values and paternalistic ways, Pan began to associate with an Asian gang who accepted him, cared for him, and seemed knowledgeable about his new country. When his family learned of this, they were ashamed and embarrassed and demanded that he leave

Case Study Continued

their home. Pan became depressed and started to burn himself with cigarettes. His drug and gang involvement intensified, resulting in his being hospitalized for a heroin overdose.

In examining the life experiences of southeastern refugees, Harper and Lantz (1996) underscore the need to examine problematic events before, during, and after their flight to America. Listening to Pan helped the worker understand that before immigrating to America, his family lived in abject poverty, his father was the unquestionable authoritarian head of the household, and Pan, the only male child, was severely beaten for misbehavior, but his sisters were not. Prior to immigration, an older sister committed suicide rather than tell the family that she was pregnant, with no hope of marriage to the father of her child.

The social work student understood Pan's need for a family to love and accept him within his new cultural context and that, in his mind, the gang affiliation provided just that. The gang leader was authoritarian, as was Pan's father, and Pan did as he commanded, which included drug trafficking and drug use. Although this "new family" clearly exploited Pan, they also financed his legal fees when he was initially committed to the Department of Youth Services.

Process Recording

The following excerpt from treatment illustrates how the worker tries to understand what is culturally specific to Pan's experience, and what might be deviant.

Pan: My father used to hit me in Vietnam; he used to hit me a lot.

Worker: Can you tell me more about that?

Pan: He hit me because I was bad; he made me lie down on the floor and he hit me.

Worker: Tell me, Pan, what is your sense of why this was happening?

Pan: Well, usually my father hit me when he was drinking and then he would get angry. He wouldn't stop hitting me even when I cried.

Worker: So, drinking caused your father to act in ways that he might not otherwise behave. . . . Am I getting this right? Did he also hit you when he wasn't drinking?

Pan: Sometimes, if I did something bad . . . but he usually hit me a lot when he was drunk—and usually for no reason.

Worker: Did he stop hitting you when you cried when he wasn't drinking?

Pan: Yes, because he would be afraid of hurting me.

Worker: So, drinking made your father so angry that he wouldn't stop hitting you even when you cried because he was hurting you?

Pan: That's right.

Worker: Did this confuse you as a young child—maybe even now? It seems that your father sometimes hit you because he cared about you and it was his way of getting you to obey. And this type of discipline is customary among Vietnamese families, am I right?

Pan: Yes.

Worker: But then there were times when your father was drinking and hitting you for no reason or for reasons you couldn't connect with caring. Is this what made you begin to feel that you must be the problem, instead of your father's drinking? Is this what made you feel that you were bad?

Pan: I got to believe I was always bad even when I wasn't. But maybe some of the problem was my father's drinking.

(continued)

Case Study Continued

Worker: The important thing to remember is that you weren't always bad. What's confusing is that your father cared about you but may have also mistreated you when he was drinking.

Pan: Yeah, well, I could never look at it in any way besides I was bad and he didn't care about me—but I could never say anything to my family about this because we don't talk about these things. It's the way.

Worker: I understand . . . and it's important for you and I to talk about these things, even though it may be difficult to talk to a stranger about this—especially when you were not able to talk about it within the family.

The student acts as a "participant observer" (Anderson & Goolishian, 1992, p. 384), questioning Pan about cultural practices to help to clarify his confusion (and her own) as to whether his father acted out of harshness or caring. She offers clinical impressions tentatively and with the understanding that they may be influenced by her own personal and cultural values. She tries to locate the problem outside of Pan or his father by introducing "drinking" as the variable that may have separated the normative from the deviant forms of discipline within Pan's Vietnamese culture. Later in the treatment, the student tries to help Pan attend to the conflicts in his family about acculturation.

Pan: My family hates my long hair—they think it means I am bad.

Worker: Why is that?

Pan: Because all good people in Vietnam have short hair.

Worker So if Yours truly, had short hair, your family would think of you in a better way?

Pan: That would be a beginning. They would also want me to show respect and not get into any trouble.

Worker: What else would your parents want you to do?

Pan: They want me to hang out with Vietnamese people like they do.

Worker: It sounds like you and your parents have different thoughts about life in America. You seem to want to make some changes but your family would like you to keep to your cultural ways. That often happens in families with teenage children who come to the United States.

Pan: Really? I thought it was just my family thinking I was bad again.

Worker: Well, understanding each other's point of view is important.

Pan: I can't talk to them about this. They would say I was being disrespectful.

Worker Well, then how can you get them to see you in the way you would like to be seen? Do you think getting in trouble with the law will help them view you in a positive way?

Pan: No. I think they will see me in a good way if I get a job.

Worker: That may be a good first step.

Pan: Sometimes I feel confused about everything.

Worker: I'm sure you do and that is understandable. You've gone through a lot of changes these past several years and so has your family. I think some of these struggles have to do with coming from a different country. It takes a while to adjust to a new place. What do you think about this?

In this segment, the student worker attempts to understand and value Pan's Vietnamese culture as well as his personal struggle to fit in and be accepted in a new culture.

Case Study Continued

Our last excerpt, a termination session, shows Pan beginning to understand his relationship with his family within its cultural context.

Worker: Now that you are ready to move on to your next program, what do you think you have learned about yourself here?
Pan: I learned that even though I made a lot of mistakes, I was not born a bad kid.
Worker: What have your learned about your family, Pan?
Pan: Well, my dad had some problems. . . . I don't think he felt good about not being able to take care of our family in Vietnam. I think he took some of his frustrations out on me because I was the only boy. He wouldn't hit my sisters.
Worker: You are recognizing that some problems in your family had nothing to do with you and that some of your father's problems were caused by struggles he faced both in Vietnam and here after your family moved.
Pan: I think they did what they could. My father made mistakes. But I think my family wanted the best for us. After all, that's why they left Vietnam to begin with. I was always so angry. I don't feel so angry any more.
Worker: What are your goals now, Pan?
Pan: I want to get a job and show my family that I am doing the right things. I hope they will start talking to me when they see that.
Worker: I hope so too, Pan. We both worked hard to get you where you are now and I will always remember you. I have a gift for you, so you can remember how much you have learned here. It is an amethyst stone. The stone and the color purple mean sobriety. So when you are feeling unsure of yourself, I want you to rub this stone and remember you are a great Vietnamese spirit with a goal to reach.

Conclusion

Some of the issues faced by the Vietnamese population have been cited in the literature and include survivor's guilt, sense of obligation to rescue family members left behind, adjustment of roles within the family, and intergenerational conflict caused by differential acculturation and social misunderstandings between refugees and members of the dominant culture left behind (Bemak, Chung, & Bornemann, 1996; Chung, Bemak, & Okazaki, 1997; Timberlake & Cooke, 1984). Tu (1985) notes that the suffering of an individual family member was second to the importance of the family name. As Pan began to construct a new narrative, he came to recognize that his family had tried to act in his best interest by talking with him about how his behavior would affect his future, letting him live with a family friend, bringing him to the hospital after a heroin overdose, and, ultimately, allowing him to feel the full weight of the court by his commitment to the Department of Youth Services. Narrative therapy within the context of culturally competent practice helped Pan reconstruct his life story so that he no longer blamed himself or his family. In the story that he and the worker created, Pan gained an increased understanding of his family and the difficulties they faced living through the Vietnam War and their journey and life in refugee camps in America. Now Pan had a more accurate view of the realities of his life and of theirs and a greater appreciation of his family's concern for him. This new narrative has helped Pan become closer to his family and to his origins.

Source: Adapted from Lesser and Eriksen (2000).

Example of Culturally Specific Practice: Research across Cultures

We undertook the following international study in collaboration with the Jamaica Association of Social Workers in West Kingston, Jamaica, West Indies, where poverty, drugs, and migration are significantly associated with crime and violence ("The Caribbean's Tarnished Jewel," 1999; Crawford-Brown, 2001; Dunn, 2001; Ricketts, 2000; Williams, 2001). We sought to gather information on the effects of violence on the families and children living in this area in order to develop clinical interventions that would help our Jamaican colleagues better serve the traumatized children and families and that would be culturally relevant. (For a more detailed discussion of qualitative research, see Chapter 14.)

The impetus for this study was the relationship that developed between one of us and a visiting professor from the University of the West Indies who spent a year teaching at the northeastern school of social work where the author was also on faculty. The visiting professor and I are experienced practitioners in the area of child welfare, with specific interest in physical and sexual abuse of children. Through our conversations about our respective work with traumatized children, both in Jamaica and in the United States, we created what Strong (2002b, p. 246) refers to as a *borderzone*—a fruitful context in which to construct new ways of talking and to reflect on accustomed ways of talking in generative new ways. Anderson (1997), cited in Strong refers to listening "ethnographically" when speaking with individuals from cultures that may be different from our own (p. 254). This challenges us to hear beyond what is culturally familiar and helps to create a mutual basis for collaboration.

I continued to correspond with my Jamaican colleague after she returned to the West Indies, and was then invited to be the keynote speaker at a conference sponsored by the Jamaica Association of Social Workers in Kingston. Attendees at the conference shared their concerns, and dialog opened on how we could establish a further collaborative relationship and bring further expertise to our Jamaican human service workers. A collaborative research study began, drawing on the experiences of Jamaican human service providers, with the goal of the development of culturally specific training for treating trauma in children. The treatment intervention would be culturally specific and would use theoretical and conceptual models of practice specific to the Jamaican clients' cultural group. Joshi (1998) writes about the significant role of research in international trauma work but stresses that the prime objective should not be the gathering of research data that might serve to subsume the interests of the affected population beneath the agenda of research (p. 183). Our research therefore included the local professionals and experts and was conducted with a commitment to further teaching and clinical care as well. Our approach to this research was relational, using competencies of "skilled dialogue" (Barrera & Corso, 2002, p. 105). The components and skills are listed, followed by a discussion of the research.

Skilled Dialog

The three main components of skilled dialog are respect, reciprocity, and responsiveness (see Figure 5.3).

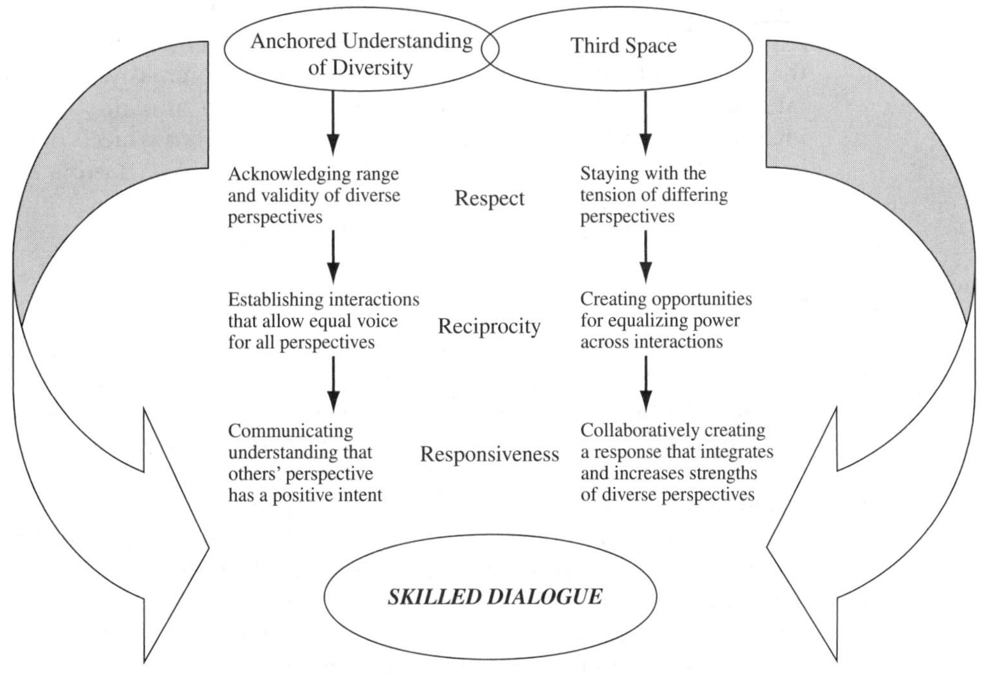

FIGURE 5.3 ***Skilled Dialogue Qualities and Component Skills***

Source: I. Barrera & R. M. Corso, *Skilled dialogue: Strategies for responding to cultural diversity in early childhood* (Baltmore, MD: Paul H. Brookes Publishing Co., 2003), p. 42. Reprinted by permission.

Respect. Respect refers to an awareness of the boundaries between persons who support trust and connection. Both emotional boundaries, which identify when words or actions convey insult or praise, and cognitive boundaries, which determine what people believe to be true, are included within this contextual use of respect.

Reciprocity. Building on respect, reciprocity balances power between persons in dialog with each other. It requires an acknowledgment and trust that the experiences and knowledge each person brings to the relationship are of equal value.

Responsiveness. Being responsive is being open to new possibilities and to "not knowing for sure" (Barrera & Corso, 2002, p. 107). This is particularly important when we enter cross-cultural situations with preconceived or misinformed ideas or judgments.

The two skills that promote and sustain the preceding three components of skilled dialogue are anchored understanding of diversity and third space (Barrera & Corso, 2002, p. 106).

Anchored Understanding of Diversity. This skill generates compassionate knowledge that evolves from active and intentional, face-to-face engagement with those from whom one differs.

Third Space. When people anchor their understanding of differences, both experientially and cognitively, they move from an "either-or" frame to a mindset that is able to hold two different perspectives simultaneously. This is a fundamental shift from a "dualistic and exclusive perception of reality to an integrative, inclusive perspective that focuses on the complementary aspects of diverse values, behaviors, and beliefs, which can lead to a third choice" (Barrera & Corso, 2002, p. 109). This choice is considered the *third space*.

The Research

I invited this book's coauthor, with a skill set different from my own, to join me and my Jamaican colleague. Together, we designed an explorative, qualitative case study based on naturalistic inquiry and well suited to cross-cultural research. Murphy et al. (2009, p. 36) caution about the challenge not to treat marginalized groups as "the other" when conducting research to "homogenize their experiences, or erase the complexity and uniqueness of their experiences under the guise of generalizability." Here, we present an overview of the study to highlight the cross-cultural collaboration.

The purpose of this research study was to explore the experiences of Jamaican human service providers and educators who have endeavored to help children exposed to violence in one community in Jamaica. Individual interviews and focus groups were conducted to obtain information and address any misunderstandings based on cultural differences. Our Jamaican coinvestigator took a lead role in recruiting the study participants. Although the Jamaican human service workers and my coauthor and I spoke English, it was also necessary for her to, on occasion, translate between us due to our different "accent." She was able to do this based on the 15 years she had spent living and working in the United States and on her greater familiarity with the English spoken in the United States.

Through active engagement and cross-cultural collaboration and research, a powerful human voice was added to the sobering sociological challenges facing Jamaica. Our colleagues and study participants spoke directly and openly about the violence embedded in the culture and the ensuring trauma that has affected children and families. We believe this was aided by the trusting relationships that had developed between my Jamaican colleague and myself, during months of discussion after the initial visit, funding to conduct the research, our willingness to personally visit and speak with the people in the community affected by the violence, and the enormous respect for authority and overall graciousness of the Jamaican people. We were mindful of the power differences in relationships when we prepared for and conducted the research—differences in race, social class, and education between the researchers, Jamaican coresearchers, and study participants.

Working together, we were able to harness the strengths in the culture and use the findings of the research to develop training in the treatment of trauma behaviors in children. We returned to Jamaica four months after conducting our study to provide the training and to conduct a second phase of research, concentrating on the personal experiences of parents and children who reside and receive services in West Kingston. The different discourses we had with our coinvestigator as well as those who participated in the interviews and focus groups were "the conversational building blocks" that encouraged us to build other discourses (Barrera & Corso, 2002, p. 259). Our collaborative relationship continued, as we used the data from the second phase of our research study to develop training for indigenous community workers who will provide psychoeducational support to parents and children through group and community interventions.

Summary

Cultural competency is a requisite condition for good clinical practice. Social workers from all backgrounds need to be trained to understand the value systems of other cultures. Studies such as those noted in this chapter remind us of the necessity of understanding the culture of our clients, and developing interventions that are culturally relevant and culturally sensitive. Social work professionals must create for their clients an atmosphere of trust and comfort, where sensitive issues can be examined and processed. When the social worker stretches to understand the client's racial and cultural experiences, he or she becomes more authentic and truly empathic. It is then that the therapeutic relationship provides the context in which growth—for both client and therapist—may occur.

6

Object Relations Theory: A Relational Psychodynamic Model

Object relations theory emerges from Freudian psychoanalytic theory and ego psychology and includes a wide range of contributions from both American and British psychoanalysts. Detailed descriptions can be found in many books on psychoanalytic theory, and the reader should refer to these books to obtain a historical perspective (see, for example, Bacal & Newman, 1990; Greenberg & Mitchell, 1983; Pine, 1990). This chapter highlights the major contributors from the British object relations school because of its pioneering attempt to connect the intrapsychic and the interpersonal worlds. The concept of internal and external "objects" to social work helps clinicians understand and treat abused children and adult survivors of childhood abuse.

Object relational theory is dense, and the wording may appear outdated. The theory still clings to the word *object*, which is mechanistic and understandably distancing. The word, however, does have historical significance in psychoanalytic psychotherapy. It was coined within the context of Freudian drive theory when the focus was not on relationships but instead on "objects" that satisfied biological needs. Although the term is anachronistic, it is important to remember that early psychoanalytic theorists were pioneers in their time, crafting from numerous clinical encounters an understanding of early childhood interactional experiences that have withstood the test of time, if not of language.

The Work of Melanie Klein

The Internal Object: The Subjective Experience

Melanie Klein is considered to be the first to offer a complete object relations theory. She introduced the concept of the "internal object" (Bacal & Newman, 1990; Klein, 1964; Segal, 1974), which is the subjective experience of the infant based on her interactions with significant external objects in the environment. Klein believed that the infant, from birth, had an elaborate fantasy life, not based on the reality of the environment. These fantasies were destructive and guilt inducing, and because they were not tolerable to the infant, they were projected outward—particularly onto caregivers. With this theory, Klein retained an allegiance to Freudian intrapsychic drive theory, but she also created a bridge to a later object relational theory that gave primary importance to the infant's actual experience of the surrounding environment.

Splitting and Projective Identification

Klein introduced the concepts of splitting and projective identification. *Projective identification* is motivated by the self's need to be rid of unwanted or dangerous aspects. A part of the self is split off and fantasized as being put into an external object (the other person). This is done to control the object and so prevent it from doing further psychical harm. This process of *splitting* (keeping apart two contradictory feelings, such as love and anger) (Goldstein, 1995) then leads to an identification by projection; that is, the object becomes an extension of the self. As a consequence of projective identification, persecutory fears (of the external object) result (through identification with the bad parts of the self). Klein felt that good parts of the self were also projected, motivated by the need to establish the object as good by identifying it with the good aspects of the self. However, projecting either a good or a bad part of the self can potentially weaken the ego and lead to an impoverishment of the self.

The Internal Object and Child Abuse

With social work's emphasis on the person in the environment, it would be easy to dismiss Klein's work—as it is so replete with inner objects and bizarre fantasies. Nonetheless, Klein's theory of the internal object and its subsequent development by other object relational theorists has been of great value, particularly in social work practice with vulnerable client populations. Klein provided insight into how many internal experiences of objects from the past can influence, if not dominate, clients' worlds, distorting current relationships and seriously compromising their self-esteem. We see this most vividly in our work with abused children who are unable to detach from the abusive parent and who often experience even well-meaning caregivers as potentially dangerous. They then engage in behaviors that would seek to confirm a vision of their own inner badness, often leading to rejection by the well-intentioned adult. The concept of the internal object provides a guide in the complex treatment that these children require to overcome their early experiences.

The Internal Object and Internalized Oppression

Klein's concept of the internal object has been expanded to include wider sociological phenomena. Gainor (1992) applies the concept to the discrimination experienced by black women as members of a minority group in U.S. society. She cites Pheterson (1986, p. 148) in suggesting that these women may suffer from an "internalized oppression," which is defined as "the incorporation and acceptance by individuals within an oppressed group of the prejudices against them within the dominant society." These women then experience feelings of self-hatred, an inability to trust those similar to themselves, and a sense of powerlessness in confronting the sources of the oppression.

The Work of Ronald Fairbairn

The Internalized Bad Object: The Environmental Influence

Ronald Fairbairn (1952a, 1952b) was influenced by Klein's theory of the internal object. Unlike Klein, Fairbairn regarded internal objects as reflections of real experiences with people, not of fantasies. Fairbairn considered the internal object to be a source of psychopathology. Briefly stated, Fairbairn believed that the child could not allow himself to think of his caregivers as bad, as it would threaten his sense of security. Instead, he takes the bad object into himself. (He internalizes it.) Thus, the child protects himself from the reality of an externally bad environment and creates a reality of a tolerable environment. Fairbairn also highlighted the clinical importance of recognizing that the child (and later, the adult) experiences shame through his associated relationship with the bad object. Clinical symptoms are manifestations of the child's attempts to rid himself of internal bad objects without really losing them, because, in the child's mind, bad parents are better than no parents at all. The child manages the conflict associated with separating from the important object (i.e., caregiver) by this process of internalization.

Introjection and Self-Blame

Introjection (another concept introduced by Klein that is important in understanding abused children) of the bad object leads to self-blame. Self-blame occurs because the confused child needs to have some cognitive control over the abuse. How else could she understand that the person she needs and loves could hurt her? Self-blame is only a temporary coping mechanism, however, because it leads to depression and low self-esteem. The child needs to see that the caregiver is responsible for the abuse, not the child. If the abused child persists in the belief that she is responsible for the abuse, she will not be able to leave the relationship.

Trauma Bonding

Fairbairn's work on the internalized bad object laid the foundation for understanding the concept of trauma bonding in contemporary child abuse treatment. A trauma bond is the internalized set of expectations and cues that a child develops when an adult intermittently harasses, beats, threatens, or abuses the child (DeYoung & Lowry, 1992; Dutton & Painter, 1981). These bonds allow the child to defend against abusive acts while feeling and remaining safe. These cues motivate the child to behave in ways that are acceptable to the abusive adult. The child thus accommodates to the situation but suffers from anxiety, muted affect, cognitive constrictions, and overcompliance. These behaviors, in addition to the obvious power imbalance inherent in abusive relationships, result in the child's increased feelings of low self-esteem. Paradoxically, the child develops a strong affective bond to the abusive person. Because of the child's obvious need for the relationship, treatment is complicated (James, 1989, 1994). Separation from that person can intensify the bond, increase the idealization of the relationship, contribute to the victim's sense of psychological powerlessness, and result in an inability to form another primary relationship. James (1989) cautions that a child–parent relationship must not be evaluated on the basis of connection alone—the connection may be a strong trauma bond and not a secure attachment relationship.

The Work of Harry Guntrip

The Internalized Good Object

Harry Guntrip (1969, 1971) elaborated on Fairbairn's ideas and focused on the importance of the object in ego development. He felt the "self" was at the core of the individual and at the center of psychoanalytic theory. This self was thought to grow in the context of meaningful personal relationships. This thinking bridges the gap between object relations theory and self-psychology (see Chapter 7). It is through the experience of a good object (relationship) that the child discovers herself as a person and ego development proceeds firmly and with self-confidence.

Object Loss and Ego Weakness

When external objects (relationships, the environment) significantly fail to respond to the child's needs, the surviving ego—the essence of the true self—experiences fear and shame and must retreat. This leaves the child unable to have strong feelings for another person, since the presence of that person triggers the wounded child's defenses, resulting in an emotional withdrawal that may include coldness, hostility, and lack of interest. These individuals sometimes fear positive relationships more so than negative ones because there is greater likelihood of feeling smothered or overwhelmed by the good experience, thus losing oneself in the process. Guntrip (1969, p. 288) referred to the way in which persons manage these relationships as the *schizoid compromise*. The individual struggles to have a relationship in such a form that it does not involve full emotional connection, by being both in and out of a relationship simultaneously.

The Work of Donald Winnicott

The Internal Object(s) and Interpersonal Relationships

Winnicott (1965), a pediatrician, focused on the mother–child relationship. The mother, in a state of "primary maternal preoccupation," provides a "holding environment" that enables the child's psyche to grow. Her caring functions toward her infant were considered to be the most significant determinants of psychological health. Although Winnicott rendered a heavy burden to mothers in his theoretical formulation of the primacy of the mother as caregiver, he also coined the term *good enough mother* to describe mother as a caregiver with human faults and failings. Mother did not have to be perfect—just "good enough" to recognize and respond to the wide range of the infant's biological, psychological, and social needs while not harming her infant in any way. Winnicott felt that the "true self" of a person emerges as a result of this relationship with a "good enough mother" who was able to give the infant a sound start in ego development by providing "ego coverage." Thus, personal object relationships are the starting point of all human life and all subsequent relationships. Like other object relational theorists, Winnicott felt that caregiver functions are internalized by the child and become the building blocks for psychic structure. Contemporary theory (Siegel, 1999) proposes that the mind develops at the interface of neurophysiological processes and interpersonal relationships. Interpersonal experiences play a pivotal role early in life and in the ongoing emergence of brain functions because the circuits responsible for social perception are the same as—or tightly linked to—those that integrate the important functions controlling the creation of meaning, the regulation of bodily states, the modulation of emotion, the organization of memory, and the capacity for interpersonal communication (p. 21).

The Transitional Object

Winnicott was interested in how children experienced simultaneous separateness from and connection to the outside world. He introduced the concept of the "transitional object," which described how infants and young children use inanimate objects—such as blankets, articles of clothing, and stuffed animals—to hold on to images of important others while not in their presence. These objects must retain their original form. If they are washed, or torn pieces are sewn or replaced, they no longer contain their original qualities and the child becomes distressed.

The Interpersonal School

The Significance of the Therapeutic Relationship

Henry Stack Sullivan (1953), writing contemporaneously with the object relational theorists, introduced an interpersonal theory of human development that also emphasized an important theoretical shift from drive theory (Freud, 1905/1953, 1915/1957) to an interactional theory that looked at the relationship between the caregiver and the developing child, moving from a one-person (intrapsychic) to a two-person (interpersonal) psychology. Sullivan can be credited as an early theorist in changing the conceptual framework of the therapeutic relationship, making it a more collaborative, interactional process. He felt that the greatest source of knowledge about the patient occurred in the interaction between the therapist and the patient. He introduced the concept of the therapist as a participant observer, working within the context of a "detailed inquiry" (DeLaCour, 1996, p. 208). The detailed inquiry raised questions about the patient's history and current problems. The information obtained would then help the therapist present himself as different from the original primary figure in the patient's life. Sullivan clearly stated that the therapist had a role in the patient's transference distortions and that these were not solely determined by the patient's childhood experiences. He felt that the therapist would be induced by the patient to reenact early and current interpersonal experiences. This "interpersonal countertransference" provided a type of "role responsiveness" to the patient (Sandler, 1984, p. 149). The therapist, working within an object relational framework, needs to recognize how he and the patient are fostering a replication of the patient's earlier dysfunctional relationships. Sullivan redefined the role of the therapist and reformulated the psychoanalytic concept of anxiety, viewing it not as an intrapsychic process, but as a result of interactions between two people. Sullivan noted that patients avoid certain clinical material in an attempt to preserve self-esteem. The therapist's role is to lessen the patient's anxiety by establishing himself as a respectful, sensitive person.

Eight Stages in Object Relations Theory and Practice

Klee (2000–2005, p. 2) developed an eight-stage model of object relations practice, which is depicted in Figure 6.1. He defines object relations practice as being focused on process as opposed to a series of techniques. Klee writes, "Without understanding the process of human relationships, the therapist is unable to truly understand or connect with the patient. . . . It is this understanding and use of process that makes therapy meaningful and effective for the patient."

Stage 1: Preliminary Diagnosis of Relational Pattern. The therapist's goal is to assess the patient's patterns of interaction across the life span (beginning with the most recent relationships and working back to the earliest). These interactional patterns provide clues to the patient's personality structure.

Stage 2: Building the Therapeutic Alliance. The therapist focuses on the here and now and the healing quality of the relationship with the patient. The therapist demonstrates focused attention, skill, humanity, acceptance, and training in this regard and avoids judgments that could derail the building of the relationship with the patient.

Stage 3: Identifying the Maladaptive Relational Pattern. The therapist must sort out her own countertransference responses during this stage, such as noting whether her reaction to the patient is based on unresolved relational issues from her own life or whether she is responding to something in the patient's relational style.

Stage 4: Patient Expresses Maladaptive Pattern. This is considered the most intense stage of the therapy. In this stage, the patient is fully immersed in relating to the therapist with the same maladaptive patterns that have caused him difficulty. The therapist is cognizant that the patient is not aware of his relational pattern and therefore the therapist does not interpret the pattern, but engages in a continuous process of exploration of the nature of the therapeutic relationship in order to bring the pattern into more conscious awareness.

Stage 5: Therapist Generates Empathic Confrontation. The therapist empathically refuses to participate in the patient's maladaptive relational pattern (once the patient becomes aware of it). In other words, there will be a natural tendency on the part of the patient to engage the therapist in his "internal drama of object relations" that are the product of disappointing relationships in the patient's early childhood (Klee, 2000–2005, p. 1). The patient projects these split-off parts of himself onto the therapist and tries to engage the therapist into experiencing the corresponding affective states. The therapist must consistently and empathically "confront" the patient with this relational style and avoid taking part in it.

Stage 6: Working through the Confrontation. This is a difficult time for the patient who may feel disappointed in the therapist and/or uncomfortable with the therapy. The therapist must remember that the maladaptive relational pattern has served as a defense for the patient. The therapist must remain firm, consistent, and empathic as the patient struggles to change his relational style.

Stage 7: Generalizing the Therapeutic Relationship. The therapist shares with the patient her experience of being induced into the maladaptive relational pattern by the patient, allowing the patient to understand how he has affected other people in his life. The patient can now begin to explore relationships from this new perspective, making conscious efforts to change his conflicted methods of relating. The patient has been strengthened through internalizing the positive relationship with the therapist and is therefore more likely to take risks with others.

Stage 8: Separation and Termination. This is a time for reviewing the relationship and it often produces anxiety in the patient He now begins to appreciate that although the relationship with the therapist is at an end, the relationship continues in his own self-structure.

FIGURE 6.1 ***Eight-Stage Model of Object Relations Practice***

Source: Klee (2001–2005). Reprinted by permission.

Object Relations Theory and Brief Treatment

Strupp and Binder (1984) developed a model of time-limited dynamic psychotherapy (TLDP) that is rooted in an object relations framework. According to object relations theory, images of the self and others evolve out of human interactions rather than out of biologically derived tensions. TLDP interpersonal perspective reflects a larger paradigm shift within psychoanalytic theory from a one-person to a two-person psychology. Levenson (2003, p. 302) suggests that TLDP has an integrationalist perspective (with its focus on interpersonal relatedness, corrective emotional experiences, and transactional processes) that integrates theoretical developments in self-psychology, cognitive-behavioral, and systems approaches.

Time-limited dynamic psychotherapy is applicable to a wide range of clients including those who may have had difficulty forming good working relationships with their therapists. Within this model, the focus is on the maladaptive relational problems that a person has learned in the past, maintains in the present, and could potentially reenact in the therapeutic relationship. The goal of TLDP is not on the reduction of symptoms but on changing ingrained patterns of interpersonal relatedness or personality style. The TLDP model uses the relationship between the therapist and the patient to discuss and change the ways in which the patient interacts. Levenson and Strupp (2007, p. 7) discuss five inclusion/exclusion criteria that should be considered to determine if TLDP is appropriate for a particular patient. First, the patient must be in some type of emotional discomfort so he is motivated to engage in a challenging change process. Second, the patient must come for appointments and be willing to talk and engage with the therapist. Third, the patient must be willing to consider that he has some difficulties relating to others. Fourth, the patient must have the ability to emotionally distance from his feelings so that they can be examined with the therapist. Finally, the patient should be capable of engaging in a meaningful relationship with the therapist.

Levenson (2003, p. 304) presents five basic assumptions that underscore TLDP:

1. Maladaptive relationship patterns are learned in the past: Relationships with early caregivers will become organized, and both affectively and cognitively encoded as interpersonal schemas through which the child, and later the adult, filters the world.
2. Such maladaptive patterns are maintained in the present: Although a dysfunctional interactional style is learned in childhood, it must be supported in the adult's current life for the interpersonal difficulties to continue.
3. Dysfunctional relationship patterns are reenacted in vivo in the therapy: The patient interacts with the therapist in the same dysfunctional way that characterizes her interactions with others in her life and tries to enlist the therapist in playing a complementary role.
4. The therapeutic relationship has a dyadic quality: The relational-interactionist position of TLDP is that the therapist will experience an "interpersonal countertransference" that involves her acting in a way that the patient expects. The therapist must recognize this replication of the patient's earlier dysfunctional relational pattern and use this information to change the nature of the interaction in a more positive way.
5. The TLDP focus is on the child problematic relationship pattern: The emphasis in TLDP is on assessing and intervening what is patient's most pervasive and problematic style of relating.

Cyclical Maladaptive Pattern

Strupp and Binder's *cyclical maladaptive pattern* (CMP) is an organizational framework for understanding the presenting problem, determining treatment goals, and guiding clinical interventions. The CMP is composed of four categories. The first category, acts of the self, includes the thoughts, feelings, motives, perceptions, and behaviors of the patient that are interpersonal in nature. The second category, expectations of others' reactions, focuses on how the patient imagines others will react in response to her interpersonal behavior. Acts of others toward the self is the third category, and it focuses on the actual behaviors of other people as observed and interpreted by the patient. The fourth category is acts of the self toward the self. This category includes all the patient's behaviors or attitudes toward herself. Levenson (2003) has contributed to the further development of this fourth category of the TLDP model with her attention to self-care, self-empathy, and self-compassion. Fosha (2004) concurs with Levenson's attention to the clinical domain of a patient's relationship with self as "an essential dimension along which the effectiveness of treatment ought to be evaluated . . . as traumatic interpersonal experiences acquire their psychotoxicity through their internalizations" (p. 75). Levenson (2006) added a fifth category to the CMP called *interactive countertransference*. The clinician considers her own reactions to the patient as they work together. For example, "When I am with a client, I ask myself what it is like to try to relate to this person? Am I pushed or pulled to respond in a certain way? Am I anxious, solicitous, or withdrawn?" (p. 4).

Multicultural Considerations

The therapist must consider that the client's CMP is an amalgamation of her sociocultural and interpersonal life contexts as well as life stages, personal values, and strengths (Levenson, 2006, p. 8). This includes awareness of and focused attention to how cultural factors may be playing a role in the patient's lifelong patterns and in interpersonal difficulties, including those that may occur between the patient and the therapist. Levenson and Strupp (2007) write, "As part of this understanding, the therapist should have some comprehension of the normative interpersonal behavior and expectations for people with similar backgrounds . . . and this should be distinguished from the individual's idiosyncratic CMP" (p. 8). The examination of the relationship in the here and now between the therapist and the patient has the potential to positively influence work between the therapist and patients from different sociocultural backgrounds. This is similar to what Barrera and Corso (2002, p. 109) refer to as the *third space* where the therapist and the patient hold two different perspectives simultaneously and together create a third, "integrative, inclusive perspective" (see Chapter 5 on multicultural practice). It also has the potential to result in cultural transference–countertransference reenactments (p. 9) that must be distinguished from interpersonal problems that the patient may be having in her life. Levenson (2006) and Levenson and Strupp (2007) also stress that it is important that the therapist work with the client to depathologize his CMP. Maladaptive and dysfunctional behaviors are explained as ways individuals learned to adapt to situations that threatened their interpersonal relatedness (Levenson, 2006, p. 3). Again these styles of coping must be understood within the larger sociocultural, historical, and political contexts of patients' lives.

The following case illustrates how TLDP was used in a 25-session treatment with an adult survivor of severe physical abuse. The case demonstrates how Jane developed a CMP that was undermining her life.

Case Example: Using the Present to Transcend the Past

Client Information

Jane is a 29-year-old single white female treated for depression in a community mental health clinic. The client came for help because a recent breakup with her boyfriend triggered memories of severe childhood paternal abuse. As a result, Jane had difficulty sleeping and could not concentrate at work. Most recently, Jane was very frightened that "someone would break into her apartment and hurt her." She also reported that although she "knows it's not real," she sometimes "feels as though she can hear the loud voice of her father threatening her." When this occurs, she plays loud music to distract herself and "drown out his voice."

History of Presenting Problem

Jane had been involved in a relationship with this recent boyfriend for approximately two years, and they had been living together for the past 15 months. Jane describes the relationship as a "stormy one." Her boyfriend had been highly critical and demeaning, and on several occasions he had "pushed her around." Jane reported that he told her this happened because "she made him reach that point," and although she objected, she "believed this was true."

Case Example Continued

Jane also described chronic, conflictual relationships with women roommates in which she felt exploited and disrespected. On a number of occasions, her possessions were taken without her permission and her roommate(s) spoke "rudely" to her. These tense living arrangements contributed to her decision to move in with her previous boyfriend, although Jane did recognize that he was verbally abusive.

Family and Social History

Jane is the youngest of three children from a working-class Irish American family. Her mother had been hospitalized for psychiatric problems on several occasions. The first hospitalization was for two months and occurred shortly after Jane's birth. Because of her mother's emotional problems, Jane's abusive father became her primary caregiver. Jane reports one vivid memory of being stripped to her waist by her father, beaten with a belt, and hung from her feet. She remembers her father waking her up in the middle of the night when he was intoxicated and yelling at her for not doing household chores. Her father's abusive behavior escalated when she was a teenager. It was during this difficult time that Jane began to use drugs and alcohol "just to get away from it all." Jane left home at the age of 20—at which time she stopped abusing substances. She had two relationships with men, and both were abusive.

Case Assessment

Time-limited dynamic psychotherapy based on object relation constructs provides a conceptual framework that helps explain the impact of Jane's early childhood trauma on her adult life. Jane's current interpersonal problems were assessed within the context of CMP.

Acts of the Self

Jane had been involved in a number of conflictual relationships in which she was verbally and/or physically abused. For example, she felt (and had been, on occasion) exploited by female roommates who did not respect her privacy and borrowed her belongings without permission. She described her first relationship with a live-in boyfriend as "okay; he wasn't abusive," but he was not someone she could really talk to. Finally, she became involved with a man who replicated her relationship with her father. She loved him and felt that if she had only behaved differently, he would not have physically hurt her. Jane began to remember the childhood abuse by her father when her boyfriend ended their relationship.

Jane's current relationship with her parents also remains problematic. Jane reported that her mother ignores her needs and does not listen when Jane tries to set limits around their contact. Even now, Jane's mother/parents are unable to put her feelings and needs first, although Jane keeps hoping that "this time would be different." This is the childhood longing to integrate the good/bad object split. However, once again, the parents disappoint Jane and are unable to engage in the type of empathic relationship that would provide a new experience for her.

Expectations of Others' Reactions. The early childhood task of understanding that the same caregiving person may be both gratifying and frustrating was severely compromised for Jane as she had to reconcile the loved object (her father) with his abusive behavior. Additionally, due to her own problems, Jane's mother was emotionally unavailable to her during the

(continued)

Case Example Continued

important time of infancy and early childhood. In Winnicott's model of psychic development, the capacity to internalize feelings of soothing, pleasure, or comfort in response to the caregiver can be sustained or summoned in the absence of the caregiver with increasing facility as the child matures. Jane, however, was primarily dependent on an alcoholic, abusive father whom she both feared and needed. It was within this context that Jane developed behaviors that object relational theorists describe as the "building blocks of what will become organized, encoded, experiential, affective, and cognitive data informing one about the nature of human relatedness and what is generally necessary to sustain and maintain emotional connectedness to others" (Levenson & Strupp, 1997, p. 86).

Acts of Others toward the Self. Jane's expectations of others' behavior is based on her past history of childhood abuse and relational style of accommodation to that abuse experience. Jane expects that others will get angry with her if she is unaccommodating. This is illustrated in the process recording in this chapter. In accommodating others, Jane replicates her original relationship with her abusive father, wherein she compromised her own integrity for her father's intermittent affection and/or to avoid cruel punishment.

Acts of the Self toward the Self. Jane has internalized the bad self-object (introject) causing problems in her self-concept and disturbances in her adult interpersonal relationships. Although she is somewhat aware of what she does, or what she does not wish to do, Jane ignores her feelings or thoughts and acts in a manner that is contrary because she experiences her own needs as secondary. Jane's behavior also indicates the absence of a protective presence, or internalized "good enough" caregiver, that foresees possible hazardous consequences of certain behaviors. Jane has developed a relational style based on accommodation to others. Her self-esteem is damaged because she has internalized blame for the abuse and, in doing so, carries the introject of the bad object within.

Goals of Treatment

The two goals of treatment within a TLDP framework were to give Jane a new understanding of her interpersonal problems and to provide her with a new relational experience (the therapist). The therapist needed to help Jane cognitively understand what happened in her life and how it contributed to her interpersonal style of relating. She needed to provide a new relational experience for Jane by sharing her understanding of Jane's struggles and by inviting her to talk about what she may be feeling in therapy. Within this new relational dyad, Jane would have the opportunity to develop a different understanding of herself, of the therapist, and of their interaction. Thus, Jane's internalized bad object would be replaced with an internalized good object (i.e., the therapist). Through this process, Jane would relive early memories in a safe, supportive presence; mourn the childhood she never had and can never reclaim; and experience mastery over her conflicts. Levenson (2006) points out that differentiating between the ideas of new experience and a new understanding helps the clinician attend to aspects of the change process that are most helpful in formulating and intervening as efficiently and effectively

Case Example Continued

as possible. The therapist did this with Jane by pointing out repetitive patterns that originated in her experience with past significant others, with present significant others, and in the here and now with the therapist (p. 308).

The therapist who works with survivors of childhood abuse may initially respond more to the client's damaged relational style than to the trauma itself. Therapy would be an affective learning process in which the therapist would try to alter Jane's internalized working model of a relationship by witnessing, with "interpersonal empathy" (Strupp & Binder, 1984, p. 87), what Jane has endured.

Treatment

Working with Jane's Accommodation to Childhood Abuse Experience. In the beginning phase of treatment with Jane, the therapist focused on trying to help Jane see the ways in which she accommodated her father's abuse. The following dialog from an early session demonstrates this.

Clinician: How are you doing today, Jane?

Jane: Well, last night I went out to a bar with two other women and all they wanted to do was to pick up guys. I wanted to hang out with them and relax, so the only way I could get through the night was to drink. We met this one guy who was kind of good looking and he was attracted to me. I wasn't really interested, but he was buying all of us drinks and so it became my job to flirt with him so we could drink for free.

Clinician: What happened after that?

Jane: I left the bar with the guy and my friends stayed. I just wanted to go home and go to bed. I didn't want to sleep with him but I knew that if he wanted to sleep with me, then I would. I always feel that if a guy buys me drinks and spends the night talking to me that somehow I owe him. The guy walked me to my car and started kissing and touching me. I didn't want to make him mad, so I let him.

Clinician: It seems as though you were frightened and immediately thought of a way to give him what he wanted even though you didn't feel good about it.

Jane: Right; otherwise, he might get mad and hurt me.

Clinician: It's understandable that you would be afraid under those circumstances.

Working with Jane's Internalized Self-Blame. The "good father," needed for appropriate affection and attention, was kept in Jane's consciousness as long as she assumed responsibility for his abusive behavior. Jane was able to protect herself from the "bad father" who behaved so cruelly by shifting the blame to herself. Her father's erratic behavior was difficult to psychically integrate within Jane's childhood mind, for how does one reconcile feelings of love with those of fear? The therapist focuses on the multifaceted nature of Jane's internalized self-blame to help her give up responsibility for her own abuse. In the following passage, the therapist works with Jane to shift responsibility for her abuse experience from herself to her father.

(continued)

Case Example Continued

Jane: At home, when I think I hear my father's voice, I get very scared.
Clinician: What do you do when you get scared?
Jane: I lock all the doors and hide in my closet on the floor.
Clinician: Does that make you feel better?
Jane: Yes.
Clinician: I'm glad it helps you, Jane. Did you hide from your father in the closet when you were a little girl?
Jane: (quietly) Yes . . . I hid in the closet for a long time.
Clinician: Tell me about that little girl hiding in the closet.
Jane: I could hear him cursing, yelling, and calling my name. I knew he was drunk and that I had better stay out of his way. I kept trying to figure out what I did wrong. I was getting tired in the closet. I kept trying to figure out when it would be safe to come out. I listened and listened so I could hear if my father stopped yelling—then he was usually nicer to me—maybe he would even be sleeping.
Clinician: You protected yourself very well during those times, Jane—and in the only way a little girl could. But it wasn't right that you had to have such a tough job; you were a child.
Jane: But why did he act that way? I tried really hard not to upset him. . . . Sometimes it worked and he was nice.
Clinician: As a child you felt that your behavior was causing your father to be so angry and hurtful. Many children who are abused feel that way. But it wasn't your fault, Jane. Your father had some serious problems. . . . One of his problems was drinking. It was alcohol, not you, that caused many of his angry moods.
Jane: Sometimes I feel that way and other times I still feel that if I had been a different child, he wouldn't have hurt me so much.
Clinician: You wanted him to love you and not to hurt you. And that's so understandable. He was your father.

Jane hides in the closet and takes on the burden of monitoring her father's behavior. Here, we see Jane assuming responsibility in order to cope with her fears. The therapist works with Jane to help her to understand that this was a survival skill that she needed when she was a child. She then gently but directly addresses the self-blame that Jane has internalized. Here again, the therapist dually focuses on the cognitive and affective levels, providing new information for Jane in a way that is both understanding and respectful of her coping mechanisms. It is noteworthy that Jane describes hiding in a closet in response to current fear. The feelings associated with the time of the abuse are summoning old coping strategies. Because Jane has not internalized self-soothing, her fears overwhelm her in adulthood. The therapist is presented with the challenge of providing a soothing presence through direct eye contact, softly spoken words, and focused empathy while Jane speaks of potentially shaming matters.

Working to Help Jane to Gain Mastery over Her Abuse Experience. In the following excerpt from the middle phase of treatment, the therapist makes a clinical error. She moves too quickly in trying to help Jane gain mastery. The cognitive blame that becomes associated with the internalized bad object causes guilt and emotional paralysis. Jane's internal psychic

Case Example Continued

structure is not mature enough to envision a confrontation with the powerful, internalized bad object.

Clinician: Did you ever tell your father how afraid you were of him?
Jane: No, never. I couldn't do that.
Clinician: Do you think you could pretend in my office to tell your father why you are afraid of him?
Jane: No, I couldn't.
Clinician: I could help you. I would be right here and we could do it together.
Jane: I'm sorry, I can't. . . . I'm too scared.

The therapist is well intentioned in her desire to help Jane gain mastery over her internal terrors; however, she urges Jane to take action beyond her ability. This may not be helpful to someone who carries the abuser within. The introject of self-blame is too powerful. James (1989, p. 22) writes, "This self blame is embedded in the child's cognitive understanding and in his affective, sensory and muscle memory. . . . The cornerstone of treatment is to help the child understand, mind, heart and soul, that it is not his fault." The therapist must address the legacy of self-blame and shame and help Jane gain mastery. In the following excerpt, the therapist gives Jane some distance from the internalized bad object:

Clinician: Talking about your father is very difficult and very scary. I can see that. Let's try to understand what this is about.
Jane: I feel he's here in the room with us when I talk about him.
Clinician: In what way is he here in the room?
Jane: I don't know—I can feel his presence somehow.
Clinician: Do you ever feel his presence when you aren't talking about him?
Jane: (softly) Yes, lots of times, especially when I'm alone.
Clinician: What happens when you're alone, Jane?
Jane: I remember the things he said and did to me. . .. Why did he do those things?
Clinician: When you ask that question, it makes me wonder if you are once again feeling that you caused his abusive behavior.
Jane: But why else would he do those things?
Clinician: I think he did those things because he had many problems and was drinking heavily. He needed to feel powerful in ways that were very, very wrong, Jane. I know for sure that nothing you did caused your father to be mean to you.

The therapist, acting like a "good enough" surrogate mother, recognizes Jane's fears and offers her a way to talk about them. This will make it less frightening for Jane to relinquish her earlier style of survival by accommodation.

Working with Jane's Abuse Experience. In the next excerpt, the therapist focuses directly on Jane's abuse by her father. Only after issues of self-blame have been addressed can Jane work through the trauma of the actual abuse experience.

(continued)

***Case Example* Continued**

Clinician: We've talked a lot about the ways you tried to understand and control your father's behavior. We have also worked on ways you could feel less frightened when you remember your father. You now seem able to understand what you couldn't possibly understand as a child—you were not to blame for the things your father did.

Jane: Yes, I can really see that sometimes, and then at other times, I lose it and can't really believe it wasn't my fault.

Clinician: Jane, I think that happens because you get very scared. I'd like to try to talk about that with you.

Jane: I'm getting scared now.

Clinician: Tell me about it.

Jane: Well, I remember how mean and big he was.

Clinician: Yes, he was mean and big—a lot bigger than you. Jane, what would have happened to you as a little girl if you hadn't felt you could control your father's behavior?

Jane: (very softly crying) It's too scary. . .. It was too scary . . . because then he might have really hurt me and he might even have killed me.

Clinician: Yes, and you see now why you couldn't face that as a little girl—but you can look at it as an adult because your father doesn't have that same power over you. No one does.

Working with the Therapeutic Relationship

Object relations theory helps the therapist understand that if the client cannot part with her bad psychic objects because of guilt and fear, the therapist must become the good object whose care helps the client find her own true self. The therapist must be a sufficiently real person to give Jane the chance to rid herself of the internal bad object, freeing her to become a real person. In the following dialog, the therapist talks to Jane about how she is feeling about her—the therapist—and their relationship.

Jane: Before I started therapy, I didn't always feel so afraid of my father.

Clinician: Do you think that something is happening here in therapy that is making you afraid?

Jane: I feel like you are making me talk about things that are too hard for me to discuss.

Clinician: So, in some ways you're feeling that I am not putting your needs first.

Jane: That's right . . . just like everyone else.

Clinician: I can see how you would be feeling that way, Jane. We are talking about painful things and I say this will be helpful but right now it hurts.

Jane: That's right . . . it hurts a lot to talk about the past.

Clinician: You know, maybe when we talk about the past and it hurts, maybe you get confused about whether I am really helping you—or hurting you—just as you were confused as a child over what kind of a father you had—was he a loving dad or a hurtful one?

Jane: That's right (moves beyond the therapeutic impasse). There were times when he would bring me candy and be really nice to me. And then when he was drinking he got really mean.

Clinician: And so, sometimes it may be hard for you to accept my help, even though you may want to.

Case Example Continued

Jane: Yes, even though I really want to.
Clinician: I believe that happens, Jane, when you get frightened. Your trust in other people was betrayed a lot when you were a child. It will take a while to rebuild that trust.

Jane forgets that it was her escalating fears of her father that brought her to therapy. Instead, in the moment, she experiences the therapist as causing her this pain of remembering. Fairbairn understood this to happen because the patient does not want to be reminded of the pain experienced with a bad object. He also cautioned that there is shame associated with the internalized bad object. We may also be witnessing the projection of the internalized bad object onto the therapist as Jane attempts to escape its force. The therapist must also consider that Jane's mistrust of her occurs after they have experienced a good relationship and after Jane has been relieved of some internal self-blame. This is a poignant illustration of the dilemma Jane faces—she fears trusting the therapist as a good object even though she yearns for this connection.

Evaluation of Practice

Time-limited dynamic psychotherapy provided an important framework that enabled Jane to look at her experience of childhood abuse through adult eyes within the context of a nurturing relationship. In doing so, Jane was able to understand that she was not responsible for her father's actions. Jane began to attend Al-Anon meetings where she became further educated about alcoholism and its effects on family members. She was also able to let her parents know that she was attending these meetings in spite of the fact that they continued to deny her father's problem with drinking. Jane had difficult moments in therapy when the pain over what she had endured as a child seemed overwhelming. She was sustained during these times by the supportive presence of the therapist who, with ongoing self-reflection and focus, remained a good object.

Therapy helped Jane make different types of relational choices. Her post-traumatic symptoms decreased. She started to consider new employment possibilities. Jane now recognized that her boyfriend had been very abusive toward her. She speculated about what a nonabusive relationship would be like and knew that she would like to have one. At the end of treatment, Jane and her therapist both felt that she had made a great deal of progress and could now be optimistic about her future.

Time-limited dynamic psychotherapy, specifically the contribution of the therapeutic relationship to psychotherapy outcome, has been empirically tested. A number of studies were conducted using single-case design and the development and application of several scales to explore the process of therapy and the therapist–patient relationship. A consistent finding in all of these studies was that the quality of the therapeutic relationship was an important predictor of treatment outcome (Vanderbilt Psychotherapy Alliance Scale, Gomez-Sanchez, 1978; the Vanderbilt Therapeutic Alliance Scale, Bein, Levenson, & Overstreet, 1994; Hartley & Strupp, 1983; Hartmann & Levenson, 1995; Levenson & Bein, 1993; O'Malley, Suh, & Strupp, 1983; Windholz & Silberschatz, 1988) Treatment tended to be successful if the patient felt accepted, liked, and understood by the therapist.

Source: Case material supplied by Jennifer Cass Markens and Connie Crain.

Research Perspectives

Research shows that object relations continue to develop from immature dependency to mature respect and love until adolescence, then continue to grow and change through adult life experiences (Carlson & Kjos, 2002). Most useful research to help therapists think about families from an object relations point of view comes from attachment research (Berlin & Cassidy, 1999; Slade, 1996) and the "specificity of its predictions about individual differences and its arguments that mental representations (internal working models) underlie the associations between early attachments and subsequent close relationships" (Berlin & Cassidy, p. 688). (For further discussion of attachment theory and attachment research, see Bowlby, 1969/1982, 1973; Brisch, 1999.)

Clinicians can use attachment theory to help conceptualize assessment and treatment. It can be used in assessment to evaluate strengths and weaknesses in the client's capacity for relating and also in methods of engagement. Attachment theory guides the treatment as the therapist develops the therapeutic relationship by providing a secure base from which to work. As Scharff (1998) states, "We can view our participation in therapy as a dynamic interplay between the therapist's attachment organization and the patient's. As clinicians, we are objects of attachment and detachment, actively interpreting how the patient, in the transference, uses us to replay interactions of internal objects as they come to light in the transference and counter transference."

Summary

In summary, object relations theory has made a significant contribution to clinical social work because it provides a conceptual framework for understanding the development of the ego in early, as well as later, interpersonal relationships. The patient must experience the therapist as a good object in order to feel secure enough to risk giving up the internalized bad object. Once this occurs, a mature relationship becomes more of a possibility for them. As Guntrip (1969, p. 3), eloquently wrote, "They [clients] can now embark on two way relations between emotional equals, characterized by mutuality, spontaneity, cooperation, appreciation and the preservation of individuality in partnership. . . . The relationship is the same both ways . . . each goes on being and becoming because of what the other is being and becoming, in their personal interaction and mutual knowledge."

7

Self-Psychology: A Relational Psychodynamic Model

Self-psychological theory is particularly applicable to social work practice because many vulnerable client populations have suffered injury to their self-esteem through traumatic life experiences. The worker's conscious use of self provides empathic and growth-producing new experiences for clients, and a commitment to avoiding the repetition of past injuries that have left clients feeling emotionally injured (Elson, 1986). This chapter includes a discussion of self-psychology as a relational theory and its application to brief therapy. Case examples illustrate the major principles and techniques.

Self-Psychology as a Theoretical Framework

In self-psychological theory, developed by Heinz Kohut (1971, 1977), a person's sense of self (and self-esteem) is described as dependent on the quality of relationships with parental figures who serve as self-objects. A *self-object* is a person who is experienced intrapsychically as providing an enduring sense of availability to an infant, which fosters the developing self. Kohut introduced three specific self-object relationships as notably important to achieving a healthy self: the *mirroring*, *idealizing*, and *alter ego*. The *mirroring* self-object recognizes a child's unique capabilities and talents. The *idealizing* self-object links a child with the admired caregivers. The *alter ego* (also called *twinship* or *partnering*) self-object provides a sense of sameness with the self-object that is essential to psychic growth, attainment of skills, and sense of competence (Wolf, 1988).

The self-objects in a young child's life perform the adaptive functions of soothing and tension regulation (Hilke, 1998). Through a process Kohut called *transmuting internalization*, the individual is gradually able to perform these psychological functions himself, even in the absence of the original self-objects. When the child does not have important self-object experiences, the internalization of psychic structures cannot occur. Shame and humiliation result from the helplessness experienced as a result of ongoing self-object failure (Siegel, 1996). Conflicts arise when the individual fears that his own expression of needs will diminish whatever self-object experiences are available. The individual, anxious for the support of the self-object, may falsely comply with the needs of the other at the expense of the development of a true self.

A merger bond with the caregiver is created that is actually an accommodation to the needs of the self. Failure to accommodate to this position leaves the individual feeling isolated and depressed, with no self-object support for one's true self (Bacal & Newman, 1990; Siegel, 1996; St. Clair, 2004). This results in early, appropriate narcissistic needs remaining unnourished. The child (and later, the adult) is on a continual search for self-object experiences that will provide what is lacking. As the self becomes strengthened through self-object responsiveness (most notably in the therapeutic relationship), it becomes less shameful of these self-object needs, and more capable of giving without feeling anxiety about the needs of another. Self-psychology defines *maturity* as the ability to evoke and engage in mutually enriching self-object relationships with others throughout the life span (Wolf, 1988). An emotionally healthy individual has the ability to choose self-objects based on adult developmental levels, instead of early, narcissistic needs.

Empathy

Kohut felt that healthy psychological development grew out of and was dependent on a basic attunement between the self and its self-objects. This repeated attunement gradually builds the internal psychic structures that enable the individual to move from early, narcissistic or self-referenced developmental needs to attachments based on empathic connections appropriate to life cycle stages.

In his progressive hallmark paper, "Introspection, Empathy and Psychoanalysis: An Examination of the Relationship between Mode of Observation and Theory," Kohut (1959/1978) developed an empathic-introspective model of psychological investigation that he considered essential to the psychotherapeutic process. Kohut referred to empathy as "vicarious introspection" and defined it as the ability of the therapist to investigate the inner world of the patient. He considered empathy to be the tool with which the therapist gathers psychological information (Siegel, 1996). In the empathic introspective model, defense and resistance are viewed as normal attempts at self-protection in a person anticipating pain or injury. The therapist assumes there are valid reasons for resisting the therapist or the therapy and tries to find out what the patient fears in life and in the therapeutic relationship. Thus, every aspect of the therapeutic encounter is framed within the context of empathy.

The Role of the Therapist in Self-Psychology

Kohut was a pioneer in his time. He didn't subscribe to the Freudian view of the neutrality of the therapist. The classical drive or one-person psychology model addressed transference as arising from forces solely within the patient. The patient's experiences of the therapist were then felt to be distortions based on projections that the therapist interpreted (Bacal & Newman, 1990; Greenberg & Mitchell, 1983). Self-psychology shifted this view to a two-person psychology model in which the patient's feelings are viewed as determined by past experiences, current behaviors, and the relationship with the therapist in the present. Kohut (1959/1978) suggested that an exclusive focus on the patient's experience may not always be empathic or helpful and that the therapist needed to share her experience of the patient with the patient.

According to Kohut, patients come to therapy seeking admiration, guidance, and the opportunity to merge with the calmness and competence of an idealized figure through whom their own worth and capability can take form. Through the process of transmuting internalization, the patient gradually gains capacities that were not achieved earlier in life. The major capacities are the ability to self-soothe, self-comfort, and self-empathize. These capacities are initially provided by the therapist. Elson (1986, p. 49) talks about this therapeutic process as the "healing function to be played in the present by the therapist as a new self-object." Within the environment of the therapy, a compensatory psychic structure emerges in the patient. This new structure enables the person to seek and find more mature self-object relationships in life.

Kohut noted that there would be times when the therapist would not be able to provide all that the patient required in the way of self-object needs—because perfect empathic attunement was not possible. He believed that no great harm would come to the patient so long as the therapist recognized and acknowledged his mistakes and communicated, without judgment or criticism, an understanding of the impact of this empathic failure on the patient (Siegel, 1996). These minor experiences of the therapist's empathic failures, which Kohut called *optimal frustration*, actually contribute to the building of intrapsychic structure. The patient learns to tolerate frustration and is helped to develop internal capabilities in much the same way as young children are helped by parents who do not gratify every need. With these new intrapsychic structures in place, the individual can move from the earlier childhood need for idealizing, mirroring, and twinship self-object experiences to more mature, emotionally healthy relationships throughout life. The individual can also choose emotionally sustaining self-objects and be able to provide such experiences for others.

Self-Psychology and the Treatment of Children and Adolescents

Elson (1986) and others (e.g., Young, 1993) apply self-psychology to the treatment of children. Elson writes about the need for children, given their immature psychic equipment, to have functions performed by others (self-objects) so that they can develop a primary self-structure. Childhood disorders of the self (with concomitant behaviors such as rage, depression, clinging, disturbances in impulse control, and inhibition in the capacity for learning and the development of social skills) can result from persistent failures in phase-specific responses by caregivers to the child's appropriate needs and wishes. In other words, the child often demonstrates compulsive efforts to fill in missing psychological and self-regulatory functions. Driven, repetitious behaviors from a self-psychological perspective are viewed as desperate attempts to achieve recognition and response to vital needs for affirmation of a mirroring self-object and to merge with the strength and wisdom of an idealized self-object. The therapist's task is to understand the self-object needs presented by the child.

Young (1993, p. 80) writes about children who seek a mirroring response by showing aspects of themselves that can be admired. This same child may at another time seek a twinship type of relationship by directing the therapist to draw alongside her, but separately. Young cautions against interpreting the child's behavior, which can precipitate a narcissistic injury, but instead to respond to what the child needs.

Elson (1986) discusses the more entrenched structuralization of defenses to cover over deficits that are often present in older children and adolescents. She shares the example of a 12-year-old boy who vacillated between clowning and aggressive behaviors to engage his peers, resulting in rejection and a vicious, repetitive cycle. Through "innumerable, infinitesimal experiences of optimal frustration" between the client (self) and the therapist (new self-object), this child's needs for mirroring and merging with an idealized self-object were transmuted into reliable self-structure (p. 90).

The adolescent years bring turmoil not only to the developing youngster but to his or her parents and caregivers as each copes with the simultaneous "intensifying and loosening of the ties to primary self-objects" (Elson, 1986, p. 92). Parental self-objects are compared to self-object peers as the adolescent struggles both cognitively and affectively with familial values and ideals. Parents must demonstrate both strength and flexibility during these years as they examine the importance of their own values within the context of newer social norms. This is, as Elson (p. 93) notes, "the unique significance of the simultaneous ongoing process of the experience of self and other in parents and children."

Self-Psychology and Learning Disorders in Children and Adolescents

A number of authors have written about the relationship between learning disorders including attention deficit/hyperactivity disorder (ADHD) (see the *Diagnostic and Statistical Manual of Mental Disorders* [American Psychiatric Association, 1994] for a description of this condition) and disorders of the self from a self-psychological perspective (Mishna, 1996; Mishna & Muskat, 2004; Palombo, 1995, 2001a, 2001b; Rosenberger, 1988; Shane, 1984). Palombo writes about the subjective experience of the child, the impact that learning disorders have on development, and their contribution to personality formation. He clarifies that disorders of the self do not *cause* learning disorders, since the latter are neurologically based. He focuses specifically on the effects of neuropsychological weakness on a child's development, factors that give rise to a disorder of the self when a child has such weaknesses, and the modifications of the way the treatment process is conceptualized when a child has a learning disorder. Palombo clarifies that children with learning disorders are often misunderstood by caregivers, educators, and therapists who do not appreciate that the child's thoughts and behaviors are neurologically based and not motivated by psychological factors. This conceptualization also shifts the focus away from the impact of early caregiving on the child's development to appreciating that some of these caregiving responses may be in reaction to the child's difficulties.

It is important that the therapist and the child's caregivers become partners in the child's treatment to avoid perpetuating a situation "in which the environment continues to make demands that the child cannot meet" (Palombo, 2001a, p. 7). When a child is not able to make sense of her experiences and when there is additionally a discordance between the personal meanings the child ascribes to her experiences and the beliefs others (including parents, family members, and educators) have about the child's experiences, the child becomes vulnerable to problems ranging from struggles with self-esteem to disorders of the self. Concerning the self-object relationship for children with learning disorders, Rosenberger (1988) says, "Direct verbal explanations to clarify a confusing situation, soothing guidance on how to deal with a problem or at least to calm down, as well as an emotionally calm presence to stem the spread of anxiety, all bespeak a reliable alliance of immediate assistance to the child" (p. 274). Elson (1986, p. 93) describes this phenomenon as the "unique significance of the ongoing process of the experience of self and other in parents and children."

Treatment of children with learning disorders from a self-psychological perspective revolves around the centrality of the child's self-experience. This includes working with children (and their caregivers) to identify high-risk areas and the development of maladaptive defenses before they become part of the structure of the personality. The therapist must be a self-object for both the child and the caregiver, serving as an interpreter of experience and an intercessor with teachers, doctors, extended family, and other members of the child's community (Amerogen & Mishna, 2004; Rosenberger, 1988, p. 278).

Self-Psychology and Self-Harm in Adolescents

Straker (2004, p. 95) suggests that adolescents who self-injure—deliberately inflict harm on their bodies without suicidal intent—may be trying to put together the different parts involved in the building of self-identity. This represents a means of communication when there are deficits in the adolescent's capacity to process feelings through language. Deiter, Nicholls, and Pearlman (2000, p. 179) write that from a self-psychological perspective, self-injury behaviors are compulsive efforts that can serve as a substitute for the self-regulatory functions that are missing as a result of persistent failures in phase-specific responses to the child's self-object needs by caretakers. Lesser (2011) wrote about a self-psychological group therapy approach for immigrant mothers of adolescent girls who engaged in cutting behaviors. The purpose of the mothers' group was to strengthen the parents through empathic understanding of their experience and to promote the parents' empathy for the child's experience (Levine & Mishna, 2007). These parents were experiencing the turmoil of raising daughters in a country and a culture different from the one where they spent their teenage years. They were not able to provide their adolescent daughters with the self-object parental experience they needed, especially from their mothers. They were inadvertently inserting a wedge in their relationships with their daughters at a crucial developmental juncture (Elson, 1986). During one group meeting, the therapist says, "I hear that your experiences as teenagers in your countries have been very different from your daughters'. Would it be helpful to talk about your experiences? What was it like when you were 15 where you grew up?" After engaging the parents in conversation about their younger lives, the therapist uses "informed empathy" (Palombo, 2001a, 2001b) to educate the parents about the cutting behaviors. "I think maybe your girls are struggling because their life is so different from yours and you are very important to them. They love you but may feel you cannot completely understand what they are coping with as American teenagers. And so I can appreciate what a struggle this is for all of you as parents and for your daughters also. You grew up in one world . . . they are growing up in another world. I am wondering if we can figure out a way that you can talk with your daughters about this . . . like we are talking here."

Self-Psychology and the Elderly

The developmental task of the last phase of the life cycle is to maintain self-esteem in the wake of biological, psychological, and social stresses (Cath, 1976; Meissner, 1976). Lazarus (1993) cites the following manifestations of disorders of the self in the elderly:

1. Sensitivity to perceived slights and insults
2. Reactive anger and withdrawal/depression in response to disappointment or rejection
3. Wide vacillations in self-esteem
4. A propensity to self-consciousness, shame, and embarrassment
5. Hypochondriasis
6. Overdependency on others for approval
7. A tendency to view other persons not as objects separate from the self but as self-objects or extensions of the self that serve to stabilize a precarious self
8. An overemphasis on physical attractiveness, possessions, and past accomplishments to cope with feelings of diminished self-esteem

One of the major goals of therapy with the elderly is the restoration of self-esteem. The therapist may do this by engaging with the patients in reminiscing about past accomplishments, mourning the loss of self-object relationships, or listening to past narcissistic injuries suffered by the patient.

Self-Psychology and Brief Treatment

Self-psychology is quite applicable to brief treatment. Its proponents (see, for example, Balint, Ornstein, & Balint, 1972; Gardner, 1999; Goldberg, 1973; Lazarus, 1982, 1988; Ornstein & Ornstein, 1972; Seruya, 1997) feel that patients seek treatment because of a loss of self-object experiences that weaken the sense of self. The goal of treatment from a self-psychological perspective is to enhance the patient's self-esteem and restore the level of functioning prior to the loss. Through empathic investigation, the therapist provides the mirroring, idealizing, and twinship functions introduced by Kohut (1959/1978, 1971, 1977) that remain central to the development of the self. Understanding the patient's subjective experience enables the therapist to offer the needed self-object responsiveness, which, in turn, restores self-cohesion and decreases symptomatology. The therapist helps the patient appreciate the legitimacy of his needs and feelings, promoting awareness, understanding, and self-acceptance. The relationship with the therapist as a self-object serves as a bridge to reestablishing a supportive self-object environment outside the treatment arena (Gardner, 1999; Lazarus, 1982, 1988).

Case Example: Brief Treatment of an Individual from a Self-Psychological Perspective

This case illustrates how brief treatment based on self-psychology helped an aging mother accept her son's gender change. The therapist's nonjudgmental, empathic approach contributed to the mother's ability to appreciate that although her son's outward appearance was not the same, her daughter remained her child.

Client Information

Mrs. W., a 68-year-old white Catholic woman, consulted a therapist in private practice in a small northeastern city. Mrs. W. was widowed from an alcoholic husband. She had two grown sons, Jonathan and Lawrence. Her eldest, Jonathan, age 35, was undergoing transgender surgery, and Mrs. W. was sad and afraid. She described Jonathan as bright and somewhat shy as a child. She felt he was always different from the other children, although she couldn't exactly comment on how or why. When Jonathan was 14, Mrs. W. began to discover articles of her clothing missing and on occasion found nylon stockings and undergarments hidden in various locations. She said that somehow she "instinctively knew it was him and not his brother, Lawrence." When she approached Jonathan, he confided that he felt "drawn to her clothing" and that he "dressed up when he was alone." Mrs. W. told him that his behavior was not "normal" and that he should not continue it or she would tell his father. She never did share this with her husband as she "feared his reaction" and never found additional clothing missing or hidden. She decided to consider what had occurred as only a "stage."

Jonathan left home to marry by age 22. He and his wife had two children. The marriage ended in divorce after six years. Neither Jonathan nor his family have contact with his children. Mrs. W.'s younger son, age 30, has been married for 10 years and is the father of three children. Several years following his divorce, Jonathan confided to Mrs. W. and his brother and sister-in-law that he was "terribly unhappy living as a man" and that he was thinking of pursuing sex reassignment surgery. He had been talking about his gender dysphoria with a psychiatrist for a number of years and wanted his family's support and understanding. Although not surprised that he "was inclined to be feminine," Mrs. W. said she suspected he was gay—"something I could accept more easily." She found the idea of her son having surgery to become a female "shocking" and became depressed and withdrawn. Neither she nor her other son rejected Jonathan, but they were not able to offer any emotional support to him.

Shortly after telling his family, Jonathan had the surgery and changed his name to Leslie. The first time Mrs. W. saw her new daughter was very difficult for her; she felt that she couldn't call Jonathan "Leslie" and that although Jonathan was now a woman, he was still her "son." It was during this intense period of confusion, when the relationship with Jonathan had become very strained, that Mrs. W. decided to seek help.

Clinical Assessment

Initially, Mrs. W. expressed feelings of shame, anxiety, and sadness, which had been present since her son had begun "dressing like a woman in public." Because of the stigma associated with transgenderism (Emerson & Rosenfeld, 1996; Herdt, 1994), Mrs. W. felt isolated and unable to confide in her friends and family. She feared their judgment of her family, and she judged herself to be a bad mother. She was also worried about continuing

(continued)

Case Example **Continued**

to include Jonathan in family gatherings. She was concerned about the reaction of her three young grandchildren when they learned that their Uncle Jonathan was now their Aunt Leslie.

It was clear that Mrs. W.'s own self-esteem was compromised by her son's sex reassignment surgery and that she blamed herself. She talked quite a bit about "whether she should have left his father" because Jonathan felt he "never acted like a real father." She wondered if things would have been different if "his father had taken him fishing or to ball games like other fathers." She thought she had not protected Jonathan enough from his father's verbal abuse and that somehow this had damaged his sense of self-esteem and identity. Mrs. W.'s strong sense of responsibility and shame led her to be secretive about her son's sex change, diminishing her social supports at a time when they were most needed. Mrs. W. was experiencing self-object failure and loss in her role as a parent. This was heightened because of her previous experience of self-object failure in her marriage to an alcoholic husband wherein she felt she compromised her self-esteem as a wife. Now she felt inadequate as a parent. It was important for the therapist to provide idealizing, mirroring, and twinship self-object experiences in the therapeutic encounter to restore Mrs. W.'s sense of worth. Goals for treatment were to decrease her depression, enhance her self-esteem, help her grieve the loss of the relationship with her child as she knew him, and enable her to build a new relationship with her child as a daughter.

Treatment from a Self-Psychological Framework

Beginning Phase of Treatment. The therapist's initial focus was to provide an accepting and validating place for Mrs. W. to talk about her son and her grief over what had happened—to be the mirroring self-object that she lacked. This would be the first step in the journey to help Mrs. W. establish a relationship with her new daughter and to reestablish relationships with caring friends and family where possible. The therapist used empathic inquiry to explore Mrs. W.'s thoughts and feelings about transgenderism. Mrs. W.'s feelings of secrecy and shame were validated by acknowledging the stigma and lack of knowledge associated with transgenderism in society. The therapist mirrored an understanding of Mrs. W.'s feelings that she may be "the cause" and provided reassurance that she was not to blame. Finally, the therapist offered a twinship experience—the human understanding and connectedness so important during this time of shame and emotional isolation—by telling Mrs. W. that their counseling sessions would help her learn more about transgenderism. The following dialog is from the initial meeting:

Therapist: What brings you to counseling at this time?

Mrs. W.: It's really very hard for me to talk about this. I don't even know how to say it.

Therapist: (listening, nodding encouragingly) What's making it so hard to discuss?

Mrs. W.: (sighs) Well, my son had a sex change operation and now he wants me to call him Leslie. I can't bring myself to do it—to me he will always be my son, Jonathan. Do you think I'm wrong?

Therapist: I feel sure it isn't a question of right or wrong but more a struggle you're having over what has happened. Let's try together to sort out some of your feelings or concerns.

Case Example Continued

Mrs. W.: Well, is this somehow my fault? I don't understand what has caused this to happen. He says he always wanted to be a woman and that he couldn't live as a man any longer. . . . Is this normal?

Therapist: It seems as though you don't have a lot of information about what is involved in a person's decision to pursue sex reassignment. I'm not an expert on the topic but I can certainly assure you it is not something that parents cause to happen, although I can see how that is worrying you. I can give you some names of organizations to contact for more information. I would even be glad to get the information for you. For now, I'm concerned about the fact that you seem to believe you did something to cause Jonathan's decision to become a female.

Mrs. W.: Well, mothers get blamed for everything, and I can't help but feel like it's all a reflection of me and our family.

Therapist: You seem to be ashamed of what your son did. Again, I think it will be important to learn more about transsexualism. That might help you appreciate the fact that you were not the cause. . . . Would that help with the shame?

Mrs. W.: I don't know—maybe a little—but I'm so afraid to talk to anyone about this.

Therapist: What is your fear?

Mrs. W.: That people will be disgusted or horrified.

Therapist: Those are powerful feelings and it's understandable that you haven't been able to reach out to anyone with those fears. I'm glad you decided to come in today to get some help even though it was very hard to do. Hopefully, together we can help you with your feelings.

This excerpt demonstrates how, as a mirroring self-object, the therapist empathizes without judgment with Mrs. W.'s feelings as well as provides educational information. The counselor forges a twinship self-object experience for Mrs. W. who, at this juncture, feels alone with her shame. This is done by talking in terms of "we" rather than "you" as the therapist presents herself as a companion to Mrs. W. on this new journey.

Middle Phase of Treatment. In this challenging phase of treatment, the therapist struggles to keep the primacy of Mrs. W.'s feelings in sharp relief while showing concern for her son and their relationship. The therapist walks a clinical tightrope—at moments empathically falling short of Mrs. W.'s desire for unconditional support. Mrs. W. clearly needs the opportunity to grieve the loss of her son, Jonathan, while moving toward acceptance of her daughter, Leslie. Mrs. W. confided that although she knew that Leslie had suffered before the surgery and really craved acceptance, she felt torn nonetheless. She would call her son "Leslie" when they were together but she could not bring herself to do that with anyone else.

Mrs. W.'s ongoing sense of shame and fear of social rejection were primary concerns. Although attention initially focused to her son's needs for an accepting parent, self-psychological theory helped the therapist understand that Mrs. W. was not able to be the self-object her son wanted at this time. The counselor needed to reframe her response and focus once again on Mrs. W. (providing the appropriate mirroring self-object experience). She let Mrs. W. know she appreciated Mrs. W.'s feelings and shared her own feeling of

(continued)

Case Example Continued

"wanting to be respectful of her son's decision as did Mrs. W. but also understanding that Mrs. W. needed help and time to feel comfortable moving forward." In this way, the counselor joined with Mrs. W. in the twinship experience that would help her build a relationship with Leslie. This is conceptualized as *optimal frustration* (Kohut, 1971, 1977) or *optimal responsiveness* (Bacal, 1985). In optimal frustration/responsiveness, the therapist is empathically attuned enough to provide certain psychological functions but is momentarily unattuned as well. At this point in the treatment, the counselor reviewed her own values, particularly because she too had been influenced by a larger society that regards transgenderism as unnatural. It was important that the therapist's decision to refer to Leslie as a "he" was a self-psychological intervention to help Mrs. W. in her initial stage of grieving and not a collusion with society's devaluation of transgenderism.

Mrs. W.: I think what makes this all so difficult is the reaction that you get from other people.

Therapist: What are your concerns?

Mrs. W.: Well, they wouldn't understand. They might laugh, feel sorry for me, or wonder what kind of a family we have.

Therapist: In many ways, you are right to be concerned. Transsexualism is not very well understood and people get uncomfortable with what they don't understand. What would someone's laughing or not understanding mean to you?

Mrs. W.: (crying) It would hurt because he is still my son and I raised him the best way that I could. I also feel sorry for him because he hasn't had an easy life.

Therapist: You seem to really appreciate some of the difficulties your son has faced and what may have contributed to his decision to have the surgery. Have you shared these feelings with him?

Mrs. W.: Not really—it's just all been so hard for me and I'm afraid I might also say the wrong things.

Therapist: Well, you have a lot of feelings but a good place to start may be to let your son know that you are trying to understand him and his life better.

Mrs. W.: But I still worry about the other people. If I told someone and they laughed, it would just about kill me.

Therapist: What would be a helpful response from people if you were to share this with them?

Mrs. W.: I guess just to listen and be supportive without judging him, our family, or me.

Therapist: That makes a lot of sense to me. When you've sorted out your own feelings enough to take a risk sharing with others, it may make you feel less burdened. Right now, you are carrying a "secret" that keeps you in isolation.

Mrs. W.: Do you think I should be telling people?

Therapist: When you are ready I think it may be helpful to no longer feel you need to keep this a secret. But again, we need to be realistic about who you should initially share with and what kinds of reactions people may have.

Mrs. W.: I did get the information we spoke about. I guess I myself never realized this type of thing existed—it makes me feel as though it's not only my son or my family.

Case Example Continued

End Phase of Treatment. With encouragement, Mrs. W. moved from her initial period of adjustment and showed an increased willingness to refer to Jonathan as "Leslie." She was also very anxious that Leslie be accepted by the family and took a leadership role by providing information to her other son and his wife about transgenderism. With assistance from the therapist, she told them what to tell her grandchildren. Mrs. W. was no longer concerned about Jonathan's sex change as a reflection of her parenting. She was even able to confide in one of her sisters about Leslie. At this turning point, Mrs. W. had taken a chance, reached for a self-object outside the therapeutic relationship, and found support. Mrs. W. gave information on transgenderism to her sister, offering herself as a self-object, much as the counselor had provided this experience for her. She decided not to share with other family members whom she felt would be critical and hurtful. This was another sign of enhanced self-esteem as Mrs. W. made self-object choices that were appropriate for her at the time.

Mrs. W.: Well, we all got together at my other son's house last week and this was the first time Jonathan—Leslie—came over.

Therapist: How did things go?

Mrs. W.: It was okay—it seemed strange at first partially because to me he still sounds like Jonathan. And I could see the older children were confused and uncomfortable. The little girl was totally loving because she doesn't really know what is happening; she was hugging and kissing Jonathan. He was great with her, too.

Therapist: Perhaps we can all learn from how your youngest granddaughter was dealing with the situation, by simply relating to the person around her. This little girl actually may help pave the way for others in your family.

Mrs. W.: I hope so because it would kill my son—I mean, my daughter—if the kids didn't want anything to do with her. I guess we all have to try hard or we'll fall apart as a family over this.

Therapist: I don't think you are going to fall apart. We'll continue to work together with other members of the family to make sure that doesn't happen.

In this final exchange, the therapist again used the language of twinship to provide a merger self-object that helped support Mrs. W. as she wondered if her family would ever reunite.

Evaluation of Practice

According to self-psychological theory, the essence of cure resides in the patient's ability to identify and seek out appropriate self-objects in her surroundings and to be emotionally sustained by them. Like its theoretical predecessor, object relations theory, self-psychology places the therapeutic relationship at the center of treatment. Therapy provides the corrective emotional experience of being understood in an empathic manner and nontraumatically frustrated in a way that promotes a solid sense of self-identity and self-esteem. Kohut felt that the internal world can and should be studied only through the instrument of the therapist's empathy. In other words, the therapist uses empathy to collect data, immerse

(continued)

Case Example Continued

himself in the patient's experience, and reflect on the meaning of that experience (Siegel, 1996). Treatment conducted from a self-psychological perspective may therefore lend itself to heuristic research and qualitative methodology, where the question of validity is one of meaning. In such studies, the researcher shares her understanding of the participants' experiences with them and seeks their verification. In self-psychology, the therapist must be able to understand the patient's subjective experience, share that understanding with the patient, and be willing to listen and change therapeutic directions if the patient does not feel his experience is fully appreciated. Kohut (1984) wrote, "If there is one thing I have learned during my life as an analyst, it is the lesson that what my patients tell me is likely to be true—that many times when I believed that I was right and my patients were wrong, it turned out, though often only after a prolonged search, that my rightness was superficial whereas their rightness was profound" (p. 94, cited in Siegel, 1996).

Although a formal research study was not conducted, several important outcomes of Mrs. W.'s treatment were evident. Mrs. W. learned that transgenderism is misunderstood and devalued in society and that it is not something that a parent can cause. She was able to tell her sister about her son's operation and then introduce her to her niece, Leslie. Mrs. W. began to call Jonathan "Leslie," and facilitated her daughter's acceptance by her brother, sister-in-law, and their children. Mrs. W. was involved in a number of senior groups where she was able to be selective regarding whom she could tell about her daughter and whom it might be best not to tell. This reflected Mrs. W.'s increasing ability to choose appropriate self-objects that could continue to emotionally sustain her. Finally, at the end of therapy, Mrs. W. was able to empathize with Leslie's experience rather than remain focused solely on her own feelings. In this regard, Mrs. W., after having empathic self-object experiences with her therapist and others, was able to be an empathic self-object for her daughter.

Brief Psychotherapy with Women

I have used the group modality and brief treatment from a self-psychological perspective in treating a number of women with self-esteem problems. This evolved from my experiencing these women as having a paucity of appropriate self-object relationships in their lives. The following clinical case example describes a 12-week group devoted to women in abusive heterosexual relationships.

Case Example: Group Brief Treatment

The Group

This group was composed of eight women ranging in age from 25 to 45 who came from similar socioeconomic and educational backgrounds. Each of the group members had previously been in individual treatment with the same therapist because of past and present involvement in abusive relationships. The group goal was to provide an opportunity for women who shared similar problems to work together toward change. The group met on a weekly basis for $1^1/_2$ hours for 12 consecutive weeks.

Case Example Continued

Stages of Group Development and Role of the Therapist

Beginning Stage. The two major themes that emerged in the beginning stage were trust and shame (Hartling, Rosen, Walker, & Jordan, 2000). The women were understandably concerned with whether they would be accepted by other members of the group. The clinician took an active role at this early stage by addressing and diminishing the group members' anticipation that they would be shamed. "I appreciate everyone's taking a big chance with the unknown and coming here today. I know it wasn't easy. Beginnings can be hard and meeting new people isn't always easy. Now that we all know each other's names, I'd like to ask each of you to try to share any particular concerns you had about joining the group. You may find you share some common worries."

The members' responses reflected their feelings of shame and vulnerability:

> "I felt very afraid because I was never in a group and I wasn't sure if my problems were real enough."
>
> "I was worried that someone I knew might be here and that would be embarrassing for both of us."
>
> "I was anxious—worrying about what I would say and whether I would sound stupid."
>
> "I was afraid of what would happen. . . . What if someone got really upset and I couldn't help, or if I got really upset and no one could help me."

The therapist validated the women's feelings and reframed them as self-protective responses. She then suggested other ways the women could experience themselves and each other: "It occurs to me that each of you is really talking about the way in which you tried to prepare yourself to enter the group—maybe how to be ready to protect yourself from hurt just in case others didn't understand your feelings." The therapist also introduced the idea that their feelings of fear and shame might also come up in our group.

"Let's talk about how we can help if we think someone is ashamed to talk about a problem in group or worried about what others might say or think. Hopefully, we'll be able to feel comfortable enough to talk about those fears so that you can be helpful to each other. . . . My job is to try to help you with that." In this way, the therapist established a safe and empathic self-object environment where the women were able to feel understood by each other. She engaged the members in making connections with new self-objects in the group.

Middle Stage. In sessions 4 through 9, the therapist focused on helping the members remain attuned to each other's affective states and continued to validate experiences that might be different from their own. She also helped them recognize each other's uniqueness, thereby beginning the process of restoring damaged self-esteem. The women became sensitized to potential shame in other members and began to assume the role the therapist had modeled in the initial stage of the group. An example of this occurred when one member responded to an apology by another who felt unable to leave an abusive male partner:

> "Sue, you don't have to apologize for staying with your boyfriend. No one here is judging you—we understand how scary it is to be alone."

(continued)

Case Example **Continued**

One woman consistently provided counsel to others in the group and spoke of her problems as being "in the past." The first woman became defensive and angry. She said, "If you don't want me here, I'll leave." Before the clinician could intervene, another group member said, "Maybe Jane is ashamed to talk about her problems even here in the group. . . . I still feel that way sometimes." At this, Jane told the group that her boyfriend had been drinking and was verbally abusive to her again. She was ashamed to tell this to the group because she had said in an earlier meeting that she would leave him if he drank again. "I feel like everyone else here is changing but I'm stuck. . . . I'm always stuck . . . . My family says they weren't surprised and never expected me to leave." At this point, the therapist addressed the issue of shame again: "We need to help each other in whatever way possible and be mindful of how shame continues to make us feel badly about ourselves. . . . Let's agree right now to challenge shame to leave the group—the rest of us can stay."

Using the language of twinship (Elson, 1986; Kohut, 1971, 1977), the therapist provided the context for a common human bond. This was especially important because talking about shame can itself be a shaming experience. She reminded members of the time frame, encouraged them to review what had taken place thus far, and restated goals for the remaining sessions: "We are at the midpoint in our group meetings. Let's take some time to check in and see where everyone is at." The therapist also raised the possibility that members may feel like leaving the group before the actual termination date particularly as concerns around separation and loss were raised: "There may be moments when people feel like it would be easier to just not come back. The reason I say this is because endings can be hard."

End Stage. During sessions 9 through 12, the clinician helped the women identify ways to transfer their learning from the group experience to their daily lives: "I'm interested in having us share ways in which members of this group will continue to get support when the group ends. You've all experienced support here and you now know what it feels like and what to look for. . . . That's the first step to finding it."

The members talked about what they would need to look for in relationships and what they needed to avoid:

> "I need someone who lets me talk without telling me I don't know what I'm saying."
>
> "I know I'm not crazy now and I want someone to respect me. I need someone who can listen instead of talk."
>
> "I'll never be involved with someone who only wants to control me. That's definitely over."
>
> "I won't take any verbal abuse; it hurts too much. I want a man who talks to me like I'm worth something."

The group used role-plays to practice directly expressing feelings and setting limits on inappropriate behaviors. The therapist actively facilitated these behaviors by playing the abusive partner:

> "Right now, I will be your boyfriend. . . . Can you try to tell me exactly how you are feeling?"

Case Example Continued

As the women become more relaxed with this exercise, the therapist suggested they try to play different roles for each other. The women agreed that they would like to have something in writing when the group ended so they could periodically review the important points they were practicing. The clinician supported this group decision and talked about it as a way "you will be holding onto the group experience concretely as a reminder when you are feeling shaky inside." During this end phase of group, fear and grief were prominent themes. The clinician was concerned about possible retraumatization of earlier injuries to the self due to the withdrawal of the self-object(s) of the group as the women began to talk about past losses and relationships that left them feeling depleted and rejected. They expressed some anger toward her as they were experiencing the termination of the group as a rejection. They also expressed fears that the end of the group would mean the end of psychosocial support:

> "I have had so much loss in my life and this group is really important to me. I feel angry that the group can't just continue. . . . I'm not sure I understand why it can't."
>
> "I feel sad, too, but I also have to say that this time it's different. I feel sad—but not like I'm a terrible person or that I did something wrong. That's the way I usually feel when a relationship ends—like it was my fault."
>
> "When something upsetting happened during the week, I didn't get as anxious because I knew I was going to come here and tell people about it and they would listen and help me. I wasn't alone."

The therapist made a decision at this time to address the veiled feelings of anger and disappointment behind the termination statements. She gave the women the important message that she had heard their feelings, and in doing so, continued to provide an important self-object experience: "I think it may be important to talk about some possible disappointment that I am not continuing the group—maybe even some anger about that."

In the final session of the group, each member had the chance to talk about what the group had contributed to her life:

> "This is our last meeting—a time for ending but also for new beginnings. How has the group helped with those new beginnings?"
>
> "I will always remember the kindness, especially when I couldn't be kind to myself. . . . I won't let people put me down like I used to."
>
> "I'm not the only one who makes mistakes. . . . I don't have to always feel lousy about everything I do and say."
>
> "I learned that I deserve to have people in my life who really like me and want me to do well."

A follow-up meeting was scheduled for the next month. Excerpts from this group illustrate some of the confidence the women gained from their experience and some of the struggles they had yet to overcome:

> "It is so good to see everyone again. I really missed all of you—but I have to say I also feel pretty good about my life right now. My family has backed off—basically because I told them I wasn't going to be treated badly any more."

(continued)

***Case Example* Continued**

"My boyfriend tells me that I have changed and I'm not so timid anymore. In the beginning I wasn't sure he liked this but now we actually seem to be getting along better."

"I'm still afraid to meet someone or get involved in a relationship—that will be the real test of whether I have made any changes."

"Whenever I felt myself slipping into old patterns, I thought of this group and remembered what it was like to really be understood and accepted. I really want that in my life."

The inner strength that members had gained from the group experience sustained them. Confidence replaced shame and doubt.

Countertransference

The therapist was challenged during this group as she struggled to provide an appropriate self-object environment where the members felt validated by her and each other. She sought consultation from peers who were able to be validating self-objects for her during these times. The therapist felt relieved when, during the middle stage of the group, the women began to listen and respond to each other in ways similar to how they had initially experienced her. During the termination phase, when the women wanted to continue meeting, the clinician felt guilty. She wondered about the time limit she had imposed and whether this was sound practice or a capitulation to a managed care environment. The therapist shared her feelings with the women: "I'd like to let you know how much you have all helped me in my work as a therapist. You taught me something new about the courage it takes to change and about how capable people are of making their lives better with some help and support. I will take this experience I have had with you to my work with other women. In this way, I will always remember each of you and the special journey we took together. Thank you for giving me the chance to work and to grow along with you."

Source: Adapted from Lesser (2000).

Summary

Empathy, in self-psychological theory, is more than the therapist feeling for the patient—it is listening in such a way that the therapist hears the patient's story and is able to communicate her understanding of that story and its impact on the patient's life. Being understood by another person (the therapist) gives the patient the affirmation so vital for establishing other meaningful relationships. Elson (1986, p. 3) aptly sums this up by saying, "The practitioner has only one tool and that tool is herself." This statement underscores the primacy of the therapeutic relationship in clinical social work practice from a self-psychological perspective.

8

Relational Theory

Jay Greenberg and Stephen Mitchell's publication of *Object Relations in Psychoanalytic Theory* in 1983 linked together, for the first time, interpersonal, object relations, and self-psychology theories under a "relational" paradigm. Psychic reality was now viewed as a relational matrix, encompassing both the intrapsychic and the interpersonal worlds. Intrapsychic or mental representations contain the imprint of interpersonal living as it is experienced by the individual and include a representation of the self, the other, and the interaction between them. Intrapsychic relational processes, once formed, reshape interpersonal processes that, in turn, alter intrapsychic processes. These changing patterns of interaction perpetually transform themselves and each other (Fonagy & Target, 2003). Mentally healthy persons can integrate, express, and satisfy their various needs in a way that maintains a positive sense of self (good representations of self) and positive feelings about others (good representations of others). This facilitates the formation of solid interpersonal relationships and the ability to use relational capacities fully (Fairbairn, 1952a, 1952b; Klein, 1948; Kohut, 1977; Mitchell, 1988; Stern, 1977; Stolorow & Atwood, 1992; Sullivan, 1953).

The Therapeutic Relationship

Transference, Countertransference, and Intersubjectivity

At the root of relational theory is the concept of the therapist being a "participant in a shared activity" with the patient/client (Fonagy & Target, 2003, p. 222). Mitchell (1988, p. 3) writes, "The basic unit of study is not the individual as a separate entity whose desires clash with an external reality, but an interactional field within which the individual arises and struggles to make contact and to articulate himself. The mind is composed of relational configurations . . . the person is comprehensible only within this tapestry of relationships past and present."

The relational therapist brings her authentic self into the treatment, resulting in greater participation than in classical psychodynamic models of therapy. Relational theory emphasizes clinicians' authenticity—their honest and relatively open subjective reactions to the therapeutic process. The focus, of course, must always be on the client and the issues she brings to treatment. Self-disclosure is considered an important aspect of mutuality, and subjectivity in the therapeutic relationship but only when it relates to the client's needs. It may involve sharing countertransferential feelings as well as disclosures of the therapist's thinking process in relation to helping the client recognize his impact on others (Goldstein, Miehls, & Ringel, 2009, pp. 45–46).

Transference and Countertransference. In classical psychoanalytic therapy, *transference* is viewed as the patient's distortions of the therapist based on past relationships. In relational therapy, transference is seen as a real social response to the actions of the therapist, and therefore it contains both transference and nontransference components. *Countertransference* includes the therapist's subjective experiences of the therapeutic relationship and, in particular, of the patient's transference.

Relational theory enlarges the interactional field because transference and countertransference now form a system of reciprocal influence and mutual recognition known as *intersubjectivity* (Meissner, 1996).

Intersubjectivity. Intersubjectivity is the reciprocal influence of the conscious and unconscious subjectivities of two people who cocreate the relationship they live and talk about (Natterson & Friedman, 1995). The intersubjectivists enlarge the concept of countertransference to include the ways that the therapist's subjectivity shapes the relational experience and the patient's transference. The primary clinical question changes from "what does it mean" to the client, to "what is going on between client and therapist" (Fonagy & Target, 2003, p. 211).

Relational Theory and the Third Space

Ogden (1982) and Benjamin (1990) have used the concept of the third space to describe the interactional field created when the subjectivities of the therapist and the patient come together. Goldstein, Miehls, and Ringel (2009) write about "the third" as being a transitional space that allows the client to practice new ways of interacting with another (p. 52). Mattei (1999) describes how the culture, race, and ethnicity of both the client and the therapist influences the treatment and how the interaction between client and therapist is transformed into a new, third dimension. Walls (2004, p. 6) describes seeing the interpersonal as *fundamentally cultural* and writes how we must also help our patients gain insight into the dynamics of internalized societal relations and clarify the unconscious accommodations our patients may be making to existing exploitative and oppressive social structures (in their jobs, marriages, political and market structures, and freedom to change those accommodations). Therapists should examine how the structure of society is expressed in our work, and how injustices and inequalities may be implicitly enacted through our therapeutic practices (Dimen, 2000; Mattei, 1999; Spivak, 2001; Walls, 2004; Stracker 2004). The entire range of racial, sociocultural, and political identities and subjectivities that therapist and patient bring to their relationship, including issues of oppression and privilege, then become topics for therapeutic conversation.

Relational Mindfulness

Several authors (Safran & Readin, 2008; Surrey, 2005) relate the concept of intersubjectivity to the experience of connection in mindfulness-based relationship therapy. Safran and Readin describe mindfulness as "the process of locating and directing one's awareness to the present moment as it unfolds" (p. 122). Mindful practitioners listen deeply, attentively, and empathically. This can be integrated into our work as therapists through the ongoing discipline of meditation practice (Hicks, 2008, cited in Lesser & Pope, 2010, p. 73).

Surrey (2005), writing from a feminine perspective, incorporates mindfulness into cultural relational psychotherapy. In addition to paying attention to her own feelings, thoughts, memories, and sensations, the therapist is paying attention to the experience of the patient as the object of awareness, using these perceptions to facilitate the movement—or flow—of the relationship (Lesser & Pope, 2010, p. 73). This is called *tripartitie awareness* (self, other, and the flow of the relationhip); a type of "comeditation" beween the therapist and patient allowing the therapist's empathic attunement and acceptance to provide the patient the possibility of remaining emotionally present with difficult feelings (Surrey, 2005, p. 94).

Case Example: Cross-Racial Relational Therapy and African American Women

The Cross Model of African American Racial Identity Development

The Cross (1971, 1978, 1991, 1995) model helps explain black racial identity development and the relational dynamics of African American women living in white communities. The five stages of the Cross model are pre-encounter, encounter, immersion/emersion, internalization, and internalization/commitment. In the *pre-encounter* phase, the black woman has absorbed many of the beliefs and values of the dominant white culture, perhaps unconsciously internalizing negative black stereotypes. Denial helps her to selectively screen out awareness of information that affirms she cannot really be a member of the dominant racial group (Helms, 1984) and thus she seeks assimilation and acceptance by white society. Crisis events such as social rejection by whites precipitate movement into the *encounter* phase, where the black woman is forced to focus on her identity as a member of a group targeted by racism. In the *immersion/emersion* stage, she surrounds herself with visible symbols of racial identity, making everything of value black or relevant to blackness. In the *internalization* and *internalization/commitment* stages, the woman is ready to build coalitions with members of other oppressed groups and has a general sense of commitment.

Clinical Example of Carol

The following case illustrates how the therapist, a white middle-class social worker who came from a working-class background, and the client, an upper middle-class African American professional, also from a working-class background, work together within the context of a cross-racial therapeutic relationship.

Carol, a 28-year-old African American woman, grew up in a small southern town. Her family had great expectations of their only child. Her mother was the only one of

(continued)

Case Example Continued

13 children who went to college—her siblings either worked in the steel mills or were day workers. Her father was a government employee. After high school, Carol elected to attend a black women's college, and while there, she gained admission on a master's level to a prominent eastern university, where she earned an advanced degree. Although she achieved, she felt it was a matter of luck and that she was seen as a "token" by her predominantly white classmates. She performed well and was recruited by a prestigious New York corporation after graduation. In spite of her accomplishments, Carol was unhappy. She felt isolated in a large city and misunderstood by family and friends back home. Plagued with self-doubts, feelings of being alienated from family and friends, and conflicts at work, she entered treatment. This process continued over two years, during which time Carol began to resolve conflicts related to divided loyalties.

Initial Phase of Treatment. The only woman of color at her prestigious firm, and brighter and more experienced than many of her colleagues, Carol, in the early stage of treatment, had talked of her discomfort in asserting herself. Recently, she had been invited to become a member of the Board of Directors of a major international corporation, but her own company refused to support this initiative. The company stated that it was a matter of policy, but Carol was not convinced. She felt that the issue had to do with race, and she felt angry, vulnerable, and exposed. This brought up earlier memories of childhood in her small southern town. The following process recording is taken from an early interview:

Carol: I saw this movie on TV the other night—it's old and very famous, called *Imitation of Life*. Did you see that?

Social Worker: No, I have not. Would you like to tell me about it?

Carol: It's about a black girl who wants to be white. She passes, but pays a big price. She has to leave her family, and she's always afraid that she'll be found out and rejected and have no where to go. In high school I remember thinking that it would be easier if I were white or not there at all. I felt invisible. I got good grades. I looked good because my mother always dressed me well. The school was mainly white—my parents wanted me to have the best education so they sent me to parochial school. I had a friend named Betsy; she was very pretty and popular and I thought that if I were with her, people would like me. My mother chastised me, told me I was acting like I thought I was white. I told her that we don't recognize color here, we're all the same. She told me I was kidding myself, that color was always there. One day Betsy's cousin from New York came to visit. When she saw me, she refused to play with me because I was black. Betsy went off with her and left me standing there.

Social Worker: She betrayed you. You must have felt very hurt and alone.

Carol: I was so startled I couldn't speak. I wanted to run and hide. But I didn't say anything. And I feel that way now—I lose my voice at work when I feel I'm not being seen for who I am. I make all this money and I feel I don't deserve it. So I keep to myself, I don't socialize.

Social Worker: You still are feeling lonely.

Case Example Continued

Carol: Yes, but at least I don't have to feel like a fraud. I don't fit in anywhere—not in the white world, or the Black world either. I feel like I live life on the fence.

Social Worker: I would like to hear more about your feelings.

Carol: Have you ever seen the old movie *Splendor in the Grass?* I feel like Dini. She's this pretty girl in a small town. Her parents are extremely strict, and she falls in love with this great-looking guy, has sex, and later a nervous breakdown. She recovers and then moves away. She becomes really affluent after leaving her small town, but when she returns to find her former lover married, with kids, as if nothing has changed, she wonders what she's really left behind, and if she's really happy.

Social Worker: I did see the movie—I remember feeling very sad.

Carol: I feel I could be Dini and have a breakdown. Sometimes I feel like I live on the edge. It's so hard to pull myself together.

Social Worker: Are you wondering whether you'd be happier back home?

Carol: At least I'd feel a sense of belonging.

Social Worker: It sounds like your present situation at work has brought back feelings you had as a young girl. You were told that you didn't fit into one world and then you were having a hard time fitting into another world. Your loyalties are still divided, and you are trying to find an identity that feels right for you.

In this dialog, Carol struggles with living on the boundaries of two separate cultures. Rather than betray a part of her identity to live in the dominant culture, she isolates herself from both, which leaves her pained and alone. Also evident is how she has not internalized her success, but rather feels fraudulent in her white world of work. This is a common theme among professional women of color—the more successful they become, the more alienated they may feel from their ethnic and racial communities (Comas-Diaz & Greene, 1994). Bell and Nkomo (2001) write about the success of African American professional women coming at least in part from their resilience in handling the microtraumas of the everyday racism that occurs in routine encounters at work. Having absorbed many of the beliefs of the dominant white culture, Carol appears to be in the early stages (pre-encounter) of racial identity development. Although there is conflict, she avoids the pain aroused by having to confront racial identity isissues by retreating from both cultures.

The social worker tries to talk with Carol within a relational framework. However, what has been missed in this early stage of counseling is any discussion of the cross-racial helping relationship. Powerful countertransference issues kept the worker from discussing race. There were certain similarities between the worker and the client—both had crossed class boundaries to achieve success. In fact, Carol's salary was more than double that of the worker, making it difficult for the worker to view Carol as a victim of discrimination and herself as a woman of privilege. The social worker appears color blind, a stage of white identity development that Sue and Sue (2003) describe as not recognizing herself as a racial being. This contributes to her inability to see the difference between herself as a white woman and Carol as an African American woman. The worker's attempt to understand Carol's feelings by referring to her childhood sound intellectualized and lacking in relational authenticity and unwittingly replicate the unbalanced power relationship between blacks and whites in American society.

(continued)

Case Example Continued

Middle Stage of Treatment. As treatment progressed, Carol spoke more openly about her conflicting loyalties and just how wide the gap between her past and present had become. She described how angry she was at her parents for pushing her to enter the white world, yet denigrating her when she assimilated at the expense of her own racial heritage. The following process recording from the middle stages of treatment illustrates her continued struggle with racial identity development and the challenge both Carol and the worker face in maintaining relational authenticity.

Carol: January 15th was Martin Luther King Day and I went to work. A group of colleagues asked me why, and I didn't know how to answer. It made me stop and think. Why did I work? My Jewish colleagues take time off for the Jewish holidays.

Social Worker: How do you feel about this? What did Martin Luther King Day mean to you?

Carol: I don't know (shifts uncomfortably). I can tell you something else that happened. I belonged to this group of professional black women at my previous job. When I left, I didn't keep up the contact. Recently, I ran into one of the women. She was angry at me—she said we had to stick together. I felt uncomfortable. I am very busy, yet I did get in touch with a former white colleague recently. So now I feel torn.

Social Worker: Do you feel that you have to stick together with other black women?

Carol: Well, in some ways—the more I continue to advance, the wider the racial gap becomes. I go to this upscale university, and my 16-year-old cousin back home has three kids and is still not married. Yet I don't want to work in the ghetto. I realized that if it weren't for Martin Luther King and the struggle of the 1960s, I wouldn't be where I am now—I'd probably be where my cousin is.

Social Worker: So, you are talking about racism and where this all leaves you because as an African American woman you have had some opportunities, but many other African American women—and men—continue to struggle a lot.

Carol: (crying) I feel so guilty. It's awful. My parents didn't achieve as much because they didn't have the opportunities, but I just want to live my life. Sometimes I feel that it means forgetting that I'm black. And yet at work, I feel very black.

Social Worker: How do you feel about being black?

Carol: (angrily) How do you feel about being white?

Social Worker: I didn't mean to make you angry. To be honest, I'm glad I'm white. I think it's really hard to be black in this country.

Carol: Right, and so you don't get to ask me how I feel about being black, okay? I feel proud a lot of the time but right now it's a burden. Many people still think that African Americans are inferior. I don't, but then again you have to question why black people have never been able to rise above the slavery issue. It's all mixed up within me. Sometimes I feel that all I've done, I've done for my parents. At other times, however, I feel as though I am leaving them behind. I just want to live my life . . . like a white person gets to do.

Social Worker: Carol, sometimes I wonder whether I can understand your feelings enough to help you. How do you feel about working with me? Do you wonder whether

Case Example Continued

I can understand or appreciate your feelings? Or do you feel you might get more understanding from a black therapist?

Carol: (crying) In some ways it is difficult to talk to you but I would like to tell you about my experiences. In all the time I have spent with white people, I feel I have never really been honest about who I am. Sometimes, I don't even know who I am. It's important for me to be honest with you and for you to be able to hear what I have to say. Working with you gives me a chance to practice being a black woman in a white world—but in a real way. I just want you to be honest with me.

Social Worker: Okay, this is hard but I will be honest. Would it surprise you to know that sometimes I feel jealous of you . . . even though I said I was glad I was white . . . we came from similar backgrounds and I didn't have a lot of the educational opportunities you did because you were African American. I also feel a sense of shame as a white person for what white people have done to black people in this country and I get that they deserve more opportunities than white people . . . but it's hard . . . because sometimes I guess I feel like they deserve more opportunities than only some white people. So I get confused also.

Carol: I appreciate your honesty. I never thought about it this way I guess. I always felt white people have all the advantages.

Social Worker: I'm not saying they don't . . . only that sometimes things get complicated. I appreciate your honesty as well.

In this interview, Carol has moved into the immersion/emersion stage of racial identity development by demonstrating a conflict between appreciation and deprecation in her attitude toward her race (Sue & Sue, 2003). However, vestiges of the pre-encounter phase (Cross, 1991) are apparent in her negative stereotypical thinking about blacks and her continual strivings toward acceptance by the white culture. The denigration of Carol's own racial group may be a defense against internalized racism (Greene, 1993) and also allows her to feel superior, which enhances flagging self-esteem. This denigration also engenders guilt, as it further separates her from her family and heritage. The worker has entered a new stage in her own identity development as a white person when she openly talks about her feelings of conflict and shame. Suchet (2004, p. 431) refers to race as one of the "most charged discourses in our society." This brief exchange illustrates some of the pain but also the growth of mutuality and enlarged connection between Carol and her therapist who are now beginning to authentically discuss their relationship. The worker struggles with the racism inherent in her identification with African Americans—in believing that her class issues and Carol's race issues somehow make them kindred spirits (Bodnar, 2004, p. 593).

Brown (1998) suggested that girls (and women like Carol) may "ventriloquate" the voice of the dominant culture in order to please or stay in relationships with others (in this case example, the worker) who align themselves with the dominant culture. This ventriloquated voice, although initially consciously spoken, may in time become less conscious and begin to replace the girls' own voice. The therapeutic relationship described in the case presentation has allowed Carol to find her voice—and to experience relationship authenticity—considered, by cultural relationship theorists, to be the hallmark of mental health.

Self-in-Relation Theory or Cultural Relational Theory

Cultural relation theory suggests that women are oppressed by the patriarchal social structure where their relational bonds are devalued and labeled as dependent. Miller, Stiver, and Surrey (1991) and Miller (2002, 2003) present a model of female developmental theory originally referred to as *self-in-relation.* This model challenges the earlier psychoanalytic concept of separation individuation in favor of a perspective that stresses relationship differentiation. These authors, as Chodorow (1978) and Gilligan (1982) before them, note that female infants do not separate, but instead develop a "self-in-relation" to others. Problems in development occur in this new model because of difficulties women have in remaining relationally connected while trying to assert a differentiated sense of self (Enns, 1991; Miller, 1987), and not because of a failure to separate.

Constructs of self-in-relation theory are the following:

Mutual Empathy. This is a reframing of the concept of empathy from its introduction in self-psychological theory (Kohut, 1959/1978, 1971, 1977) where empathy was unidirectional (i.e., from caregiver to child). Empathy is now a mutual, interactive process, suggesting a way of joining together in which each person is emotionally available, attentive, and responsive to the other in the relationship.

Relationship Authenticity. This is the ongoing challenge to feel emotionally real, connected, vital, clear, and purposeful in a relationship (Surrey, 1991, 1997). It describes the need to be seen and recognized for who one really is. Being able to say what you see, think, feel, and need—to find one's voice—is of the utmost importance (Gilligan, 1982). Dialog is between two active individuals—speaker and listener—initiating and responding to each other, creating truth.

Relationship Differentiation. The third concept of cultural relational theory is relationship differentiation (Jordan, 1997a, p. 61). The word *relationship* in this context is defined as the ongoing, intrinsic awareness and responsiveness to the continuous existence of the other or others and the expectation of mutuality in this regard. The capacity and the willingness of each person to change and grow fosters development.

Self-Empathy. Developing an inner sense of relationship, or self-empathy, is difficult for women, who are often more comfortable in the role of caregiver to others. Engagement in a relationship with a therapist promotes the building of a mutually empathic bond in which the patient feels understood by the therapist. The therapist facilitates the development of self-empathy as he or she joins the patient in a process of empathic witnessing and acceptance (Surrey, Kaplan, & Jordan, 1990, p. 13).

Self-in-relation theory was renamed to cultural relational theory when a number of authors (Canon & Heyward, 1992; Coll, 1992; Coll, Cook-Nobles, & Surrey, 1995; Jordan, 1997b; McRae, 2000; Spencer, 2000) expanded the theory to include the influences of culture. Comas-Diaz (1994), moving away from the original emphasis of the theory of the mother–daughter relationship, highlights the variance of child-rearing practices among different racial and cultural groups. McRae (2000) integrates concepts such as acculturation, cultural identification, use of language, socioeconomic status, experiences of racial and social oppression, minority identity development, and acknowledgment of power differentials in the therapeutic relationship as well as other relationships in the lives of women of color.

Cultural Relational Theory and Women's Groups

Schiller (1995) offers a stage model particular to women's groups, based on cultural relational theory. This author highlights how connection influences the way in which women approach conflict in groups. Stage 1 of the relational model, preaffiliation, is fairly typical of other group therapy models. Stage 2, establishing a relational base with peers, is in contrast to moving into a phase of power and control more common in groups. This is a time when the women discover shared experiences and seek approval and connection from the members and the group leader. This sense of connectedness to others in the group is what contributes to a sense of safety. Stage 3, mutuality and interpersonal empathy, is an extension of stage 2, when the women are able to develop trust as they share and begin to respect differences. The therapist does this by helping the women find ways to understand each other even when they may differ. Jordan (1991) refers to this as a type of empathic attunement marked by intimacy and mutual intersubjectivity. Stage 4, challenge and change, is when the women more directly begin to question themselves, each other, and the leader. They are able to risk the direct expression of anger and disappointment because they feel secure in the connections that have been established. Stage 5, termination, is in keeping with standard practice of endings with groups.

Group Example: Women's Support Group—New Connections

Introduction

Cultural relational theory was used as a framework for an eight-week group for white, heterosexual women in their fifties and sixties who came from working-class backgrounds. They were raised in traditional female gender roles to be caregivers of husbands, children, and aging family members. Most had not worked until after their children were grown and then found employment in factory and service jobs. Their husbands, the primary breadwinners, were skilled and unskilled blue-collar workers.

Cultural relational theory posits four elements that contribute to depression in women, each of which was quite evident during the individual screening interviews the practitioner conducted: experience of loss, inhibition of anger, inhibition of assertion, and low self-esteem (Kaplan, 1986). The women were disappointed in their relationships with significant people in their lives, most notably husbands or adult children. They were unable to express their anger and disappointment because they felt the relational bond would be broken. They consequently doubted their own relational worth and were left feeling ineffectual in their roles as wives and mothers. The absence of intimacy was experienced as a

(continued)

Group Example Continued

failure of the self as well as failure of love from another. The therapist believed that a group would provide a chance for these women to see that they were not alone in their experiences. Through sharing personal and family histories, they might begin to understand how they had decided that taking care of themselves meant that they were selfish. The group would hopefully provide a safe place to begin to talk about how they would feel about being in roles other than caregiver.

Role of the Therapist

Enns (1991), writing on the importance of social intimacy to identity development, suggests that the experience of connecting with a counselor and with other women may be the most important corrective experience for women who have not had the chance to take part in mutually affirming relationships. Fedele (1994) highlights three essential relational paradoxes that the therapist needs to work within women's groups to facilitate this process.

The *first paradox* is the ongoing dialectic between the desire for gratifying connections and the need to maintain strategies to stay out of connection for fear that one's feelings will not be understood. This was most evident in the first stage of the group, as illustrated in dialog from the initial meeting.

Seven women agreed to participate in the group and they all attended the first meeting. The therapist greeted them in the waiting room where she immediately noticed that each woman sat alone, either reading a magazine or staring straight ahead. She said, "Hello everyone. I think you're all here for the women's group—why don't we go inside and get acquainted."

The women acknowledged the therapist but continued to avoid looking at each other. As they filed past, she extended her hand and personally greeted each one in a similar manner: "Hello, Anne, I'm glad you're here; nice to see you tonight, June."

This meeting was very important because if the women felt connected and safe, they would look forward to returning. The practitioner introduced herself as the group leader, saying, "I've had the opportunity to meet each of you. I'm very happy we are all here tonight. I put this group together as a place for women to have a chance to talk about their lives, their concerns, and their relationships with important people in their lives. I decided to do this because it is sometimes difficult for women to talk about their disappointments in people they care about—either to the individuals themselves or to other people. Sometimes women have trouble letting others know they are angry. Instead, women tend to blame themselves and keep their feelings inside. But this can lead to sadness, poor health, and lots of other problems. I hope this group can be a place where each of you will feel comfortable sharing your feelings and finding your voices over the next eight weeks. Now, I'd like to ask each of you to introduce yourself. Please tell us your name, something about your life, and what made you decide to come to this group. Let's begin on my right and go right around in a circle. Remember, it may feel a little uncomfortable at first, but it will get easier."

The therapist gave a rather long introduction to the group before asking the women to speak. This set the tone for the group, establishing the common relational ground that will enable the women to feel safe sharing. And so it begins with June:

> "I feel a little foolish being here because my life is supposed to be going well right now—I just retired. I was always able to handle things in the past—I

Group Example Continued

adopted and raised three children, my husband had a drinking problem—I was always able to handle things but now I'm falling apart. I'm depressed and anxious all the time. Everyone is sick of listening to me. I need a place to talk."

Looking directly at June, the clinician says, "Well you came to the right place." She then looked at each of the women in the room and ask, "Isn't that right, ladies?" For the first time, the women smiled and began to look at each other.

Debra says, "You sure did. Let me tell you what happened to me. After 35 years of marriage, my husband decides to leave me for another women—a young one, of course. He cheated on me all our married life and I always took him back—I thought that was what I was supposed to do—but this time when he wanted to come back, I said no and I got a divorce. I know I did the right thing but I feel lousy." Silence. The therapist interjects, "Well, maybe some of these other women will help you figure that out, Debra. I'm glad you decided to come to the group. Let's hear from Mary."

Mary shares that her husband won't support her in trying to set some limits with an adult daughter who recently returned home to live, without a job and with a young child. Lucy is afraid even to speak to her husband of 25 years because she wants to avoid confrontation at all costs, despite the fact that he leaves her alone most of the time. She is perhaps the most traditional of the women, raised in a very religious home to believe that the man is the head of the household. Abby married late in life and is taking care of an aging parent with dementia. Her brother does not help, and she suffers from caregiver stress. Donna, married for 20 years, simply says, "My husband won't talk to me; whenever I try to tell him something he just rolls his eyes and walks away." And Anne is married to a man who abuses alcohol on a daily basis. She continues to cook his meals and take his verbal abuse when he is intoxicated because "I don't know what else to do or where else to go."

As the therapist listened to the women tell their stories, she considered the ways in which they would be able to connect with each other. She saw clearly how much they wanted to belong and to be understood, and she also saw how frightened they were of being judged. She said, "What really strikes me as I listen to each of you is how much you have in common—maybe we can talk more about that. I'll begin by saying that it's clear how very hard each of you has tried to take care of so many people—and situations—in your lives." A couple of the women smile—two of them start to tear and there is silence in the room. This time, however, it feels like a silence of connection, not disconnection, because the clinician has struck a chord that resonates with the caregiver role each knows so very well. And so, the tone is set for validation of the women's experiences, development of self-empathy, and mutuality—three of the four most curative factors in women's groups. The fourth factor, empowerment to act in relationships, will hopefully come at a later stage of the group (Fedele & Harrington, 1990).

The *second paradox* introduced by Fedele (1994) is between similarity and diversity. This takes place in the middle phase of group, during stages 2 and 3 of Schiller's model. The women have discovered shared experiences, and made a connection with peers.

The therapist continues to focus on creating a safe context so that there will be mutuality and shared empathy. If the women feel connected, they will be able to develop trust. This is illustrated by the following dialogue from the fifth group meeting.

(continued)

Group Examplee Continued

Mary is crying and talking about how disappointed she is in her daughter, who returned home for the second time with her 7-year-old child. "She doesn't respect me at all—she comes and goes as she pleases and even though she sees how hard I work, she doesn't pay any rent or give money for food. She wants me to babysit and if I don't, she takes my granddaughter with her. I don't like this either because I don't know who her friends are or where she is going."

June responds tentatively, "I know what you're going through. I had a lot of problems with my daughter; she got involved with drugs. I hate to say this but maybe your daughter is taking drugs."

Mary quickly interjects, "No, I don't think she's taking drugs."

June replies, "It was hard for me to accept and maybe your daughter isn't—I hope not—but whatever . . . I finally just got tough and said she couldn't live at home any more. It was the hardest thing I ever did."

Mary cries softy, "I don't know if I can do that—how did you find the strength?"

The therapist feels somewhat anxious during this exchange because Mary and June are sharing different experiences and expressing different emotions. She's worried about whether they can talk about their differences and remain connected. As she grapples with this, she realizes that she is moving away from the group process and experiencing what Miller and Stiver (1995) suggest are the therapist's own paradoxical struggles for connection and disconnection that emerge throughout the group's development. As a woman, the therapist has also found it difficult at times to remember she can express differences and remain connected to others. And so she says, "You know, there are ways in which your situations with your children differ but what's so important is that you share in your struggles as mothers—not always knowing what to do and feeling the pain and loneliness this brings." The clinician sees that June hears Mary's pain and is trying to find a way to show her. And Mary may not do things exactly as June did but knows now that she is not alone in her disappointment and may find comfort in knowing that another mother found a way out that was right for her. "Can anyone else share any moments of difficulty as mothers to their adult children?"

The *final paradox, conflict in connection*, involves the ways in which the leader sets the tone for group members to discuss feelings of anger without judgment. In this way, the group provides the opportunity for the women to experience disconnection within a context of connection, making reconnection a possibility. In the following exchange from the sixth group meeting, the therapist identifies the strong emotions being expressed in a calm, accepting, and nonjudgmental manner, modeling authenticity and connection in the midst of tension.

Lucy is the quietest member of the group. For the first three meetings, she said only that she was married and had three grown children. When the other women spoke, she tentatively asked questions or tried to make supportive comments. Now, she tells her story: "I don't know what to do anymore—my husband doesn't listen to me at all. Our house has been under construction for about five years because he won't finish the work and he won't let me get anyone else to do it either. I can't have anyone over; even my children don't want to come any more."

Group Example Continued

Debra, recently divorced after a long marriage, immediately says, "I don't think you should take that. Why do you stay with him? You need to leave."

Abby says, "Maybe if you show him you're not going to take it anymore, he'll get the message."

Lucy, looking somewhat shaken, replies, "I can't get divorced—he's my husband. Besides, where would I go? I don't have any money of my own."

The therapist interjects, "Some of you are angry at what Lucy is going through with her husband—and that's okay. As women, we should be angry when we see other women being hurt."

Carol, married to an alcoholic, takes Lucy's hand, and says, "I know how you feel, Lucy, because I feel the same way. I feel too old and afraid to start over. At least I know what I've got with Joe."

Abby responds, "I didn't mean to sound harsh; it's just that after a while you have to take some action."

The clinician says, "I can see this is a tough subject and brings up strong emotions. Let's try to understand what this is about. Lucy is expressing some feelings of helplessness in her life. Have any of you ever felt you were helpless to change a situation?"

Debra (who had initially been quite angry when confronting Lucy) was the first to speak: "I felt helpless for years but finally I had enough. I took abuse for a long time. It was hard for me to get a divorce—I was raised to believe that marriage was forever. A long time ago I even went to a priest and told him what my husband was doing and he said I should pray but marriage was forever. I know they don't talk that way now but I went through hell. I don't think you have to stay (crying now). I just don't want to see you or anyone else go through what I did for such a long time. I had to get tough—I have to be tough or I'll fall apart."

June adds, "I know what you mean; my husband drank for 20 years. When I look back, I don't know how I took it—but I had three children. Today, women don't take these kinds of things—but Lucy is from our generation."

Donna says, "My husband isn't abusive and I know he loves me in his own way but he doesn't listen to me either. But I wouldn't leave either because we've been together a long time—we raised children together. But he didn't cheat on me—I can understand why Debra left but I can also understand why Lucy stays."

Throughout the remaining sessions the women began to grow in connection to one another. Termination took place after eight weeks, as contracted, although no one, including the therapist, really wanted the group to end. And so they agreed to continue to meet in the same format once a month for the next four months, to provide further relational development and support. At the point when the therapist left the group, most of the women had become empowered to act on their own without her leadership.

At the last meeting, the women decided to meet on their own every few months for continued validation and support. They get together at restaurants, or meet at each other's homes. Recent feedback from some of the women in the group revealed that this continued social intimacy has not only provided connection but has also been instrumental in furthering the development of their personal identities.

Summary

Relational theory and practice is a postmodern perspective that calls for active engagement between client and clinician. The therapeutic relationship is an interactive, alive process—empathic, authentic, and mutually growth enhancing. It has application for clinical work practice across cultures, across races, across genders, and even across social classes, for all clients need to be validated and responded to within a context of truth if they are to better understand themselves, others, and the world in which they live.

9

Cognitive Theory: A Structural Approach

History and Definition

Cognitive theory began in 1911 when Alfred Adler (1964), came to disagree with Freud's structural theory and the concept of conflict between the id and the superego. Adler viewed the personality as a unified whole, which later became known as the *holistic* approach. Adler concluded that it was inaccurate perceptions, and not underlying unconscious processes, that resulted in a person's inappropriate behavior. For almost 20 years after his death in 1937, there was little interest in Adler's ideas, because Freudian thought reigned supreme in western analytic circles. Today, when practice is frequently dominated by brief treatment modalities, there is a renewed interest in cognitive therapy.

Cognitive theory is based on the concept that there is a reciprocal interaction between what one thinks, how one feels, and how one behaves. People's thoughts determine their feelings, which then determine their behavior. Cognitive theorists deal with current realities, not unconscious conflicts. Cognitive practitioners work to change clients' conscious thought processes so that their perceptions are more accurately grounded in reality. It is a skills-based therapy in which clients acquire new techniques and strategies that foster healthier ways of thinking and communicating.

The Therapeutic Relationship

The relationship between client and therapist in the cognitive realm is based on collaboration. The therapist is not assumed to be an authority who holds all the answers, but a trusted teacher, trainer, and coach who enables the client to actively participate in solving problems and meeting goals. The therapist engenders mutual respect and openness and inspires confidence by being highly professional and exemplifying positive qualities. Beck and Young (1985) point out that part of the process of developing a good collaborative relationship involves working together with the patient to set therapeutic goals, determine priorities, and develop an agenda for each session. The clinician and the client develop a theory and test the validity of automatic thoughts, or schemas, or the effectiveness of patterns of behavior (Bermudes, Wright, & Casey, 2009).

The cognitive therapist gives an adequate rationale for a treatment procedure, as well as elicits regular feedback from the patient to determine if the patient is complying with instructions. Cognitive therapists are especially skilled at seeing events through the client's perspective (accurate empathy), and they are logical thinkers. They can spot the subtle flaws in someone's reasoning and skillfully elicit a different interpretation of the same events. Cognitive therapists are active/directive in their approach, and they can plan strategies and anticipate desired outcomes.

Although cognitive theory has not consistently underscored the therapeutic relationship as an important variable in the change process, the empirical evidence points to the fact that patients perceive the relationship as crucial, even if their therapists do not.

Research Perspective

Cognitive therapy has been widely researched and stands out as an evidenced-based practice. Many of the empirical studies of cognitive therapy have been with depression (see, for example, Gottlib & Hammen, 2002; McCollough, 2003), but there has been an extension of the aims and principles to other disorders such as anxiety (see, for example, Barlow, 2002; Beck & Emery, 1985), social anxiety (Hope, Heimberg, & Turk, 2006), generalized anxiety disorder (Brown, O'Leary, & Barlow, 1993), and obsessive-compulsive disorder (Abramowitz, Franklin, & Foa, 2002). Cognitive theory has also been especially useful in the treatment of substance abuse and personality disorders (Beck, 1995).

Client Characteristics

It is as yet unknown what client characteristics respond best to cognitive therapy. Clients with delusions, dementia, or thought disorders would make poor candidates. Clients who are good planners, conscientious about carrying out responsibilities, and well organized are predicted to have more rapid success with cognitive therapy. On the other hand, clients who are excessively angry and rigid in their thinking may not be good candidates for cognitive therapy. Findings, especially with depression, suggest that age is not an obstacle, as older adults seem to benefit as much as younger persons (Gallagher-Thompson, Hanley-Peterson, & Thompson, 1990), although mildly to moderately depressed patients are more likely to benefit than more severely depressed patients (Klosko & Sanderson, 1999). Recent literature addresses the effectiveness of cognitive therapy with children and adolescents (Friedberg & McClure, 2002; Reinecke, Datillo, & Freeman, 2003), particularly for management of ADHD, ODD, chemical dependence, low self-esteem, eating disorders, and academic skills problems.

A Structured Approach

Cognitive therapy interviews are structured, and each session usually begins with an agenda that the client has set and ends with the provision of feedback and assignment of homework. Some cognitive therapists write summaries of sessions, whereas others make audiotapes for clients to take home with them. Sessions must include a review of the homework to underscore its importance to the therapeutic process. Homework helps clients practice skills learned in therapy sessions and generalize them to daily life. If clients fail to complete homework, cognitive therapists do not speak of a client's lack of motivation or resistance; rather, they consider that there are obstacles to progress. Because cognitive therapy requires courage and can be extremely painful and difficult to undertake, therapists need to be extremely supportive when discussing these obstacles. Sometimes there is role rehearsal within the session, to play out events or thoughts that might get in the way of the client's completion of assignments:

> ***Worker:*** Can you think of any reasons why you wouldn't be able to complete the homework?
>
> ***Client:*** No. I will do it.
>
> ***Worker:*** I know that is your intention, and that's good, but sometimes we don't get to do all that we intend.
>
> ***Client:*** I'll do it.
>
> ***Worker:*** Let's talk about when you will do it—that might give us some clues to things that could get in the way.
>
> ***Client:*** Well, I'll do it when I come home from work, with the kids before they have dinner.
>
> ***Worker:*** Will the children require your attention at that time?
>
> ***Client:*** Well, they might. I could do it sometimes with them, and other times maybe in the morning or evening.
>
> ***Worker:*** It's good to get a routine established for doing the homework. Some people like to do their homework right before bed. This works especially well if you are keeping a log of the events of the day and want to recapture them and write them down during a quiet moment. Homework is really important, because the more that you can do between sessions to practice the skills that we've talked about, the faster you will progress. That's why you need to give it an important place in your life.

Some therapists use prompts between sessions—spontaneous "hello" telephone calls to clients. Often, hearing the therapist's voice serves as a reminder to the client that homework needs to be done.

Cognitive therapists make sure that clients take credit for the changes they make and do not attribute their success to the practitioner. This is important because it reinforces the client to undertake further change without the help of the therapist.

Rational Emotive Therapy

In 1955, Albert Ellis founded rational emotive therapy (RET, or REBT—rational emotive behavioral therapy, as it is sometimes called). Although Ellis was trained in psychoanalytic methods at the Karen Horney school, he acknowledged his debt to Adler's

(1964) central concept that social interest has a primary role in determining psychological health. The concept of rationality is central to understanding RET. The term *rational* means that which aids and abets people in achieving their basic goals and purposes. The term *irrational* means what does not aid and abet people in achieving their basic goals and purposes. Ellis believes that people can rid themselves of most of their emotional or mental unhappiness, ineffectuality, and disturbance if they learn to maximize their rational and minimize their irrational thinking (Ellis, 1962). Rational emotive theory posits that people vary in their ability to be disturbed. Ellis noted that some people emerge relatively unscathed psychologically from uncaring or overprotective parents, and others emerge emotionally damaged from more "healthy" child-bearing practices.

The ABCs of RET

Ellis is famous for his concept of the ABCs of RET. *A* stands for an activating event or the perception of the event, *B* for the way that perceived event is evaluated, or the person's beliefs, and *C* for the emotional and behavioral consequences that stem from *B* (Ellis, cited in Mahoney & Freenab, 1985). How people feel also affects their beliefs. So there is a constant interaction within the social and material environments. Ellis identifies a number of irrational ideas that are elaborated on by Werner (cited in Turner, 1986, pp. 108–109). These ideas are taught and transmitted by culture, family, or significant others:

1. It is a dire necessity for an adult to be loved and approved by most of the significant people in his environment.
2. A person is not worthwhile unless he is virtually perfect in all respects.
3. Certain people are bad and should be blamed and punished for their badness.
4. It is terrible when things are not the way people would like them to be.
5. Human unhappiness is externally caused and people have little ability to control their sorrows.
6. A person should keep dwelling on the possibility of dangerous things happening and be deeply concerned (e.g., being in a car accident).
7. It is better to avoid difficult situations or responsibilities than to face them.
8. A person should depend on someone else, for every person needs someone stronger on whom to rely.
9. A person's past history is an all-important determiner of present behavior, and a significant past event will indefinitely continue to influence us.
10. People should become quite upset over other's problems or disturbances.
11. There is a correct and perfect solution to human problems, and it is catastrophic if the perfect solution is not found.

Frequent Disturbances in Thinking

Ellis, who is known for his irreverence and sense of humor in his work with clients, also evolved a concept he called *musturbation*. This was borrowed from Horney's (1950) ideas on the "tyranny of the shoulds." Humans, Ellis believed, make absolutistic evaluations of the perceived events in their lives, couched in the form of dogmatic "musts, shoulds, have tos, got tos, and oughts" that lead to psychological disturbances. Distortions in thinking almost always stem from the musts. Some of the most frequent disturbances in thinking and their examples, according to Dryden and Ellis (cited in Dobson, 1988), are the following:

1. *All-or-None Thinking.* "If I fail at an important task, as I must not, I'm a total failure and completely unlovable."
2. *Jumping to Conclusions and Negative Nonsequiturs.* "Since they have seen me dismally fail, as I should not have done, they will view me as incompetent."
3. *Fortune Telling.* "Because they are laughing at me for failing, they know that I should have succeeded, and they will despise me forever."
4. *Focusing on the Negative.* "Because I can't stand things going wrong, as they must not, I can't see any good that is happening in my life."
5. *Disqualifying the Positive.* "When they compliment me on the good things I have done, they are only being kind to me and forgetting the foolish things that I should not have done."
6. *Allness and Neverness.* "Because conditions of living ought to be good and actually are so bad and so intolerable, they'll always be this way and I'll never have any happiness."
7. *Minimization.* "My accomplishments were the result of luck—unimportant. But my mistakes are unforgivable, and I should never have made them."
8. *Emotional Reasoning.* "Because I have performed so poorly, as I should not have done, I feel like a total nincompoop, and my strong feeling proves that I am no damned good."
9. *Labeling and Overgeneralization.* "Because I must not fail at important work and have done so, I am a complete loser and failure."
10. *Personalizing.* "Since I am acting far worse than I should act, and they are laughing, I am sure they are only laughing at me, and that is awful."
11. *Phonyism.* "When I don't do as well as I ought to do and they still praise and accept me, I am a real phony and will soon fall on my face."
12. *Perfectionism.* "I realize that I did fairly well, but I should have done perfectly well on a task like this and am therefore really an incompetent."

Rational emotive practitioners hold that clients must be helped to discover the illogicalities and the unconditional shoulds, oughts, and musts, if change is to take place. The cognitive technique is a Socratic one—disputing irrational beliefs, debating, and looking for evidence. Clients are encouraged to listen to tapes of therapy sessions and dispute their own irrational beliefs. Rational self-statements are written on cards, such as "I want my boyfriend's love but I don't need it," to be reviewed between sessions. Imagery (having a client close her eyes and visualize) is used to change a negative feared event to a positive one or to see that life goes on after the awful event. This helps a client recover and continue to pursue his or her original goals or develop new ones. Rewards and penalties are used to encourage clients to undertake uncomfortable assignments. Behavioral techniques include activities to help clients tolerate discomfort while remaining in uncomfortable situations for a long period of time. Antiprocrastination exercises encourage clients to push themselves to start tasks sooner rather than later while tolerating the discomfort of breaking the habit.

Rational emotive therapists strive to unconditionally accept their clients as fallible humans who do self-defeating things. They are patient and reassuring when obstacles occur, but not unduly warm, because Ellis believes that a client's self-acceptance should not depend on the therapist's approval. The template in Figure 9.1 provides a model for identifying and disputing irrational beliefs.

Constructive Perspective

A constructive perspective (CNP) on cognitive theory focuses on the stories that people tell themselves and others about important events in their lives, but adds a cognitive component. For example, constructivists do not believe that clients are depressed because they "distort reality" since there may be a number of different realities. The goal is to help clients understand how and why they constructed their particular reality (or story) and the consequences of that particular construction (Lesser & Pope, 2010). As in narrative therapy (see Chapter 11), these accounts help a client make sense of distressing events and integrate those events into a coherent whole so that they become part of the patient's lived experience. The client's opening up and sharing the various perspectives of her story is intended to help change the way the story is viewed, as opposed to particular thoughts or beliefs. A cognitive reframing of the dramatic events enables clients to rescript their reactions and "re-cast their roles" (Meichenbaum & Fitzpatrick, 1993), giving attention to strengths and resilience. This is considered to be more empowering than challenging the "irrationality" of the clients' thoughts and beliefs (Meichenbaum, 1996a).

Taylor (1990) and in Meichenbaum (1994a) identified five positive cognitive mechanisms or narrative processes that people report using to cope with distressing situations:

1. Comparing oneself with those who are less fortunate
2. Selectively focusing on positive attributes of oneself in order to feel advantages
3. Imagining a potentially worse situation
4. Constructing benefits that might derive from the victimizing experience
5. Manufacturing normative standards that makes one's adjustment seem "normal"

Individuals who *do not* cope as well, and who evidence continuing distress, tend to:

1. Have difficulty retrieving positive memories
2. Continue to search for meaning and fail to find satisfactory resolution
3. Make unfavorable comparisons between life after and before the distress
4. See themselves as blameworthy
5. See themselves as victims and have little hope that things will change

A (Activating Events or Adversities)

Briefly Summarize the Situation as Objectively as Possible:

Critical A (What I Was Most Disturbed About):

Examples:
- A can be internal or external, real or imagined
- A can be an event in the past, present, or future

- **Situation:** "My wife and I disagreed about something"
- **Critical A:** "She criticized me badly"

C (Consequences)

Major Dysfunctional/Unhealthy Negative Emotion (Feeling): ______

Maladaptive/Unhelpful Behaviors (and/or Action Tendencies): ______

Dysfunctional Negative Emotions include:

- Anxiety/fear
- Shame/embarrassment
- Rage/anger
- Guilt
- Depression (depressed mood)
- Problematic jealousy
- Problematic envy
- Hurt

Maladaptive Behaviors include:

- Social avoidance
- Not taking care of yourself (e.g. not exercising, not resting)
- Being aggressive

GOALS

B's (Beliefs): Irrational (Unhelpful/Dysfunctional) Beliefs

To Identify Irrational Beliefs, Look for:

1) **Demands** (musts/absolute shoulds/oughts)
2) **Awfulizing/Catastrophizing** (It's awful, terrible, horrible!)
3) **Frustration Intolerance** (I can't stand it!)
4) **Self-Downing, Other-Downing, or Life-Downing** (I'm bad or worthless, He/she is bad or worthless, or Life is not worthwhile)

D's (Disputation): Debate Your Irrational (Unhelpful/Dysfunctional) Beliefs

To Change Irrational Beliefs, Ask Yourself:

- Where is holding this belief getting me? **Is it helpful** or getting me into trouble?
- **Where is the evidence** to support my irrational belief?
  - Is it really awful (as bad as it could be)?
  - Can I really not stand it?
  - Am I really a totally bad person?
- **Is it logical?** Does it follow from my preferences?
- **Use metaphorical disputation** (e.g. metaphors, stories, humor)

E's (Effective): Rational (Helpful/Functional) Beliefs

To Think More Rationally, Strive for:

1) **Flexible Preferences** (e.g. I want to do well, but I don't have to do so.)
2) **Anti-Awfulizing** (e.g. It may be bad or unfortunate, but it is not awful, and I can still enjoy some things.)
3) **High Frustration Tolerance** (e.g. I don't like it, but I can stand it, and I can still enjoy many things.)
4) **Self-Acceptance, Other-Acceptance, Life-Acceptance** (e.g. I can accept myself as a fallible human being.)

F's (Functional): Major Functional/Healthy Emotion and Adaptive/Helpful Behaviors

(Goal): New Functional/Healthy Negative Emotion:

(Goals): New Adaptive/Helpful Behaviors:

Functional/Healthy Negative Emotions Include:

- Concern
- Disappointment
- Healthy anger/annoyance
- Remorse/regret
- Sadness
- Healthy concern for relationship
- Healthy envy
- Sorrow

Adaptive/Helpful Behaviors Include:

- Meeting friends or seeking support
- Exercising
- Assertive behaviors

FIGURE 9.1 ***REBT Self-Help Form***

Source: Reprinted by permission of The Institute of Rational Emotive Therapy.

A cognitive constructivist intervention helps the client make sense out of distressing events so that he does not get stuck in the story by trying to answer "why" questions for which no acceptable answers can be found. In the reframing of the event, the client comes to view the trauma as something he has survived and finds meaning in his ability to overcome obstacles and to prevail.

Beck's Model of Cognitive Therapy

Beck's model of cognitive therapy also aims at correcting dysfunctional thoughts, and, at a deeper level, at uncovering underlying schemas that frame the client's experience and form the basis for the cognitive distortions. These are similar in breadth to Ellis's irrational beliefs (DeRubeis & Beck, 1988). These schemas are not as readily available to the person as are automatic thoughts, but become apparent as the client and therapist identify the themes that run through the client's upsetting instances. Beck, like Ellis, initially operated from a classically Freudian perspective, but following several systematic studies (Beck, 1961; Beck & Hurvich, 1959) he came to reject Freud's concept of the depressive syndrome (melancholia), a model based on the premise that in the depressed client, anger is turned inward toward the self. Instead, Beck believed that depression stems from the depressed person's negative thinking.

In sessions, using Beck's model, the client focuses on the content of his cognitive reaction. By carefully considering this content, the client can arrive at a different view. He is then encouraged to view this belief as a hypothesis—a possibility but not necessarily a fact (Hollon & Kriss, 1983). Reframing a belief as a hypothesis has been called *distancing*—a technique that helps the client look at the belief more objectively.

Beck teaches that there are several kinds of errors of thinking that occur more frequently during affective episodes. These errors can be labeled by the therapist to remind the client of maladaptive thought processes that are taking place. The following are included in the types of cognitive errors:

1. *Arbitrary Inferences* refer to the process of drawing a specific conclusion in the absence of supporting evidence, or when the evidence is contrary to the conclusion.
2. *Selective Abstraction* consists of focusing on a detail taken out of context and conceptualizing the total experience on the basis of that detail.
3. *Overgeneralization* refers to a pattern of drawing a general rule or conclusion on the basis of one or more isolated incidents and applying it across the board to related and unrelated situations.
4. *Magnification and Minimization* are errors in evaluating the magnitude of an event. They are so gross as to constitute a distortion.
5. *Personalization* is the client's tendency to take things personally even when there is no such connection.
6. *Dichotomous Thinking* is the client's tendency to place experiences in one of two opposite categories, for example, viewing people as either saints or sinners (DeRubeis & Beck, 1988, p. 7).

The client must take an active role in questioning his thoughts while he is in the midst of emotional upset or shortly thereafter. Much of the work in Beck's model of cognitive therapy centers on the use of a device called the *Daily Record of Dysfunctional Thoughts* (see Beck, Rush, Shaw, & Emery, 1979), which is reprinted in Figure 9.2.

On this daily record, the client reports situations, thoughts, and emotional reactions, preferably at the time of the event. Using this template, intervention can begin. Intervention consists of coming up with rational responses to these automatic thoughts by examining the inferences made when the client is emotionally upset. The simplest method of uncovering automatic thoughts is for the therapist to ask the client what went through her mind in response to a particular event. This questioning gives the client a model for exploration that she can use on her own. Imagery is also used to help the client picture the situation in detail. The client can describe the distressing event as she relives it in her mind in the therapist's office. If the upsetting event is an interpersonal one, role-play can be utilized. The therapist plays the role of the other person in the situation, while the client plays herself. This further helps elicit automatic thoughts.

	Situation	**Emotion(s)**	**Automatic Thought(s)**	**Rational Response**	**Outcome**
	Describe: 1. Actual event leading to unpleasant emotion, or 2. Stream of thoughts, day dream or recollection leading to unpleasant emotion.	1. Specify sad/ anxious/angry, etc. 2. Rate degree of emotion, 1–100%.	1. Write automatic thoughts that precede emotion(s). 2. Rate belief in automatic thoughts, 0–100%.	1. Write rational response to automatic thought(s). 2. Rate belief in rational response, 0–100%.	1. Rerate belief in automatic thought(s), 0–100%. 2. Specify and rate subsequent emotions, 0–100%.
Date					

Explanation: When you experience an unpleasant emotion, note the situation that seemed to stimulate the emotion. (If the emotion occurred while you were thinking, daydreaming, etc., please note this.) Then note the automatic thought associated with the emotion. Record the degree to which you believe this thought: 0% = not at all; 100% = completely. In rating degree of emotion: 1 = a trace; 100 = the most intense possible.

FIGURE 9.2 ***Daily Record of Dysfunctional Thoughts***
Source: DeRubeis R., & Beck, A. (1988). Cognitive therapy. In K. S. Dobson (Ed.). *Handbook of cognitive - behavioral therapies*. New York: Guilford. Reprinted with permission.

The therapist is careful to note any mood changes that occur during the session, such as tears or anger, and ask the clients what thoughts occur prior to the shift in mood. This helps the client make the connection between mind and mood, and furthers the teaching of identification of automatic thoughts.

Testing of Automatic Thoughts

Testing of automatic thoughts is done by asking clients to list the evidence from their experiences for and against the hypothesis under consideration. It is sometimes necessary to help clients operationalize a word. For example, the recurring automatic thought, "I'm a failure in math," could be narrowed down to being unable to achieve a grade of C after investing an average amount of studying time. Now the client could examine past evidence and test the validity of the hypothesis. This process helps clients see the all-inclusiveness of their negative self-assessments and the idiosyncratic nature of their thoughts (Young, Beck, & Weinberger, 1993).

Schema Theory

Beck also addresses the schema, or underlying cognitive structures or core beliefs, that organizes the client's experience and forms the basis of disturbances in thinking. Schemas originate in childhood, through the experiences of the developing child. They may not be as readily accessible as automatic thoughts, but become clear to the client and therapist as both strive to identify the consistent themes that run through the client's disturbing events. This schema work has been elaborated on Young, Klosko, and Weishaar (2002), who identified the following 23 sets of core beliefs and their umbrella categories:

1. **Disconnection and Rejection**
   The expectation that one's needs for security, safety, stability, nurturance, empathy, sharing of feelings, acceptance, and respect will not be met in a predictable manner. Typical family origin is detached, cold, rejecting, withholding, lonely, explosive, unpredictable, or abusive.
2. **Emotional Deprivation**
   The expectation that one's desire for a normal degree of emotional support will not be adequately met by others.
   a. *Deprivation of Nurturance.* Absence of attention, affection (physical or emotional), or warmth from others.
   b. *Deprivation of Protection.* Absence of strength, direction, or guidance from others.
   c. *Deprivation of Empathy.* Absence of understanding, listening, self-disclosure, or mutual sharing of feelings from others.
3. **Abandonment/Instability**
   The perceived instability or unreliability of those available for support and connection. Involves the sense that significant others will not be able to continue providing emotional support, connection, strength, or practical protection because they

are emotionally unstable, unpredictable, unreliable, and erratically present; because they will die imminently; or because they will abandon the patient in favor of someone else.

4. **Mistrust/Abuse**
   One's expectation that others will hurt, abuse, humiliate, cheat, lie, manipulate, or take advantage of him or her. Usually involves the perception that harm is intentional or the result of unjustified and extreme negligence.

5. **Social Isolation/Alienation**
   The feeling that one is isolated from the rest of the world, different from other people, and/or not part of any group or community.

6. **Defectiveness/Shame**
   The feeling that one is inwardly defective, flawed, or invalid; that one would be fundamentally unlovable to significant others if exposed; or a sense of shame regarding one's perceived internal inadequacies.

7. **Impaired Autonomy and Performance**
   Expectations about oneself and the environment that interfere with one's perceived ability to separate, survive, function independently, or perform successfully. Typical family origin is enmeshed, undermining of child's confidence, overprotective, or failing to reinforce child for performing competently outside the family.

8. **Dependence/Incompetence**
   The belief that one is unable to handle one's everyday responsibilities in a competent manner, without considerable help from others (e.g., take care of oneself, solve daily problems, exercise good judgment, tackle new tasks, make good decisions).

9. **Vulnerability to Harm and Illness**
   An exaggerated fear that disaster is about to strike at any time (natural, criminal, medical, or financial) and that one is unable to protect oneself. May include unrealistic fears that one will have a heart attack, get AIDS, go crazy, go broke, be mugged, crash, and so on.

10. **Enmeshment/Undeveloped Self**
    An excessive emotional involvement and closeness with one or more significant others (often parents) at the expense of full individuation or normal social development. Usually leads to insufficient individual identity or inner direction. May include feelings of being smothered by or fused with others.

11. **Failure**
    The belief that one has failed, will inevitably fail, or is fundamentally inadequate relative to one's peers in areas of achievement (school, career, sports, etc.). Often involves beliefs that one is stupid, inept, untalented, lower in status, less successful than others, and so forth.

12. **Impaired Limits**
    Deficiency in internal limits, responsibility to others, or long-term goal orientation. Leads to difficulty respecting the rights of others, cooperating with others,

making commitments, or setting and meeting realistic personal goals. Typical family origin is characterized by permissiveness, overindulgence, lack of direction or a sense of superiority rather than appropriate confrontation, discipline, and limits in relation to taking responsibility, cooperating in a reciprocal manner, and setting goals. In some cases, the child may not have been pushed to tolerate normal levels of discomfort or may not have been given adequate supervision, direction, or guidance.

13. **Entitlement/Self-Centeredness**
The insistence that one should be able to have whatever one wants, regardless of what others consider reasonable or regardless of the cost to others. Often involves excessive control over others, a demanding nature, and lack of empathy for others' needs.

14. **Insufficient Self-Control/Self-Discipline**
A pervasive difficulty exercising sufficient self-control and frustration tolerance to achieve one's personal goals or to restrain the excessive expression of one's emotions and impulses. Once the client begins to recognize situations in which these core beliefs exist, he can be taught to consider alternative inferences.

15. **Other Directedness**
An excessive focus on the desires, feelings, and responses of others, at the expense of one's own needs in order to gain love and approval, maintain one's sense of connection, or avoid retaliation. Usually involves suppression and lack of awareness regarding one's own anger and natural inclinations. Typical family origin is based on conditional acceptance. Children must suppress important aspects of themselves in order to gain love, attention, and approval. In many such families, the parent's emotional needs and desires—or social acceptance and status—are valued more than the unique needs and feelings of each child.

16. **Subjugation**
An excessive surrendering of control to others because one feels coerced—submitting to avoid anger, retaliation, or abandonment. The two major forms of subjugation are the following:
a. *Subjugation of needs: Suppression of one's preferences, decisions, and desires.*
b. *Subjugation of emotions: Especially anger.*
Usually involves the perception that one's own desires, opinions, and feelings are not valid or important to others. Often presents as excessive compliance, combined with hypersensitivity to feeling trapped. Generally leads to a buildup of anger, manifested in maladaptive symptoms (e.g., passive-aggressive behavior, uncontrolled outbursts, a temper, psychosomatic symptoms, withdrawal of affection, acting out, substance abuse).

17. **Self-Sacrifice**
An excessive voluntary focus on meeting the needs of others at the expense of one's own needs and preferences. The most common reasons are to avoid guilt, to prevent causing pain to others, to gain in esteem, and to maintain the connection with others perceived as needy.

18. Approval-Seeking/Recognition-Seeking
Excessive emphasis on gaining approval, recognition or attention from others, or fitting in at the expense of developing a secure and true sense of self. One's self-esteem is dependent on the approval of others. May be an overemphasis on status, appearance, social acceptance, money, or achievement as a means of gaining approval and admiration, or frequently results in major life decisions that are inauthentic or unsatisfying or in hypersensitivity to rejection.

19. Overvigilance and Inhibition
Excessive emphasis on suppressing one's spontaneous feelings, impulses, and choices or on meeting rigid, internalized rules and expectations about performance and ethical behavior, often at the expense of happiness, self-expression, relaxation, close relationships, or health. Typical family origin is grim, demanding, and sometimes punitive; performance, duty, perfectionisms, following rules, hiding emotions, and avoiding mistakes predominate over pleasure, joy, and relaxation. There is usually an undercurrent of pessimism and worry that things could fall apart if one fails to be vigilant and careful at all times.

20. Negativity/Pessimism
A pervasive, lifelong focus on the negative aspects of life (pain, death, loss, disappointment, conflict, guilt, resentment, unsolved problems, potential mistakes, betrayal, things that could go wrong, etc.) while minimizing or neglecting the positive or optimistic aspects. Usually involves an exaggerated expectation that things will eventually go seriously wrong or fall apart. Usually involves an inordinate fear of making mistakes that might lead to financial collapse, loss, humiliation, or being trapped in a bad situation. Because they exaggerate potential negative outcomes, these individuals are frequently characterized by chronic worry, vigilance, complaining, or indecision.

21. Emotional Inhibition
An excessive inhibition of emotions or impulses because one expects one's expression to result in loss of esteem, harm to others, embarrassment, retaliation, or abandonment. May result in loss of spontaneity and warmth, flatness of affect, mishandling of anger, obsessive-compulsive symptoms, and so on.

22. Unrelenting/Unbalanced Standards
The relentless striving to meet high expectations of oneself, at the expense of happiness, pleasure, health, sense of accomplishment, or satisfying relationships.

23. Punitiveness
The belief that people should be harshly punished for making mistakes. Involves the tendency to be angry, intolerant, punitive, and impatient with those people (including oneself) who do not meet one's expectations or standards. Usually includes difficulty forgiving mistakes in oneself or others, because of a reluctance to consider extenuating circumstances, allow for human imperfection, or empathize with feelings.

Cognitive Processing Therapy

Cognitive processing therapy (CPT) was originally developed as a combination treatment for specific symptoms of PTSD in sexual assault trauma survivors, but it has since been tested with other populations. It can be delivered in individual or group formats, in 12 structured sessions. The clients are introduced to PTSD symptoms and the therapy, and then asked to write an impact statement of how their worst traumatic event affected them. They focus on the self-blame aspect and the effects of the event on their beliefs about self and others (Resick, Monson, & Rizvi, in Barlow, 2008). This statement helps traumatized people understand how they may have distorted the cause of the event or overgeneralized its meaning, compromising their functioning. The client is further taught to recognize the connection between events, thoughts, and feelings, and then asked to write a detailed account of this traumatic event and read it to herself every day. The therapist helps the client to challenge and question a single thought, then look for patterns of problem thoughts, and finally, to generate alternative more balanced thoughts about the event, oneself, and the world. In the last five sessions, clients are given modules that assist them in thinking about specific themes that are commonly disrupted after traumatic events, such as trust, safety, power, control, esteem, and intimacy (Resick et al., in Barlow, 2008).

Positive Psychology

Since World War II, a disease model of human functioning with emphasis on psychopathology has permeated the thinking of the mental health profession. In the past five years, the science of positive psychology has emerged, and we include it here as it has implications for cognitive social work practice.

Positive psychologists believe that a complete science and practice of psychology should include an understanding of suffering and happiness, as well as their interaction, and validate interventions that both relieve suffering and increase happiness (Seligman, Steen, Park, & Peterson, 2005). Positive psychologists, like social workers, embrace a strengths perspective. But social work can learn from positive psychology how to "broaden and build positive emotions as a means to achieving psychological growth and improved psychological and physical well being" (Fredrickson, 2004). This has important implications for treatment as well as prevention; for prevention, researchers have discovered that there are human strengths that act as buffers against mental illness: courage, future mindedness, optimism, interpersonal skill, faith, work ethic, hope, honesty, perseverance, and the capacity for flow and insight, to name several (Seligman & Csikszentmihalyi, 2000).

Peterson and Seligman (2004) have written a counterpart to the *Diagnostic and Statistical Manual of Mental Disorders* (*DSM*) (1994) that describes and classifies strengths and virtues that enable human thriving. This, *Character Strengths and Virtues: A Handbook and Classification* (CSV) (2004), relies on six overarching virtues that almost every culture endorses: wisdom and knowledge, courage, humanity, justice, temperance, and transcendence (Seligman et al., 2005). Under each virtue is a list of strengths.

1. Wisdom and knowledge
   a. Creativity
   b. Curiosity
   c. Open-mindedness
   d. Love of learning
   e. Perspective
2. Courage
   a. Authenticity
   b. Bravery
   c. Persistence
   d. Zest
3. Humanity
   a. Kindness
   b. Love
   c. Social intelligence
4. Justice
   a. Fairness
   b. Leadership
   c. Teamwork
5. Temperance
   a. Forgiveness
   b. Modesty
   c. Prudence
   d. Self-regulation
6. Transcendence
   a. Appreciation of beauty and excellence
   b. Gratitude
   c. Hope
   d. Humor
   e. Religiousness

Positive psychology attends to the deliberate cultivation of strengths that contribute to fulfillment and life satisfaction. Some positive psychology interventions that have been evaluated and proven effective are the following:

1. Burton and King (2004, in Duckworth, Steen, & Seligman, 2005) employed a random-assignment, placebo-controlled design to test the effect of a writing intervention on mood and physical health. For 20-minute intervals on three consecutive days, participants in the intervention wrote about intensely positive experiences, whereas the control group participants wrote about neutral subjects such as their schedule, their bedroom, and their shoes. Writing about positive experiences caused a short-term boost in mood and made fewer visits to the health center over the next three months.
2. Emmons and McCullough (2003, in Duckworth et al., 2005) found that participants randomly assigned to a gratitude intervention showed increased positive effect relative to control participant. They were asked to write about five things for which they were thankful, every week for 10 weeks. In two control conditions, participants wrote about either daily hassles or neutral life events. Relative to the control groups, participants in the gratitude condition reported feeling better about their lives in general, more optimistic about the coming week, and more connected to others. They also demonstrated more positive affect and less negative affect as measured by a 30-item survey. On follow-up, gratitude journals were kept daily for two weeks and the positive effects found in the first study were replicated.
3. Lyubomirsky, Sheldon, and Schkade (2005, in Duckworth et al., 2005) did a "count your blessings" intervention. Participants in a no treatment control condition were compared with participants who counted their blessings either once per week or three times per week. After six weeks, only those who counted their blessing once per week were happier, suggesting a "less is more" philosophy that may prevent habituation.

4. Lyubomirsky et al. (2005, in Duckworth et al., 2005) also reported a six-week kindness study where participants were asked to perform acts of kindness all in one day, compared to those who performed five acts of kindness over a week. The authors speculated that the passage of time between acts of kindness kept the exercise fresh, preventing habituation. The intervention "dose" was larger and more concentrated when performed all in one day.

All of the above interventions are simple to reproduce, and social workers using cognitive therapy might consider incorporating them in their repertoire of cognitive therapy techniques. (Barlow, 2002).

Case Example: Cognitive Treatment for Anxiety

The following case illustrates theory and techniques from both Albert Ellis and Aaron Beck.

The client, Linda, is a 32-year-old woman who functions well in her work and social milieus. However, she described "getting very crazy inside" whenever she was waiting for the appearance of someone important to her, often her boyfriend Carl. She would feel frightened and fantasize various catastrophic events that might have occurred. If in a public place, such as a restaurant, Linda would be able to hide her reactions, but if alone, she would become physically restless, pace, peer out the window, and sometimes survey the phonebook to determine the number of hospitals she would have to call to search for Carl. She also engaged in ritualistic behaviors in attempts to calm herself, such as counting the number of cars passing her window and telling herself, "By the time I get to two dozen cars, Carl will be here."

Linda had tried to manage these anxious feelings with alcohol and marijuana, but has been sober and in Alcoholics Anonymous for four years. When asked if she could identify any thoughts she had immediately before the anxious feelings began, Linda was able to find a pattern common to these experiences. In session, the worker attempted to help Linda identify her underlying schema, first helping her to relax and then to try to remember the origin of her fears.

Worker: Linda, we're going to work on trying to identify your core beliefs, or schema, that have led to your distressing thoughts. These beliefs originate in childhood, so I'm going to ask you, in a moment, to close your eyes and think of something that happened when you were very young. Does that seem all right with you?

Linda: OK.

Worker: Now just close your eyes and let yourself relax. Picture yourself somewhere in the distant past and describe the scene to me.

Linda: I'm in my living room, with my younger brother, and it is starting to get dark.

Worker: Go on.

Linda: It feels chilly, like November or sometime when the days get shorter.

Case Example: Continued

Worker: Yes.
Linda: I see my younger brother playing with some toy cars. I'm about 7 or 8 years old.
Worker: What are you feeling?
Linda: I think I'm scared. I don't like being alone when it starts to get dark. I'm thinking I want my mom to come home, and what to do if she doesn't.
Worker: And then?
Linda: I'm starting to walk around the house. Like I'm looking for her, even though I know she's not there. I'm trying not to cry, because I don't want my little brother to get scared. I feel it getting darker, and I'm listening for my mom's car in the driveway. I'm looking out the window now, just sitting on the sofa and staring out the window. I feel my heart beating faster, and I'm worried that I'll get sick or something and be all alone.
Worker: How do you feel now?
Linda: Really anxious, like it's happening all over again.
Worker: You've done a good job of visualizing this, Linda. Now in just a moment I will count to three, and you can open your eyes. You'll be here with me in my office and you'll feel very safe.

It was not difficult to see how this anxious thinking began for Linda at an early age and how it would fit into an overall schema Linda had put together around her early experiences of being responsible for her sibling, feelings of abandonment, and the lack of supervision and structure. Using Bricker and Young's schema outline, one could say that Linda's maladaptive schema is in two primary areas: Abandonment/Instability and Vulnerability to Harm and Illness. Linda's sequence of events and feelings can also easily be viewed through the format of Ellis's ABC theory of emotions: The activating event (*A*) is that someone important is supposed to be with her at a given time, (*B*) is Linda's belief that she has to know what to do if that person doesn't arrive, and (*C*) represents the consequences, which, for Linda, include uncomfortably high levels of anxiety. Linda also mentioned a tendency to avoid situations that might evoke this sequence.

Linda was acknowledged for her courage in attempting to take on this difficult problem. She was told that her obsessive thinking usually started out as an effort to massage a thought or situation into a less scary shape, but that it then takes on a life of its own and becomes the problem. The mutually agreed on goal was to break this habit of reacting with obsessive thinking, high anxiety levels, and anxiety-provoked behaviors and to replace this pattern with more comfortable thoughts, feelings, and actions. When asked what she would "like it to look like" when the goal had been met, Linda said that she wanted to react as most other people did to lateness, specifically, "annoyance at the worst" while being able to relax or use the time spent waiting productively.

Linda was asked to keep a daily record describing the situation, emotion, automatic thought, and actions taken, based on the model described by Beck (1995). She was also asked to rank her emotional state on a scale of 1 to 10, with 1 indicating low emotional arousal and 10 indicating high emotional arousal. Three events are printed in Linda's daily record (see Figure 9.3).

In the next session, Linda was asked about her overall experience with completing the thought record. She said that she thought the act of keeping the log had made her very

(continued)

Date	Situation	Emotion	Automatic Thought	Action
	Describe the: 1. act or event leading to the anxiety 2. stream of thoughts or fantasies	1. the specific emotion 2. rate the degree on scale of 1–10	1. the thought that precedes the emotion 2. rate belief in the thought on 1–10 scale	Describe what actions are taken.
5/26	*Waiting for Carl. I noticed the time and started to plan how long until I would get really worried, then how long until I would take action.*	*Anxious.* ***7***	*What will I do if he doesn't come home? I have to know what I'm going to do.* ***9***	*Got physically restless. Could not sit still.*
5/28	*I was on the phone with a friend and noticed the time. I couldn't really pay attention to her after that, but Carl came home before I finished the call and I was okay then.*	*Anxious.* ***7***	*He's not here. I have to stop talking and figure out what to do if he doesn't come.* ***9***	*Started walking around with the phone. Tried to listen to her and listen for him at the same time.*
5/31	*Dinner was almost ready and no Carl. Imagined myself being told Carl had been killed and life without Carl.*	*Anxious and then panicky.* ***10***	*What am I going to do if he doesn't come home?* ***10***	*Did things with the food, then paced. Looked at the number of hospitals in New York in the telephone directory.*

FIGURE 9.3 ***Linda's Thought Record***

Case Example: Continued

aware of her thoughts and feelings. In two of the episodes recorded that week, the anxious thinking began when Linda noticed that it would soon be time for Carl to come home. In the third instance, she did not begin to worry until his usual time of arrival because she was involved in preparing a complicated dinner and had not noticed the time. Linda's automatic thoughts all revolved around the need to know what to do if Carl did not come home. Her behaviors then became anxious; she paced and counted the number of hospital emergency rooms she would call if Carl failed to appear.

Intervention

The core of the treatment process was to have Linda identify her irrational thoughts and underlying beliefs and to debate them for truth or falsehood. The worker would help Linda discriminate between her rational and irrational beliefs. The underlying schemas that would be addressed would include the beliefs that others cannot be counted on to remain available to support, nurture, or protect her and that disaster could strike at any time. Linda was given other suggestions to interrupt obsessive worrying. She was told to visualize a stop sign in her head and to carry a 3 by 5 inch card with the word *STOP* written on it to remind her to use this technique. She was also advised that she could wear a rubber band on her wrist and snap it whenever the obsessive thinking started, followed immediately by directing her attention elsewhere. An example would be to pick up a small object and study it (Seligman, 1990).

Exploring Automatic Thoughts in an Interview. The following session demonstrates the process of exploring and disputing automatic thoughts:

Worker: Linda, what about the automatic thoughts, the need to know what to do? What do you notice as you think about them now?

Linda: Well, it's always the same thing. And it feels really urgent.

Worker: Do you notice anything missing?

Linda: Missing?

Worker: Missing compared to what others might think. You often mention your friend Gerri as being a logical thinker. What would Gerri say back to you, for example, if you were saying those thoughts out loud to her?

Linda: Ha. Well, she'd think I was crazy, but that's why I don't tell her, of course. Hmmm . . . I guess she'd point out that I don't know why he's late, it could be anything. Oh, that never occurs to me, does it?

Worker: Right. Because people are late for all sorts of reasons, even super on-timers like you (both smile). So if it did occur to you, what might you come up with for Carl? Or whomever?

Linda: Well, I suppose there are reasons why he usually is late when he's late. With Carl, it's mostly the subway or work. Or sometimes he stops somewhere or forgets to tell me about something.

Worker: What about other people? If they might be late?

(continued)

Case Example: Continued

Linda: I suppose it would depend on who. If it were Gerri, it's because she's just more casual about time than I. You know "on time" for her means within 5 or 10 minutes after the appointed time. Other people. . . .

Worker: Just generic or ordinary reasons why people are late.

Linda: Yeah, like the subway or transportation. . . . Why don't I think of things like that?

Worker: Well, you can now. You can begin to tell yourself that kind of stuff. What way of doing this would work for you?

Linda: I could ask myself, "What would Gerri say?" That would be good. Because I know what kind of things she would say. I can even picture how she would feel when she was saying it, you know, by how she looks, just calm and sort of casual.

Worker: You could make yourself a card for your bag: "What to do when someone might be late." What could you tell yourself? The card could ask, "What would Gerri say? And how would she act?"

Linda could now dispute her irrational thoughts by putting herself in the role of Gerri, intuiting her reactions, and putting her answers into action. Linda was also encouraged to ask herself, "What would I be doing if I weren't worrying?" She would then proceed to put the answer into action. Linda was also taught a relaxation technique called *circular breathing*. In this technique, Linda counts to eight (or higher as one becomes practiced) on an inhalation, then to eight on the exhalation, but without a pause at the "top." The long "loops" of circular breathing give the body a message of safety. This breathing technique was used in addition to cognitive techniques. Relaxation methods are known to help clients with anxiety disorders. Such clients tend to take shallow breaths when anxious, which increase physical symptoms and escalate anxiety.

Daily Record Sheets. Linda was given new daily record sheets, which included additional columns for recording her new "rational responses" to automatic thoughts, as described by Beck (1976). See Figure 9.4 for a copy of Linda's completed Daily Record of Automatic Thoughts.

Exploring Underlying Assumptions. In the following session excerpts, the previously revealed automatic thoughts and underlying assumptions or schemas are explored:

Worker: It's interesting that when people are late, you always start thinking and planning about what you're going to have to do about it.

Linda: Yeah . . . (looks blank).

Worker: You always have to plan that you're going to go into action. It seems there's an assumption underneath those "what-am-I-going-to-do" thoughts.

Linda: Well, right. I guess I'm assuming it's something really bad, tragic. If someone is late, they must have been in an accident. They've been killed. They aren't coming back (Linda becomes teary). Because if it goes on long enough, if I have to wait long enough, I start imagining all of that, you know, the funeral. Even what I'll wear (smiles). And what it would be like if they really were dead, how much I'd miss them. Then I'm scared

Date	Situation	Emotion	Automatic Thought	Action	Rational Thought	Outcome	Action
	Describe the: 1. act or event leading to the anxiety 2. stream of thought or fantasies	1. the specific emotion 2. rate degree on scale of 1–10	1. the thought that precedes the emotion 2. rate belief in the thought on 1–10 scale	Describe what actions are taken.	1. Write rational responses to the automatic thought. 2. Rate belief in the rational response.	1. Rerate belief in the automatic thought on 1–10 scale. 2. Rate degree of subsequent emotion.	Describe what actions are taken.
6/2	*Meeting Carl at a restaurant and he's not there first. Started to think about how long I should wait until being really scared.*	*Anxiety* ***6***	*Something might have happened to him (more an image than a thought).* ***7***	*Clenched hands under table.*	*What would Gerri be thinking? She'd assume he was on his way. The most she'd be worried about was whether he'd be crabby when he got there, from being late.* ***5***	*Belief = 5* *Anxiety = 4*	*None, because I was in a restaurant.*
6/4	*Waiting for Carl to get home from the gym. I noticed the time and started trying to figure out what was a reasonable time to expect him.*	*Anxiety* ***6***	*Seeing myself waiting and no Carl. Have to figure out how to find out what happened.* ***8***	*Started to pace.*	*Did the 3-interp. exercise. Did circular breathing.* ***6***	*Belief = 4* *Anxiety = 4*	*Cleaned out my junk drawer!*
6/7	*Waiting for my Mom's weekly call. Started thinking about what I'll have to do when she dies.*	*Anxiety* ***5***	*If she doesn't call, what should I do to find out if she's okay.* ***7***	*Was restless, but didn't do anything in particular.*	*Told myself she often calls late and she doesn't know I worry.* ***4***	*Belief = 4* *Anxiety = 3*	*Watched a video.*

FIGURE 9.4 ***Daily Record***

Case Example: Continued

and sad. But nothing has happened yet. It doesn't get that far too often because most of the time they show up before I get to that point. Whew! What a lot of stuff from something that's probably due to a subway delay.

Worker: People suffer a lot from thinking that's just plain illogical. One of the people who writes about this has a chapter title that really fits: It's called "The Alarm Is Worse Than the Fire" (Beck, 1976, p. 132).

Linda: Yeah, you're right. I guess an accident could happen. I mean, they do happen to people. But I'm setting off the alarm every time somebody lights a match, aren't I?

Worker: Right. What you automatically imagine is always a catastrophe.

Linda: So it's not just, "If they're late, I have to know what to do." It's "If they're late, something really bad happened." Really bad, because if it goes on long enough, I always get to the seeing myself at the funeral part. I plan as if, well, if they're late, they're dead. But that doesn't follow. And you're right, I do at least partly know it doesn't make sense, because I could certainly never say that aloud to anyone (smiles).

This session demonstrated that Linda has understood the underlying beliefs driving her obsessive planning. Her ability to smile at herself is a sign that she knows there is irrationality behind her obsessive thinking. The worker points this out and acknowledges Linda's hard work.

Conclusion

Linda's therapy was completed in six sessions. Using single-subject design methodology to demonstrate effectiveness, the worker created a graph measuring Linda's anxiety, the frequency of her thoughts, and her belief in these automatic thoughts.

The two baseline weeks (*B*) measure weekly frequency of occurrence and levels of anxiety and of belief in the automatic thoughts. The two intervention weeks (*I*) measure frequency and Linda's degree of anxiety and belief in the automatic thought following her use of one or more of the interventions. The graph in Figure 9.5 shows that the levels of belief in the automatic thoughts and the degree of anxiety seem to parallel. The limitations of this study are that the worker was able to obtain only 2 to 4 baseline points (7 to 10 are considered desirable to ensure that the baseline is stable, as problems do fluctuate over time) (Bloom & Fischer, 2009), and there are no statistical calculations to help analyze the data. However, a quick "eyeballing" of the graph notes a clear reduction in anxiety and belief levels following the interventions and a one-third decrease in frequency.

In order to achieve pervasive and long-lasting change, in future sessions Linda will be assisted in revealing and understanding the ways in which this particular cognitive error fits in with her overall schemata. It is possible that a core belief underneath her feeling that "If they are late, they must be dead" is, perhaps, "If they don't come home, I'll die." If so, disputing it will help Linda understand that today, as an adult, although the death of a loved one would be painful and tragic, it would not threaten her existence. Linda can come to further appreciate her own very real and well-developed capacity to survive.

Source: Case material supplied by Catherine Boyer.

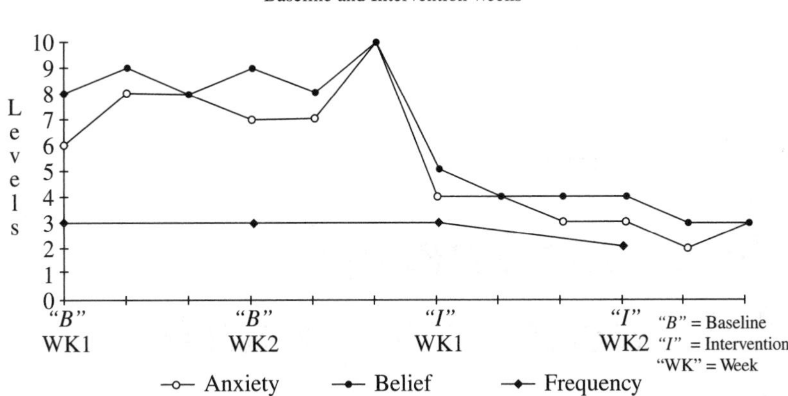

FIGURE 9.5 ***Linda's Automatic Thoughts***

Summary

Cognitive theory is well suited for contemporary clinical social work practice. Because cognitive therapy is a structured approach, it provides a focus for both the clinician and the client as they work together to prioritize problems and set therapeutic goals. Finally, cognitive therapy enables clients to achieve a sense of mastery as they continue to use the techniques they have learned after the therapeutic relationship has ended.

10

Behavior Therapy: A Structural Approach

The Three Generations or Three Waves

Behavior therapy can be divided into three generations or waves: traditional behavior therapy, cognitive behavior therapy (CBT), and the most recent "third generation" of relatively new approaches that emphasize contextual and experiential change strategies in addition to more direct and didactic ones.

Traditional Behavior Therapy

Traditional behavior therapy consisted of the systematic application of techniques that facilitate behavioral change. The word *systematic* is key, for it is the planned arrangement of behavioral contingencies (those events that happen before and after specific behaviors) in relation to specific goals, and the evaluation of outcomes, that characterize a behavioral model. In this behavior therapy, there are no differences between what is labeled normal or abnormal behavior. The same learning principles give rise to both. Human behavior is viewed largely as a function of past and present circumstances, and emotional problems are seen as problems in living or maladaptive ways of behaving. Since behaviors are learned, they can be unlearned, and therapy is, essentially, a learning process. Behavioral therapy is therefore an empowerment therapy: Clients gain mastery over their lives and increase self-esteem through their own actions that bring about behavioral change.

Behavioral techniques are based principally on learning conditioning theories. B. F. Skinner, considered to be the father of behavioral theory, and his followers developed radical behaviorism, which is the philosophy of science that underlies behavioral work. At the heart of Skinner's theory is the concept of reinforcement. Skinner and his followers state that the operant (or voluntary) behavior of a person can be increased in frequency if it is positively reinforced. Alternatively, the frequency of a behavior can be decreased by either administering punishment or withholding reinforcement, a process referred to as *extinction*. The essence of the Skinnerian, or operant, model of human behavior relied heavily on an understanding of the environmental (behavioral) events that preceded and/or followed the behavior(s) under consideration (Thomlison & Thomlison, 1996).

Another important name in behavioral theory is Ivan Pavlov, whose behavioral learning process is referred to as *respondent conditioning*, which remains as the fundamental theoretical explanation for a variety of anxiety and phobic disorders. Pavlov developed his theory by placing food (an unconditioned stimulus) in view of a dog. Salivation (the conditioned response) was elicited by the arbitrary event of ringing a bell. Over a number of such pairings, the bell (a conditioned stimulus) took on the power to elicit the response of salivation (the conditioned response) (Thomlison, 1984).

Although both of these explanations of human behavior have been refined as a result of research and clinical experience, the interaction between behavior and the events that precede and follow the behavior remains the foundation of most contemporary behavior therapy.

Albert Bandura (1977, 1986) is credited with advancing modern social learning theory. Believing that behavioral theories were too mechanistic, Bandura set out to link behavior and internal processes. Bandura's four key components of social learning theory are observational learning, reciprocal determinism, cognitive processing, and self-efficacy.

New learning takes place in *observational learning* by the respondent paying attention to the behavior, retaining the model of the behavior, reproducing the behavior, and having the expectation that he will receive positive reinforcement, which produces motivation to continue the behavior.

The concept of *reciprocal determinism* suggests that learning is influenced by a reciprocal interaction of the environment, behavior, thought, and emotion. Three types of interactions reciprocally influence each other: person and behavior interaction, person and environment interaction, and environment and behavior interaction.

Social learning theory focuses on cognitive capabilities, and *cognitive processing* consists of four cognitive capabilities: (1) forethought capability, or the ability to anticipate future behavior and reinforcement; (2) symbolizing capability, or the ability to transform and store images for later retrieval; (3) vicarious capability, or the ability to set goals based on one's beliefs and values and to monitor one's progress in achieving these goals; and (4) self-reflective capability, or the ability to reflect on one's inner thought processes.

Self-efficacy refers to one's ability to effectively cope with a given situation. This concept is particularly useful in understanding self-esteem regulation. Persons with high self-efficacy see challenges as something they can overcome, and each success builds further confidence. Persons with low self-efficacy doubt their abilities and don't perceive themselves as competent to deal with their environment. The strength of one's efficacy expectations is considered to affect whether one will try to cope with a given situation, and the degree of coping—the effort that people will expend and how long they will persist in the face of obstacles and aversive experiences (Bandura, 1977, p. 194). There has been much exploration into the role of self-efficacy in the treatment of addictive behaviors and in the prevention of relapse.

Behavioral Assessment

Behavioral assessment consists of a thorough evaluation of either behaviors that need to be increased or shaped (e.g., lack of assertiveness) or behaviors that need to be extinguished (e.g., temper tantrums). Assessment and selection of intervention methods are closely related in behavioral therapy. Quantitative data about the frequency, magnitude, or duration of a behavior, thought, feeling, or other outcome is collected before intervention and is then compared with the frequency, magnitude, or duration after the intervention. Standardized tests (such as depression and anxiety scales) as well as subjective measures (i.e., client logs, diaries, and charts) are good assessment tools. Behavioral therapy is ideally suited to evaluation because clients can act as their own evaluators by gathering data on their problem behaviors before, during, and after an intervention. Behavioral treatments are individually tailored; there is a specificity of treatment approaches for each subproblem. Social workers practicing behavior therapy can therefore go to the literature on the problem at hand (e.g., social phobia) and follow the treatment protocol verbatim to achieve results.

Cognitive Behavior Therapy

In CBT, the added emphasis is on cognition. CBT resulted from an integration of three schools: behavior therapy, cognitive therapy, and cognitive and social psychology. The theory is built on the framework of social learning theory (Bandura, 1977, 1986). The basic tenet of social learning theory is that it is partly through their own actions that people produce the environmental conditions that can affect their behavior in a reciprocal fashion. Behaviors that are the focus of change are known as *target behaviors. Antecedent behaviors* are events that precede the problematic behaviors. Events that follow are known as *consequences*. The use of positive consequences (reinforcement) to change maladaptive behaviors is at the crux of social learning theory. The experiences generated by behavior can also partly determine what individuals think and can do, which, in turn, affects their subsequent behavior, cognitive processes, and environmental factors. In social learning theory, thoughts and feelings can both cause and explain behavior. This is in contrast to radical behaviorism, which views thoughts and feelings as covert behaviors that may be part of chains of behavior but do not have an initiating role. In social learning theory, thoughts and feelings may elicit emotional reactions or provide discriminative cues for operant behaviors or negative or positive consequences (Gambrill, 2004).

There are three overlapping schools of CBT: rational emotive therapy, cognitive therapy (Beck, 1963), and self-management strategies. The first two schools were discussed in detail in Chapter 9. Self-management strategies have a conceptual scheme of self-efficacy (Bandura, 1977, 1980, 1996); self-instructional training, developed by Meichenbaum and colleagues (Meichenbaum, 1977, 1996; Meichenbaum & Goodman, 1971), and stress inoculation training (SIT) (Meichenbaum, 1975, 2007) will be discussed here. The major application of self-management strategies has been to problems of impulse control (e.g., weight, alcohol, drugs, impulsivity in children).

Self-Management Strategies. Bandura (1977, 1996) suggests that people who have a high degree of perceived self-efficacy believe that they can master difficult tasks. Repeated successes in particular situations give rise to self-efficacy expectations, whereas failures tend to lower them. Observing another person performing the behavior of interest can also influence a person's efficacy expectations. Verbal persuasion is another valuable tool in changing a person's efficacy expectations; however, because it is not founded on experience, it may be easily dismissed by the client (Rehm & Rokke, 1988). Bandura, Reese, and Adams (1982) have conducted several studies that show a strong association between perceived self-efficacy and the subsequent level of performance accomplishment. Bandura believes psychological treatment of any form is successful in part because it alters a person's expectations of personal self-efficacy. Self-management approaches teach skills that can be implemented on one's own (Chaney, O'Leary, & Marlatt, 1987).

Self-instructional training is a form of self-management that focuses on the importance of a person's self-statements, because maladaptive self-statements may contribute to a person's problems. The learning and application of more adaptive self-instructions is the goal of self-instructional training (Rehm & Rokke, 1988). Meichenbaum (1977) describes imaginal techniques to help the worker assess the client's self-statements. The client, with eyes closed, is asked to imagine a difficult situation and to describe her internal dialog to the social worker. They then discuss the quality of these self-statements and how they affect the behavior. Self-monitoring can be used with more formal record keeping or simply by telling the client to listen to herself. Conducting initial sessions in this way enables the therapist and client to conceptualize the problem and introduce a credible treatment rationale.

The second phase of self-instructional training is called *trying on*, or allowing the client to test the logic of the rationale to see if it applies. The essence of the treatment is to teach the client more adaptive self-statements so that the problem can be changed. The third stage of treatment is directed toward promoting change. The client and social worker together develop some self-statements that are conducive to coping, to replace the maladaptive self-statements that promote negativity and hopelessness. Meichenbaum and Goodman (1971) outlined their procedures for training impulsive children in self-instructional techniques. This was a five-step process. First, an adult modeled a task while talking to himself out loud, thus modeling self-statements to the child. The child performed the same task under the therapist's direction (using the same or similar statements). The child then performed the task while instructing himself out loud. The self-instruction was gradually faded so that the child repeated the task while whispering the instructions to himself, and finally while guiding his performance by private (covert) speech.

One of our favorite methods of instructing children to resist their impulses, developed by Meichenbaum and Goodman (1971), is called "The Little Turtle Story." It goes something like this: "The little turtle didn't like school and vowed to stay out of trouble but always found it. Then he'd get angry and rip up his papers. Luckily, he met a tortoise who told him that he was carrying the answer to his problem in his shell. He could hide in the shell whenever he got the feeling that he was angry. Then he could rest a moment and figure out what to do."

The therapist or teacher can then demonstrate the turtle reaction. Relaxation skills can be taught to the child, to be used while in his or her "shell." Counting from 1 to 10 while tensing and relaxing muscles can help to control strong feelings. The turtle method is combined with problem solving—once safely inside the "turtle shell," the child then thinks of an appropriate way to handle the situation. This might include self-instructional training, such as having the child talk to himself in his head, using language such as "I'm going to cool down now. Getting all upset about this never works, it just makes things worse. I don't need to let my anger get the best of me; I can keep cool, relax, and think of what to do." Meichenbaum and Goodman (1971) found that self-instructional procedures, compared to placebo and assessment control conditions, resulted in improved performance for impulsive children on the Porteus Maze, the Performance IQ, and the WisC, and on a measure of cognitive impassivity.

These self-instructional procedures can be applied to adults with a variety of problems such as anger, anxiety, pain, and schizophrenia (Meichenbaum, 1977). The most important features of self-instructional training are the education about the specific problem and the modeling and rehearsal of relevant behavioral and cognitive skills. Strategies such as relaxation training, systematic desensitization, and assertiveness training could all include a self-instructional component.

Stress Inoculation Training. SIT is a form of CBT that aims to bolster clients' intra- and interpersonal coping skills as well as their confidence in applying these skills in stressful situations. SIT was developed by Meichenbaum in 1975 and researched by Meichenbaum and colleagues over 30 years (Meichenbaum, 2007). In the first phase of SIT, the client's story is solicited, with narrative accounts of stress and coping identified, and stressful situations broken into specific behaviorally prescriptive problems. The second phase is skills training. Skills that are directed at the modification, avoidance, and minimization of the impact of stressors are taught (e.g., cognitive restructuring, self-instructional training, communication, assertiveness, problem solving, anger and anxiety management, parenting, and study skills). Problem solving helps identify possibilities for change. Palliative coping skills, such as perspective taking, and adaptive modes of affective expression including humor, relaxation, reframing the situation, acceptance, and selective attention–diversion procedures are also introduced. Clients then rehearse the skills, using coping modeling (either live or videotape models), self-instructional training, and discussion and feedback. In the third phase, the client is prepared for the application of skills by being exposed to graded stressors through imagery. Relapse prevention procedures are then employed. These include identifying high-risk situations, anticipating possible stressful reaction and rehearsing coping responses.

Treatment is gradually phased out and booster and follow-up sessions are planned. The client is encouraged to develop coping strategies to recover from failure and setbacks.

A Typical Cognitive Behavioral Approach. A typical CBT assessment and intervention includes the following steps:

1. *Specifying the Problematic Behaviors.* Here, one needs to be as specific as possible as to the "target" (key) behaviors that are to be the focus of change. Indicate which

behaviors are excessive and need to be extinguished (i.e., temper tantrums, overeating, smoking) and which behaviors are underdeveloped and need to be shaped (developed), such as lack of assertiveness and too little motivation.

2. *Data Collection.* Assessment includes monitoring of behaviors that require attention by keeping logs, journals, or notecards on a daily basis and looking at the antecedent events that arouse the behaviors and their consequences. Clients need to learn to evaluate their behavior, monitor their behavior, read signs of their own feelings (anger and hostility), label their feelings, and evaluate their acts as social or antisocial. This also includes identifying patterns and themes that have occurred. Diaries are useful tools wherein the client can write what happened, what was said, what she did, and how comfortable she was with the results. Scaling (applying a numerical value from 0 to 100) can help the client identify the intensity of the response. The client can then evaluate how satisfied she was with her actions and what she would do differently if that event was to occur again. Additional comments can be recorded if applicable, such as thoughts and feelings. Therapists can also monitor the therapist–client interactions, as can others in the client's life, such as a parent or teacher. Standardized tests are also useful monitoring tools.
3. *Goal Setting.* The therapist and client work collaboratively to set goals for change.
4. *Intervention.* Behavioral interventions include numerous techniques that are specifically tailored to enable the client to reach the goal that has been set. Many existing protocols can be found in the literature and can be accessed by problem definition or clinical syndrome.
5. *Homework.* Giving homework assignments helps clients practice the skills they are learning in therapy and provides continuity from session to session.
6. *Reinforcement for Change.* The acquisition of new, positive behaviors needs to be met with positive reinforcement. This is usually done by significant others, but clients can be their own reinforcers by giving themselves rewards for engaging in new behaviors. Behavioral clinicians and researchers have taken a leading role in designing intervention methods that use only positive reinforcement and in advocating against the use of aversive methods that inflict unnecessary stress or physical discomfort on the client (LaVigna & Donnellan, 1986; Meyer & Evans, 1989, cited in Gambrill, 2004).
7. *Taking Credit for Change.* Clients need to credit themselves with change that takes place, instead of attributing the change to the therapist. In this way, they learn to feel that they can engage in changing behavior on their own, which leads to greater self-control, mastery, and self-esteem enhancement.
8. *Relapse Prevention.* It is much more difficult to break a habit than to form one. Plus, old habits tend to come back, particularly when a person is under stress. Clients need to be prepared for the possibility of relapse and should strategize as to how they will handle slipping when it does occur. This is common in treatment of problems of impulse control regarding drinking, overeating, and smoking. Self-management strategies such as coping skills training and using self-statements help prevent relapse.

Some of the more common behavior therapy techniques that can be utilized within specific interventions are the following:

1. *Reinforcement.* Positive reinforcement is something the person wants, such as praise. It increases the probability that the behavior will occur again. In behavior therapy, the therapist and client both create opportunities for the client to receive rewards for the new behaviors. For some clients, just engaging in new, positive behaviors has merit of its own. Sometimes reinforcements have to be earned, as with token economies—a work payment incentive system in which participants receive tokens when they display appropriate behavior. At some specified time, these tokens are exchanged for a variety of backup reinforcers (items and activities). Tokens such as stickers are used in classrooms to help children earn points that can later be exchanged for small toys, treats, and other rewards. They are used with great success in special settings with children who are disabled or who are developmentally delayed, and with patients in mental hospital settings who are emotionally disturbed (e.g., five days of earning tokens for appropriate behaviors can be exchanged for a pass to go off grounds).
2. *Punishment.* This is a controversial technique that requires some consideration. An extreme form of punishment, known as *aversion therapy,* has been used with injurious behaviors to self and/or others, such as head banging, induced vomiting, self-mutilation, and child molesting. However, punishment not only goes against social work ethics but it is also generally not effective. Because punishment doesn't usually coincide with the actual behavior, but happens afterward, the subject doesn't connect punishment with the deed. Punishing rewards the punisher, helps maintain dominance, and induces guilt and shame (Pryor, 1985). Negative reinforcement, more acceptable than aversion therapy, differs from punishment in that it occurs during the behavior, and the consequence is immediate. (Time out for a disruptive child is a negative reinforcer. This procedure has been used quite effectively and is well known to most parents and practitioners.)
3. *Social Skills Training.* This technique is frequently used to coach children in a variety of socially acceptable skills. The skills usually covered are listening, speaking, and verbal and nonverbal communications (Pryor, 1985). Training in social skills teaches children to see others' points of view. Prosocial behavior is modeled, such as making positive comments to another child who is playing constructively. Praise is given for exhibited appropriate social behavior and the child is encouraged to adopt a sociable personality. (For example, "Let's talk about some ways to have fun with other children when you play games. One way is for everyone to take turns." The therapist then clarifies what "taking turns" means.) The child is also encouraged to identify some good and bad examples. (For example, "waiting until others have finished before you begin" would be a good example of how to take turns. "Always trying to go first" is not a good example of how to take turns.) The child receives feedback about what she has learned and how she performs.
4. *Assertiveness Training.* These skills help clients to discriminate accurately between aggression, assertiveness, and slavish conformity or deference. Clients practice assertiveness training by making statements that are direct and to the point, firm

but not hostile, considerate, and respectful. They are taught to recognize the other person, accurately reflect their goals, and offer a short explanation rather than a series of excuses. They are helped not to include sarcasm, pleading, whining, or blaming others.

5. *Relaxation Training.* This technique is useful with clients suffering from anxiety disorders and panic attacks. Different scripts abound, but most include progressive muscle relaxation where the client, with eyes closed, focuses on the different parts of the body while tensing and relaxing the muscles for 15 to 20 minutes.

There is a breadth of behavioral interventions specific to clinical syndromes such as generalized anxiety disorder, depression, panic disorder, agoraphobia, social phobia, social anxiety, obesity, and eating disorders. We refer you to a comprehensive text offering specific protocols: *Clinical Handbook of Psychological Disorders* by David H. Barlow (2008). Barlow's contributors give thorough assessment and research evaluation information, plus step-by-step instructions on how to intervene with a wide range of psychosocial disorders.

The Third Generation of Behavior Therapy

The second generation of behavior therapy (CBT) broke away from the first generation of behavior therapy because operant and classical learning principles were not sufficient to account for human cognition. Thus, cognition became an essential component, and CBT evolved. In the third generation or third wave, therapies were inspired, in part, by the meditation practice of observing thoughts without getting attached and tangled up in them. We will discuss one of the third-wave therapies, ACT (acceptance and commitment therapy), and refer the reader to Chapter 9 for two other examples of third-generation therapies—dialectical behavior therapy (DBT) and mindfulness-based cognitive therapy.

Acceptance and commitment therapy was developed by Hayes and colleagues (see, for example, Hayes and Smith, 2005; Hayes and Strosahl, 2004; Hayes, Strosahl, and Wilson, 2003). Third-wave therapies have an existential bent. They balance both acceptance and change. They teach acceptance of suffering as part of the human condition. ACT is based on psychological flexibility (Hayes, Barnes-holmes, and Roche, 2001)—the process of contacting the present moment fully as a conscious human being and changing behavior in the service of human values.

Acceptance and commitment therapy commonly employs six core principles to help clients develop psychological flexibility (Hayes, Luoma, Bond, Masuda, and Lillis, 2006):

1. *Cognitive defusion:* Learning to perceive thoughts, images, emotions, and memories as what they are, not what they appear to be.
2. *Acceptance:* Allowing thoughts to come and go without struggling with them. It is an alternative to avoidance and fosters increasing actions based on one's values.
3. *Being present:* Awareness and openness to the here and now, experienced with openness, interest, and receptiveness.

4. *Observing the self:* Accessing a transcendent sense of self, a continuity of consciousness which is unchanging.
5. *Values:* Discovering what is most important to one's true self.
6. *Committed action:* Setting goals according to values and carrying them out responsibly.

Taken as a whole, each of these processes supports the others. All target psychological flexibility, the process of contacting the present moment fully as a conscious and aware human being and changing behavior in the service of human values. (Harris, 2006).

The Therapeutic Relationship

In behavioral therapy, the therapist is viewed as a consultant, teacher, and trainer who is there to help clients learn about themselves and change maladaptive behavior patterns. Corrective learning experiences are emphasized. Clients acquire new coping skills and improved communication competencies, or learn how to break maladaptive habits and overcome self-defeating emotional conflicts. Behavioral therapists have not consistently credited the relationship as an important variable in behavioral change, but there is a growing empirical literature that demonstrates that clients perceive the relationship as crucial. Safron and Segal (1996) cite the following works: Sloane, Staples, Cristol, Yorkston, and Whipple (1975), who all found that patients successful in behavior therapy felt that the personal interaction with the therapist was the single-most important element in the treatment; Rabavilas, Boulougouris, and Perissaki (1979), who correlated therapists' attitudes of understanding, interest, and respect with favorable outcome in the treatment of 36 obsessive-compulsive patients; and Johnston, Lancashire, Matthews, Munby, Shaw, and Gilder (1976), who studied agoraphobic patients and ranked their therapists' encouragement and sympathy as more important than the practicing component of the treatment.

Research Perspectives

Social learning theory is well known and widely researched. The most famous study (Bandura, Ross, & Ross, 1961) is that of the "Bobo." In this methodologically rigorous experiment, children witnessed researchers acting aggressively toward a doll. The researchers then left the room and allowed the children to play with the doll. These children modeled the researcher's aggressive behavior and extended the aggression to their other toys. The Bobo doll study has been replicated many times with similar findings, indicating explanatory power for social learning.

Single-subject design methodology has also been widely used to demonstrate effectiveness of behavioral interventions. For more information on this design, please refer to Chapter 14. CBT has the largest evidence base today (Ost, 2008). The third-wave therapies described in this chapter have attracted a great deal of interest, but so far there has not been an independent review of the evidence base of treatment outcome studies done on these therapies.

Case Example: A Behavioral Approach to Obsessive-Compulsive Disorder

The following case illustrates behavioral treatment of a client with obsessive-compulsive disorder (OCD). Several behavioral techniques are demonstrated: modeling, exposure, response prevention, the construction of an anxiety hierarchy, use of client self-statements, homework, and self-monitoring. Single-subject design methodology was used to evaluate the effectiveness of the interventions.

The client, a 26-year-old woman, was handicapped by severe washing, checking, and counting rituals. During the course of a typical day, she performed approximately 54 rituals, which impaired her ability to function vocationally and socially and caused her great suffering and misery. She awoke at 4:00 A.M. in order to do all her morning rituals and still be at work by 9:00 A.M. Not surprisingly, she was frequently late for work. Although the client recognized that her ritualizing was senseless, she felt compelled to continue to do so. Originally treated with psychodynamic psychotherapy for several years, she experienced no relief in symptom reduction. The therapist treated her psychodynamically for two additional years, with no change in her ritualizing behavior. Depressed and discouraged, the client happened to see a television program on OCD that spoke of a successful behavioral treatment. She asked her therapist if she could help her with the approach described on the show. Since the therapist was not a behavioral therapist at the time, she began her own research and discovered some protocols on the treatment of OCD. The result was astounding—after nearly five years of psychodynamic therapy, the change to a behavioral treatment approach resulted in an elimination of the client's rituals in just eight weeks.

Assessment Phase

To prepare for the behavioral treatment, the clinician discussed the rationale for the protocol with the client: "OCD is considered an anxiety disorder. Some people feel that it is biological in nature and that it has to do with the uptake in the brain of a chemical called serotonin. Others believe that it is a maladaptive way of managing anxiety—that feeling of calm. Perhaps you were feeling anxious one day, and you washed your hands and felt better. So, the next time you felt anxious, you washed your hands, and this pattern continued until suddenly, without thinking about it, you were washing your hands all the time. Then this washing behavior began to enter into other aspects of your life. Soon, you started showering for longer periods of time. The ritual seemed to grow in size as well as frequency, until it took on a life of its own. Now, instead of feeling less anxious, you begin to feel more anxious because of all the time you were spending washing in an attempt to ward off bad feelings. That is what happens with OCD—the ritualizing begins to spread into other areas of your life. Pretty soon, you forget the reason that you started ritualizing in the first place. The treatment we will undertake is called exposure and response prevention. I will expose you to those things that you fear, and help you to face your fears. By preventing you from ritualizing we will break the automatic bond between the discomfort and the ritual. It won't be easy, but I will be here to help you each step of the way."

The client was given some reading material on OCD and behavior therapy, and the client and the therapist started the assessment process. This entailed looking at all the external stimuli that gave rise to obsessive-compulsive behavior, the content of the rituals, the length of time taken to perform them, the sequence in which they were performed, and the situations that were avoided to prevent ritualizing. The client identified 54 rituals that she performed

(continued)

Case Example Continued

with regularity. Some examples included glancing into cups, glasses, and corners of doorposts of a room; looking up common words in a dictionary to ascertain that they were spelled correctly; and counting the number of times she swallowed or gulped while drinking a beverage.

The client and therapist constructed a hierarchy of anxiety. This was done by asking the client to rank on a scale from 0 to 100 (0 indicated no anxiety and 100 signified intense anxiety) how anxious she would feel as she was confronted by each item that engendered the urge to ritualize. From this hierarchical list, the worker developed assignments to eliminate the rituals. To determine the effectiveness of the treatment, the worker selected three rituals for monitoring: (1) repetitively opening and shutting makeup cases, which the client did after daily use to listen for a clicking sound that would indicate that they were closed; (2) excessive rinsing in the shower after soaping, which lengthened her shower time to over an hour; and (3) counting her belongings (e.g., tote bag and pocketbook) each time she carried them from place to place. The client predicted that the anxiety she would have if faced with the first item while not being allowed to ritualize would cause her to experience a discomfort level of 30 to 40 on the anxiety hierarchy. The assignment developed for eliminating the ritual became "Open and close makeup cases only once, and don't listen for a click or other signs that they are closed." According to the client, lowering the rinsing time (item 2) in the shower to 15 minutes (considered normal) would result in an anxiety level of 50 to 60. The therapist developed an assignment accordingly. The client rated eliminating the counting of belongings (item 3) at a discomfort level of 90 to 100. The assignment for extinguishing this ritual was stated as, "When you move from place to place and carry your belongings, do not count them." As can be noted, there is no particular reason why the elimination of one ritual would cause more anxiety than another—it is all part of the senseless nature of the disorder.

The Measurements

A single-subject design with a multiple-baseline approach was used to monitor the effectiveness of the treatment. The client identified 54 rituals that she regularly performed. The three target behaviors were systematically monitored, although the intervention addressed all 54 items.

The Behavioral Techniques

Modeling, exposure, and response prevention were the three treatment techniques applied. First, the clinician modeled (demonstrated) the appropriate way that a person would respond in different situations (e.g., when putting on makeup). In sessions, the client was exposed to those items that caused her to ritualize. She was told to bring to session her makeup cases. The clinician showed the client how to apply each makeup item, closing each case only once (modeling). The client was then instructed to do the same. This, at times, engendered considerable anxiety, as noted in the following dialog from an early session:

Worker: Now I will put on mascara. (I begin to do so.) Notice how I open the wand, apply the product to my eyelashes, close the wand, and return it to my makeup case. Now you do the same. (I hand her the wand.)

Client: No, I can't do it.

Case Example Continued

Worker: Yes, you can. I know it's hard, but I assure you, nothing bad will happen. I did it just a moment ago, and nothing bad happened to me.

Client: That's easy for you to say. What if something does happen? It's too difficult for me, I need more time. I'll do it next week. I need to think about it.

Worker: We've already thought about it, and you've come to recognize that these rituals don't make any sense. You think they will comfort you, but in actuality, you have become much more anxious since taking them on. Here, take the mascara; I know you can do it.

Client: (becoming more frightened now) No, I can't. You can't make me. It's all too much for me. I should never have let you talk me into this. Stop pushing me. I need more time.

Worker: We could put it off, but it won't get any easier. Sometimes you just have to forge ahead. Just think about how good you will feel when you can put on your mascara like everyone else. Remember, no harm will come to you. I'm living proof that a person can put on mascara and not have anything bad happen. Just take my example. I have complete confidence in you. (I again hand her the wand.)

Client: (takes the wand and looks at it)

Worker: That's the way. Now just apply it to your eyelashes. Just remember, worrying about things like mascara takes too much time and energy. What's the worst thing that will happen? Maybe some will spill. Maybe you'll have to clean it up. But you can't spend your days worrying about every little thing.

Client: (takes the wand and finally applies her mascara) See, I did it. Are you happy now?

Worker: You did a very brave thing. I know how hard that was for you. Now let's see if we can apply the other makeup items.

The therapist then proceeded to expose the client to the other makeup items that caused her to ritualize. The client was able to follow the clinician's example and apply each item, with considerably less anxiety than she had first experienced. Homework was assigned, consisting of daily practice sessions of exposing herself to her makeup and applying it without ritualizing, for a total of 40 minutes of practice time, Monday through Friday. Self-instructional training was also used, and together the client and the therapist constructed a script that she would practice and say to herself when she became anxious. Included in these self-statements were some of the following:

"There's no need to feel anxious now. I know the correct way to put on makeup. I know how to close the case just once. What difference does it make if I don't close it perfectly? What is the worst that could happen? So maybe a little bit of makeup will spill inside the bag. So what? It's not a catastrophe. It won't hurt anyone. All this closing and listening is senseless—just time-consuming nonsense that prevents me from doing important things. I will choose to stop this ritualizing. I can do it. It might be hard, but I can do hard things."

The client was also instructed to practice correctly closing, pressing, and twisting items such as bottles, jars, and containers to foster generalization from makeup items to other items that required closing. The client kept a homework book and recorded exactly how, and how often, she practiced each item. After intervention, self-monitoring (recording) continued for each targeted ritual six more times over six weeks, as an after-measure.

(continued)

Case Example Continued

This continuation of self-monitoring provided a basis for measuring change between the pretreatment and posttreatment phases, and gave the therapist feedback on the success of the treatment. Follow-up reporting took place at three- and six-month intervals. At both follow-up sessions, the client reported that ritualizing remained extinguished for makeup cases. The same treatment principles were applied to all 54 items on the list to eliminate all ritualizing behavior.

Conclusion

Complete data analysis with graphs is found in Chapter 14, "Integrating Research and Practice." The official behavioral therapy protocol ended after eight sessions. Talk therapy continued, and together we worked on reducing the frequency of the 12 remaining rituals, and in the next two months, 9 of the remaining rituals were reduced by half and 3 were eliminated completely. Treatment then terminated, as the client had reached her goal. By the three-month follow-up, 45 of the 54 rituals had been eliminated. The nine that remained were reduced in frequency by at least half. The client was extremely pleased with her progress and felt that for the first time in years she was leading a normal life.

The treatment protocol for OCD has been established to be effective (Clark, 2003; Franklin and Foa, 2008; Swinson, Antony, Rachman, & Richler, 2001). The overall success for the combination of exposure and response prevention has been consistently high—about 75 percent of patients have markedly improved (Steketee, 1987).

Source: Cooper, M. (1990, June). Treatment of a client with obsessive-compulsive disorder. *Social Work Research & Abstracts*, 26(2), 26–32.

Empirical Evidence

Acceptance and commitment therapy is generally considered to be an empirically oriented psychotherapy. However, most clinical trails have been done on small samples. Despite this, ACT is considered an empirically validated treatment for depression by some organizations, such as the American Psychological Association, with "modest research support" (Murrell & Scherbarth, 2006). Hayes (www.contextualpsychology.org/state of the act evidence) states that ACT has shown preliminary evidence of effectiveness for a variety of problems including chronic pain, addictions, smoking cessation, depression, anxiety, psychosis, workplace stress, and diabetes management.

Ost reviewed 13 randomized clinical trials (RCTs) both in ACT and DBT, 1 in CBASP (cognitive behavioral analysis system of psychotherapy), 2 in IBCT (integrative behavioral couples therapy), and none in FAP (functional analytic psychotherapy). He concluded that the third-wave treatment RCTs used a research methodology that was significantly less stringent than CBT studies, that the mean effect size was moderate for both ACT and DBT, and that none of the third-wave therapies fulfilled the criteria for empirically supported treatments.

Bear in mind that to claim a theory is empirically proven, one must rely on a far greater number of clinical trials that these therapies have undergone. Time and further research will tell if there is a strong evidence base for their effectiveness.

Summary

Behavior theory has value for social workers because of its practical application to case situations. It is particularly useful when working with children, who respond extremely well to positive reinforcement techniques. This highly structured arrangement is comfortable for both clients and workers. In addition, social workers can immediately learn the effectiveness of the treatment. Finally, behavioral practice lends itself to evaluation, as noted in the single-subject design method described in this chapter. Behavioral practice is, therefore, evidence based—a concept of growing importance as social workers are being urged to become more rigorous in examining their practice.

11

Narrative Therapy

A Postmodern Approach

Narrative therapy began with the family therapists in Australia and New Zealand, originating with the work of White and Epston in the 1980s. Their approach became popular in North America with the 1990 publication of their book, *Narrative Means to Therapeutic Ends.* These authors were influenced by the social philosopher Michael Foucault (1972), who wrote extensively about the oppressive cultural discourses of everyday life.

Narrative therapy is a brief treatment modality. It can be accomplished in seven or eight sessions, but it does not have to be limited to that time frame. The emphasis in narrative therapy is on understanding and meaning, which makes it particularly relevant to social work practice with diverse populations. The clinician does not presume a way of being, but instead aims to understand the client's reality within the client's social and cultural contexts. Narrative therapy is strengths based, and thus resembles the solution-focused therapy of Berg and de Shazer (de Shazer, 1991). Narrative therapy is about knowledge and how the client has "storied" her life to make sense of it. Often this story is "saturated" with problems. Through a process known as *deconstruction,* the dominant dysfunctional story line is given new meaning, based on an understanding of other truths and alternative realities (Drewery & Winslade, 1997; Kelly, 1996; Morgan, 2000).

Narrative theory is rooted in postmodern theory. Philosophically, postmodern thinkers are concerned with the nature of reality and being (metaphysics and ontology) and the nature and acquisition of human knowledge (epistemology; Carpenter, 1996; Dean, 1993). This conceptual framework asserts that (1) the individual is an active participant in the construction of his or her reality; (2) cognition, affect, and behavior are interactive; (3) an individual's development across the life span is significant; and (4) internal cognitive and affective structures (including meaning systems, narrative and life stories) determine behavior and behavioral change (DiGiuseppe & Linscott, 1993; Mahoney, 1988; Neimeyer, 1993, cited in Franklin & Nurius, 1996, p. 323). Narrative therapists enlist the client's problem-solving capacities by focusing on successful ways that the client has coped in the past.

The Language of Narrative

Because reality is constructed through social discourse, the use of language plays a central role in the postmodern paradigmatic shift from objective to subjective reality (Real, 1990). Rather than acquiring the facts about the client's life (taking a psychosocial history), the therapist listens to the client's stories. Therapeutic dialog becomes a conversation as the therapist and client are engaged in the making of a new story called "meaning making or narrative creation" (Peller & Walter, 1998, p. 74). Language is used to build on the client's strengths, not to correct pathology or cognitive distortions. Walter and Peller (1992) write about the therapist taking an "inviting" stance that conversationally elicits what the client may be willing to and/or prefer to talk about. This sends a message of curiosity about the client's perspective, knowledge, resources, competencies, and imagination that encourages engagement—referred to by some narrative authors as "conversational resources" (McNamee, 1996). The intent behind the use of language is to present different ways of thinking using familiar words but "in unfamiliar sequences and juxtapositions" (Hayward, 2003, p. 186). The complexities and contradictions of popular language are therefore highlighted and cultural assumptions about the location of problems are challenged.

There have been criticisms about the language of narrative therapy (Crago & Crago, 2000; Flaskas et al., 2000). These include the avoidance of realities that are uncomfortable and the use of rhetoric.

The Structure of Narrative: Narrative as Metaphor

Narratives are reformulations or constructions of memories in the client's life that change over time. They form the center of treatment from a constructivist perspective. The process of understanding and organizing life events and experiences (whether historical or current) within their social and cultural contexts constitutes a narrative. Narratives provide structure and meaning that help people understand their own roles in relation to the wider social and cultural environment. The individual's self (identity) develops within this context.

The use of the story metaphor instead of history has several implications. First, the therapist is hearing a reformulation of the client's memories and not necessarily the historical truth. The therapist assumes that every person's life story is filled with contradictions and makes use of that fact in therapy. Second, narratives about the same event can change over time. Finally, the telling of the narrative is influenced by the therapist's participation in the process as a "participant observer" (Anderson & Goolishian, 1988, p. 384) and the context in which the narratives are told and heard. The therapist tries to ask questions that expand on the client's story and, when relevant, attempts to clarify the story in ways that may be important to the client. This "discourse-sensitivity" (Lowe, 1991, p. 43) assumes center stage in narrative therapy where attention is focused on the ways in which the conversation between the therapist and the client unfolds. In this interpersonal relationship between the therapist and the client, the client's narrative or life story will change in meaningful ways (Morgan, 2000; White, 2000, 2001; Wingard & Lester, 2000).

Hoffman (1992, p. 78) describes the therapeutic encounter in narrative practice as a dialectic process between the activity of patients constructing problems in their lives, the social and environmental forces contributing to and/or encasing these problems, and the patients' present experiences (in the immediacy of the relationship with the therapist). Real (1990, p. 260) describes the collaborative process of conversing, stressing both the facilitative and the participatory role of the therapist in "the process of change through conversation." Through this type of interaction, both the client and the therapist change in some way (Hayward, 2003; Strong, 2000a, 2000b). Noble and Jones (2005), for example, write about how the narrative therapist can help individuals who are facing experiences of loss. They write, "Putting the experience of illness, dying and death into story form helps to identify concerns and anxieties and the person to make sense of what is happening at a time of emotional turbulence."

There are a number of strategies that narrative therapists can use to collect stories from individuals during the interview process. Jackson (2002, p. 25) offers some suggestions regarding introductory questions that can be used in a structured interview with African American clients regarding their experiences with mental illness: (1) What is the one thing that you love about yourself? (2) When were you first diagnosed with a mental illness? (3) What experiences stand out most for you related to being labeled mentally ill? (4) What was your most positive experience with the mental health system? (5) What was your most negative experience with the mental health system? (6) How did/does your family and friends respond to your emotional crisis? (7) What helps you to heal? Have you ever used nontraditional (nonmedical model) interventions to support your recovery? (8) What, if any, impact did being African American have on the manifestation of behaviors labeled as mental illness in your treatment? (9) Knowing what you know now, what would you do differently about your contact with the mental health system? (10) What do you feel is important for African Americans to know about mental illness, treatment, and recovery?

The Deconstruction of Narrative

Narrative therapy views the client's problems as products of discourse that have placed her in problematic positions in the story she is telling about her life. The narrative counselor looks for alternatives to the problem story, and in doing so, helps the client develop a clearer perspective, which allows the client to reposition or reclaim her own voice. The process of listening to the client's story in this way is called *deconstruction*.

An important component of the deconstruction of narrative is the deconstruction of social power that dominates people's lives in more ways than they often realize. Clients are invited to talk about the effects of these familiar practices of power and the hold that they have on their lives—what these practices have caused clients to feel about themselves and their relationships with others. In this way, clients come to appreciate the degree to which these practices of power influence and diminish their lives and the lives of those around them (White, 1995).

In the deconstruction stage, the client is encouraged to take responsibility for her own behaviors and to fight the effects of the problem. Clients are not seen as "resistant" or "unmotivated." It is essential that the therapist believe and respect the client's words and not dispute the story as untrue. It is through discussion, analysis, and interpretation that the story is given meaning (White, 1986, 1988b).

Externalizing Conversations

One of the distinctive qualities of narrative therapy (and the deconstruction of narrative) is the use of externalizing conversations (Nylund, 2000; White & Epston, 1990). Through this process, the problem becomes objectified—placed outside the person—rather than internalized. The therapist encourages the client to trace or understand the influence that these perceptions have had on her life, her view of herself, and her relationships with others. The therapist tries to understand the client's perceptions of the problem, and how other persons may have been recruited (or drawn) into sharing these same views. Separating the client from the problem helps the client explore alternative, more positive experiences and gain self-knowledge. She is now open to the many possibilities of whom she might become. For example, in working with a young child who experiences urinary frequency, Epston (1997, p. 64) writes, "Your habit is trying to trick you into thinking you are a weakling . . . it is not so! You are a powerful young man, but your problem is weakening you and making you miserable, making you not sleep at night."

Another example of how the concept of externalizing is used in narrative practice is illustrated in White's (1991, p. 24) work with a couple experiencing marital discord. White says he needs the couple to "help me understand how they had been recruited into this pattern of responding to differences of opinion over particular issues."

These externalizing interventions help clients "disidentify from and reflect on the effects of these meanings and rules in their lives" (Strong, 2002a, p. 224). This allows the clients to unite with the therapist (and each other) in challenging the problem, instead of fighting and blaming each other, and results in a "conversational accomplishment." Hayward (2003) notes that "externalizing has emerged as a recommended 'technique' in many behavioral and systemic approaches."

The following case example uses narrative therapy with a group of middle school children diagnosed with attention deficit/hyperactivity disorder (ADHD) (Lesser, 2010, pp. 289–322). The therapist borrowed the term *detective club* from Debra Brooks (1998, cited in Nylund, 2000) and incorporated Nylund's (2000, p. 50) five-step SMART approach to working with these children:

1. Separating the problem of ADHD from the child through the use of externalizing conversations;
2. Mapping the influence of ADHD on the child and the family;
3. Attending to the exceptions to the ADHD story;
4. Reclaiming special abilities of children with ADHD;
5. Telling and celebrating the new story including the engagement of others in the child's life to corroborate and highlight the new story.

Case Example: The Detective Club: A Narrative Approach to Group Work with Middle School Children Diagnosed with ADHD

An excerpt from the first meeting of the Detective Club illustrates how the leaders use "separating the problem" of ADHD from the child through the use of externalizing conversations (Nylund, 2000, p 76):

Leader: I am going to ask you to help me out with understanding something. I put this club together because others have told me and you also have told me when I met with each of you that something called ADHD is causing problems in your lives. Can you become detectives along with me to figure out a few things about ADHD? Let's get started, okay? Oh, I have something for each of you (I give each child a gold handmade detective badge printed with each child's name and I also put on one with my name)

Children (Looking interested and happy about the badges, putting them on. . .)

Leader: First question for our detectives: "How does ADHD get in the way in your life?"

Melissa: "I can go first. It gets in my way when I start fighting with my sister and I can't stop. The other night I threw something at her and had to go to my room."

Jennifer: "It gets in my way at school sometimes because I get really bored and then I start tapping my pencil or my foot, and the teacher walks by my desk and puts her hand on it to remind me to stop, but I can't always stop."

Leader: "These are great examples of how ADHD gets in your way. Anybody have any other examples to share?"

Ashley: "Yeah. ADHD gets in my way during recess sometimes when I get a time out from the monitor because she says I am getting 'too wild.' That really makes me mad, because this is the time we are supposed to be free right?"

Leader: "Well what do some of you other girls think about this. Ashley is describing a way that ADHD gets in the way of her having fun. Does this happen to anyone else?"

Emily: "Well I think it gets in the way sometimes when I am with my friends. I don't know. My mom tells me that sometimes I get bossy when I am with my friends, or don't always listen to what they want to do."

(The dialogue continues for awhile with other children joining in with examples of how ADHD gets in the way.)

Jamie: Sometimes I think my friends are making me mad but maybe ADHD makes me too mad and I can't seem to stop myself.

Leader: "Well how does ADHD convince you that you can't do anything to stop yourself? I mean that you can't do anything about it when it is making you get too mad?"

Jamie: "I don't know . . . it just comes over me."

Emily: "Me too . . . my dad says that sometimes I just change into another person."

Leader: "Well it sounds to me like ADHD is making you sometimes do things that you might not want to be doing, but I think as detectives we can figure out a way to show ADHD that it can't just do things to you that you can't do anything about. What do you think? Shall we try to figure out some ways to fight back at ADHD?"

Therapeutic Strategies

Real (1990, p. 270) discusses five techniques used in postmodern therapy. Since these strategies are not linear, they can be used at any time during a therapy session.

1. *The Eliciting Stance.* Here, the therapist invites the client to share his ideas about the presenting problem and shows curiosity about aspects of the problem definition that may have previously received little attention. Real suggests that the therapist use questions that would encourage the client to expand on his thinking. A parent began therapy recently. Her 11-year-old son had been stealing money from her purse and was being disruptive in school. She was at her "wit's end" because she had taken away many of his privileges—all to no avail. The therapist asked, "What's your thinking about what is happening with your son at this time?" She replied, "I don't know, I think he's angry." "What might he be angry about?" asked the therapist. "Do you have any ideas?" The parent replied, "I just think he's angry and trying to get attention. I work long hours and he doesn't like that."
2. *The Probing Stance.* The therapist offers alternative descriptions to those offered by the client. These descriptions are discrepant enough from preexisting descriptions so as to be useful, but not so wildly discrepant as to be offensive and therefore rejected out of hand. Continuing with the preceding dialog, the therapist uses a probe, "I'm wondering if John's behavior could be sending you a message that he is sad as well as angry?"
3. *Contextualizing.* The therapist moves away from language that focuses on the individual client and moves toward language that connects the client to others in her life. The focus moves from a state of "being" to a state of "showing"—for example, "When your son is angry, to whom does he show his anger?" "What happens then?" "What would happen if your son showed his anger to . . . (another person)?"
4. *The Matching or Reflecting Stance.* The therapist mirrors back what has been told to her: "I see. You're worried about there being more tension in the family if your son's behavior continues."
5. *The Amplifying Stance.* The therapist attends to a particular emotion, behavior, or idea that has worked well for the client in the past. "I am impressed that in spite of your fears about further tension in the family, your concern for your son has prompted you to get some help."

Reauthoring

The narrative therapist invites the client to evaluate alternative outcomes. He asks if the client considers them to be significant and preferred and the reasons why this may be so. The therapist assumes a position of not knowing. Genuinely curious about these alternative outcomes, he engages the client in a retelling of her original story, called *new meaning making.* The client assumes the role of primary author. The therapist becomes the coauthor whose participation depends on important information and feedback from the client about her experience with the therapy. The therapist asks the client directly why certain ideas that have emerged during the therapy are of more interest to her than others. The client is encouraged to evaluate how therapy has affected her life and her relationships to others. She is also asked if her current relationships are preferable to those she had before entering therapy, and to what extent. The therapist engages in different types of questions in this process of reauthoring:

1. *Landscape of Action Questions* address the past, present, and future. For example, questions referencing the past are raised to generate new meanings of a client's history (other than the problem-ridden perception she may have about her life). White (1991, p. 31) provides some useful examples of questions that generate "alternative historical landscapes":

> "What can you tell me about your history that would help me understand how you managed to take this step?"
>
> "Are you aware of any past achievements that might, in some way, provide the backdrop for this recent development?"
>
> "I would like to get a better grasp of this development. What did you notice yourself doing, or thinking, as a younger person, that could have provided some vital clue that this development was on the horizon of your life?"

2. *Landscape of Consciousness Questions* encourage the client to verbalize and try out alternative or preferred personal and relational qualities, beliefs, and meanings about her life. Such questions generate optimism because clients are encouraged to reflect on their life stories. Examples of useful questions include the following (White, 1991, p. 31):

> "What do these developments inform you about what suits you as a person?"
>
> "Let's reflect for a moment on these recent developments. What new conclusions might you reach about your tastes; about what is appealing to you; about what you are attracted to?"
>
> "What do these discoveries tell you about what you want for your life?"

3. *Experience of Experience Questions* help the client reflect on another person's experience of her. They can be oriented to alternative landscapes of action or alternative landscapes of consciousness (as discussed). They can encourage the client to consider future developments in these two realms—for example (White, 1991, p. 32):

> "If I had been a spectator to your life when you were a younger person, what do you think I might have witnessed you doing then that might help me understand how you were able to achieve what you have recently achieved?"
>
> "How do you think that knowing this has affected my view of you as a person?"
>
> "Of all the persons who have known you, who would be the least surprised that you have been able to take this step in challenging the influence of problems in your life?"

Positions

Narrative theory posits that it is possible for an individual to hold more than one position within each discourse (or conversation), each with a different meaning. A sister and daughter, for example, would be two different positions within the single discourse of a family. This is complicated by the fact that an individual may also hold positions within different discourses at the same time. (For example, the sister/daughter may have a position in a school in addition to her position in a family.) These different positions or discourses may hold different sets of expectations, which may be in conflict with each other. In the case that follows, Mrs. G. is a daughter to a mother (position within her family of origin) who struggled with mental illness and was abusive toward her. She is a student (position within educational institution), working toward a degree in human services, and she is the mother of two adolescent children (position within current family). We include a genogram and an ecomap in this chapter to illustrate Mrs. G.'s many positions within her family and the other varied discourses in her life.

Narrative therapy suggests that individuals do not always have control over the positions or discourses wherein they find themselves. Unfortunately, these stories, developed from the positions available to individuals, can lead to difficulties contemplating other stories. The conflict and stress that result are often what bring individuals into therapy.

With regard to the therapeutic relationship, positioning involves what Strong (2002a, p. 223) describes as "being able to hear and speak from within different discourses; being generous in one's positioning means not committing one's therapeutic ear to solely one form of discourse." By listening and speaking in such a way, the therapist is able to elicit exceptions (previously described) to the problem discourse.

Definitional Ceremony

Narrative therapy is structured as a context for "thick description" of people's lives. Thick description is achieved through tellings and retellings of life stories. There will be an initial telling, a retelling of the telling (first telling), a retelling of the retelling (second retelling), and so on. Through these retellings, people's lives are "thickened," shared themes emerge, and alternatives are generated. This process contributes an understanding about their lives that would otherwise be inaccessible. The therapist and the client discuss who else in the client's life might be invited to participate in the definitional ceremony as affirming witnesses to the client's preferred claims about herself. The therapist (and any other outsider witnesses) engage with the client (and with each other) in conversations about what they heard and their responses. This provides the opportunity for all the participants (including the therapist) to participate in a new experience—one that hopefully contributes to their emotional growth. Most recently, Michael White (2000) is exploring the use of reflective teams within the context of the definitional ceremony.

Caldwell (2005, p. 172) takes a creative twist on the definitional ceremony in narrative therapy. This author integrates techniques from the expressive arts therapies such as bibliotherapy, journaling, memory books, self boxes, life maps, time capsules, and videography to assist elderly clients with life review (see Butler, 1963, for further information on life review with aging clients; Appalachian Expressive Arts Collection, 2003). Caldwell writes, "A central task of the therapist is to assist with picking up and picking out strands of memory and collaborating with the client, the family, and even the client's community in a re-creative and co-creative process" (Grimm, 2003).

Therapeutic Documents

A therapeutic document (White, 1995, p. 199) can be a letter written by the therapist, a statement of position written by the client, or a letter of reference from an affirming person in the client's life. The worker and client discuss confidentiality concerns and determine who should be involved in preparing the document. Additional decisions to be made are who reads the document and under what circumstances and when might the document be consulted. (See, for example, the narrative letter(s) in this chapter written by the therapist to the client between sessions as a source of affirmation and support. The client can consult this letter during periods of self-doubt or stress.)

The therapist invites the client to consider the consequences of consulting the therapeutic document by asking, "What effect do you imagine this consultation could have on your responses to the problem and on your relationships in general?" (White, 1995, p. 211). Events that take place between sessions are explored to identify those times when the client felt a need to consult the therapeutic document. The client is asked to consider how her prediction about these consultations (e.g., Will it be helpful?) compares to the actual events that occurred (e.g., Was it helpful?). If the predictions were accurate, the client is asked to reflect on the significance (e.g., the letter did help; the letter helped because . . .; the letter did not help; the letter did not help because . . .). If a review of events contradicts the client's predictions, the therapist and client can discuss what important information may have been missing from the documents and how these documents might be revised in the future. Some clients report that each narrative letter is worth as many as four therapy sessions (White, 1991). These letters can also be used as case notes for the clinician.

Cross-Cultural Counseling

Steier (1991, p. 4) defines an *individual* as "a person in a culture" whose self-definition is influenced by the way in which he is viewed by others in that culture. Narrative therapy has been considered effective in cross-cultural counseling (see Chapter 5) because this therapeutic framework views identity as a socially constructed phenomenon (Lee, 1996). In narrative therapy, the client's way of seeking help is understood within a sociocultural context. Lee and Greene (1999, p. 30) discuss this as "accessing the culturally embedded, unique meaning of the client's perceived problem and solution." Solutions generated between the therapist, the client, and the therapist's professional values are offered in ways that are both culturally specific and culturally respectful. Akinyela (2002a) suggests that culture is constructed in the constant process of dynamic change as more powerful relationships between and within groups contend for positions of power and privilege. She writes, "Black people in the United States have not been the passive objects of a process of de-Africanisation on the one hand and the helpless victims of Americanisation on the other. Black people have been active subjects in the process of Africanising the European culture that they encountered, and reshaping their own African culture in relationship to the new cultural practices they found themselves related to" (p. 34).

Case Example: The G. Family

The following case demonstrates a narrative therapy approach that extended over a period of eight months. The therapist is an Anglo male and the client is a Latina female. Each was raised and educated within different sociocultural contexts, making the choice of narrative therapy a good one. Although the therapy was conducted primarily in English, both the client and the therapist are bilingual, and they were able to introduce Spanish words when English was not sufficiently descriptive. As the Latino definition of *self* is one of being in relation to family (Garcia-Petro, 1982; Lee, 1996; Lee & Greene, 1999), individual and family interventions were combined.

Mrs. G. is a 45-year-old woman who grew up in a small town in Puerto Rico. She lived with her parents and two other siblings until the death of her father, which occurred when the client was 13 years old. Her father was described as "abusive" and "an alcoholic," and Mrs. G. felt life as a child was chaotic since the family often moved. Mrs. G. migrated to mainland United States in 1990, after experiencing dissatisfaction and disappointment in her marriage. She is the only family member to have left Puerto Rico. (See Figure 11.1 for a genogram of Mrs. G.'s family of origin and Figure 11.2 for a diagram of Mrs. G.'s family upon marriage.) Since living in the United States, Mrs. G. has become fluent in English. She graduated from college with a degree in human services and refers to this as "my one achievement in life." (See Figure 11.3 for an ecomap of Mrs. G.'s family.)

Mrs. G. went to counseling to seek help in parenting her two adolescent children: a daughter, age 16, and a son, age 13. She felt overwhelmed by her son's school difficulties and out-of-control behaviors and her daughter's incessant demands. The therapist chose narrative therapy as the modality and introduced the use of therapeutic documents, specifically narrative letters, as an important component of the work. The narrative letter is a "record of a session or sessions and its impact on the client, in addition to an account of the client's abilities and talents as identified in the session. The letter emphasizes the client's struggle and draws distinctions between the problem story and the developing preferred story" (McKenzie & Monk, 1997, p. 111). Mrs. G. was able to consult these concrete affirmations of the positive elements of her life story at times when she began to doubt herself.

Using the Narrative Letter

Session with Mrs. G.: Preparing for a School Conference. After several initial sessions, the therapist and Mrs. G. met prior to a school conference to discuss the difficulties her son was having in school, including explosive and unpredictable behavior, the need for one-on-one support, his tendency to get into various kinds of trouble, and an unwillingness to do the work. The therapist notes, "Mrs. G. felt very pessimistic about getting change from the school today. We discussed various aspects of that. . . . She doesn't want to get out of control and become emotional." Dialog from the therapeutic letter he writes after the session illustrates how the therapist asks questions that help the client reauthor her story.

Narrative Letter. "Our conversation today covered several important issues of concern to you. You told me how lonely you feel when you confront situations, such as the school conference for Juan, which you felt you could not handle. You remarked, 'I miss my family' for the 'boundary' it provides. You are indeed far from your family in Puerto Rico. Many people are able to hold powerful images in their mind of those they miss, which

(continued)

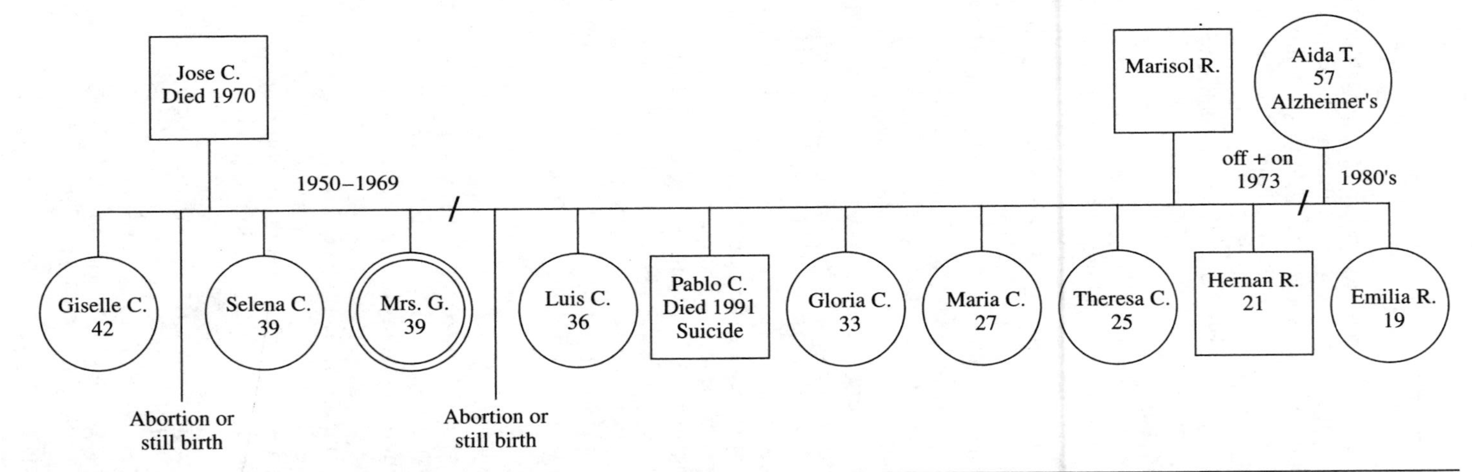

FIGURE 11.1 ***Genogram of Mrs. G's Family of Origin***

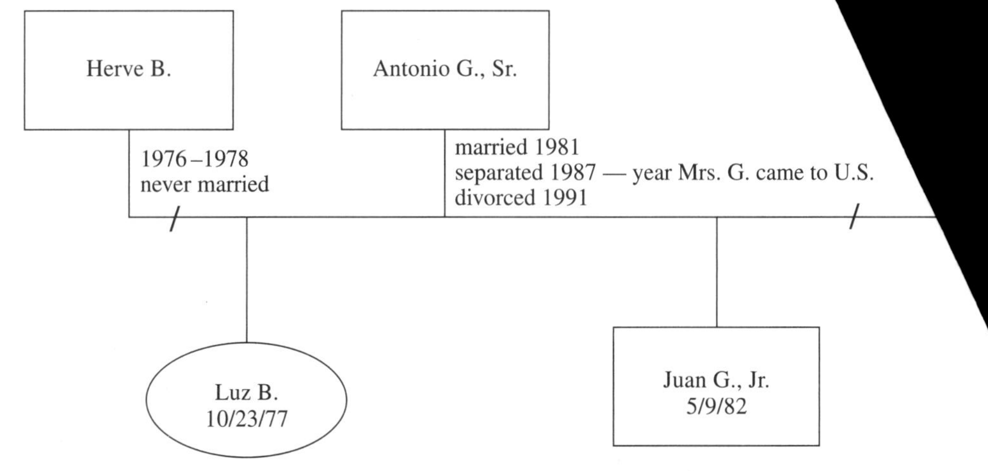

FIGURE 11.2 *Mrs. G.'s Family (Upon Marriage)*

Case Example Continued

enable them to get through tough situations. *I'm wondering how you will view your difficulties and what images you will choose to help you."*

Here, the therapist assumes an eliciting stance (inviting the client to share her ideas about the presenting problem) and uses a *landscape of action questions* (addressing the future). These questions are framed so as to suggest that Mrs. G. may be able to construct new meaning—a meaning that will help her feel secure.

Narrative Letter Continues. "How extraordinarily special you are to your mother that she always knows when you will call. What joy to hear her laughter with Juan! There is a deep and rich connection of joy and sharing between three generations. This is the positive side of your relationships. The idea of possible inherited mental illness continues to worry you. I want to remind you of all the ways you are different from your mother and how you are not crazy. You worry that Juan may have inherited some of your mother's characteristics. I'm wondering if it would be helpful to examine Juan and his ancestors by asking yourself, *How is Juan different from his relatives who have suffered from mental illness?"*

Here, the worker is *probing* (helping the client find alternative explanations) and *contextualizing* (using language that connects her to others in her life). He is again using a *landscape of action questions* (this one addresses the past) as he tries to help Mrs. G. consider an alternative way of "storying" her family background. He encourages a strengths model, rather than a deficits perspective, which Mrs. G. finds empowering.

In another session, Mrs. G. shared some painful feelings about her relationship with her son. Following the session, the therapist wrote this letter to her:

(continued)

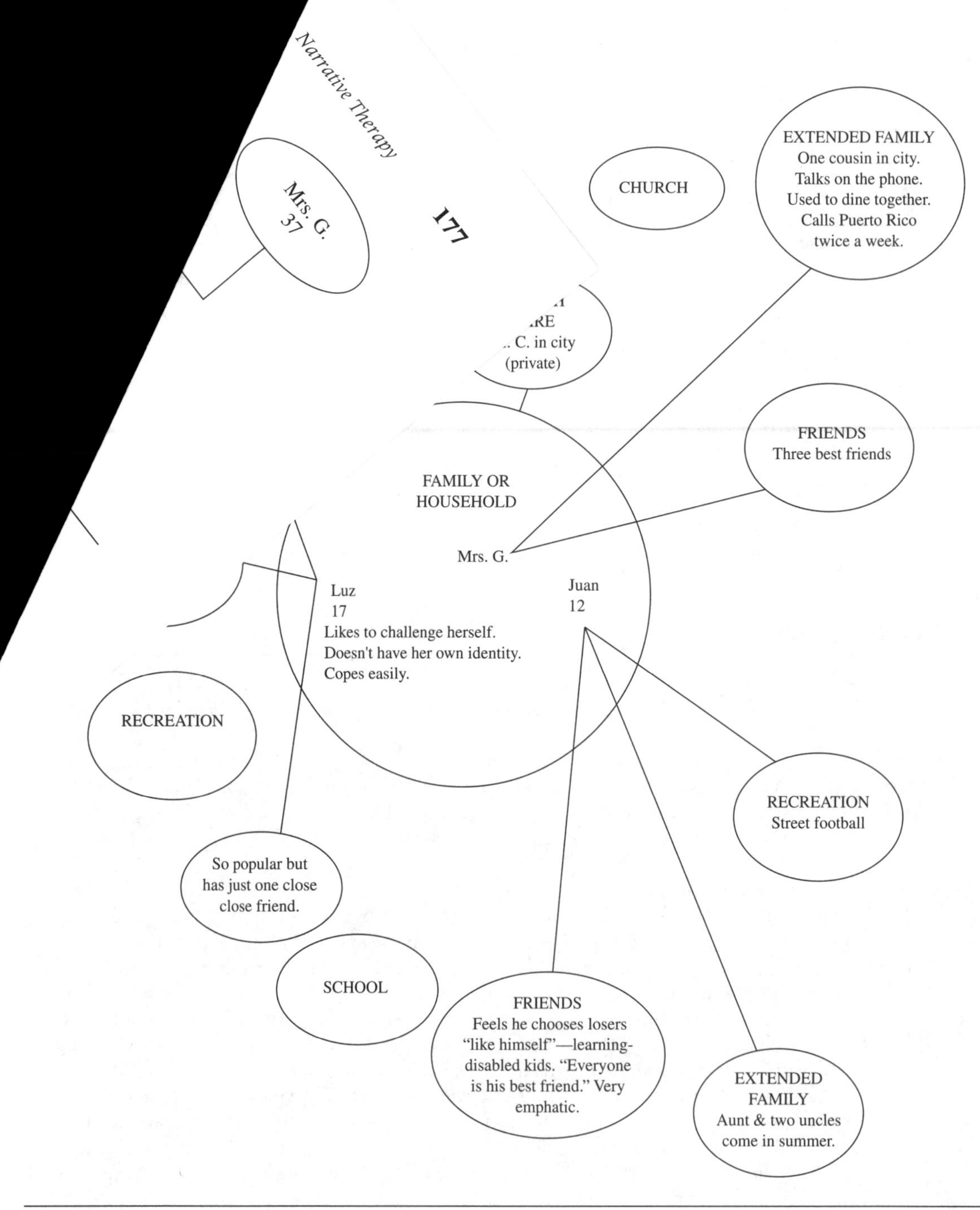

CHURCH
EXTENDED FAMILY
One cousin in city.
Talks on the phone.
Used to dine together.
Calls Puerto Rico
twice a week.
FRIENDS
Three best friends
FAMILY OR
HOUSEHOLD
Mrs. G.
Luz
17
Likes to challenge herself.
Doesn't have her own identity.
Copes easily.
Juan
12
RECREATION
RECREATION
Street football
So popular but
has just one close
close friend.
SCHOOL
FRIENDS
Feels he chooses losers
"like himself"—learning-
disabled kids. "Everyone
is his best friend." Very
emphatic.
EXTENDED
FAMILY
Aunt & two uncles
come in summer.

FIGURE 11.3 *Ecomap of Mrs. G.'s Family*

Case Example Continued

Narrative Letter. "You talked about the difficult transition Juan is facing in his new behavioral class and of your continuing effort to help Juan be successful in his new school. How painful it was for you to have Juan openly say 'I hate you' during your school visit. You requested that I speak with him, and I will soon schedule a visit to your home. I continue to be amazed by your growing *confianza* in me. You are indeed very committed to the process of counseling to help you unravel the difficulties that confront you and your children.

"How have you talked to Juan this week about his anger? What did you discover about your relationship with Juan? What do these discoveries tell you about what you want for your life?"

The therapist is now *amplifying* (attending to a particular emotion—Juan's anger) with a *landscape of consciousness questions* (engaging her to verbalize and reflect on alternative meanings and beliefs). This encourages Mrs. G. to verbalize and consider preferred ways of interacting with her son.

Community Practice (home visit)

The therapist made a home visit to the G. family and met with Mrs. G., her daughter, Luz, and her son, Juan. The purpose of the visit was to facilitate communication between family members, particularly between Mrs. G. and Juan. "Community based practice refers to practice grounded in a recognition of the profound interdependence of individual and community well being, an understanding that the health of one is highly influenced by the health of the other" (Lightburn and Sessions, 2006, p. 4). The hostility between mother and son was immediately evident. Mrs. G. repeatedly interrupted the therapist in his conversation with Juan, making critical comments about the boy. Luz twice sided with her mother. Success came when Juan's cousin and best friend, Jose, came to visit. The therapist asked Jose to join the meeting (with the family's permission) and attempted to recruit him as an ally who might be more affirming of Juan. During this family meeting, Mrs. G. noted that Juan reminded her of his father. Juan's father left her because he could not live up to "her high expectations."

Narrative Letter Following Home Visit. "Mrs. G., in the past you shared with me some of your emotional experiences of childhood. 'I wasn't showed how to love anybody. I wasn't taught to love, just to survive. I think I'm the only one in the family who expresses feelings.' Then you connected this to your daughter Luz. 'I feel overwhelmed when Luz gets so close to me. She demands too much.' Your ability to build deep and lasting relationships is extraordinary—precisely because you continue to believe quite often that you are unlovable or isolated. You wonder how capable you are of being loved. I don't think these beliefs are part of your real and authentic self. Where do these ideas come from? You will be able to more readily determine the answer when you are speaking for yourself than when that belief is running the show. *I wonder if you feel Juan demands too much, in different ways that also touch on your childhood experience of love?"*

In this example, the therapist is *reflecting, contextualizing,* and *probing* and poses a *landscape of consciousness question* to try to help Mrs. G. consider new ways of thinking about her past. He writes, "You are so often able to see connections and apply what you experience in one part of your life to another. We have spoken in the past of your relationship

(continued)

Case Example Continued

with Juan. I asked if your conflicts with him might in some way be related to your profound hurt and disappointment about his father. You did not feel this to be so. You are so often able to see connections and apply what you experience in one part of your life to another. You have 'been there' for Pablo (a friend of Mrs. G.'s). You said, 'By expressing how strongly I'm there for him, how much I care for him, I have seen how important these expressions are. So I now support my children and express my love to them.' You continue to evaluate your present and past relationships. It will be fascinating to listen to this dialog with yourself and see where you go. As you said, 'My goal is peace of mind.' *Would it be helpful to explore your relationship with each of your children through the theme of expectations? You spoke of how Luz 'lived up to my expectation.' You feel 'so proud of her . . . so close.' How has Juan's inability to live up to your expectations changed your relationship with him? How has it affected his relationship with himself (with how he feels about himself), and how he feels toward you? How can you act now, Mrs. G., to improve this? How can I help you?"*

The therapist continues *probing* and *amplifying*; this series combines a *landscape of consciousness questions*, a *landscape of action questions*, and *experience of experience questions* (helping the client reflect on another's experience of her) as he ties Mrs. G.'s past to her present and gives her optimism for the future.

In another session, Mrs. G. tells the therapist that she is thinking of putting Juan in foster care because she cannot handle both him and the stress of her new job. After the session, the therapist writes the following:

Narrative Letter. "You certainly face very difficult decisions at home. You are determined not to lose your job because it is so central to your definition of yourself. You have said, 'If I have to quit because of Juan, I will be a complete failure.' I sense your despair of being trapped by a deficit model, a half-empty glass. This feeling is very much underscored by our culture and the values that are dominating the political process in our country, tending to be destructive to the poor and working class of this country. You seem to feel that there is only enough of you to either succeed at work or to hold things together unhappily at home. You told me, 'I will give up Juan before I give up my job. I have no one to care for me. I will not go back on welfare. Juan has disability insurance,' implying that he will be okay because he will have financial support. How sad for parents to have to think about choosing between keeping their children and keeping a job they love. Your lack of practical resources has you facing this choice. For next week, I would like you to do an experiment on alternate days. One day you will think and feel as if you have given up Juan. The next day you will think and feel as if you have decided to keep Juan and have found a way to combine work and family. Then go back to thoughts of giving up Juan. It will be important for you to write down your thoughts, ideas, and feelings each day. The forces of despair will try to convince you that you could never successfully combine work and family (days 2, 4, and 6). Don't let them fool you! Call me if you need reinforcing."

Following the letter, Mrs. G. tries to get Juan's father to take charge of him for a while. When the father refuses to help, she makes the decision, in spite of her frustration, to keep him at home with her. She does not feel that she can give up on him. As the situation develops, Juan does better in his new school, and because Mrs. G. learns to

Case Example Continued

modify her expectations, set limits, and be more expressive of her love for him, their relationship improves. As the client's goals have been reached, the worker moves toward termination.

Narrative Letter Following Termination. "As we talked about the end of our work, you have been able to describe the remarkable progress you have made in our eight months together. You described some of the powerful decisions that you have been able to make:

1. You confronted Juan's father.
2. After months of consideration, you made the decision to leave Pablo and you found a new apartment.
3. You didn't let Luz and Juan 'walk' all over you.
4. You learned to tell yourself, 'I'm not a supermom, I guide my children, but I can't control their choices. . . . I'm not going to take responsibility for their actions.' I asked you if this was tough love and you replied, 'No, it's real love. I think I have found myself.'

What rich roots have you rediscovered that have nurtured your rapid growth these last few months? What experiences have you had in the past that made it possible to predict these recent changes, that let you know you were capable of these many recent changes? What new knowledge of yourself do you have that makes growing easier and easier? What are you learning about the process of making life-changing decisions? How can you make it easier on yourself to make such decisions?"

As therapy with Mrs. G. terminates, the therapist continues *amplifying* and *contextualizing* and introduces several *landscape of consciousness questions* to review the past work and empower Mrs. G. to think about the future.

Narrative Letter Continues. "You have long struggled with a deeply felt sense of aloneness. The end of my work with you, of course, raises these feelings again. But during your time alone this summer, you went from feeling empty to being able to make a triumphant statement, 'I'm me alone.' Do you understand the power of that statement? You are whole; you are complete. You went on to say, 'I want to be alone, to explore myself, to be independent.' When we meet for our last counseling session, I will read this letter and we can reflect on it further. I suggest that we try to talk more fully about my leaving and how that makes you feel. Although I am leaving you, I am NOT leaving without telling you. I continue to be amazed by your skillful sculpting of your future.*Is that a useful analogy, of yourself as a sculptor, carving yourself in a new image?"*

The therapist concludes therapy with Mrs. G., *reflecting, contextualizing,* and *amplifying* their work together. He uses *experience of experience questions,* encouraging Mrs. G. to give new meaning to her history, her current life, and her future.

Collective Narrative Practice

Denborough (2008, p. 192) writes about the use of "collective narrative practice" to respond to groups and communities who have experienced trauma and in contexts where one-on-one counseling is not possible or appropriate. Two examples of collective narrative practice follow:

1. *Collective Narrative Documents:* Narrative documentation is taken from several different people who are challenged by the same issues. Four questions used to generate material are (1) what is the name of a special skill, knowledge, or value that sustains you or your family through difficult times? (2) what is the story about this skill, knowledge, or value and the story about a time when this made a difference to you or to others? (3) what is the history of this skill, knowledge, or value? How did you learn this? Who did you learn it from? and (4) is this skill or value linked in some way to collective traditions and/or cultural traditions? Are there proverbs, sayings, stories, songs, images from your family, community, and/or culture with which these skills and knowledge are linked? (Denborough, 2008, p. 29).
2. *Convening Definitional Ceremonies:* There are a number of definitional ceremonies that are relevant to collective narrative practice. These can include storytelling, public rituals, ceremonies, meetings, murals, and protest marches, among others. One example of a definitional ceremony took place in Kingston, Jamaica, when a group of children who had been sexually abused decorated white tee shirts with messages of empowerment such as "I am not afraid of you any more" and displayed these on a clothesline outside the protected house in which they lived—a display of their resiliency to the community (Lesser, 2010).

Narrative Theater

Sliep, Weingarten, and Gilbert (2004) write about a unique interactive community approach to addressing the issue of domestic violence in a refugee camp in northern Uganda. This approach, called *narrative theater* (NT), integrates concepts from narrative therapy and forum theater, also known as "Theater for the Oppressed," developed in Brazil by Augusto Boal (1995, cited in Sliep et al., p. 310). In forum theater, the facilitator and the audience are mutually engaged in a "scene" that is recognizable to all present. They are then "invited" to provide commentary on what they have witnessed. Members of the audience are able to replace any of the actors at any point in the presentation in order to share their own unique perspectives about the scene. (For further information about forum theater, see Boal, 1992, 1995.)

The NT approach draws on the collective community—"the network of relationships and interpersonal processes that operate in particular activities and social practices" (Sliep et al., p. 311). The authors describe this approach as helpful in challenging certain positions and cultural practices that seem natural, but actually subjugate and oppress. For example, they write about a scene enactment of a woman seeking help because her husband felt it was his right to hit his wife. The audience, witnessing the domestic violence scenario, was able to revisit the woman's position as well as collaborate as a community regarding their own local values and build a structure of accountability.

Research Perspectives

Narrative research should value difference, thick description, metaphor, individual perception, and the voice of the client over the voice of the researcher (Carlson & Kjos, 2002). It should not care about cure rates, as studies using measurement are not what narrative research is about. Rather, qualitative approaches that honor the assumptions of the narrative perspective and that thicken description and capture diversity would be consistent with the narrative perspective. Citing Gergen (1999), Carlson and Kjos state:

> Required are the kinds of analysis that enable us to understand what is taking place from multiple standpoints, that will help us engage in dialogue with others from varied walks of life, and that will sensitize us to a range of possible futures. Most important, social analysis should help us generate vocabularies of understanding that can help us create our future together. For the constructionist, the point of social analysis is not then to "get it right" about what is happening to us. Rather, such analysis should enable us to reflect and create. (p. 195)

Many qualitative researchers, however, do not subscribe to the postmodernist approach. They disagree with the notion that all information is interpretation. Padgett (1998, p. 7), in taking up this point, states, "Clearly, the logic of postmodernism and cultural relativism can be taken to an extreme; the 'many realities' approach becomes a hall of mirrors where all knowledge is suspect. In this context, we can never verify how many died in the Nazi Holocaust or in the Serbian massacres in Bosnia in the 1990s because these horrific incidents can be seen via many interpretive standpoints—none being privileged." Citing Lofland and Lofland (2006), Padgett continues, "This statement may seem far-fetched but it follows a line of reasoning consistent with postmodern assertions regarding the fictitiousness of facts."

Summary

The case example provided in this chapter illustrates the concepts of narrative therapy and, in particular, the use of the narrative letter as a therapeutic tool. These narrative letters advance the work of the therapy between sessions, affirm the client, and enable her to reframe the "problem-saturated story" into a new and empowering narrative. Carpenter (citing Colapinto, 1985, p. 30, in Turner, 1996) points out that we may choose not to accept versions that are congruent with the perpetuation of racism, domestic violence, school dropouts, runaway teenagers, and other destructive interactions and try to change "uglier versions of reality." This is consistent with the mission of social workers and the value base of the profession. Equally important is that workers don't deny the harsh realities of their clients' lives. Social workers must help these individuals find the strengths and coping capacities that have been ignored in their problem-saturated dominant story line and challenge the power that these harsh realities have been given. Such is the work of creating new narratives.

12

Solution-Focused Therapy

A Postmodern Approach

Solution-focused therapy originated in the late 1970s. Its founders were Steve de Shazer, Insoo Kim Berg, and their colleagues at the Brief Family Therapy Center of Milwaukee. The model was influenced by Milton Erickson's view that the client, not the therapist, defines the problem (O'Hanlon, 1987). Initially, the model was conceptualized around a problem orientation and emphasized the importance of intervening in problem patterns as a prerequisite to constructing solutions.

From its inception, a unique feature of solution-focused therapy has been its emphasis on looking for exceptions to the problem. Examples of these exception-finding questions would include "What's better with your situation?" "What else are you doing differently that seems to be making a difference?" and "What will you continue doing so this happens more often?"

In its later development, solution-focused theory stated that it was not necessary to have a connection between the problem and the solution. The model shifted then from identifying problems, to identifying exceptions to problems, and finally, to identifying solutions to problems. This movement is illustrated later in this chapter, with the revision of the future-focused miracle question, developed by de Shazer (1988).

Solution-focused therapy, like narrative therapy, is rooted in postmodern or post-structural thinking. This model operates within a conceptual framework that views people living and creating new narratives about their lives that extend beyond their problem-focused ones. Unlike narrative therapy, whose name is conceptual and suggests process, the term *solution focused* may lend itself to being misinterpreted as being a set of techniques only. This belies the importance in solution-focused therapy of the collaborative process—therapist and client working together to construct a solution, not merely giving simple solutions to complex problems (DeJong, 2002).

An important technique in solution-focused therapy is the miracle question. The following illustrates how the miracle question moves the problem focus to goaling talk.

> Suppose tonight while you were sleeping a miracle occurs, and life is the way you want it to be. But because the miracle happened while you were sleeping, you didn't know it happened. What would be the sign to you that this miracle had occurred? (Peller & Walter, 1998, p. 84)

Since its origin, the miracle question has undergone revisions.

Another variation of the miracle question helps the client consider the progress he or she may be making (Peller & Walter, 1998, p. 85):

> Suppose when you leave here tonight after this appointment, life is the way you want, or you are on track to putting your life together in the way that you want. What signs would you notice that would let you know?

In addition to the miracle question, presuppositional questions can be used to help clients define the "who," "what," "how," and "where" of goal attainment. Examples may include "How will you know that the problem is really solved?" "How will you know when you don't have to come here any more?" and "If you were to gaze into my pretend crystal ball and see your family one month down the road, what will we see happening that is different?"

Exception questions imply that "nothing is always or never" (Becvar & Becvar, 2009, p. 266), and there are circumstances and times when the problem is not being experienced. Focusing on exceptions such as "What is different or better?" helps the client see that some good things are happening, and the problem may seem less oppressive.

Kiser, Piercy, and Lipchik (1993, p. 240) offer questions that address clients' emotional needs in solution-focused therapy sessions with individuals, couples, and families. Examples are "What do you suggest you do when you are feeling this way?" "What can your partner do that will help you be more loving to him or her?" and "What are you likely to be doing together the next time you all find yourselves laughing?"

Scaling questions can help determine a quantitative measurement of the client's problem prior to treatment, such as "Where would she like to be at the end of . . . (a certain period of time), on a scale of 1 to 10?" or "How confident is the client that he will be able to resolve the problem (on a scale of 1 to 10)?" In the following excerpt, the student uses a scaling question to help the client define the progress she has made since coming to therapy. We can see how the student supports the client's ability to make future changes by reinforcing the fact that it is the client herself who has made the changes in her life.

Student: If you had to rate how things have gotten better on a scale of 1 to 10, with 1 being the lowest and 10 the highest, how would you rate yourself when you first came here?

Client: I'd say I was a 4.

Student: And how would you rate yourself now?

Client: I'd say I was a 7 now.

Student: That's a significant amount of change. How have you managed to take such a strong stand for yourself?

Problem-tracking questions are used in work with families (Selekman, 1997). Members are asked to give a detailed description of how each person interacts with each other and with other people. These questions are particularly useful in "interactionalizing" (viewing problems as interactive) rather than locating problems within any one individual. Problem-tracking questions can be used with individual clients as well—for example, "When your daughter won't listen to you and refuses to go to bed, what do you do? What does she do in response? What happens next?"

The Editorial Reflection

The solution-focused therapist varies the traditional psychotherapy hour. She may take a break during the session so that she and the client each have an opportunity to reflect on what has been transpiring in the session. The consultant may use this time to compose a thoughtful reflection on what has transpired during the session and also to invite the client to share her reflections. In addition, the consultant uses this time to select appropriate tasks for the client or family members and to consider how she might compliment the client(s) on problem solving or coping strategies that may have been helpful at some point. Berg and DeJong (2005, pp. 51–52) discuss three different types of complimenting that are particularly helpful in engaging clients: direct, indirect, and self-compliments. When giving *direct compliments,* the therapist observes what has been successful for clients and brings these observations to the client's awareness in a direct statement. *Indirect compliments* are those the therapist elicits from clients by asking questions that are posed through the lenses of those who know them and therefore may considered credible (e.g., a best friend). *Self-complimenting* involves asking questions in a way that places clients in the position of describing their hidden abilities, rather than their problems. As these authors write, "Complimenting begets gratitude and reciprocal complimenting" (p. 55).

Some solution-focused consultants work with reflecting teams who are available to offer different points of view about what transpired in the session. (Reflecting teams observe sessions from behind a one-way mirror.) After the break (whether it has been with a reflecting team or alone, in self-reflection), the consultant shares her thoughts with the client. She may, at that time, offer suggestions for how to work on those things she would like to do differently or suggest keeping a list of times when the problem behavior is not occurring. A specific question, originating in the pioneering days of solution-focused therapy, is the Formula First Session Task (FFST): "Between now and next time we meet, I want you to observe, so that you can tell me next time what happens in your life (or marriage, family, or relationship) that you want to continue to have happen" (Molnar & de Shazer, 1987). This is not a homework assignment. The strategy is presented as "clues" suggested by the consultants who may help the client make desired changes (de Shazer, 1988; Friedman, 1995).

Postassessment Session and Self-Reflection

During this phase, the solution-focused therapist reflects on her work with the client or family, considering both the interventions she made and any other interventions she might use in the next meeting. Examples of self-reflective questions, suggested by Selekman (1997, pp. 70–71) in his work with families, include "If I were to conduct this session all over again with the same family, what would I do differently?" "What family members do I need to spend more time engaging in the next session?" "Have I been sensitive to cultural issues?" "Are there power imbalances around gender in this family?"

Solution-Oriented Family Assessment

Selekman (1997, p. 32) designed a "solution-oriented family assessment format" consisting of five components that the therapist and family participate in during their initial meeting.

1. *Problem Defining and Clarification.* Although seemingly contrary to solution-focused therapy, Selekman feels it is important to show interest in how the family views its struggles (as problems) and to work with the family to establish a focus for what members are most interested in changing (i.e., finding a solution for). He uses future-oriented questions to help find this focus: "Suppose we were months down the road, long after we successfully completed counseling together, and you each proceeded to tell me the steps you took to get out of counseling. What would you tell me you did?" In addition, the therapist might interject collaborative problem identification questions, such as "Which of these (presenting) problems do you want to change first?" or "If we were to break that problem up into small pieces, what part of the problem do you want to focus on changing first?"

2. *Meaning Making.* Meaning making elicits the family story. Once the family's view of the problem is known, the therapist uses the language of solution-focused therapy to begin to inquire about and understand the important themes in their stories. Selekman reminds us that "there are multiple meanings to the words that family members use to describe their problem situation" and that "their problem stories are stories" (p. 41). He gives particular attention to the reasons why people seek therapy and may engage in conversational questions to seek this information: "If you were to work with the most perfect therapist, what would he or she do that you would find to be most helpful?" If a family has been in prior counseling, the therapist might be interested in exploring their experience further by asking a question, such as "Have former therapists tried something with you that you found helpful? We could try doing the same" or "You have seen a therapist(s) before me; what, if anything, has he or she missed with your situation? What, if anything, would you like me to do differently?"

3. *Assessing the Customer(s) for Change in the Client System.* Here, Selekman draws on de Shazer's (1988) delineation of three possible therapist–family relationship patterns.

These are essentially the ways in which the therapist determines how motivated the clients may be and the ways in which she can best respond and engage them in the therapy. The first group is called *visitors.* They are generally those individuals (such as children and adolescents) who may be brought to counseling because someone else in the family thinks they have a problem. Sometimes, entire families can be considered visitors. Visitors require warmth, empathy, and acceptance by the therapist of whatever goal the family (or individual members) may wish to pursue. *Complainants* are those who express their worry or concern and are often hoping that the therapist will correct the problem, as they see it. To engage complainants in the treatment process, it is useful to give them some type of observational task that requires their involvement in a positive way (e.g., writing down what their child did during the week that was encouraging or writing down ideas about how to be encouraging to the child). Finally, *customers* are those who are most concerned about the identified client's problematic behaviors and most willing to work with the therapist toward new solutions.

4. *Goal Setting.* Solution-focused consultants encourage the client to talk about how she would envision a future without problems. The miracle question(s), presuppositional questions, scaling questions, and problem-tracking questions are used to set goals. Selekman (pp. 64–65) also offers examples of how to use scaling questions within the context of family therapy: "How confident are you today on a scale of 1 to 10 that you will resolve your son's temper tantrums?" "Let's say we get together in one week's time and you proceed to tell me that you took some steps and got to a 7. What will you tell me you did?"

5. *Collaborative Treatment Planning.* Family sessions are generally structured so that the therapist meets with the family as a whole, with the parents alone, and with the identified child alone. It is important to remember that others outside the immediate family may also be important collaborators in the treatment process (i.e., concerned relatives, schools, family doctors, etc.). The therapist informs the family members that they will be encouraged to do certain tasks and experiments between meetings. The collaborative process extends to empowering families to determine how frequently they feel counseling should occur, when they may need some time away from counseling to practice on their own, and even what *DSM-IV* diagnostic code they feel would be most applicable. When a diagnosis is required for his purposes, the consultant invites the client to discuss the diagnosis that he feels is most appropriate, within a reasonable choice of possibilities.

As with narrative therapy, the therapist works with the family to externalize *DSM-IV* codes that label individual members as identified clients. For example, "How did this problem begin to make trouble for you in school?" may be one way to talk to a child (family) who is brought to counseling for behaviors associated with attention deficit disorder. Other externalizing-the-problem questions Selekman offers are "Have there been any times lately where you stood up to . . . (name the problem; e.g., distraction) and didn't allow it to get the best of you?" or "What do you do to achieve victories over . . . (name the problem)?" In all these ways, solution-focused therapy is committed to client empowerment.

Interdisciplinary Collaboration

Selekman (1997) extends a solution-focused approach to interdisciplinary collaboration with other professionals involved in working with a particular family. He cautions that the family consultant needs to be open to other perspectives and opinions (just as she is in working with the family as the client system). This involves a genuine interest in what the other professionals have to say and a willingness, if necessary, to alter one's own views. Selekman raises the important point that professionals from different disciplines speak different languages; therefore, solution-focused consultants must either be versed in these different languages or be willing to ask questions nondefensively. In this day of technological advances, it is important to remember that collaboration can be done via instant messages, email, speaker phone, written correspondence, skype, and/or fax (with the family's consent and attention to confidentiality matters).

An interesting twist on interdisciplinary collaboration is the involvement of the child or adolescent client's friend(s) as consultants. This is similar to White and Epston's definitional ceremony (see Chapter 11 on narrative therapy) and Saleebey's (2009) concept of viewing the entire community as a potential resource to be enlisted on behalf of clients. Friends are called on to offer helpful advice concerning what could be done to make things better for their pal. These friends can also participate in role-plays and offer the support and encouragement of a peer.

Solution-Focused Strategies

Introduced by de Shazer (1985, 1988, 1991), these rather creative strategies can be used with children, adolescents, adults, or families. They engage the clients in becoming more aware of what works and help them move forward to new solutions to old problems. With the *Prediction Task,* the consultant invites the client to "predict" whether the next day (or other defined period of time) would be a good day, and then to consider and report what made it good. In the *Do Something Different Task,* particularly suited to work with families, the parent(s) or the child(ren) is asked to do something other than what others around them would expect them to do (in response to a particular problematic situation). The idea behind this strategy is that often when one person in the system changes his or her behavior, others respond differently as well. The client is asked to observe and report on how the other person responds to him or her at that time. The *Pretend the Miracle Happened* strategy suggests to the client that he or she engage in what the other person would consider a miracle behavior. Selekman (1997) suggests that parents use positive consequences (rather than negative consequences) as a strategy to employ with children who have pushed the limits. Positive consequences might incorporate skills the child has shown mastery over, such as babysitting for a neighbor or helping make dinner for several nights. This is in keeping with the solution-focused notion that attention needs to be given to incorporating more of what works (strengths) into making what doesn't work better. These solution-focused strategies bear some resemblance to White's (1991) narrative concept of "eroticizing the domestic," since they are all geared toward making the familiar different.

Selekman (1997, pp. 111, 180) offers two other variations on the miracle question with the following question he addresses to parents during the course of family therapy:

> Suppose I had an imaginary time machine sitting over here, and I asked each of you to enter it and take it wherever you wished to travel in time. Where would you go? Who would you be with? What would you do there? What difference would that make in your life? Suppose you were to wake up tomorrow and find yourselves in Parentland, where parents are totally fulfilled by their important roles, are regarded by society as its most important citizens, and have well-behaved children. What would you observe these parents doing for themselves and their children that makes them feel so fulfilled as parents?

These interventions may be particularly helpful in those challenging family situations where parents (and children) feel stuck, guilty, angry, and helpless. It offers them a sense of empowerment and perhaps a vision (from the imaginary vantage point) of future possibility. It also interjects some lightheartedness in the work—which is often sorely lacking for many of these parents and families.

Solution-focused therapy has expanded beyond its original family focus to include strategies that are geared toward specific groups and settings such as child protective services, mental health intervention in school settings (Gingerich & Wabeke, 2001), chronic and severe mental illness (Eakes, Walsh, Markowski, Cain, & Swanson, 1997; Kok & Leskela, 1996; Rowan & O'Hanlon, 1999), group therapy, couples counseling (Hoyt & Berg, 1998; Weiner-Davis, 1992, 2001), and adolescent abuse survivors (Kruczek & Vitanza, 1999). Solution-focused treatment with trauma and mandated clients are described next.

Solution-focused brief therapy with trauma. Seligman (2002) in his experiments with animals inflicted with pain noticed that those who had no control over the electric shocks became passive and developed depressive symptoms. He proposes that expectations are powerful predictors of behavior. Expectations of continued adversity lead to helplessness, withdrawal, passivity, anxiety, depression, and health problems. In contrast, expectations of control engender persistence, coping capacities, and resilience to depression and physical health problems. Seligman shifted his attention from learned pessimism to learned optimism. Bannink (2008) proposes that in working with solution-focused brief treatment with traumatized patients, the therapist looks at how the person was able to survive. Exploring the client's resilience, those factors that enabled him to cope and successful coping patterns in the past, helps promote a more positive view of the self. He writes that psychotherapy with traumatized clients should shift from impossibilities to possibilities and from post-traumatic stress to post-traumatic success. Citing O'Hanlon (1999), a solution-focused therapist who introduced the term *post-traumatic success,* he gives some guidelines for therapy with survivors:

1. Find out what the client seeks to gain from treatment and how she will know that treatment has been successful.
2. Make safety contract and provisions.

3. Do not assume that the client needs to revisit traumatic memories. Some will, and some won't.
4. Look for strengths and resources. Focus on what enabled the client to cope, survive, and thrive since then. Look for healthy support systems and current skills. Have the person talk about how he refrained from acting on destructive impulses, got himself into therapy, and so on despite the enduring after effects of trauma.
5. Stay focused on the goal of treatment rather than getting lost in the gory details.
6. Gently challenge self-blaming or invalidating identity stories that the person has accepted from others.

Citing Tedeschi and Calhoun (2004), Bannick offers some important words on post-traumatic growth. While trauma is not desirable in any way, nor necessary for growth, growth and distress can coexist, and the growth in trauma survivors emerges from the struggle with coping—not from the trauma itself. The worker must have empathy for the pain and suffering of trauma survivors, while helping them to develop in meaningful ways in the aftermath of trauma.

Solution-focused brief therapy with mandated clients. DeJong and Berg (2001) describe the use of solution-focused interviewing as a way to engage involuntary and mandated clients. The term *mandated* evokes strong feelings in practitioners. It conjures up images of resistant, difficult, uncooperative, hostile, and negative clients—clients who frequently see practitioners against their will. Mandated clients expect to be judged harshly for the events that brought them to your service, which makes the engagement process extremely challenging. DeJong and Berg propose that solution-focused interviewing invites these clients to be their own authority on what they want changed in their lives, and how they want the changes to happen. The practitioner is encouraged to ask several questions that draw out what the client perceives the mandating agent expects to be different and what the client thinks about the expectations. This puts the client in charge of describing them in detail and on her own terms. It sets the stage for the construction of cooperation. Ask about what outcomes the client wants from service, rather than telling mandated clients what they have to do. Gather details about the client's successes and strengths, and compliment the client on these. Convey that the client has competencies and that the solutions to his difficulties will arise from these. By listening to mandated clients' expertise about their mandated context in relation to their hopes for the future, we help them to open up new possibilities for doing something different, and cooperation will happen naturally. DeJong and Berg end by noting that client resistance is not contrariness, but represents a client's unique way of being and perceiving. "Perceived resistance, then, should prompt us to struggle to formulate and ask more not-knowing questions about what clients have just said to us, not to educate or confront. Doing so will keep the door open for continued co-construction and cooperation" (p. 19).

Case Example: Initial Meeting with the Drew Family

The following example demonstrates an initial family meeting. The consultant conducts the assessment according to the solution-focused format suggested by Selekman (1997). This schema appears in bold type within the dialog.

Overview

Mrs. Drew initiated the counseling session. In a brief telephone conversation, she reported that her 12-year-old son Donald could not be controlled. She identified his problem behaviors as "lying and stealing." She also stated that she and Donald's father had divorced when Donald was 5 years old. She was remarried, and she and Donald's stepfather live with Mr. Drew's 15-year-old daughter. Donald's older brother, age 18, lives with Donald's father and stepmother. Donald sees his father on a very regular basis, but the relationship between the two families is strained.

Before meeting with Mr. and Mrs. Drew and Donald, the practitioner obtained Mrs. Drew's permission to call Donald's father to ensure his support and involvement. Mr. Drew and the therapist determined that they would meet together on a separate occasion.

Solution-Focused Family Assessment with Mr. and Mrs. Drew and Donald

In keeping with Selekman's suggested format, the therapist greeted each member of the Drew family warmly, introducing herself and taking the time to let them know that she was pleased that the family decided to seek some help for whatever was troubling them. The practitioner then says, "We'll be meeting for about an hour. We'll spend the first half of our time together talking about your concerns and then we'll turn our attention to some solutions that you might like to see happen."

Mrs. Drew immediately begins to tell her reasons for seeking help at this time. She speaks rapidly and with obvious frustration, "I'm at my wit's end with Donald. His behavior has been getting worse and worse over the past couple of months. My husband and I don't know what else to do. We have tried taking privileges away but he doesn't even care any more. I apologize for not coming sooner but I was hoping that things would get better."

In an attempt to involve Mr. Drew and Donald in this discussion and to get further information about why they decided to seek help at this time, the therapist asks, "Who was the first person who got the idea that you should seek help?" **(meaning making and eliciting the family story)**

Mrs. Drew: What finally prompted me to call was a recent incident when Donald got into trouble again because he signed my name to a test with a failing grade.

Consultant: Who else thought counseling would be helpful now? **(eliciting other meanings)**

Mr. Drew: I did. This was not the first time Donald had lied to us. He seems to be lying more and more to cover up things that aren't going well. Donald also hoards food. He's been doing this since we tried to offer him a healthier diet. His pediatrician suggested that we do this because Donald is gaining weight at a rapid rate. We find empty bowls of cereal and candy wrappers hidden in his room. We suspect that Donald is buying candy with money he periodically steals from his mother's purse.

Case Example Continued

Mrs. Drew initially presents herself as a **complainant** who has tried all she could to help Donald but now feels that professional help is warranted. The therapist will try to involve her, at a later point in the session, in some type of encouraging, **observational task** concerning her son's behavior—a task she can identify. Mrs. Drew clearly wants the practitioner to do something to make their situation better. Mr. Drew is a **customer**, conveying concern about Donald and a willingness to engage in a team effort to make changes.

While Mr. and Mrs. Drew speak, Donald looks down and appears sullen and uncommunicative. Clearly, Donald is a **visitor** at this session, brought because his mom and stepdad feel he has problems that require professional attention. It is time to reach out to him:

Consultant: Donald, what's your theory about why this problem exists? **(problem-finding question)**

Donald: (looks somewhat surprised; responds by shrugging his shoulders) I don't know. . . . I think I'm afraid of getting into trouble.

Consultant: Well, that makes a certain amount of sense to me. Now, let me ask you two questions, Donald. How long has this lying about your troubles been taking charge of your life? **(externalizing the problem so that it does not define Donald)** Have there been any times lately where you have stood up to lying and didn't allow it to get the best of you? **(finding exceptions to the problem)**

Donald (and his parents) smile for the first time and Donald begins to share his story. It becomes clear as he speaks that this young boy is having a very difficult time in school—both academically and with his peers.

Donald: The work was hard this year, especially because I started middle school and got confused when I had to change classes. Then the kids started making fun of me because of my weight. They do it when the teachers aren't looking and it makes me sad. They also think I'm dumb because it takes me a long time to do the work, especially math. I don't like school. I'm afraid to bring my work home because my parents will be upset or take away some privilege so I try to hide it from them. And then suddenly I just started lying about everything.

Consultant: Yes, I can see that lying seems to have taken hold of you somehow. Now, can you or you (turning to parents), Mr. and Mrs. Drew, think of any times in the past when Donald was struggling to handle something? What did you do to help him get back on track?

Mr. Drew: Well, we know that the punishment isn't helping because Donald is very sensitive. He just gets upset or shrugs it off and says he doesn't care.

Mrs. Drew: When he was little, I used to bribe him to do things—that would work.

Consultant: You mean using rewards for jobs well done?

Mrs. Drew: Yes.

Consultant: (turning to Donald) Donald, can you think of anything your Mom and Dad could do to help you get this monkey—this lying monkey—off your back?

Mr. Drew: (jumping in) We could try to be more understanding and not be so quick to punish Donald when he gets a bad grade or makes a mistake.

Donald: (smiling) That would help because sometimes I feel like everybody is against me.

(continued)

Case Example Continued

Mr. Drew: Perhaps Donald and his mother and father should have a meeting with you. Maybe that would help.

(Here the consultant moves from **meaning making** into the process of **goaling**.)

Consultant: These are all good suggestions. I think that by meeting together as we have done today, we can come up with some good solutions to help get family life back on track. Would you like to meet with me again next week? (All agree. The therapist introduces an **observational task**.) Mr. and Mrs. Drew, I would like you to observe Donald over the coming week and write down anything Donald does that is encouraging to both of you and anything you do that is encouraging to Donald during this difficult time. (The therapist uses a **scaling question**.) On a scale of 1 to 10, where would you like to be in a week's time when we meet again?

Mr. Drew: I would be happy with a 4 or a 5.

Mrs. Drew: I agree—that would be nice.

Consultant: (asking a **presuppositional question**) Let's say all of you are eating dinner tonight and you are talking about how successful today's meeting had been. What will have changed with your situation?

Mrs. Drew: (responding immediately) Donald wouldn't be lying—that's the biggest thing in my mind because I would like to be able to trust him again.

Mr. Drew: I agree.

Donald: I wouldn't be in so much trouble any more.

Consultant: (speaking to all three) Would you like to participate in an experiment that I think might help Donald kick this lying habit that has taken hold of him?

The family agrees and seems curious. The consultant introduces the **Do Something Different Task** hoping to get these three people to begin to act differently as they deal with Donald's problematic behaviors.

Consultant: Donald, I would like you to bring home any school papers no matter whether the grade is good or bad. I'd also like you to leave candy wrappers or empty cereal bowls out in plain view rather than trying to hide them away. And Mr. and Mrs. Drew, I'd like you to let Donald know that you appreciate it when you find the candy wrapper or empty cereal bowl he's left out and to thank him when he shows you a grade that he's not too proud of.

As the session with this family is drawing to an end, the therapist offers Mr. and Mrs. Drew and Donald a framework for making the changes they have discussed. The **FFST** a good way to do this:

Consultant: Between now and next time we meet, if you would like to do so, I want you to observe what happens in your family that you want to continue to have happen. This is very important because sometimes, when people are working hard to make changes, they forget about the positive experiences they have together. Donald, you need to be a detective and really help me out by closely watching, maybe by writing it down and reporting back to me next time, so that I will know what works well in your family. Then, we'll all try to figure out how to make more of those good times happen. You can do this

Case Example Continued

on your own sometimes or you can talk it over with your mom and stepdad. Next time, I'd like to first meet alone with you for a while and we'll have a chance to go over what you have observed. Afterward, we'll all meet together again and talk about how you each made out with trying the new things we discussed earlier. How does that feel to you?

The Drew family agree to work on this task, and to meet again in one week's time.

Postassessment Session and Self-Reflection

Following the sessions, the practitioner begins to think about their meeting and develops ideas for their next session. As can clearly be seen from the vignette, Donald is a **visitor** to the counseling session and initially not a happy visitor. Although he did admit to having some problems as the meeting progressed, he was brought to see me because his parents felt he had a problem. In today's session, the therapist made some headway by helping Donald become a **customer**, by reaching out to him in an empathic manner. She was very conscious of how small he appeared to be, sitting in between his concerned but quite upset mother and stepfather, and of his rather desperate attempts to let his family know he wasn't feeling all that happy.

Following this first meeting with the Drew family, the consultant considers the interventions she chose and whether there might be others that she could have used or would use in the next meeting. She made a positive connection with each family member, but more needs to be done to engage Mrs. Drew. The therapist believes that if Donald's behavior continues, Mrs. Drew would be unable to ignore it and would become quite punitive. She decides that next time, she will introduce the idea of **positive consequences**. Mrs. Drew has noted that when Donald was little she used to "bribe him" and this got results. **Positive consequences** will enable the Drews to set limits on Donald's behavior in ways that will draw on his strengths and help the family out of this vicious cycle of poor behavior and negative consequences.

The consultant considers Mr. Drew's suggestion about having a session with his wife and Donald's father. She thinks it is still too early to do this but makes a mental note to try to find a way to open up this line of communication in the future. She hopes that the Drew family will be able to follow through on the assignments they discussed so that the tension among them can abate. The therapist hopes to work with Donald alone to give him an opportunity to talk further about his feelings and perhaps help him find more adaptive coping strategies. Perhaps she will ask Donald how he feels about **inviting one of his friends to the session**—someone who might have some helpful suggestions to offer. The consultant will, of course, have to be sure that Donald feels comfortable with this approach. She makes a mental note to get permission to talk to Donald's teachers and to get their perspective on the problems Donald appears to be having in school. She also thinks it will be important to talk with Donald's pediatrician.

Conclusion

As is illustrated in the Drew family case, solution-focused therapy is a strengths-based model of practice. In this initial assessment, the consultant reaches out to this troubled family with optimism to establish a collaborative working relationship. She respects their right

(continued)

Case Example Continued

of self-determination, invites the family members to discuss their goals for the consultation, and obtains permission for her interventions. She demonstrates her belief that they are capable of change and growth by engaging them in a discussion of ways they have coped with problems in the past. She helps the family give new meaning to Donald's "lying and stealing," reframing these behaviors as alien to him as well as to his parents. In the future, the therapist will use interdisciplinary collaboration to further her understanding and marshal additional resources. Together, the clients and the clinician will construct a solution that will help this family replace their anger and frustration with empowerment and hope.

Crisis Intervention

Greene, Lee, Trask, and Rheinscheld (2000) promote the solution-focused approach to working with clients in crisis situations. They emphasize (1) joining with the client, (2) eliciting the client's definition of the problem, (3) eliciting the client's desired outcome goal, (4) identifying solutions, (5) developing and implementing an action plan, and (6) conducting termination and follow-up. The crisis worker relies on the use of questions as a primary intervention strategy, and the important task of assessing risk is done "in the course of joining, defining problems, and identifying goals and solutions" (p. 69). In addition to the miracle question (previously discussed), the dream question (Lee, Greene, Mentzer, Pinnell, & Niles, 2001) is used to help set goals:

> Suppose that tonight while you are sleeping, you have a dream. In this dream you discover the answers and resources you need to solve the problem that you are concerned about right now. When you wake up tomorrow, you may or may not remember your dream, but you do notice you are different. As you go about starting your day, how will you know that you discovered or developed the skills and resources necessary to solve your problem? What will be the first small bit of evidence that you did this?

Focus is given to coping questions that offer a sense of empowerment to clients at a time when they lose sight of potential resources. Attention is also given to the development of indicators that will tell clients when they may need help in the future, perhaps before a crisis situation develops.

Research Perspectives

Although there are not many studies of either the efficacy or the effectiveness of solution-focused brief therapy, there is some evidence that this is an effective treatment approach (M. Lee, 1997; Lee et al., 2001; Lindfross & Magnusson, 1997; McKeel, 1997; Weiner-Davis, de Shazer, & Gingerich, 1987). A research study done on solution-focused therapy ($n = 64$, eighteen months after completion at the Milwaukee Brief Family Therapy Center) showed that 84 percent of families experienced long-term improvements. All of these families received fewer than 10 sessions of therapy, with an average of 3 sessions (Wylie, 1990). Research done in Sweden found that 80 percent of clients completing solution-focused therapy accomplished their stated treatment goals, and the average length of treatment was five sessions (Andreas, "A Follow-Up of Patients in Solution-Focused Brief Therapy," paper presented at the Institution for Applied Psychology, University of Lund, Sweden, cited in Carlson & Kjos, 2002).

Lipchik, Becker, Brasher, Derks, and Volkmann (2005, p. 55) are working to understand the "fit and incompatibility" of this postmodern theoretical framework with contemporary advances in neuroscience (Cozolino, 2002; Damasio, 2003; Siegel & Hartzel, 2003). They are looking, for example, at the process of dual-track thinking, whereby solution-focused therapists monitor their emotional state and thoughts to avoid getting caught in their clients' emotional and cognitive reactions. They are speculating that this dual-track thinking may involve "mirror neurons," discovered by neuroscientists as important in understanding the development of empathy in therapy. (See Lipchik, 2002, for further information on the integration of neuroscience and solution-focused therapy.)

Summary

Solution-focused therapy, with its thoughtful and creative use of language, offers a range of new clinical possibilities. Its focus on solutions rather than diagnoses makes it well suited for work with clients of all ages and backgrounds. Solution-focused therapists use a wide range of techniques to engage their clients in collaborative therapeutic relationships. Such relationships are especially helpful when working with children and adolescents who are often in counseling at the request or insistence of others. The solution-focused model also offers concerned families the opportunity to see that their children are doing some positive things. Finally, solution-focused therapy embodies the values of the social work profession as the client's innate strengths and resiliency factors are supported and enhanced in the therapeutic contact.

13

Clinical Practice with Children and Adolescents

Clinical treatment of children and adolescents requires a multisystemic team approach. The team includes the child or adolescent; parents; school personnel; the pediatrician; and representatives of environmental influences such as friendship groups, religious and cultural affiliations, child welfare agencies, and the therapist. The social worker—with knowledge of developmental assessment, clinical theory, play therapy, differential diagnosis, and environmental influences—coordinates the team. In this chapter, we discuss the components of child and adolescent treatment. Case examples—using self-psychological play therapy and behavioral therapy—illustrate two different treatment models that apply to work with this population.

Developmental Assessment

Child and adolescent behavioral and emotional problems occur within a developmental context. Knowledge of child development informs assessment, diagnosis, theoretical conceptualization, and treatment planning (Altman, Briggs, Frankel, Gensler, & Pantone, 2002; McCart, Sawyer, & Smith, 2008; O'Connor & Braverman, 2009; Shirk, 1999). Webb (1996, p. 64) suggests a tripartite assessment that attends to the biological, psychological, and sociocultural factors in the child's support system. Genograms (McGoldrick & Gerson, 1985), ecomaps (Hartman, 1978), and culturagrams (Congress, 1994) are also helpful assessment tools (see Chapter 11 for examples of how these tools can be used).

Various developmental frameworks provide a context for child psychotherapy. These include Piaget's (1952a, 1952b) model of cognitive development, Erikson's (1950, 1959) psychosocial model, Freud's (1905/1953) model of psychosexual development, Stern's (1977, 1985) model of self-development, Kail's (2001) model of emotional development, and Kohlberg's (1984) model of moral development. Feminist models, multicultural developmental models, and those that address gay, lesbian, bisexual, and transgender identity development provide important insights into therapy with children and adolescents whose primary identity is different from that of the dominant culture or who may have a number of ethnic identities (Cramer & Gilson, 1999; D'Augelli, 1994; Eliason, 1996; Falicov, 2007; Gonzalez, 2002; Gusman et al., 1996; Hayes, 2008; Oetting & Beauvais, 1990; Sue & Sue, 2003; Sommers-Flanagan & Sommers-Flanagan, 2009).

All of these models provide templates for the cognitive, linguistic, physical, emotional, moral, social, and play development of children within their environmental contexts. It is important to remember that children with the same presenting problems will differ significantly in their cognitive, emotional, and social competencies as well as in the stresses they face in their everyday lives. Shirk (1999, p. 61) refers to this as a "developmental dialectic between the child's capacities and psychosocial demands."

Child Psychopathology

Symptoms of most child and adolescent disorders are manifested during different stages of development; the clinical challenge is to determine whether the behaviors are maladaptive or within the normal range. Davies (2004) presents a nicely organized chronological summary of normal child development. Infant development takes place from birth to 12 months of age, toddler development occurs at 1 to 3 years of age, preschool development occurs at 3 to 6 years of age, and middle childhood development takes place from 6 to 12 years of age.

Several authors discuss the importance of equifinality, multifinality, and heterotypic continuity in a developmental understanding of clinical practice. *Equifinality* means that a single disorder (e.g., dysthymia) can be produced through different developmental pathways (e.g., as a result of ongoing difficulties with peers or in reaction to family problems and stresses). *Multifinality* suggests that the same developmental events may lead to different adaptive and/or maladaptive outcomes. The death of a parent, for example, may result in different ways of coping. *Heterotypic* continuity implies that a given pathological process will be exhibited differently with continued development (e.g., bipolar disorder will have different behavioral manifestations in childhood and adolescence). (For further information, see Cicchetti & Rogosch, 2002; Holmbeck, Greenley, & Franks, 2003; Shirk, 1999.)

Treatment, then, cannot be guided solely by diagnostic manuals such as the *DSM-IV* because they do not attend to the developmental precursors of symptoms and behaviors. The social worker needs to understand the child's cognitive and emotional functioning within a developmental framework and note how this translates into behaviors that can be observed during the clinical interview. These behaviors may include (1) responsiveness to limit setting, (2) impulsivity, (3) distractibility, (4) level of organization in play, (5) responsiveness to interviewer, (6) mood, (7) use of environment, (8) attention span, (9) recurring themes in play and conversation, and (10) social reasoning (Hughes & Baker, 1990, p. 8). Certain conditions, such as anxiety and depressive disorders, among others, emerge during childhood and adolescence, and a social worker's knowledge of child development helps him or her identify these problems and plan for early intervention. Early identification and intervention help the child or adolescent make a healthier transition to later stages of development.

The Clinical Interview

With the Parent(s)

The clinician needs to obtain information from the child or adolescent as well as the parent. We suggest that the initial interview be conducted with the parent(s) when the child is age 12 or younger. In certain instances, the parent of an older adolescent needs to talk first, and this should be respected. Listening to the parents' concerns, answering questions, and providing education about the interdisciplinary approach fosters the therapeutic partnership. Allow time to take a detailed developmental history and to have the parents sign all necessary releases. Review the mandatory reporting laws and limits of confidentiality so that the client knows your role as a mandated reporter of child abuse and neglect.

If the parents are divorced, establish who has custody of the child and discuss how each parent (including the parent who may not be present during the initial interview) will be involved. Contact with both parents, if seen by the child on a regular basis, is always preferable (Wachtel, 1994; Webb, 1996). The initial interview with the parents is also the time to establish what other therapeutic partners might need to be consulted to complete the diagnostic picture. Request permission to talk with the child's pediatrician and obtain results of a recent health examination. Consider getting information from the school adjustment counselor or a teacher. A child psychiatrist, clinical psychologist, or speech-language therapist might be part of the treatment team, especially if the parent or the clinician suspects the presence of a learning disability, attention deficit/hyperactivity disorder (ADHD), or other problems that are manifested in childhood.

Finally, advise the parents on how to explain the therapy to their child. Use developmentally appropriate language. You might, for example, coach a parent of a 4-year-old child attending preschool and not wanting to leave the parent in the morning to say: "I met a very nice woman who plays with children who don't like to say good-bye to their mommies in the morning." Be prepared to talk with the parents about your plan for assessing the child in the child's first interview and how you will be working as you proceed with treatment. This helps the parents feel confident that their child is in the hands of a competent practitioner.

Denborough (2007, pp. 17–20) developed a questionnaire that is designed as a supplementary intake tool that recognizes the particular experiences of mothers of children with disabilities. It also contains questions for the child. This questionnaire is based upon a narrative theoretical framework and includes five parts:

Part I: A History of Care

1. When did you first come to think that your child was different from other children?
2. How did you try to respond to this knowledge?
3. What steps have you taken before coming here?
4. Why did you take these steps?
5. Were there any difficulties along the way?
6. If so, what assisted you to keep persisting—to keep seeking help? Why was this so important to you?

7. What do you think it says about you that you have taken all these steps?
8. What does it say about your commitment to your child?
9. Who would be the least surprised to know that you have this commitment to your child?
10. If they were here now, what might they say about this history of care?

Part II: Current Acts of Care

Physically

1. Are there ways in which you care/support/assist your child physically?

Emotionally

1. Are there ways in which you care/support/assist your child emotionally?
2. When he/she is upset, how do you respond?

Relationships with others

1. Are there ways in which you care/support/assist your child with relationships with others, such as siblings, or other family members?

Other people's care

1. Are there other people who assist in caring for your child?
2. If so, who are these people?
3. Why do you think they assist in this caring?
4. What do they value and appreciate about you and your child?

History of these skills

1. It seems you care for your child in so many different ways; how did you learn to care for your child in these ways?
2. Who taught you these skills? Who did you learn caring from?
3. What would they say about the ways in which you are using these skills to care for your child?

Part III: Responding to Blame and Stigma

Responding to Blame

1. Is blame a part of your life?
2. What effects does blame have on your life and what you think about yourself?
3. What effect does blame have on your relationships with other family members?
4. What effect does blame have on your relationship with your child?
5. What effect does blame have on your child's life?
6. When does it do the most harm?
7. Are there times when blame is not so powerful?
8. Are there people, friends, family members who do not support blame?
9. Who is most supportive? Why do you think they are supportive? What do they value about you? Why do they care about you?
10. Are there ways in which you have found to cope with blame? When blame is present are there any ways in which you protect yourself?

Responding to Stigma

1. Is stigma a part of your life?
2. What effects does stigma have on your life and what you think about yourself?

3. What effects does stigma have on your relationship with other family members?
4. What effects does stigma have on your child's life?
5. When is stigma the most powerful?
6. What does it do the most harm?
7. Are there times when stigma is not so powerful?
8. Are there people, friends, family members who do not support stigma?
9. Who is most supportive? Why do you think they are supportive? What do they value about you? Why do they care about your and your child?
10. Are there ways in which you have found to cope with stigma? When stigma is present are there any ways in which you protect yourself and your child?

Part IV: Questions for the Child

1. What are some times when you are most happy?
2. Can you tell me a story of a happy occasion?
3. What do you most enjoy doing?
4. Why do you enjoy this the most?
5. What are you thinking when you are doing these things?
6. Who are the most precious people to you in your life?
7. Why do you care about them?
8. Are there people who care for you, who look after you, who support you? If so, who are those people?
9. How do they care for you?
10. Is this good? Why?
11. Are there times when you try to be kind and caring to others?
12. How do you try to do this?
13. Why do you do this?
14. Do you have any favorite toys or games?
15. What do you like about them?

Part V: Offering Back a Reflection

When the interview is complete, the mother and child will be given some feedback or response that will offer a healing acknowledgment of the skills, knowledge, and stories they have shared. In an individual setting, the counselor can offer a reflection based on several questions:

1. As you listened to the mother speak, what things did she say that particularly caught your attention or sparked your imagination?
2. As you listened to her say these things, what images of her life, or of the world more generally, did you picture in your mind? What did the things the mother said suggest to you about what this mother stands for in life, about her values, beliefs, hopes, dreams, and commitments?
3. Why was this most significant to you? What is it about your own life that explains why these things caught your attention or struck a chord for you?

4. How have you been moved by hearing this mother's stories? Where has this experience taken you to, that you would not otherwise have arrived at, if you hadn't heard her stories? What difference has it made to you? What difference might this make to your work with other mothers?

In a group setting, the counselor can interview one mother using the questionnaire, while the other mothers listen. At the end of the interview, the counselor turns to the other women and asks them the four reflection questions described earlier. Each of the group members then can have a chance to answer these questions, focusing on different aspects of the story they have heard from the mother. These reflections from the other mothers can also be very helpful in providing a healing acknowledgment of the skills, knowledge, and stories of the mother who was interviewed.

With the Child or Adolescent

We recommend that the clinician meet with the parents and the child together for the first 10 to 15 minutes of the first session. During this time, the child or adolescent (who is still a minor) can hear why the parent has brought her to see the therapist (Wachtel, 1994). This meeting helps establish rapport so that later in the session, when the child or adolescent meets alone with the therapist, she knows why the parent has brought her for counseling. Then, the therapist might say, "I can see your point, but it sounds like your parents see it differently. What do you think about their point of view?" Keep toys within view when working with younger children. You may want to sit on the floor and engage in some play as you talk with the parents to find out the reason they are bringing the child to "visit" you. In a developmentally sensitive interview, the communication process may rely more on play than words (Gil & Shaw, 2009; Hughes & Baker, 1990; Lee, 2009; O'Connor, 2000; Sweeney & Landreth, 2009).

Adolescent clients are often silent in initial interviews when parents are present. Use the time to establish the boundaries of the relationship with the adolescent and the parents and refrain from pushing the adolescent to talk. Taffel (2005) suggests beginning the first meeting with an adolescent by inquiring about his or her interests in life as opposed to focusing on problems. He also emphasizes the importance of talking with adolescents about their "second family"—the peer group and pop culture. Taffel engages his adolescent clients in a "theme-specific sociogram" (p. 37). He draws a circle in the center of the page and, together with the adolescent, fills in circles with the names of friends—beginning with the person closest to the center circle, or the adolescent client. A series of questions about this second family includes "What do your friends like to do?" "Who likes to hang out with whom?" and "Who gives the best advice?" (p. 38).

Confidentiality

Review confidentiality within a developmentally appropriate context. Younger children expect parents to be involved in their lives (Wachtel, 1994), but adolescents may feel differently. We suggest being flexible when discussing the guidelines for disclosure. Use language such as, "I will be meeting alone with ________ but, from time to time, we may want to involve you (the parent) in a session." Be clear and honest with adolescents about the need to inform parents about high-risk behaviors. The following brief example demonstrates how to engage an adolescent in a discussion of confidentiality: "You're telling me some things right now that I have a lot of concern about. I know you won't like hearing this, but I feel strongly that we need to bring your parents on board for this conversation. Tell me how we can work together to tell them."

Reamer (2003, 2005) considers the standard of care as the basis for decisions regarding what information should be shared with the parents of a child or adolescent. This standard is defined as "the steps that an ordinary, reasonable, and prudent social worker should take when deciding how to handle complex circumstances involving private, confidential, and privileged information" and includes (1) consulting with colleagues; (2) obtaining proper supervision; (3) reviewing relevant ethical standards; (4) reviewing relevant regulations, laws, and policies; (5) reviewing relevant literature; (6) obtaining legal consultation when necessary; and (7) documenting the decision-making process.

Learning Disturbances

Learning problems manifest in a variety of ways. Included are problems of intelligence, specific cognitive disabilities, interrelations of specific cognitive deficits and broader psychological functioning, a specific symptom secondary to other psychological conditions, a reflection of disturbance in object relations, a part of a general character trait, a family-based disinterest in learning, or the result of the effects of poverty and social disadvantages (Elbaum & Vaughn, 2003). Palombo (2001a) suggests that dyslexia (pp. 122–123), ADHD (pp. 144–145), executive function disorders (pp. 164–165), and nonverbal learning disabilities (pp. 192–193) are most often associated with self-esteem problems because these children are often introspective, self-conscious, and sensitive to others' expectations of them. Learning and emotional disorders interface, and mental health clinicians need to team up with practitioners from other disciplines to provide comprehensive services to clients who are at risk of any of these complex disorders (Lesser & Pope, 2010). Siegel (1999, p. 21) discusses a model of "interpersonal neurobiology" that integrates scientific findings from a range of disciplines. This model conceptualizes the human mind as developing at the interface of neurophysiological processes and interpersonal relationships. Neuropsychological and educational testing is often warranted in these cases to facilitate an early and accurate diagnosis and intervention plan.

Play Therapy

Play is the child's language of expression. We concur with the definition of play therapy introduced by the Association for Play Therapy (1997) and expanded on by O'Connor (2000):

> *Play therapy* consists of a cluster of treatment modalities. It involves the systematic use of a theoretical model to establish an interpersonal process wherein trained play therapists use the therapeutic powers of play to help clients prevent or resolve psychosocial difficulties,

achieve optimal growth and development, and re-establish the child's ability to engage in play behaviors as they are classically defined in childhood. (p. 7)

The many theoretical models of play therapy include psychoanalytic (Ablon, 2001; Altman et al., 2002; Lee, 2009; Neubauer, 2001), humanistic, cognitive behavioral (Knell, 1997, 1998, 2009; M. Lee, 1997), child-centered (Sweeney & Landreth, 2009), developmental (Brody, 1997; Jernberg, 1979), and filial (Guerney, 1997; VanFleet, 1994, 2009). Each model uses play in a different way. In psychoanalytic play therapy, the therapist interprets the child's play metaphorically through the use of objects in the play. Play, in a behavioral approach, is used to reinforce or extinguish behaviors. Cognitive play therapy encourages modeling of adaptive behaviors and thought processes (O'Connor, 2000). Play therapies are further differentiated by styles. In directive play therapy, the therapist assumes responsibility for guidance and interpretation of the play (Gil, 1991). Nondirective play therapy relies on the child's ability to direct the process and pace of the play. The developmental age of the child further defines the type of play therapy plan (O'Connor, 2000). It is important to explain what play therapy is to the child's parent or guardian and to address any doubts or misconceptions they may have about this modality of treatment. The Association for Play Therapy has a website (A4PT.org) with many informative materials that clinicians may find helpful in working with parents.

Each of the theories presented in this book may contribute to an understanding of different aspects of a child's development. Behavioral protocols that involve parents are appropriate for young children. Older children with more advanced cognitive abilities may benefit from a cognitive approach that relies on the modification of cognitive structures and processes (Kendall, 2000). Research has shown that cognitive behavioral treatment for depression with adolescents is quite successful because adolescents are capable of the level of abstract reasoning central to this form of therapy (Kendall, 2000; Marcotte, 1997). Strategies that focus on self-control may also be more useful with older adolescents (Holmbeck et al., 2003). Psychodynamic models of play therapy are useful in work with young children. Play has an abreactive value, can help to establish a relationship, and is useful in gathering information related to intrapsychic conflict (Ablon, 2001; Altman et al., 2002; Lee, 2009; Neubauer, 2001). Gallo-Lopez and Schaefer (2005) offer a range of play therapy interventions geared toward adolescents that are specifically used to foster a therapeutic alliance. Older children and adolescents with some capacity for verbal expression and insight may benefit from interpretations that make the client's conflicts conscious and allow for behavioral change (O'Connor, 2000). Gil (1994) and Ariel (2005) offer suggestions on how to integrate play therapy with family therapy as it has the potential to engage all family members in meaningful therapeutic exchange. When play is included in family sessions, clinicians treat children as equally important family members rather than imposing the adult world on them by responding only to verbal communication. Finally, it is important to appreciate the significance of cultural competence in the application of any of these models to work with children and adolescents.

The following case examples demonstrate the application of two different child and adolescent therapy models—self-psychological play therapy and behavioral modification.

Case Example: Play Therapy

Rosa: A Child Suffering from Selective Mutism

Client Information. Rosa, a 10-year-old Puerto Rican girl, lives with her mother, father, and two older sisters. The family is Pentecostal, Spanish-speaking, with a large extended family living in Puerto Rico. They visit Puerto Rico at least twice a year. Rosa was referred for school-based counseling services by her teacher because she was "not speaking in school." Rosa was diagnosed with selective mutism, "a disorder of childhood characterized by the total lack of speech in at least one specific situation (usually the classroom) despite the ability to speak in other situations" (Dow, 1995, p. 1) (see *Diagnostic and Statistical Manual of Mental Disorders*, 2000, for complete diagnostic criteria). Her mother described Rosa as "only speaking in the home" and "not outside the home," even when in the company of her family. She reported that this condition began when Rosa was 4 years old, when she soiled herself in preschool after being denied permission to go to the bathroom. Subsequently, Rosa's family moved back to Puerto Rico for a four-year period before returning to the United States. Rosa, according to her mother, stopped speaking in school after the event, both here and in Puerto Rico.

Assessment of Rosa. Meyers (1984, pp. 41–42) describes several characteristics common to families where a child has selective mutism. These apply to Rosa and her family and include (1) an intense attachment to another family member, usually the mother; (2) suspicion of the residents in a low socioeconomic inner city; (3) fear of strangers; (4) language difficulties; (5) marital disharmony; and (6) mutism modeling.

Several authors (Bradley & Sloman, 1975; Eizur & Perednik, 2003; Hollifel, Geppert, Johnson, & Fryer, 2002; Steinhausen and Juzi,1996) write about a cultural component in selective mutism. They suggest that children who fail at mastering a new, second language can develop selective mutism as a way of coping. They also assert that children of immigrants are more likely not to speak in classrooms, regardless of their understanding of the dominant language.

Rosa was 4 years old and mastering language development—bilingual language development—when the bathroom incident occurred. She may have associated her "accident" with a failed attempt at language mastery and retreated into the world of silence.

Self-Psychological Play Therapy with Rosa. The clinician, a white, bilingual (English/Spanish) female, recognized the importance of language and culture in treatment of Rosa. She selected a self-psychological bilingual approach and conceptualized her role as that of a self-object who would provide idealizing, mirroring, and alter ego self-object functions (see Chapter 7). Therapy was conducted in Spanish to establish an empathic relationship. Landreth (2002) and Sweeney and Landreth (2009) emphasize the importance of the therapist's authenticity, warmth, and acceptance, as well as an ability to connect to the child's world. Miller's (1996) application of self-psychology to work with children further helps in understanding Rosa. He speaks of (1) the child's need for others, (2) the child's will to do, and (3) the principle of internal harmony. These are necessary for the development of a healthy self-structure, are present in a fragmented form by mutism, and are described in detail.

Need for Others. Rosa's need for others may not have always been optimally met outside of her home. Disruptions in language acquisition, compromised by numerous moves between English- and Spanish-speaking countries, may have contributed to difficulties in

Case Example Continued

Rosa's development of a sense of self at the crucial developmental stage when words are important in interpersonal relationships. Her parents, able to function psychologically as protectors and as providers of emotional support in the home, may not have been able to do so in the larger, English-speaking environment because of their own language constraints. How frightening this must have been for Rosa—precipitously torn from the self-object merger with her parents because of language. The idealizing relationship with the parents provides a model for the self-organization of the child. It is interesting and not surprising that Rosa speaks in her house, where Spanish is the language of the family.

Will to Do. Rosa's refusal to speak tells everyone of her power. However, her will to do is not free to focus on the normal developmental tasks of her age, such as school performance and social interaction with peers. Rosa remains caught in a bind: She can either succeed at maintaining her sense of cohesion or fail at growing up.

Internal Harmony. The principle of internal harmony is both a motivational force and the main mechanism of experience that becomes part of the self-structure. Rosa is trying her best to integrate the frustration, anger, and loneliness of unmet self-object needs with the conflicts of her developmental age, and so she stops speaking.

Rosa's need for others, will to do, and internal harmony begin to be met in new ways by the therapist through play therapy conducted in Spanish. The English-speaking therapist can negotiate the English-speaking environment on behalf of her clients and can provide an important anxiety-reducing buffer for Rosa. As a primary self-object support, the therapist becomes a role model and figure for identification (Miller, 1996). She affirms Rosa as the admired child within the context of play therapy. This admired child has a fuller command of the language (Spanish) that she and the therapist need to use to communicate. This is demonstrated in the following exchange between Rosa and the worker. The play puppets hold Rosa's voice until she is able to speak herself.

Therapist: Tiger? (speaking to tiger puppet) Do you think you can help me with my Spanish today?
Rosa: (no response)
Therapist: My Spanish is pretty bad and tigers know a lot.
Rosa: (no response)
Therapist: Tiger? Are you there?
Rosa: (walks over to the puppet box that the worker was sitting in and puts Tiger on the window of the box)
Therapist: So, will you help to teach me Spanish, Tiger?
Rosa: (nods the tiger's head yes)
Therapist: Wonderful. You know so much Spanish—I will be lucky to have your help. Thank you so much.

This type of exchange, interspersed with moments of sharing—another important part of both mirroring and idealizing relationships—continued throughout the play sessions. Miller (1996, p. 41) describes sharing "as an awareness of the underlying unity of

(continued)

Case Example Continued

self and object that defines all self object experiences." The therapist and Rosa share the experience of reading books (in Spanish), using play telephones, and writing notes. Therapy culminates with Rosa writing a book about her life, sharing it with the therapist during sessions, and reading it when it is completed.

Source: Case material supplied by Ariel Perry.

Behavioral Therapy

Behavioral therapy is particularly effective with young children because it can be taught to the parent, who then applies the method at home (Barkley, 2003a; Kendall, 2000; Kneel, 2009; Smith, Barkley, & Shapiro, 2006, 2007). The parent learns from the experience and can then take credit for being instrumental in producing change. One can obtain rapid results with behavioral therapy, and the pretreatment and intervention periods can be monitored by using single-subject design methodology (see Chapter 14 on integrating research and practice). This next case illustrates behavioral therapy for a child with temper tantrums.

Case Example: Child Behavioral Therapy

Jenny: Working with a Parent

Jenny is a 4-year-old African American child whose single mother requested help. Jenny's behavior in school was appropriate, but at home she exhibited temper tantrums whenever she did not get her way. Jenny's mother, Mrs. P., frustrated and angry, tried bribing, screaming, spanking, and punishing to end the tantrums—all to no effect. The worker determined that she would intervene with Mrs. P., and not Jenny, because of Jenny's development stage. She selected a behavioral protocol from Phelan (1995)—a simple counting method combined with a "no talking–no emotion" rule. She instructed Mrs. P. that when unacceptable behavior occurred, Jenny was to be told that the behavior was "unacceptable," followed by the words: "That's ONE." If Jenny did not respond, Mrs. P. was to say: "Jenny, that's TWO." If Jenny did not comply by the third time, Mrs. P. was to say "Jenny, That's THREE, take four minutes" (one minute for each year of her age). Jenny was then immediately sent to a time-out area to serve the allotted four minutes of time. If Jenny had a temper tantrum before the time out, Mrs. P. was instructed to wait until the tantrum was over and then request, calmly, that Jenny serve the time out. Mrs. P. was also encouraged to reinforce all of Jenny's positive behavior with praise and extra incentives such as delaying bedtime to watch a special TV movie or playing a special game. The worker developed a daily chart with Mrs. P. so that she and Jenny could keep track of Jenny's temper tantrums (see Figure 13.1). Jenny would receive a sticker on the chart every day that she did not get a time out. Seven stickers would earn her special privileges.

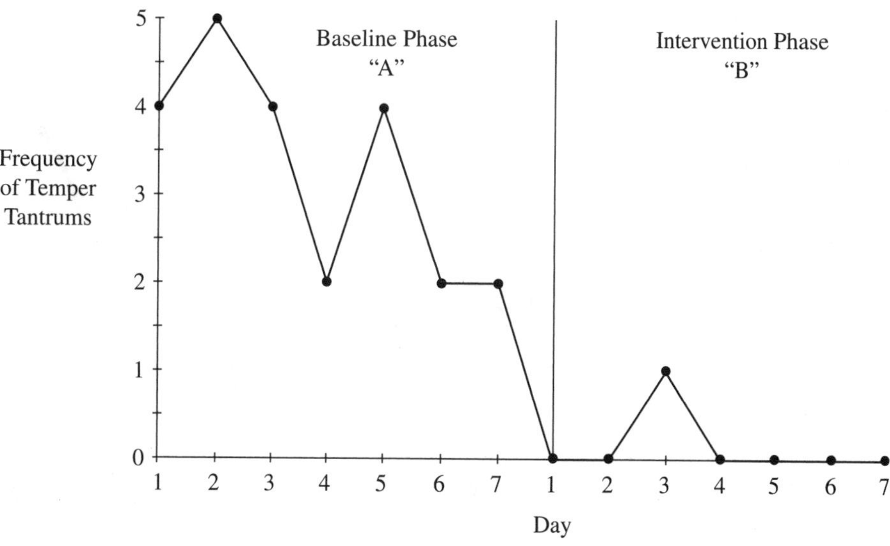

FIGURE 13.1 ***Jenny's Temper Tantrums***

Case Example Continued

Mrs. P. collected baseline data for seven days before intervention took place. The therapist and client looked at the data and learned that when Mrs. P. asked for compliance and Jenny didn't wish to obey, a tantrum followed. The program began in the second week. Jenny had a rapid, positive response. She adjusted quickly, and her temper tantrums decreased. Data on baseline and intervention phases of the work are visually demonstrated in Figure 13.1. Graphing data allows both worker and client to see, just by eyeballing, if results have been obtained. The downward direction of the trend line informs immediately that Jenny's temper tantrums have decreased.

Case Example: Adolescent Behavioral Therapy

Bruce: A Child Diagnosed with ADD and ODD

Mrs. J., a 35-year-old white, single mother, sought treatment for her 12-year-old son who was having difficulty progressing in school. Mrs. J. felt that Bruce was immature for his age and oppositional at home. Homework was a major struggle. The social worker used the multisystemic team approach (described earlier in this chapter). A psychologist and psychiatrist were consulted and evaluations were completed. Bruce was diagnosed with attention deficit disorder (ADD) and oppositional defiant disorder (ODD) and prescribed psychotropic medication.

(continued)

Case Example Continued

The social worker also met with his teachers and the child study team to help them understand Bruce's behaviors within a developmental context, and, as a result, academic adjustments were made to provide educational support services and an individualized educational plan.

Obviously, Mrs. J. needed help in parenting this difficult child. The worker might have intervened with Bruce in behavioral play therapy, but this would not have helped Mrs. J. feel empowered in her role as parent. Again, as in Jenny's case, the parent became the client. Homework was selected as the target for change and a token economy was employed as the intervention. Token economies work well with children and adolescents (see, for example, Barkley, 2002, 2003a, 2003b) because they involve positive reinforcement with tokens that can then be exchanged for privileges or material rewards.

The worker taught Mrs. J. how to develop this system with Bruce, using poker chips as tokens. Different color chips had different point values and were redeemed for rewards.

Everyday rewards had lower point values, whereas weekend and special rewards had higher values. A red poker chip, for example, was worth 5 points, and Bruce could earn one for every 20 minutes of staying on task with homework, without giving up or demonstrating oppositional behavior. (After 20 minutes, Bruce was given a 5-minute break and then instructed to return to the task.) Figure 13.2 illustrates Bruce's reward system.

During the first week (baseline), there was no reinforcement for Bruce's target behavior—staying on task with homework for 20 minutes without quitting or displaying oppositional behaviors. Bruce spent between 25 and 48 minutes on task without his behavior deteriorating during this time period. Reinforcement for appropriate behavior began in the second week. Over the next four weeks, Bruce's time spent on task gradually grew longer. Bruce was reinforced with poker chips for appropriate behavior. As the amount of time spent doing homework increased, so did the number of chips that Bruce received (see Figure 13.3).

As treatment progressed, Bruce was able to increase the weekly time that he spent on homework without arguing, crying, making demands on his mom, quitting, or otherwise displaying oppositional behaviors. As can be seen in Figure 13.4, Bruce's appropriate homework

Everyday	Weekends	Specials
½ hour of ball playing (10 points)	Eating at restaurant (50 points)	Extra trip to New York (120 points)
½ hour of video games (15 points)	Renting a video game (50 points)	Having a sleep-over (90 points)
1 hour of ball playing (15 points)	Play day (50 points)	
1 hour of video games (20 points)		
Eating at McDonald's (20 points)		

FIGURE 13.2 *Bruce's Rewards*

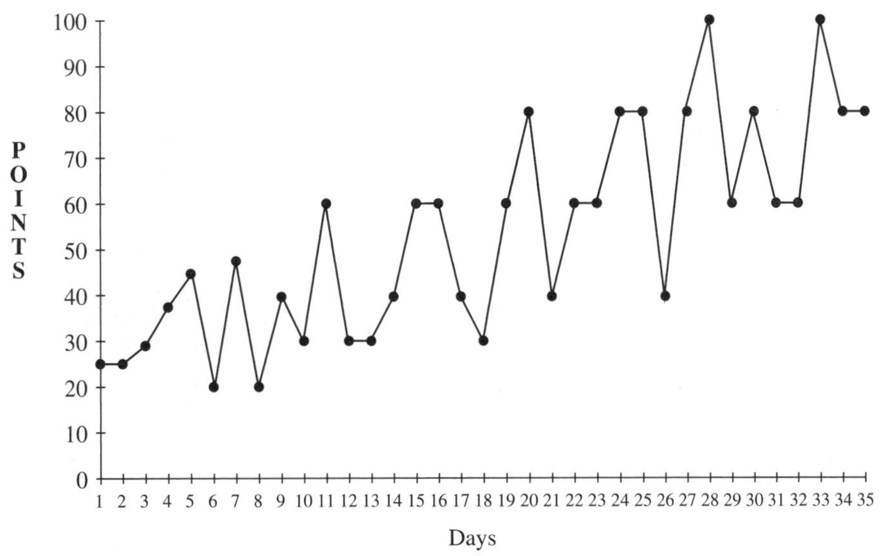

FIGURE 13.3 *Points Earned during Five-Week Intervention*

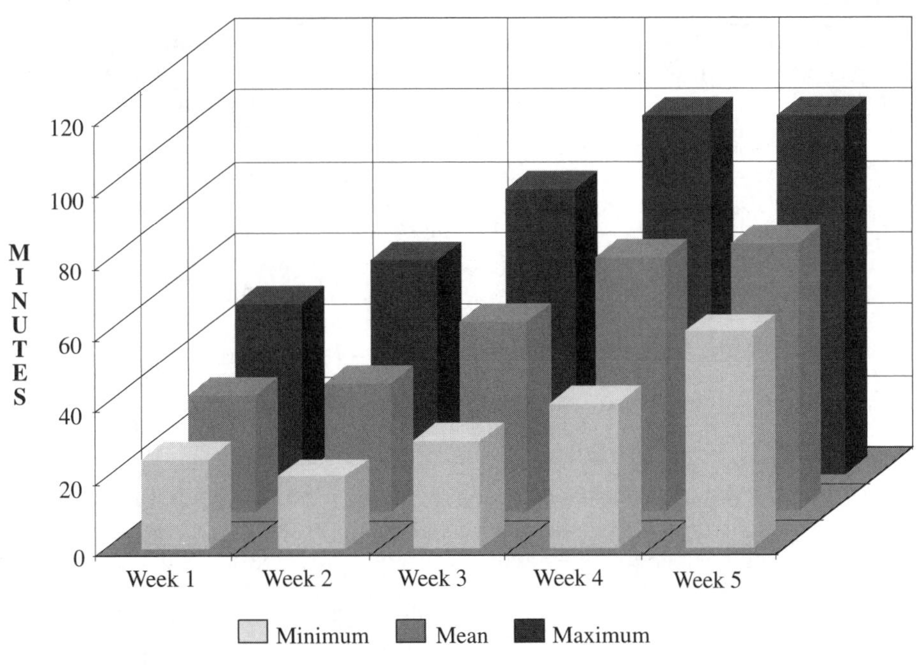

FIGURE 13.4 *Bruce's Weekly Program: Staying on Task*

Case Example Continued

behavior climbed from a weekly average of 33 minutes to a weekly average of 75 minutes (note the minutes on the vertical axis). The minimum and maximum times spent on task also increased. Mrs. J. felt relieved that Bruce was more compliant, proud of his increasing academic success, and empowered in her role as parent.

Working with Parents

It is important to discuss the emotional toll on parents of children such as Rose and Bruce. Therapists who work with children and adolescents may want to consider parent education groups to provide psychoeducation in a supportive environment. Barkley and colleagues (see, for example, 2003, 2005, 2006, 2007) write extensively about children with ADHD, and a behavioral training manual has been developed for use in psychoeducational parenting groups to manage child noncompliance (Barkley, 2002). This manual can be adapted for work with individual clients. Barkley teaches parents that children misbehave to gain positive consequences or rewards, or to escape unpleasant or boring activities such as chores. Oppositional behavior is then seen as a way to escape parental commands. Stressful events in families (single parenting, financial troubles, tension between family members) affect the way that parents manage child noncompliance. A parent under stress can increase noncompliance by giving in or responding inconsistently. A reciprocal interaction occurs, and the behavioral pattern becomes fixed. Barkley's step-by-step program for parents includes some of the following skill-building exercises:

1. *Paying Attention to Positive Child Behavior and Ignoring Negative Behaviors.* A technique called *special time* is introduced. The parent spends 20 minutes a day with the child at a designated time and the child selects the activity. The parent watches the child at play, narrating with enthusiasm the child's activities, much like a sports announcer narrates a ball game. The parent neither intrudes nor directs play. The child then develops the idea that the parent is interested in what he is doing.

2. *Increasing Compliance and Independent Play.* This skill develops parent's ability to give straightforward effective commands. Parents are taught to neutrally and directly ask the child to do something, such as "pick up yours toys" or "turn off the TV." There is no coaxing, cajoling, or asking as a favor. Praise immediately follows the child's compliance. (Hugs, thumbs up, "good girl.") The parent sets up compliance training sessions of 3 to 5 minutes a day that are almost effortless for the child. A parent might ask to "please hand me a tissue," followed by praise. These "fetching" sessions provide numerous, easy opportunities for children to comply and for parents to follow with praise.

3. *Poker Chips and Points.* The parent allows the child to get additional rewards through a token economy system as described in the case of Bruce.

4. *Time Out and Other Disciplinary Methods.* Time out consists of placing a chair facing the wall of a room. Parents are to give a command in a neutral tone and not back down. If compliance isn't immediate, the parent counts backward from 5 to 1. If the child doesn't begin to comply, the parent warns the child that "if you don't do as I say, you will sit in that chair." The parent then counts down again. If the child doesn't comply, he is told that "you did not do as I said, so you are going to the chair." The child is taken to the chair, and told

***Case Example* Continued**

to sit there "until I say you can get up." The child should remain in the chair for at least 1 to 2 minutes for each year that he or she is old. Many children beg or cajole to be released, but the parent is told not to engage. Guidelines are given for managing children who leave the chair without permission: "the child is warned she will be sent to her room and placed on the bed."

5. *Extending Time Out to Misbehavior in Public Places.* Parents are taught to use rest room areas in restaurants, crying rooms in churches, dress racks in department stores, and so on for time-out locations should the child misbehave when away from home.

6. *Improving School Behavior.* This skill is implemented along with the child's teacher to send progress reports from school to home. Poker chips or points can be earned, or taken away, depending on the positive or negative ratings on the report card.

Notice that the initial part of the program is nonpunitive and consists only of positive reinforcement. Many parents object to this, feeling that they shouldn't give praise when their child has behaved so badly. Parents need help to understand how effective positive reinforcement can be. Parents must also be reinforced by the therapist for their efforts at positive parenting.

Leone (2001, p. 278) writing from a self-psychological perspective, suggests that educating interventions should be considered within the overall context of an "empathically attuned response" to the parents' self-object needs. One such group initiated by a therapist in a private practice setting focused on providing education and support to parents with children similar to Bruce, also diagnosed with ADHD and ODD. Many of the parents in the group were initially angry and frustrated with their children. The therapist empathized with their feelings and provided information on token programs. As the parents felt accepted by the leader and by each other, they were able to share more of their worries and concerns about their children. The group was then able to move to a discussion of the many strengths their children had and how these were sometimes overlooked. The therapist facilitated discussions about the joys as well as the challenges they faced in parenting these children they loved so much.

Summary

The knowledge base of child and adolescent therapy has depth and breadth. It includes an understanding of child development, the environment, cultural, and religious factors, various theoretical models and styles of play therapy, and learning disturbances. Social workers need a multitude of skills. Additionally, social workers must be comfortable facilitating and often leading a treatment team. They need to know the community resources and the legislation that affects the lives of children and adolescents. An appreciation of the difficulties of parenting in today's complex world and empathy for parents' struggles is also imperative. Beginning workers need to be careful not to overidentify with the child client, because they may risk alienating the parent.

14

Integrating Research and Practice

New demands on social workers call for an integration of research and practice. There is a movement to develop a strong evidence base when making decisions about services to clients. Social workers also need to meet the demands of accountability by evaluating the effectiveness of their interventions. They are also called on to add to the body of knowledge about clients' lived experiences and the various agencies in which they work. This chapter addresses all three of these current areas of concern.

Evidence-Based Practice

Evidence-based social work practice (EBP) has been widely adopted in the United Kingdom and increasingly in the United States. It has origins in evidence-based medicine, whose leading figures emphasized that clinicians use their scientific training and judgment to interpret guidelines and individualize patient care (Gray, 2001). Evidence-based practice developed as an alternative to authority-based decision making. Authority-based practice relied on criteria such as consensus, anecdotal experience, and tradition for decision making (Gambrill, 2004). Whenever possible, EBP allows for the consideration of client preferences, rather than practitioner preferences, and for transparency—a candid discussion between the social worker and the client regarding the evidence presented in the research, and ethical decision making regarding the change process.

In its most general form, EBP is a major dimension of professional education and a way of attempting to arrive at a consensus about what collective bodies of research findings recommend (Witkin & Harrison, 2001). Rosen and Proctor (2002) describe EBP as the practice of selecting interventions that are based on their empirically demonstrated links to desired outcomes. McNeil (2006) and Sackett, Straus, Richardson, Rosenberg, and Haynes (2000) define evidence-based practice as an integration of clinical expertise and client values with the best available evidence from systematic research, within the parameters of agency context. Rosen, Procter, and Staudt (1999) list the domains of knowledge needed to support EBP: descriptive knowledge to conduct assessment, explanatory knowledge that examines linkages between client problems and the environment, and control knowledge that refers to the relative success of clinical interventions used in practice.

Through the use of EBP skills, social workers attempt to provide quality services to clients that are informed by practice experience and critical thinking, supported by the evidence, consistent with clients' personal and cultural values, and applied during all phases of the therapeutic work (Cournoyer, 2004, p. 19). At its best, EBP enables the development of a truly collaborative relationship between the social work practitioner and the client and respects the hallmark value of client self-determination.

The move toward evidence-based practice is not without controversy. From a practical standpoint, there are obstacles to the use of EBP in the context of agency practice. Social workers today are handling large caseloads and multiple responsibilities. They do not always have time to search out current research findings, and they cannot always gain access to current knowledge. In addition, social workers do not always find consensus in the literature on what constitutes "reasonable and adequate" scientific evidence of safe and beneficial treatment (Beutler, 2001, p. 1001). Even social workers who like the idea of EBP need considerable expertise in how to evaluate research design, methodology, and analysis (McNeil, 2006).

Many providers have contributed to the development of treatment guidelines. This approach makes sense, because clinicians are increasingly being asked why they chose particular interventions and how such choices are justified economically (Addis, Wade, & Hatgis, 1999, p. 431). However, it should be recalled that throughout this book we have emphasized that clinical social work treatment is neither static nor mechanistic. It is an interactive process between client and worker—a complex process that characterizes clinical practice as both an art *and* a science (Larner, 2004).

Careful attention to concepts such as the therapeutic alliance, client–worker collaboration, transference, and countertransference apply in all interactions with patients (Gabbard, 2001). Krupnick and colleagues (1996) demonstrated that in depressed patients, the therapeutic alliance was just as important in pharmacotherapy as it was in psychotherapy. They noted that transference-based perceptions of the therapist grounded on the internalized working models from early experience could impair the patient's capacity to form a collaborative relationship and to participate in the therapeutic alliance. By making a special effort to reach such patients through sensitive and empathic communication, Gabbard (2001) believes that health care providers may help improve treatment adherence. Luborsky, Digiuer, Luborsky, Singer, and Dickter (1993) note that some therapies require naturalistic, open treatment conditions that allow patients to seek the treatment they think would be best for them, to define the goals of the treatment, and to explore unexpected issues that emerge in the treatment process. These therapies may not lend themselves to randomized clinical trials, but they should not be undervalued. These authors further note that much of the promotion of EBP has been prompted by the demands of third-party insurance payers on providers for lowered costs and objective psychotherapy outcomes. Strupp (2001) argues strongly against EBP criteria that assume psychotherapy can be examined independent of the relational context. Bryceland and Stam (2005) caution against the possible delegitimization of psychodynamic, humanistic, and postmodern therapies that, although well supported by empirical research, do not fit the restricted criteria of EBP. Psychotherapy process research that emphasizes the importance of nonspecific factors such as the therapeutic relationship, common to all therapies, and thought to be the strongest predictor of therapeutic outcome regardless of technique, is important as well. Messer (2004, p. 589) suggests that such an approach encompasses "a theoretical formulation, empirically supported treatments (ESTs), empirically supported therapy relationships, clinicians' accumulated practical experience, and their clinical judgment about the case at hand."

Adams and Matto (2009) emphasize that the development of fundamental knowledge and skills is just as important to good practice as being updated on knowledge from an evidence base. They point out that social work espouses a unique person in environment approach, with consideration of families, communities, and larger social systems. Most medical procedures are discrete and can be followed with precision, but in social work, focus on discrete symptoms and problems is less appropriate. Beutler (2001) proposes that effective psychotherapy training should focus more on understanding the basic principles and strategies of change than on scientific knowledge. Along with Beutler and Harwood (2000), he defined six keys to success for therapists in training. Arranged in order of importance, they are (1) therapeutic attitudes of acceptance and respect, (2) knowledge of the principles of change, (3) tools to allow and motivate change, (4) techniques to implement the principles, (5) time to allow change, and (6) imagination to come up with new applications to fit new situations. Goldstein (2007) adds to this that without training social workers to understand the reciprocal interactions between theory and the evidence base, the profession will be training technicians who can find research studies and follow guidelines, but who can't appropriately apply and adapt this knowledge to their practice context.

Persons (2005) argues for an empirical approach to case formulation, driven by both empirical findings and empirical methods of working, rather than an evidence-based approach. Empirical methods include a hypothesis-testing approach to treatment, where the formulation acts as the central hypothesis about the mechanisms causing and maintaining the problem. Before treatment begins, therapist and patient set clear, measurable goals, and then carefully monitor the process and progress of the treatment at each step. The effectiveness of the intervention plan provides some evidence about the accuracy or utility of the formulation. Change strategies can be employed as the formulation is validated.

McNeil (2006) makes the following recommendations to help social workers utilize evidence-based practice:

1. Increased availability of systematic reviews of literature, including the development of practice guidelines.
2. Continued efforts to map differential effectiveness of interventions and combinations of interventions.
3. Consolidated efforts by social agencies and universities to create and translate relevant practice knowledge with specific populations.
4. Greater use of the Internet and other electronic learning techniques. An example is the Campbell Collaboration (www.campbellcollaboration.org), which seeks to inform social workers about effective interventions in the social, behavioral, and educational fields.

5. More Ph.D. prepared social workers in clinical settings to serve as knowledge brokers.
6. Greater integration of EBP in teaching curricula.
7. Research into the challenges that social workers experience when trying to implement EBP.

Evidence-based practice has much to offer the social work profession. It respects the clients' right to self-determination by providing clients with knowledge about the treatment and services they receive, and it gives primacy to ethical issues such as informed consent. It allows for collaboration in the change process. It motivates practitioners to keep current with the literature and to become "life-long learners and rigorous appraisers of practice and policy issues" (Gambrill, 2004). However, clinical practice is not pure science. It is based on principles "that allow the patient to explore new ideas in the safety of the office, to help change the person's complex and multisymptomatic life, to make the patient feel and act better, and to overcome the problems imposed by the patient's particular complex environment" (Beutler, 2001). Social work demands a conceptual model that recognizes social agency as meaningful, intentional, and interconnected (Webb, 2001). Evidence-based practice is but one piece of that model.

Research Methods for Clinical Practitioners

In the following sections, we discuss three research designs that we believe are relevant to clinical practice. The first, the single-subject design (SSD), demonstrates accountability. The second, the qualitative design, helps social workers gather information about their clients' lives and develop interventions to better meet their needs. The third, mixed-methods research, incorporates the strength of both quantitative and qualitative designs.

Single-Subject Design Methodology

The quantitative SSD is a clinical tool that helps evaluate the effectiveness of social work practice. The qualitative inquiry helps social workers add to the body of knowledge about their clients' lived experiences and the agencies in which clinicians work. Social work practitioners need to be accountable—to show what they have done. The SSD demonstrates outcomes. This is particularly critical in today's managed care environment, where funding sources insist on seeing results. SSDs are quasi-experimental designs, with $n = 1$. Several versions of this design are considered "uncontrolled" because an intervention is not systematically withheld or varied so that one might observe what happens in its absence (Bloom, Fischer, & Orme, 2009). In effect, the patient acts as her own control by use of the preintervention baseline. The most rudimentary version of this design requires little more than accurate and complete recording of what many practitioners routinely do: Conduct an assessment of a case situation, intervene in it, record interventions, and assess progress. This design evolves into a research design when the practitioner wants to learn about the effects of some type of intervention on a case situation and takes an additional step to collect systematic data on intervention targets and methods.

A core function of the SSD is to enable the practitioner to compare the level of a client's problems before and after an intervention, and to make inferences regarding causality. To do so, one systematically obtains baseline data on target problems in a pretreatment phase or preintervention phase, and then makes a comparison to data obtained in exactly the same way during subsequent time periods for the same client. This differs from the classical experimental control group design, in which the comparison is made between groups.

The SSD is a time series design. There are many forms, and for a thorough discussion of this SSD methodology, we refer the reader to Bloom et al.'s excellent text on this subject. The case illustration in this chapter uses the most basic form—the A-B design. This design yields data on change coincident with or after introducing the intervention. Central to the basic time series design is the notion of repeated measurements of a given variable over time. The baseline is the preintervention phase in which planned observations of targeted problems and events take place. This is symbolized by the letter *A*. The intervention period is another phase in which some planned effort to change the client's (or system's) problems, together with a planned observation of targeted problems and events, takes place. Intervention can be thought of as a single procedure, or a combination of techniques packaged together. It is the formal and planned nature of the intervention that distinguishes it from the baseline, or assessment period, and is represented by the letter *B*.

A variety of instruments are suitable for SSDs. For a full discussion of measures, we refer the interested reader to Bloom et al. (2009). One set of standardized measures that we highlight, the WALMYR Assessment Scales (WAS) (Hudson & Faul, 1998), is well suited for social work practice because it can rapidly assess depression, anxiety, alcohol involvement, peer relations, marital satisfaction, partner abuse, parental and child attitudes, and family relations. The scales are easy to administer and easy to score. The important point in choosing an instrument is that it needs to measure the problem for which intervention is sought. If a client appears sad in an interview, but also claims that she and her partner argue a lot, and that she feels bad about herself, look for an instrument that measures the most distressing or potentially self-injurious behavior first. In such a case, the worker should get data about the client's depression before looking at the other clinical problems.

The virtue of SSDs is that after collecting data on the behaviors, feelings, cognitions, and attitudes that are the targets of intervention, these data can be visually demonstrated on a graph. Simply by eyeballing the data—looking to see if the trend line moves up, or down, or stays the same—both the worker and the client can see results. If, for example, a client has scored high for depression during baseline, as indicated by her scores on a depression measure, the data points would be moving upward, or at least be located in the upward region of the graph. A downward trend line in the intervention period would indicate that depression was declining and that the intervention had been effective. A flat line trend would indicate that no change had taken place. Displaying results visually on a graph serves to motivate the client, who can visually see the progress she has made. It is also extremely helpful to the practitioner, as it validates that the intervention was effective, or tells him that he needs to change the course of treatment because the intervention did not work. Another benefit of SSD methodology is that statistical analysis is not required. Although there are personal computer programs that generate graphs and do statistical analysis (see, for example, Bloom et al., 2009, or the Computer Assisted Social Service [CASS] system in Hudson, 1990a, 1990b; Nurius & Hudson, 1993), this level of sophistication is not required for routine practice evaluation.

In the following case example, we illustrate the use of the SSD methodology.

Case Example: Treatment of a Client with Obsessive-Compulsive Disorder

Recall that the client with obsessive-compulsive disorder, discussed in Chapter 10, was completely overwhelmed with performing 54 rituals, such as washing, cleaning, checking, and counting, on a daily basis. To monitor the effectiveness of the treatment, the worker turned to SSD methodology. Because there were several behaviors to examine, a multiple-baseline approach, more useful in demonstrating causality than the basic A-B design, was utilized. This approach, which calls for replication, is nicely detailed in Bloom et al. (2009). Of the 54 rituals that the client regularly performed, three target behaviors were selected for monitoring although intervention addressed all 54 items. The behaviors targeted were (1) how often she opened and closed her makeup cases after application (referred to as "makeup cases"); (2) the length of time spent rinsing in the shower ("rinsing"); and (3) how she counted her belongings while carrying them with her when she moved from place to place ("belongings"). I introduced the client to the notion of self-monitoring by using language from Bloom et al. (2009) who refer to the "psychological thermometer":

"Just as a doctor needs to have specific information about the problem at hand before he attempts to treat his patient, I need to have very accurate information of a psychological nature in order to help you. A doctor might ask you to take your temperature for a while to establish a baseline before he prescribes treatment, and he might take your temperature afterward to see if the treatment is effective. If the temperature goes down, you are on the right track. Social workers can use a 'psychological thermometer.' You will be asked to make daily entries on three of your rituals, using 3″ × 5″ cards. This will tell us how frequent these rituals occur. We will take the 'makeup cases' item, the 'rinsing' item, and the 'belongings' item for our recording (one from the low end of your anxiety hierarchy, one in the middle range, and the last from the high end). Make a small vertical line on the card every time you perform the targeted behavior. (I hand her a card and demonstrate how she is to make rows of hatch marks.) I would like you to do this for a week until we meet again. Then we can see just how many times a day you are doing the ritual. To record the number of minutes spent showering, you will need to keep a kitchen timer near the shower. You've estimated that you rinse for 45 to 60 minutes after soaping. Set the timer for an hour, and when you are finished, look at the timer and write down the number of minutes actually spent rinsing."

I then discussed with the client whether she felt there would be any obstacles in the way of her monitoring. Although her thinking was quite obsessive and detailed (e.g., she wanted to know if she should count the rinsing minutes when she shaved her legs and washed her hair, and what would happen if her 3″ × 5″ cards got wet), I patiently addressed her concerns and she was able to comply with the process. The client recorded diligently.

(continued)

Case Example Continued

As we reviewed the data, she was actually surprised to learn just how much time she was spending on these sample behaviors. Because of the collaborative nature of behavioral treatment, the client could participate in setting goals, monitoring her progress, and evaluating the outcome.

Data Analysis

By eyeballing the data on the graphs, the reader can see that the behavioral techniques that were used—modeling, exposure, and response prevention—were effective in reducing the client's ritualizing (see Figures 14.1 through 14.3). Intervention on the nine makeup cases (Figure 14.1) reduced the number of clicks, presses, or twists of her makeup cases to one per makeup item. Rinsing behavior decreased to a maximum of 9.5 minutes (Figure 14.2). Before intervention on the "belongings" item, 57 percent of the time that the client carried her belongings, she was obsessively counting them. After intervention, this counting behavior stopped completely. Needless to say, she was thrilled to see the graphs of her target behaviors because they offered concrete proof of her accomplishments. As mentioned in Chapter 10, the client's rapid success is attributed to her high degree of motivation, her ongoing relationship with me (two years of psychodynamic psychotherapy prior to the introduction of behavioral therapy), as well as the demonstrated effectiveness of the treatment protocol as established in the research.

(continued)

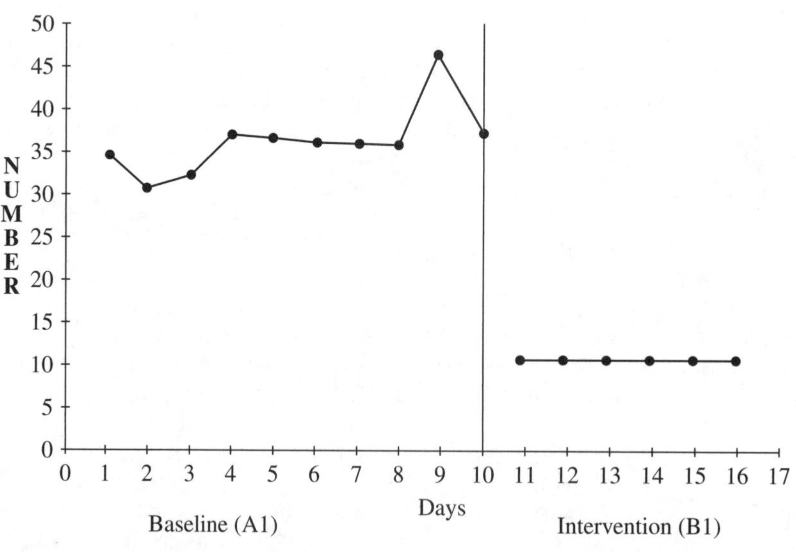

FIGURE 14.1 ***Number of Twists, Presses, and Clicks of Makeup Case by Client Each Morning at Baseline (A1) and after Intervention (B1)***

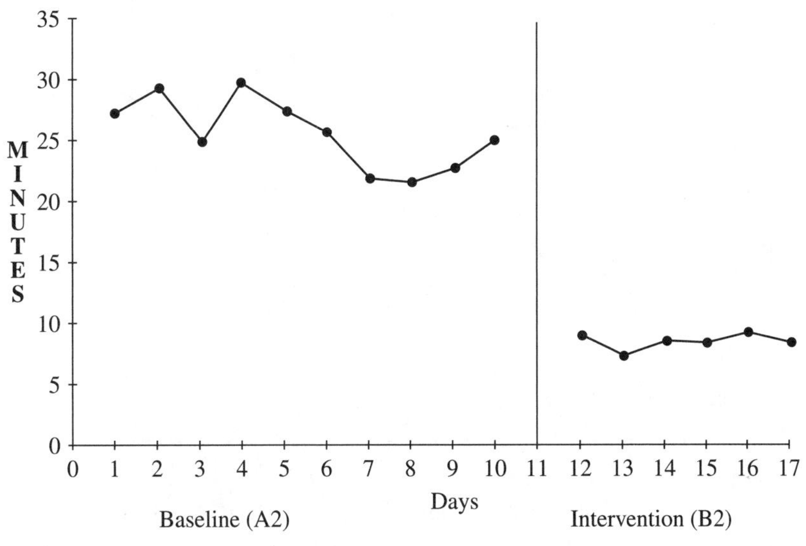

FIGURE 14.2 *Minutes Client Spent Rinsing in Shower at Baseline (A2) and after Intervention (B2)*

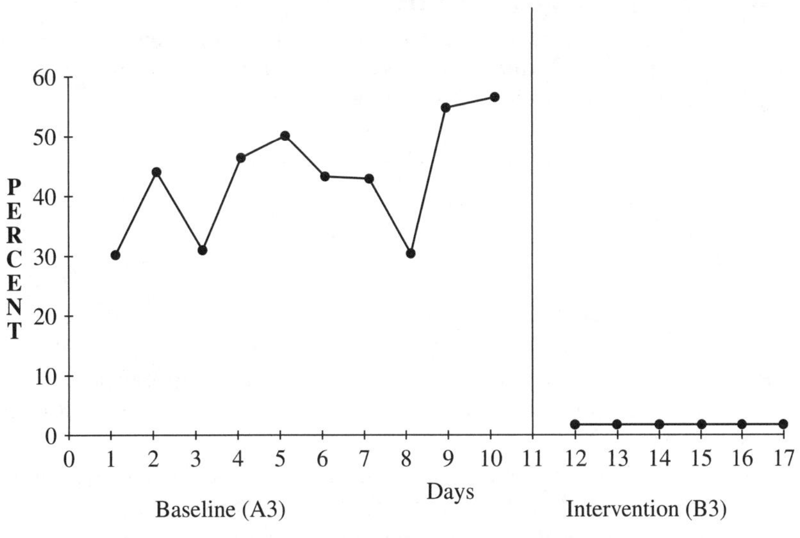

FIGURE 14.3 *Percentage of Times Client Counted Belongings when Carrying Them at Baseline (A3) and after Intervention (B3)*

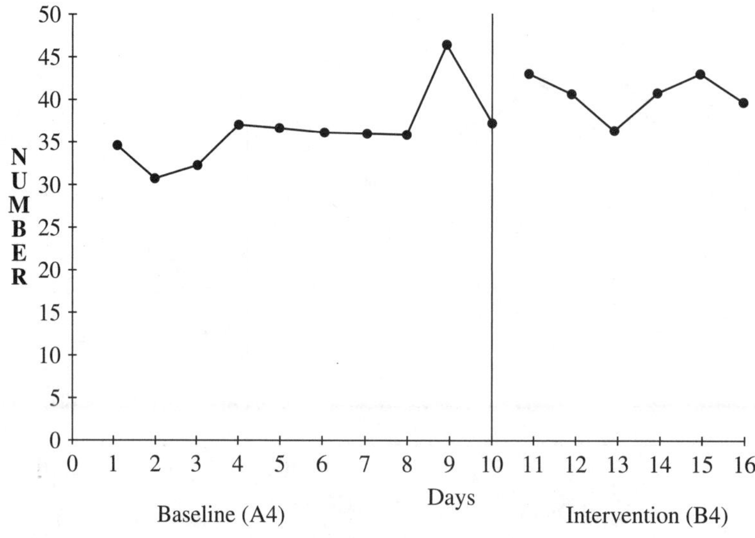

FIGURE 14.4 ***Number of Twists, Presses, and Clicks of Makeup Case by Client Each Morning at Baseline (A4) and after Intervention (B4) if intervention Was not Successful***

Case Example Continued

Graphic Illustration of Ineffectual Treatment

Let's suppose that my use of the treatment protocol had not been effective. The graph in Figure 14.4 shows how it would look if the treatment had not been successful in reducing the client's rituals on the "makeup case" item.

Qualitative Research

The next research design we will discuss is the qualitative inquiry. It is included in this chapter because of its natural fit with social work practice. Qualitative research uses the interviewing skills, concern, and curiosity of clinicians to obtain knowledge about their clients' lives and also provides clinicians with additional insight into the agencies in which they work.

Qualitative research is naturalistic inquiry. It is a human interaction, well suited to social work practice, because the researcher is also a participant who relies on conversations between himself and his respondents to understand the problem being studied. In many ways, qualitative research resembles a clinical interview. The researcher uses an interview guide and active listening skills to obtain information on his subject of inquiry. This information then generates new questions and ideas to be further explored in a continual search for meaning and understanding.

Qualitative research methods have their roots in anthropology. The method originated with the nineteenth-century ethnographers, who, like Margaret Mead and Gregory Bateson, the famous explicators of remote and exotic cultures, took copious field notes (known as "thick description") to understand their own unique experiences. There are many types of qualitative designs, and the interested reader is referred to the following sources for a detailed description: Yin (2002), Denzin & Lincoln (2000), Guba and Lincoln (1981); Lincoln and Guba (1985), and Miles and Huberman (1984). For a highly student-friendly book on qualitative research, see Padgett (2003).

How Knowledge Is Constructed

The qualitative researcher and respondent construct knowledge together. Data are gathered from individual interviews, or in focus groups (usually consisting of 7 to 10 persons, unfamiliar to each other, who come together to discuss some common concern). Qualitative research is highly labor intensive. The researcher takes abundant notes of each interview or makes video- or audiotapes that must then be immediately transcribed. Padgett (2003) notes that transcribing an audiotape of a 2-hour interview can take 10 hours and produce 30 pages of transcription data. The data are then searched for themes that must be tested out on the study participants. New data then emerge, requiring further transcription and another return to the respondents to verify the hypotheses generated by these emergent themes. This process of going back and forth between the data and the participants continues until the researcher is convinced that credibility has been achieved. The purpose of qualitative research is to get as many points of view as possible. The process is iterative and interactive—the worker tries not to make prior assumptions so as to get at the greatest breadth on the subject of inquiry.

The Researcher as Instrument

The qualitative researcher as a person is the method, the research instrument (Kvale, 1996). Although she follows an interview guide, she also uses spontaneous probes (such as "Can you tell me more about it?") to further her collection of data. The researcher is flexible as a collector of data. She can adapt to differing contexts and informational needs, which frees her to explore a given context until she is satisfied that the subjects have provided all information that is possible. The immediate transcription of interviews—usually within 24 hours—enables the researcher to change the direction of the inquiry as necessary and to return to the respondents for additional discussion.

Data Collection and Data Analysis

The detailed description of situations; events; people and interactions; observed behaviors; direct quotations from people about their experiences; attitudes; beliefs and thoughts; or excerpts from documents, correspondence, records, and case histories comprise the data sources for qualitative research (Patton, 1990, 2002). In qualitative research, data analysis is concurrent with data collection. It is an integrative, cyclical process wherein patterns and themes are generated from the data. For a detailed description of data analysis, see Glaser and Strauss (1967) and Miles and Huberman (1984).

In qualitative research, one comes up with the widest amount of data, and then culls it down to extract common themes and categories that capture the essence of the data through specific coding procedures that are described in the literature. Through this process of inductive conceptualization, the researcher develops core categories that capture the essence of the data. Coding ends when one begins to see repetition and redundancy. This is known as *saturation,* a term meaning the "cooking" process is drawing to an end. Saturation occurs when additional analysis no longer contributes anything new about a category.

This analysis of categories is written up in the form of memos—a process called *memoing*—that link different pieces of data to show their evidence of a general concept. Direct quotes from study participants can be incorporated in the memos to illustrate particular points. Thus, the researcher ensures that the analysis is grounded in the actual data and not in the researcher's interpretation. Qualitative research requires that the data be confirmed once they are obtained. Methods used to accomplish this include cross-validation strategies such as triangulation, member checks (taking the data back to the study participants for verification), and using an auditor to review the consistency of the study by checking the researcher's decision-making process and actions.

Case Example: Violence against Children and Families in Jamaica, West Indies

The following qualitative research study explores the experiences of Jamaican human service workers and educators who have worked with children exposed to violence in one community in Jamaica. To conduct the study, we flew to the homeland of the participants for observational purposes. Assisted by a Jamaican coinvestigator, we engaged in directed conversations with the participants to understand the problem being studied and to construct knowledge collaboratively. We conducted individual interviews and focus-group meetings to obtain the data. As defined by Marshall and Rossman (1989), we used holistic ethnography, which gives importance to culture by "employing . . . observation as a primary approach to gathering data . . . to uncover and document participants' perspectives" (p. 10).

Individual interviews, lasting one hour each, were conducted with a male MSW social worker, the current President of the Jamaica Association of Social Work (who was also our coinvestigator), a professor of social work from the University of the West Indies, and an educational administrator from the community school district. The interviewers used the semi-structured, open-ended topic guide shown in Figure 14.5 as a map of the subject matter they intended to cover. Descriptive, structural, and contrast questions were employed to facilitate the participants in revealing culturally relevant data. We also held three focus-group meetings. Each meeting lasted approximately an hour and a half. The groups were attended by human service workers, teachers, administrators, and members of the Jamaican Association of Social Work.

1. Structure of Jamaican child welfare system
2. Reporting system for child abuse and neglect
3. Definition of child maltreatment in Jamaica
4. Legal consequences for perpetrators of physical and sexual abuse on children
5. Service providers—identity and academic and professional qualifications
6. Mechanism for a child entering care system
7. Facilities and length of stay for children in care
8. Government resources for children in care
9. Existence of prevention programs
10. Primary access roads to care
11. Migratory patterns of Jamaicans and impact on child welfare
12. Rate of unemployment and governmental support for families in poverty and maintaining children at home

FIGURE 14.5 ***Topic Guide for Individual Interviews***

Case Example Continued

An open-ended topic guide appears in Figure 14.6. We used group member checks to summarize and confirm our understanding of their responses.

Data Analysis

All individual interviews and focus-group meetings were recorded on cassette tapes and transcribed after our return to the United States. We applied the grounded theory approach to the data analysis as described by Strauss and Corbin (1990). The primary technique used

(continued)

1. Direct experience working with abused and neglected children
2. Jamaican view of child maltreatment, specifically child sexual abuse
3. Perception by children and families of treatment providers
4. Religious and cultural beliefs of children and families that promote or forestall problem
5. Current treatment modalities, resources, and culturally sanctioned interventions
6. Cultural aspects that can be harnessed to promote change
7. Culture's effective use of support networks
8. Effects of care on children and their families
9. Prioritization and actualization of family reunification
10. Postcare support networks for children and families
11. Perception by Jamaican social service system and families of core social work values (i.e., self-determination and confidentiality)
12. Unique Jamaican practice approaches that can be incorporated in the United States to help culturally diverse clients

FIGURE 14.6 ***Topic Guide for Focus Groups***

Case Example Continued

was open coding, which involved constant comparisons to conceptualize. The coded data were then categorized into the resulting themes. One researcher read, reread, and then sorted the respondents' specific sentences under working labels that evolved into broad headings that suited the data underneath. Specifically, Microsoft Word was used to sequentially number every line in the original transcripts. Then, on the computer with the word processor, two windows were opened—numbered transcripts on the left and a blank worksheet on the right. The worksheet was used for copying, pasting, and organizing material from the left window, defining emerging themes and categorizing salient data (pieces of quotations) beneath each theme, which ultimately became the results.

After the first iteration of an entire transcript, the rater would come back, refreshed, some days later to review the grouping of data under the headings in those few cases where ambiguity existed. Because one rater with qualitative coding experience did the bulk of the analysis, Cohen's Kappa for inter-rater reliability was not applicable. Nevertheless, throughout the open coding process as the data were cut and pasted, line numbers referencing the original transcript were retained in the results. With these markers for quick contextual review, we could examine exactly where each quote had been extracted from the original interviews and establish confidence/trustworthiness in the results.

Findings

The results and supporting data of quotations are explicated next. They were culled directly from the transcripts of the focus-group sessions and individual interviews.

1. *Frequent Exposure of Children to Violence with Resulting Trauma.* The extent and pervasiveness of the violence and sexual abuse in West Kingston are for its victims not unlike the experiences and consequences of those living in a war zone. All study participants felt that this human damage can lead to a demoralizing cycle of greater violence and abuse with very serious harm to children, parents, caregivers, and society. "Violence begets violence." There was a sadness to the quality of the conversation when this topic was discussed, which must be noted as the participants referred to Jamaicans as "proud people" who have a lot of "love for the children."

> "All kinds of violence . . . murder . . . fires . . . there are lots of fires."

> "There was one night where we had a lot of shooting."

> "They experience trauma every single day because there's guns, they go to bed at night and they hear it. They wake up in the morning so all the students see, actually see, the murders right there from their school here."

> "Well, the violence really does have a serious impact on the way the children operate in school."

> "[Children's] attention span seems to be very short. They become distracted very easily and I don't think that some of them think that there is much more to their existence than, you know, just being here, going through the motions until it is time for whatever is to happen to them should happen. . . . And so we find that the students don't, many of them, don't want to sit down in class and really put their minds to what is taught in a real serious way. [They will be unable] to . . . move up the social ladder."

Case Example Continued

"It was like an innocent child said to me: He just couldn't, he couldn't take the gunshots anymore. He would just shake."

"The children . . . they're depressed. A child will say, 'I'm going to kill this person' and you say, 'Would you go to prison?' And [the child] says, 'Miss, but it's not anything.' "

"Among youngsters now . . . there are suicides a lot . . . a high level of it."

"When they play, there's so much conflict. Sometimes I'm watching and there's so much aggression."

2. *Intrafamilial Violence.* Abuse is by no means limited to occurrences between strangers but can affect a family and its members at the most basic level. People who, under "normal" circumstances, would have a very positive relationship with one another are capable of causing grievous injury. The participants all seemed to agree that this represented a breakdown in the traditional family structure that had been a mainstay of Jamaican culture and had serious implications for both the children's future and the future of Jamaica.

"The problem is . . . quite deep rooted and it's also at home. It appears it comes from home most of the time. The home environment is also what influences these situations."

"The hopelessness and the agitation a child shall experience. Going back home to the environment."

"[At home] she's a tiny little girl but her mother hit her with a cutlass [i.e., type of knife]. . . . Her mother . . . couldn't take it anymore. . . . The mother tries but that's how she punishes her . . . tries not to cut her. The mother just doesn't know what else to do."

"Her son tends to bring violence on his own sister, bringing home violence."

3. *Poverty's Role in Cultural Desensitization to Violence.* The necessities of day-to-day living, such as affording food and shelter, can cause people to make gut-wrenching compromises for the sake of survival. If repeated frequently, harmful acts can lead to a numbing desensitization until the line between normal and abnormal becomes blurred. This is a type of cultural trauma that impacts the children and families. The participants all agreed that the stark class divisions in Jamaica contributed to poverty and that this cultural desensitization to violence existed among the poorest classes in Jamaica who had very little access to a better life.

"I'll say, 'What's the matter?' 'Miss, I'm hungry.' They don't have breakfast and they don't have lunch and they don't have dinner. It's a serious problem. You are trying to work with them and they're hungry—then you have to solve the problem of hunger."

"They're provoked, they are going to retaliate so that is why . . . that's the experience of this year round and people retaliate an eye for an eye and they raise the violence. There's tolerance . . . jungle justice . . . a kind of subculture."

"They like to tease each other and they like to make the violence. They don't see a way because they don't have the skills to manage their anger."

"Sometimes what you have is that parents are not so much behind the children to take them to get this help [or medicine] because you identify factors and then you say,

(continued)

Case Example Continued

alright, and make that appointment for you to go and get some help at this appointment and you come back next week and tell them. . . . But what you find is that they tell you, I have to go to work. I don't have the time. They're not really able to spare the time and make the effort to see that the best results come for the children."

4. *Different Stresses on Different Genders.* Not surprisingly, boys and girls, women and men have dissimilar experiences and are treated differently as well. This results in both positive and negative outcomes for girls and boys; for example, boys may be punished more harshly, may be more violent, and may not be as academically motivated or encouraged. They are more often the perpetrators of sexual offense against girls. Girls may be restricted more than boys but are nonetheless exposed to greater incidents of sexual abuse. They are also achieving more academically.

"In our school . . . we have more boys who are . . . leaders, and we find that there is more aggression among that set."

"In the reading streams . . . there are more girls than boys. . . . You find a great concentration of aggression among boys. . . . I think parents pay more attention to the girls' education than boys' [education]."

"I protect my girl because I don't want her to become pregnant so she stays home. . . . The boys get the chance to run the streets because they're boys and they will not become pregnant so I have no fear, you know, but recently there is another fear with some persons who fear that they might go out there, they might pick up the guns."

"Incest also happens . . . it's just coming out of the closet now. . . . There are laws [against incest but] it's not reported."

"Sexual abuse in Jamaica among children is kept covert for many reasons."

"It is feared that the breadwinner will be lost."

"It's very hard to get a child in Jamaica to admit that they have been sexually molested. Blood is thicker than water."

"The perpetrator's in the home because we have single-parent homes in Jamaica a lot."

"There is also some amount of child prostitution. . . . Mother sends her out into places . . . where she performs acts . . . she has sex for money . . . she does [it] to support the mother and the other children in the house."

5. *Poor Societal Resources to Deal with Violence, Abuse, and Their Impact.* Poverty and lack of opportunity lead to a dearth of treatment resources and solutions. Governmental institutions that should offer relief can perpetrate additional harm and actually increase distrust and hopelessness. The participants felt that greater work needed to be done by the government to enforce policy that goes against the culture of the country. There is also a significant need for additional training and more integration between public and private services, again highlighting the class divisions within Jamaica.

"[The system] will intervene . . . if they thought it was serious then . . . the child will be taken to court and, you know, the court intervenes and decides whether or not the child can be taken away from the parent, passed on to another relative, or be placed at

Case Example Continued

the children's home. But often the laws 'have no teeth.' This is changing with the passage of the Child Care and Protection Act—it will make reporting mandatory."

"[Victims and advocates] don't want to be in the courts because the police . . . have poor, real poor, understanding of sexual abuse. They are unsympathetic in many cases. That is one of the reasons why training is so important."

"What also happens in the system many times is that the private practitioner's fees are higher than the State is willing to pay, so they end up not going to see appropriate practitioners or they end up going to Family Court or to anybody who will take it on—maybe a counselor or someone who is not necessarily a trained practitioner."

"Family Court of Probation Service . . . handles these matters. Those are not clinical practitioners."

"At the Children's Hospital they have trained psychologists who are paid by the State, but again the case load is high, so you find that many other persons like the children in this who should be benefiting from services don't get them."

"Our practitioners here are ill equipped [to treat incest] and that's why training is so important."

"[We have a] shortage of trained practitioners here in Jamaica. We have psychologists but again the psychologists' fees are expensive."

"There's a terrible lack of skill here . . . the need is so great now for the clinical aspect of treatment here. . . . It is unbelievable. . . . We really need that kind of training here because people . . . have such minimal training, like four months training, maybe a year."

6. *Hunger for Strategies to Help Break the Cycle of Abuse.* In spite of momentous challenges, affected stakeholders (parents, children, clinicians) continue to look for improvements and solutions. They are eager for additional training from credible sources. Optimism endures.

"There is a great love of young children here in Jamaica."

"There is a strong sense of spiritual and religious belief."

"Parents wanted to know how to cope. . . . How do I cope with what is happening around me?"

"There is stigma about mental health care, so we'd have to try to break it gently with them. . . . I just want a psychiatrist to come in and do something with [parents] about, you know, self-care. That's what we are calling it. Because if we call it anything else, they're not coming."

"But there are some parents who would [try mental health and medicine] because they are at their wit's end. So, of course we organized a session. And they, the parents themselves, have suggested the area that they wanted us to go into."

"Conflict resolution was one of the major things that the focus was on."

"They wanted a way to improve themselves in terms of training or to generate an income."

"Children themselves . . . are being educated to realize that . . . [incest] is wrong."

(continued)

Case Example **Continued**

"[Children surviving incest] will go through a series of counseling sessions where we try to help them. . . . That is a difficult thing, so we want to get to that stage where we can work with them. Work through the traumas and refer them to other evaluation that we feel are necessary. Work with the parents. Try to get the perpetrator in, and we have had perpetrators come in. I've had them who come in and admit. And we will refer them to the police."

"There is a national health fund and I think children are in there now. . . . So they can get the medication, but we need to inform people within this community that this exist[s]."

"We also are doing something for the teachers this semester because . . . they have been affected by the violence themselves . . . the children's behavior and their experience in the community."

Discussion and Implications

The preceding qualitative study speaks frankly to the violence that is embedded in the Jamaican culture and the ensuing trauma that has affected children and families. Despite the daunting trials faced by the focus-group participants and their peers, the island has a long history of loving and nurturing relationships between parents and children, respect for authority, and graciousness, which was clearly evident during the visit to impoverished communities and schools. We worked with our colleagues in Jamaica, who are eager for solutions, to harness the strengths in the culture. We used the findings of this research to develop additional training in the identification and treatment of trauma behaviors in children. The training was informed by trauma, attachment, and multicultural theories, as this research indicates that the primary attachments of Jamaican children have been disrupted through political, social, and economic unrest. Strategies were also provided based on constructivist cognitive and behavioral theories to help children and families manage post-traumatic stress, anxiety, depression, anger, and impulsivity, and to learn nonviolent methods of conflict resolution. Clearly, this study indicates that both micro-level and macro-level change is needed to ensure that the rights of Jamaica's most vulnerable citizens—its women and children—are protected and advanced.

Mixed-Methods Research

Mixed-methods research, described as the third research paradigm, combines both quantitative and qualitative methods (see, for example, Creswell, 2003; Johnson & Onwuegbuzie, 2003). It is formally defined by Johnson and Onwuegbuzie (2003) as "the class of research where the researcher mixes or combines quantitative and qualitative research techniques, methods, approaches, concepts or language into a single study" (p. 17). Mixed-methods research utilizes multiple approaches in answering research questions. According to the fundamental principle of mixed-methods research (Johnson & Onwuegbuzie, 2003), researchers should collect as much data using different strategies, methods, and approaches, in such a way that the resulting combination is likely to result in complementary strengths and nonoverlapping weaknesses. Thus, the product should be superior to monomethod studies.

Johnson and Onwuegbuzie (2003) recommend an eight-step process model for mixed-methods research:

1. Determine the research question
2. Determine the appropriateness of mixed-methods research
3. Select the mixed-method design
4. Collect the data
5. Analyze the data
6. Interpret the data
7. Legitimate the data (this step may include further data collection, analysis, and/or interpretation until as many rival explanations as possible have been reduced or eliminated)
8. Draw conclusions and write the final report

We urge students to try mixed-methods research because we believe that utilizing quantitative and qualitative methods within the same framework allows the researcher to incorporate the strengths of both methods and makes for a richer product as well as a more interesting inquiry for the researcher. The following is an example of a mixed-methods study of depression among Chinese elders undertaken by Roy, Cooper, and Lesser (2008). In this study, qualitative interviews of Chinese elders were added to standardized scales to give a fuller picture of the needs and concerns of this population.

Case Example: A Pilot Study of Depression among Chinese Elders

Rationale, Design, and Sample

China's aging population poses serious challenges for already strained social welfare and medical services, and China has seen disturbing increases in the rate of suicide among its elders (Chou & Chi, 2005; Yip et al., 2003). This pilot study sought to better understand levels of depression among older Chinese adults, how depression is conceptualized, and how older Chinese adults seek help for their unhappiness.

The research was a cross-sectional, descriptive study with a two-group comparison. We used a convenience sample of 108 community-dwelling Chinese adults age 60 and above who were cognitively intact. Approximately one-half ($n = 53$) resided in Boston, and one-half ($n = 55$) resided in Guangzhou, China. The researchers used a "mixed-methods" approach that included a depression scale and collection of demographic variables, as well as the use of qualitative, group-based interviews.

(continued)

Case Example Continued

Measures

We used the Geriatric Depression Scale (GDS) as our main quantitative measure. This scale has undergone psychometric validation in Chinese older adults. A one-page form was used to collect data on demographic variables. Some of the variables included in the Brief Survey Form are age, sex, education, self-reported mental health status, self-reported physical health status, and life satisfaction.

Data Collection

Both the GDS and the Brief Survey Form were translated in Chinese and administered to two groups of elders in Boston and two groups of elders in Guangzhou. Participation was completely voluntary and an elder could decline to continue at any point in the administration of the questionnaires.

Demographics and Other Descriptive Findings

Comparing demographic variables from the Guangzhou and Boston sample, we found the following (percentages have been rounded to the nearest whole percent). The Guangzhou group had more men (36% vs. 30%), were older (mean age was 78 vs. 76), and reported more years of higher education (i.e., high school, some college, and college) (29% vs. 24%). It is worth noting that the Guangzhou sample also reported more elders with no years of education (17% vs. 2%). In any case, the majority of elders from both samples reported having completed schooling only through the elementary school level.

Thirty-five percent of Guangzhou elders reported *poorer health* as compared to 14 percent of Boston elders. Again, it should be noted that the majority of elders in both Guangzhou and Boston reported *good* to *excellent health* (65% vs. 86%).

Eighty-six percent of Guangzhou elders reported being *satisfied* to *very satisfied* with their life as compared to 90 percent of Boston elders.

Our main quantitative question was, How do levels of depression compare between Chinese elders in Boston and Chinese elders in Guangzhou? We found that Guangzhou elders were more depressed (using GDS cutoff score of 11 or greater) as compared to Boston elders. In the Guangzhou group, 29 percent were depressed as evidenced by their score on the GDS as compared to 9 percent in the Boston group—a difference that was statistically significant.

We were also interested in whether there was a correlation between the dependent variable, depression, and demographic variables of age, gender, health, education, self-reported physical health, and self-reported mental health. We found one significant correlation ($r = .347$, $p \leq .05$, $n = 51$) indicating a low level association between mental health and depression. This result is informative as it tells us these two measures are consistent, with elders scoring as depressed on the GDS also reporting poor mental health as measured by our self-reported mental health measure.

Qualitative Interviews

In addition to the administration of the GDS, we used a semi-structured interview guide to obtain qualitative data from the same groups of elders. The semi-structured interview guide was administered by our Chinese Research Associate. Permission was obtained to audiotape

1. How do you know when you are feeling sad?
2. How do you show it?
3. If a man is depressed, what would he show?
4. If a woman is depressed, what would she show?
5. Is there something special about old people around here that would make them depressed?
6. Do old people talk to each other about depression?
7. If they talk to each other about it, what do they say?
8. Where do they go when they are depressed?
9. Would you trust a person outside the family to help you when you are depressed?
10. Is depression a medical or a spiritual problem?
11. What kind of person would you look for in getting help?
12. If you ever went to someone for help, what happened?
13. What would insult you when coming from a helping person?
14. If you are looking for help, what would you want this person to do?
15. How do you know when you are feeling sad? How do you show it?

FIGURE 14.7 ***Semi-Structured Interview Guide***

Case Example Continued

the group-based interviews. The questions included in the semi-structured interview guide can be found in Figure 14.7.

All focus-group meetings were recorded on cassette tapes and translated and transcribed after our return. We applied the grounded theory approach to the data analysis as described by Strauss and Corbin (1990). The primary technique used was open coding, which involved constant comparisons to conceptualize. The themes resulting from the coded data are shown in Figure 14.8.

Differences and Commonalities in Meaning between the Chinese in Boston and the Chinese in Mainland China

We also found that descriptions of negative feelings and behaviors seemed more intense and hostile among the mainland Chinese elders. They more frequently used words such as "scold," "fight," "humiliate," and "conflict" than their Boston counterparts. Those living in Boston had more familiarity with mental health services, and acknowledged the value of mental health practitioners. Those in China had less exposure, and were more skeptical. They spoke of "not having the habit" of seeking counseling, and raised issues of cost concerns and the quality of the help provided. One elder said, "Consultation fee is very expensive, and it costs 70 dollars an hour to see a psychologist. That is not a small amount, and who can afford going? Plus . . . time flies, and without knowing it, you have talked for an hour, and he (the therapist) might not even start to respond . . . but money is spent. I know that because I went before and did all the talking and he didn't even respond."

(continued)

1. Recognizing and expressing unhappiness
2. Trouble expressing negative feelings
3. Gender difference in expression of unhappiness
4. Distraction as a remedy
5. Physical health affects mood
6. Aging leads to regression
7. Views on depression (biological)
8. View on depression (environmental or psychological)
9. Views on depression (multi-rooted)
10. Treatment for depression (medical)
11. Treatment for depression (heal thyself)
12. Treatment for depression (involve family and friends)
13. Shame about one's own depression
14. Impressions of mental illness
15. Limitations of adult children, family, and friends
16. Unfamiliarity, quality, and cost concerns re: treatment
17. What do social workers do?

FIGURE 14.8 *Themes from Coded Data*

Case Example Continued

Both groups had limited appreciation of the role of the social worker, although those in Boston did view their helpfulness in delivering concrete services. Those living in China seemed less likely to blame biology as a cause of their depression, as did their Boston counterparts. They looked for multirooted causes—poor physical health, psychological disturbance, bad habits, personality shaping one's fate, and how people think. "Psychological problems are how people think . . . their thoughts are usually very pessimistic." Both groups in Boston and China expressed a great deal of belief in the power of positive thinking and positive actions as treatments for depression. The Bostonians had 53 lines of comments and the mainland Chinese had 85 lines of comments to this end. Positive thinking and engaging in enjoyable activities were seen by both as antidotes to depression. Comments such as "taking a walk," "working in my garden," and other techniques of distraction were common. Women seemed more likely to talk to their children and friends when depressed, whereas men made comments such as getting drunk or taking anger out on loved ones as coping styles.

Limitations Regarding Quantitative Findings and Questions for Further Study

For several reasons, caution is advised in interpreting the quantitative finding on depression in Chinese elders: (1) the current pilot study used a convenience sample and thus the findings are not representative of elders in Boston nor Guangzhou, (2) the sample size is small, and (3) although we used Chinese-speaking student research assistants to help administer the scale, there was evidence of language barriers during the administration of the GDS that may have reduced the reliability of the findings. It should also be emphasized

Case Example Continued

that this is a pilot study only, serving largely to assess the feasibility of conducting an international cross-cultural study.

When looking at the qualitative data, we wonder just how much the teachings of Confucius have been integrated into the thinking of Chinese elders, and have become positive coping skills when dealing with depression. Certainly the ideas of positive thinking, positive self-talk, and positive action are widely believed to be effective treatment strategies by cognitive/behavioral therapists in Western cultures. Clearly, we can learn something about treatment of depression from the positive coping styles of our Chinese elders. Lastly, we wonder if the expectations of happiness are different for Chinese elders than they are for their Western counterparts. As one mainland Chinese woman stated: "I have a clean place to sleep, good food, and friends around me . . . so I am happy."

Consistent with the literature we found indications of depression among older Chinese adults. It was evident also that regardless of where older Chinese adults live (Boston or China), they rarely participate in the Western form of help-seeking as defined by using the services of a mental health professional. Future research should continue to assess and identify depression and help-seeking behavior in the elderly Chinese population, so as to develop interventions that can lead to better coping and adjustment.

Summary

Evidence-based practice requires that social workers learn how to interpret research findings and clinical protocols in order to be accountable to both their clients and their client systems. We have endeavored to inform you about evidence-based practice, and we have presented three research designs that, we hope, will whet the appetites of our clinical students so that they will pursue them further—SSD, qualitative research, and mixed-methods research. All three methods can be quite gratifying to practitioners, and we hope that interested students will continue to learn about these designs in their research methods courses and apply them in their work.

References

Ablon, S. L. (2001). The work of transformation: Changes in technique since Anna Freud's *Normality and pathology in childhood. Psychoanalytic Study of the Child*, 56, 27–37.

Abramovitz, R., & Williams, J. (1992). Workshop 2: The pros and cons of the *diagnostic and statistical manual* for social work practice and research. *Research on Social Work Practice*, 2(3), 338–349.

Abramowitz, J. S., Franklin, M. E., & Foa, E. B. (2002). Empirical status of cognitive-behavioural therapy for obsessive compulsive disorder: A meta-analytic review. *Romanian Journal of Cognitive and Behavior Psychotherapies*, 2, 89–104.

Adams, K. B., & Matto, H. C. (2009). Limitations of evidenced-based practice for social work education: Unpacking the complexity. *Journal of Social Work Education*, 45(2), 165–186.

Addis, M., & Waltz, J. (2002, November). Implicit and untested assumptions about the role of psychotherapy treatment manuals in evidence-based mental health practice. *Clinical Psychology: Science and Practice*, 9(4), 367–378.

Addis, M. E., Wade, W. A., & Hatgis, C. (1999). Barriers to dissemination of evidence-based practices: Addressing practitioners' concern about manual-based psychotherapies. *Clinical Psychology: Science and Practice*, 6, 430–441.

Adler, A. (1964). *Social interest: A challenge to mankind*. New York: Capricorn.

Akinyela, M. (2002a). De-colonizing our lives: Divining a post-colonial therapy. *International Journal of Narrative Therapy and Community Work*, 2, 32–43.

Akinyela, M. (2002b). Reparations: Repairing relationships and honouring ancestry. *International Journal of Narrative Therapy and Community Work*, 2, 45–49.

Alexander, J. (2004). Toward a theory of cultural trauma. In J. C. Alexander, R. Eyerman, B. Giesen, N. J. Smelser, & P. Sztompka (Eds.), *Cultural trauma and collective identity* (pp. 1–29). Berkeley, CA: University of California Press.

Allen, J. G. (2001). *Traumatic relationships and serious mental disorders*. New York: Wiley.

Altman, N. (1995). *The analyst in the inner city: Race, class and culture through a psychoanalytic lens*. Hillsdale, NJ: Analytic Press.

Altman, N., Briggs, R., Frankel, J., Gensler, D., & Pantone, P. (2002). *Relational child psychotherapy*. New York: Other Press.

American Psychiatric Association. (2000). *Diagnostic and statistical manual of mental disorders* (5th ed.). Washington, DC: Author.

Amerogen, M., & Mishna, F. (2004). Learning disabilities and behavior problems: A self psychological approach to working with parents. *Psychoanalytic Social Work*, 11(2), 33–53.

Anderson, H., & Goolishian, H. (1992). The client is the expert: A not-knowing approach to therapy. In S. McNamee & K. J. Gergen (Eds.), *Therapy as a social construction* (pp. 25–39). Newbury Park, CA: Sage.

Anderson, H., & Goolishian, H. A. (1988). Human systems as linguistic systems: Preliminary and evolving ideas about the implications for clinical theory. *Family Process*, 27, 371–393.

Anderson, M. (1997). *Conversation, language, and possibilities: A postmodern approach to therapy*. New York: Basic Books.

Anderson, M. L. (2005). "Your blues ain't like my blues": Race, ethnicity, and social inequality in America. *Contemporary Sociology*, 29(6), 796–805.

Appalachian Expressive Arts Collection. (2003). *Expressive arts therapy: Creative process in art and life*. Boone, NC: Parkway Publishers.

Arrendondo, P., & Toporek, B. (2004). Multicultural counseling competencies: Ethical practice. *Journal of Mental Health Counseling*, 26(1), 44–55.

Association for Play Therapy. (1997). A definition of play therapy. *Association for Play Therapy Newsletter*, 16(1), 7.

Atkinson, D. R., Thompson, C. E., & Grant, S. K. (1993). A three-dimensional model for counseling racial/ethnic minorities. *Counseling Psychologist*, 21(2), 257–277.

Ayonrinde, O. (2003). Importance of cultural sensitivity in therapeutic transactions: Considerations for healthcare providers.*Disease Management and Healthcare Outcomes*, 11(4), 233–248.

Bacal, H. (1985). Optimal responsiveness and the therapeutic process. In A. Goldberg (Ed.), *Process in self psychology* (pp. 202–226). New York: Guilford.

Bacal, H., & Newman, K. (1990). *Theories of object relations: Bridges to self psychology*. New York: Columbia University Press.

Balint, M., Ornstein, P. H., & Balint, E. (1972). *Focal psychotherapy: An example of applied psychoanalysis*. London: Tavistock.

Bandura, A. (1977). *Social learning theory*. Englewood Cliffs, NJ: Prentice-Hall.

Bandura, A. (1980). Gauging the relationship between self-efficacy judgment and action. *Cognitive Therapy and Research*, 4, 263–268.

Bandura, A. (1986). *Social foundations of thought and action*. Englewood Cliffs, NJ: Prentice-Hall.

Bandura, A., Reese, L., & Adams, N. E. (1982). Microanalysis of action and fear arousal as a function of differential levels of perceived self-efficacy. *Journal of Personality and Social Psychology*, 43, 5–21.

Bandura, A., Ross, D., & Ross, S. A. (1961). Transmission of aggressions through imitation of aggressive models. *Journal of Abnormal and Social Psychology*, 63, 575–582.

Bannink, F. P. (2008). Posttraumatic success: Solution-focused brief therapy. *Brief Treatment and Crisis Intervention*, 8(3), 215–225.

Barbour, R. (1984). Social work education: Tackling the theory-practice dilemma. *British Journal of Social Work*, 14, 557–567.

Barkley, R. A. (2002). *Defiant children: A clinician's manual for parent training*. New York: Guilford.

Barkley, R. A. (2003a). Attention deficit hyperactivity disorder. In E. J. Mash & D. Wolfe (Eds.), *Adolescent psychopathology*. New York: Guilford.

Barkley, R. A. (2003b). *Defiant adolescents*. New York: Guilford.

Barkley, R. A., & Macias, M. (2005). Attention deficit hyperactivity disorder. In R. David (Ed.), *Child and adolescent neurology* (3rd ed.). New York: Blackwell.

Barlow, D. H. (2002). *Anxiety and its disorders: The nature and treatment of anxiety and panic* (2nd ed.). New York: Guilford.

Barlow, D. H. (Ed.). (2008). *Clinical handbook of psychological disorders* (4th ed.). New York: Guilford.

Barrera, I., & Corso, R. M. (2002). Cultural competency as skilled dialogue. *Topics in Early Childhood and Special Education, 22*(2), 103–113.

Bass, A. (2002). Historical and unconscious trauma: Racism and psychoanalysis. *Constellations, 9*(2), 274–283.

Baxi, U. (2006). *The future of human rights* (2nd ed.). New Delhi: Oxford University Press.

Beck, A. T. (1961). A systematic investigation of depression. *Comprehensive Psychiatry, 2*, 305–312.

Beck, A. T. (1976). *Cognitive theory and emotional disorders.* New York: International Universities Press.

Beck, A. T., & Emery, G. (1985). *Anxiety disorders and phobias.* New York: Basic Books.

Beck, A. T., & Hurvich, M. (1959). Psychological correlates of depression. *Psychosomatic Medicine, 21*, 50–55.

Beck, A. T., & Ward, C. H. (1961). Dreams of depressed patients: Characteristic themes in manifest content. *Archives of General Psychiatry, 5*, 462–467.

Beck, A. T., & Young, J. E. (1985). Depression. In D. H. Barlow (Ed.), *Clinical handbook of psychological disorders: A step-by-step treatment manual* (pp. 206–244). New York: Guilford.

Beck, A. T., Rush, A. J., Shaw, B. F., & Emery, G. (1979). *Cognitive therapy of depression.* New York: Guilford.

Beck, J. S. (1995). *Cognitive therapy: Basics and beyond.* New York: Guilford.

Becvar, D., & Becvar, R. (2009). *Family therapy: A systemic integration* (7th ed.). Boston: Allyn & Bacon.

Bednar, R., Bednar, S., Lambert, M., & Waite, D. R. (1991). *Psychotherapy with high risk clients.* Pacific Grove, CA: Brooks/Cole.

Bein, E., Levenson, H., & Overstreet, D. (1994). *Outcome and follow up data from the VAST project.* Paper presented at the annual international meeting of the Society for Psychotherapy Research, York, England.

Bell, E., & Nkomo, S. (2001). *Our separate ways: Black and White women and the struggle for professional identity.* Cambridge, MA: Harvard Business School Press.

Bemak, F., Chung, R. C.-Y., & Bornemann, T. (1996). Counseling and psychotherapy with refugees. In P. Pedersen, J. Draguns, W. Lonner, & J. Trumble (Eds.), *Counseling across cultures* (4th ed., pp. 243–265). Thousand Oaks, CA: Sage.

Benjamin, J. (1990). Recognition and destruction: An outline of intersubjectivity. In S. Mitchell & L. Aron (Eds.), *Relational psychoanalysis: The emergence of a tradition* (pp. 181–210). Hillsdale, NJ: Analytic Press.

Berg, I. K., & DeJong, P. (2005). Engagement through complimenting. In T. S. Nelson (Ed.), *Education and training in solution-focused therapy* (pp. 51–56). New York: Haworth.

Berkman, C., Turner, S., Cooper, M., Polnerow, D., & Swartz, M. (2000). Sexual contact with clients: Assessment of social workers' attitudes and educational preparation. *Social Work, 45*(3), 223–235.

Berlin, L. J., & Cassidy, J. (1999). *Relations among relationships: Contributions from attachment theory and research.* New York: Guilford.

Bermudes, R. A., Wright, J. H., & Casey, D. (2009). Techniques of cognitive-behavioral therapy. In G. O. Gabbard (Ed.), *Textbook of Psychotherapeutic Treatments* (pp. 201–238). Arlington, VA: American Psychiatric Publishing.

Beutler, L. E. (2001). David and Goliath: When empirical and clinical standards of practice meet. *American Psychologist, 55*, 997–1007.

Beutler, L. E., & Hardwood, T. M. (2000). *Prescriptive psychotherapy: A practical guide to systematic treatment selection.* New York: Oxford University Press.

Bien, T. (2006). *Mindful therapy: A guide for therapists and helping professionals.* Boston: Wisdom.

Bishop, S., Lau, M., Shapiro, S., Carlson, L., Anderson, N., & Carmody, J. (2004). Mindfulness: A proposed operational definition. *Clinical Psychology: Science and Practice, 11*, 230–241.

Bloom, B. L. (1997). *Planned short term psychotherapy: A clinical handbook.* Boston: Allyn & Bacon.

Bloom, M., & Fischer, J. (2009). *Evaluating practice: Guidelines for the accountable professional* (6th ed.). Boston: Allyn & Bacon.

Boal, A. (1992). *Game for actors and non-actors.* London: Butler & Tanner.

Boal, A. (1995). *Rainbow of desire: The Boal method of theatre and therapy.* New York: Routledge.

Bodnar, S. (2004). Remember where you come from: Dissociative process in multicultural individuals. *Psychoanalytic Dialogues, 14*(5), 581–603.

Bordin, E. S. (1979). The generalizability of the psychoanalytic concept of the working alliance. *Psychotherapy, Theory, Research and Practice, 16*(3), 252–260.

Bowlby, J. (1969/1982). *Attachment and loss: Vol. 1: Attachment.* New York: Basic Books.

Bowlby, J. (1973). *Attachment and loss: Vol. 2: Separation.* New York: Basic Books.

Bradley, S., & Sloman, L. (1975). Selective mutism in immigrant families. *Journal of American Academy of Child and Adolescent Psychiatry, 14*(3), 510–514.

Brisch, K. H. (1999). *Treating attachment disorders: From theory to therapy.* New York: Guilford.

Brody, V. (1997). Developmental play therapy. In K. O'Connor & L. Braverman (Eds.), *Play therapy theory and practice: A comparative presentation.* New York: John Wiley & Sons.

Brown, L. M. (1998). *Raising their voices: The politics of girls' anger.* Cambridge, MA: Harvard University Press.

Brown, T. A., O'Leary, T. A., & Barlow, D. H. (1993). Generalized anxiety disorder. In D. H. Barlow (Ed.), *Clinical handbook of psychological disorders* (2nd ed., pp. 137–188). New York: Guilford.

Browne, C., & Mills, C. (2000). Ecological model, the strengths perspective, and empowerment theory. In R. Fong & S. Suruto (Eds.), *Cultural competent social work practice: Practice skills, interventions, and evaluations* (pp. 10–32). Boston: Allyn & Bacon.

Bryceland, C., & Stam, H. J. (2005). Empirical validation and professional codes of ethics: Description or prescription? *Journal of Constructivist Psychology, 18*, 131–155.

Budman, C., & Gurman, A. (1988). *Theory and practice of brief therapy.* New York: Guilford.

Budman, C., Hoyt, M., & Friedman, S. (1992). *The first session in brief therapy.* New York: Guilford.

Burns, C. I., & Holloway, E. L. (1990). Therapy in supervision: An unresolved issue. *Clinical Supervisor, 7*(4), 47–60.

Burton, C. M., & King, L. A. (2004). The health benefits of writing about intensely positive experiences. *Journal of Research in Personality, 38*(2), 150–163.

Butler, R. (1963). The life review: An interpretation of reminiscence in the aged. *Psychiatry, 26*, 65–76.

Caldwell, R. L. (2005). At the confluence of memory and meaning—Life review with older adults and families: Using narrative therapy and the expressive arts to re-member and re-author stories of resilience. *Family Journal: Counseling and Therapy for Couples and Families, 13*(2), 172–175.

Canon, K. G., & Heyward, C. (1992). *Alienation and anger: A black and white woman's struggle for mutuality in an unjust world.* Wellesley, MA: Stone Center Working Paper Series, Wellesley College.

Caribbean's tarnished jewel, The. (1999, October 2). *Economist*, 533(8139), 37–38.

Carlson, J., & Kjos, D. (2002). *Theories and strategies of family therapy.* Boston: Allyn & Bacon.

Carpenter, D. (1996). Constructivism and social work treatment. In F. Turner (Ed.), *Social work treatment: Interlocking theoretical approaches* (4th ed.). New York: The Free Press.

Carr, A. (Ed.). (2000). *What works with children and adolescents? A critical review of psychological interventions with children, adolescents, and their families.* London: Routledge.

Carter, R. T. (1995). *The influence of race and racial identity in psychotherapy.* New York: John Wiley & Sons.

Caspi, J. (2005). Coaching and social work: Challenges and concerns. *Social Work*, 50(4), 359–361.

Caspi, J., & Caspi, D. (2003). *Task-centered personal coaching: A social work model.* Paper presented at the NASW New Jersey Annual Continuing Education Conference, Atlantic City, NJ.

Cath, S. H. (1976). Functional disorders: An organismic view and attempt at reclassification. In L. Bellak & T. B. Karasu (Eds.), *Geriatric psychiatry: A handbook for psychiatry and primary care physicians* (pp. 141–172). New York: Grune and Stratton.

Chambliss, C. H. (2000). *Psychotherapy and managed care.* Boston: Allyn & Bacon.

Chaney, E. F., O'Leary, M. R., & Marlatt, G. A. (1987). Skill training with alcoholics. *Journal of Consulting and Clinical Psychology*, 46, 1092–1104.

Chodorow, N. (1978). *The reproduction of mothering: Psychoanalysis and the sociology of gender.* Berkeley: University of California Press.

Chou, K. L., & Chi, I. (2005). Prevalence and correlates of depression in Chinese oldest-old. *International. Journal of Geriatric Psychiatry, 20*(1), 41–50.

Chung, R.C.-Y., Bemak, F., & Okazaki, S. (1997). Counseling Americans of Southeast Asian descent. In C. C. Lee (Ed.), *Multicultural issues in counseling* (2nd ed., pp. 207–231). Alexandria, VA: American Counseling Association.

Cicchetti, D., & Rogosch, F. A. (2002). A developmental psychopathology perspective on adolescence. *Journal of Consulting and Clinical Psychology*, 70, 6–20.

Clark, D. A. (2003). *Cognitive-behavioral therapy for OCD.* New York: Guilford.

Clarkin, J. F., & Frances, A. (1982). Selection criteria for the brief psychotherapies. *American Journal of Psychotherapy*, 36, 166–180.

Colapinto, J. (1985, May–June). Maturana and the ideology of conformity. *Family Therapy Networker.*

Coll, C. G. (1992). *Cultural diversity: Implications for theory and practice.* Wellesley, MA: Stone Center Working Paper Series, Wellesley College.

Coll, C. G., Cook-Nobles, R., & Surrey, J. (1995). *Diversity at the core: Implications for relational theory.* Wellesley, MA: Stone Center Working Paper Series, Wellesley College.

Comas-Diaz, L. (1994). An integrative approach. In L. Comas-Diaz & B. Greene (Eds.), *Women of color: Integrating ethnic and gender identities in psychotherapy* (pp. 287–318). New York: Guilford.

Comas-Diaz, L., & Greene, B. (1994). *Women of color and mental health.* New York: Guilford.

Congress, E. (2001). Dual relationships in social work education: Report on a national survey. *Journal of Social Work Education*, 37(2), 255–267.

Congress, E. P. (1994). The use of culturagrams to assess and empower culturally diverse families. *Families in Society*, 75(9), 531–539.

Corcoran, K., & Vandiver, V. (1996). *Maneuvering the maze of managed care.* New York: Free Press-Simon and Schuster.

Corwin, M. (2002). *Brief treatment in clinical social work practice.* Pacific Grove, CA: Brooks/Cole.

Cournoyer, B. R. (2004). *The evidence based social work skills book.* Boston: Pearson.

Cozolino, L. J. (2002). *The neuroscience of psychotherapy: Building and rebuilding the human brain.* New York: Norton.

Crago, H., & Crago, M. (2000). Editorial: The courage to enter dialogue. *Australian & New Zealand Journal of Family Therapy*, 21(3), iii–iv.

Cramer, E. P., & Gilson, S. F. (1999). Queers and crips: Parallel identity development processes for persons with nonvisible disabilities and lesbian, gay and bisexual persons. *Journal of Gay, Lesbian and Bisexual Identity*, 4, 23–37.

Crawford-Brown, C. (2001). The impact of migration on the rights of children and families in the Caribbean. In C. Barrow (Ed.),*Children's rights: Caribbean realities* (pp. 227–223). Kingston, Jamaica, West Indies: Ian Randle Publishers.

Creswell, W. (2003). *Research design: Qualitative and quantitative approaches* (3rd ed.). Thousand Oaks, CA: Sage.

Cross, W. E., Jr. (1971). The negro to black conversion experience: Toward a psychology of black liberation. *Black World*, 20(9), 13–27.

Cross, W. E., Jr. (1978). The Cross and Thomas models of psychological nigrescence. *Journal of Black Psychology*, 5(1), 13–19.

Cross, W. E., Jr. (1991). *Shades of black: Diversity in African American identity.* Philadelphia, PA: Temple University Press.

Cross, W. E., Jr. (1995). The psychology of nigrescence: Revising the Cross model. In J. G. Ponterotto, J. M. Casas, L. A. Suzuki, & C. M. Alexander (Eds.), *Handbook of multicultural counseling* (pp. 93–122). Thousand Oaks, CA: Sage.

Cummings, N. A. (1990). Brief intermittent psychotherapy throughout the life cycle. In J. K. Zeig & S. G. Gilligan (Eds.),*Brief therapy: Myths, methods and metaphors* (pp. 169–184). New York: Brunner/Mazel.

D'Augelli, A. R. (1994). Identity development and sexual orientation: Toward a model of lesbian, gay and bisexual development. In E. J. Trickett, R. J. Watts, & D. Birman (Eds.), *Human diversity: Perspectives on people in context* (pp. 312–333). San Francisco: Jossey-Bass.

Damasio, A. (2003). *Looking for Spinoza: Joy, sorrow and the feeling brain.* New York: Putnam.

Davidson, T., & Davidson, J. (1996). Confidentiality and managed care: Ethical and legal concerns. *Health and Social Work*, 21, 453–464.

Davies, D. (2004). *Child development: A practitioner's guide* (2nd ed.). New York: Guilford.

de Shazer, S. (1985). *Keys to solution in brief therapy.* New York: Norton.

de Shazer, S. (1988). *Clues: Investigating solutions in brief therapy.* New York: Norton.

de Shazer, S. (1991). *Putting difference to work.* New York: Norton.

Dean, R. G. (1993). Constructivism: An approach to clinical practice. *Smith College Studies in Social Work*, 63(2), 129–146.

Dean, R. G. (2001). The myth of cross-cultural competence. *Families in Society*, 82(6), 623–630.

DeJong, P. (2002). Solution focused therapy. In A. R. Roberts & G. J. Greene (Eds.), *Social workers' desk reference* (pp. 112–116). New York: Oxford University Press.

DeJong, P., & Berg, I. K. (2001). Co-constructing cooperation with mandated clients. *Social Work*, 46(4), 361–374.

DeLaCour, E. (1996). The interpersonal school and its influence on current relational theories. In J. Berzoff, L. Melano Flanagan,

& P. Hertz (Eds.), *Inside out and outside in: Psychodynamic clinical theory and practice in contemporary multicultural contexts* (pp. 199–221). Northvale, NJ: Jason Aronson.

DeLaCour, E. P. (1998). How has the therapeutic relationship changed in psychoanalytic psychotherapy? *Smith College Studies in Social Work*, 68(2), 171–183.

Delgado, M., Jones, K., & Rohani, M. (2005). *Social work practice in immigrant and refugee youth in the United States.* Boston: Allyn & Bacon.

Denborough, D. (2007). Talking with mothers and children: An intake questionnaire. *International Journal of Narrative Therapy and Community Work*, 3, 17–20.

Denborough, D. (2008). *Collective narrative practice: Responding to individuals, groups and communities who have experienced trauma.* Adelaide, Australia: Dulwich Centre Publications.

Denzin, N., & Lincoln, Y. (2000). *Handbook of qualitative research.* Thousand Oaks, CA: Sage.

DeRubeis, R., & Beck, A. (1988). Cognitive therapy. In K. Dobson (Ed.), *Handbook of cognitive-behavioral therapies* (pp. 273–306). New York: Guilford.

deVries, M. (1996). Trauma in cultural perspective. In B. Vanderkolk, A. MacFarlane, & L. Weisaeth (Eds.), *Traumatic stress: The effects of overwhelming experience on mind, body, and society.* New York: Guilford.

Dewan, M. J., Steenbarger, B. N., & Greenberg, R. (2008). Brief psychotherapies. In A. Tasman, J. Kay, & J. A. Lieberman (Eds.), *Psychiatry* (Vol. 2, 3rd ed., pp. 1889–1903). New York. Wiley.

DeYoung, M., & Lowry, J. A. (1992). Traumatic bonding: Clinical implications in incest. *Child Welfare*, 71, 165.

DiGiuseppe, R., & Linscott, J. (1993). Philosophical differences among cognitive-behavioral therapists: Rationalism, constructivism, or both? *Journal of Cognitive Psychotherapy*, 7, 117–130.

Dimen, M. (2000). Introduction to symposium on race. *Psychoanalytic Dialogues*, 10, 569–579.

Dow, L. H. (1995). Selective mutism. In J. S. March (Ed.), *Anxiety disorders in children and adolescents* (pp. 235–250). New York: Guilford.

Drewery, W., & Winslade, J. (1997). The theoretical story of narrative therapy. In G. Monk, J. Winslade, K. Crocket, & D. Epston (Eds.), *Narrative therapy in practice: The archaeology of hope* (pp. 32–53). San Francisco: Jossey-Bass.

Duckworth, A., Steen, T., & Seligman, M. (2005). Positive psychology in clinical practice. *Annual Review of Clinical Psychology*, 1, 629–651.

Dunn, L. L. (2001). *Jamaica: Situation of children in prostitution: A rapid assessment.* Geneva: ILO.

Dutton, D., & Painter, S. L. (1981). Traumatic bonding. *Victimology: An International Journal*, 6(1–4), 139–155.

Eakes, G., Walsh, S., Markowski, M., Cain, H., & Swanson, M. (1997). Family centered brief solution-focused therapy with chronic schizophrenia: A pilot study. *Journal of Family Therapy*, 19(2), 145–158.

Eidelson, R. J., & Eidelson, J. I. (2003). Dangerous ideas: Five beliefs that propel groups toward conflict. *American Psychologist*, 58, 182–192.

Eisenbruch, M. (1991). From post-traumatic stress disorder to cultural bereavement: Diagnosis of Southeast Asian refugees. *Journal of Scientific Medicine*, 33(6), 673–680.

Eizur, Y., & Perednik, R. (2003). Prevalence and description of selective mutism in immigrant and native families: A controlled study. *Journal of the American Academy of Child & Adolescent Psychiatry*, 42(12), 1451–1459.

Elbaum, B., & Vaughn, S. (2003). Self-concept and students with learning disabilities. In H. L. Swanson, K. R. Harris, & S. Graham (Eds.), *Handbook of learning disabilities* (pp. 229–242). New York: Guilford.

Eldridge, N., Mencher, J., & Slater, S. (1993). *The conundrum of mutuality: A lesbian dialogue.* Wellesley, MA: Stone Center Working Paper Series, Wellesley College.

Eliason, M. J. (1996). Identity formation for lesbian, bisexual and gay persons: Beyond a "minoritizing" view. *Journal of Homosexuality*, 30(3), 31–58.

Ellis, A. (1962). *Reason and emotion in psychotherapy.* New York: Stuart.

Elson, M. (1986). *Self psychology in clinical social work.* New York: Norton.

Emerson, S., & Rosenfeld, C. (1996). Stages of adjustment in family members of transgender individuals. *Journal of Family Psychotherapy*, 7(3), 1–12.

Emmons, R. A., & McCullough, M. E. (2003). Counting blessings versus burdens: An experimental investigation of gratitude and subject well being in daily life. *Journal of Personality and Social Psychology*, 84(2), 377–389.

Enns, C. Z. (1991). The "new" relationship models of women's identity: A review and critique for counselors. *Journal of Counseling & Development*, 69, 209–216.

Epstein, L., & Brown, L. B. (2002). *Brief treatment and a new look at the task-centered approach.* Boston: Allyn & Bacon.

Epston, D. (1997). "I am a bear"—Discovering discoveries. In C. Smith & D. Nylund (Eds.), *Narrative therapies with children and adolescents* (pp. 53–71). New York: Guilford.

Erikson, E. (1950). *Childhood and society.* New York: Norton.

Erikson, E. (1959). Identity and the life cycle: Selected papers. *Psychological Issues Monograph*, 1(1). New York: International University Press.

Eyerman, R. (2003). *Cultural trauma, slavery, and the formation of African American identity.* Cambridge: Cambridge University Press.

Fairbairn, W. R. D. (1952a). *An object relations theory of the personality.* New York: Basic Books.

Fairbairn, W. R. D. (1952b). *Psychoanalytic studies of the personality.* New York: Basic Books.

Falicov, C. J. (2007). Working with transnational immigrants: Expanding meanings of family, community and culture. *Family Process*, 46(2), 157–171.

Fedele, N. (1994). *Relationships in groups: Connection, resonance, and paradox.* Wellesley, MA: Stone Center Working Paper Series, Wellesley College.

Fedele, N., & Harrington, E. (1990). *Women's groups: How connections heal.* Wellesley, MA: Stone Center Working Paper Series, Wellesley College.

Flaskas, C., Stagoll, B., Larner, G., Hart, B., Doan, R., Weingarten, K., Loth, W., Hayward, M., & Pocock, D. (2000). Dialogues of diversity in therapy: A virtual symposium. *Australian & New Zealand Journal of Family Therapy*, 21(3), 121–143.

Fonagy, P. (2006). Mechanisms of change in mentalization-based treatment of BPD. *British Journal of Clinical Psychology*, 62, 411–430.

Fonagy, P., & Target, M. (2003). *Psychoanalytic theories: Perspectives from developmental psychology.* New York: Bruner-Routledge.

Fong, R. (2001). Culturally competent social work practice: Past and present. In R. Fong & S. Furuto (Eds.), *Culturally competent practice: Skills, interventions, and evaluation* (pp. 1–19). New York: Russell Sage.

Fortune, A., McCarthy, M., & Abramson, J. (2001). Student learning processes in field education: Relationship of learning activities to quality of field instruction, satisfaction, and performance among MSW students. *Journal of Education in Social Work*, 37(1), 111–127.

Fosha, D. (2004). Brief integrative therapy comes of age: A commentary. *Journal of Psychotherapy Integration*, 14(1), 66–92.

Franklin, C., & Nurius, P. (1996). Constructivist therapy: New directions in social work practice. *Families in Society: Journal of Contemporary Social Work Practice*, 77(6), 323–325.

Franklin, M. E., & Foa, E. B. (2008). Obsessive compulsive disorder. In D. H. Barlow (Ed.), *Clinical handbook of psychological disorders* (4th ed.). New York: Guilford.

Fraunce, P. S. (1990). The self-care and wellness of feminist therapists. In H. Lerman & N. Porter (Eds.), *Feminist ethics in psychotherapy* (pp. 185–194). New York: Springer.

Fredrickson, B. L. (2004). The broaden-and-build theory of positive emotions. *Philosophical Transactions of the Royal Society B: Biological Sciences*, 359(1449), 1367–1378.

Freud, S. (1912). A note on the unconscious in psychoanalysis. In J. Strachey, Jr. (Ed.), *The standard edition of the complete psychological works of Sigmund Freud* (Vols. 1–24, pp. 255–266). London: Hogarth Press.

Freud, S. (1953). Three essays on the theory of sexuality. In J. Strachey (Ed.), *The standard edition of the complete psychological works of Sigmund Freud* (Vol. 7, pp. 125–245). London: Hogarth Press. (Original work published 1905)

Freud, S. (1957). Instincts and their vicissitudes. In J. Strachey (Ed.), *The standard edition of the complete psychological works of Sigmund Freud* (Vol. 14, pp. 117–140). (Original work published 1915)

Friedberg, R. D., & McClure, J. M. (2002). *Clinical practice of cognitive therapy with children and adolescents: The nuts and bolts*. New York: Guilford.

Friedman, S. (1995). *The reflecting team in action*. New York: Guilford.

Furman, R. (2001). A radical analysis of the privatization of mental health services: Lessons for educators. *International Education Electron Journal*, 5(4). http://www.Canberra.edu.au/uc/educ/crie/2000-2—1/ieej20/leadarticle20.html

Furman, R., & Langer, C. L. (2006). Managed care and the care of the soul. *Journal of Social Work Values and Ethics*, 3(2). http://www.socialworker.com/jswve/content/blogcategory/13/46/

Gabbard, G. (2001). Empirical evidence and psychotherapy: A growing scientific base. *American Journal of Psychiatry*, 158, 1–3.

Gainor, K. A. (1992). Internalized oppression as a barrier to effective group work with Black women. *Journal for Specialists in Group Work*, 17(4), 235–242.

Galambos, C., Watt, J. W., Anderson, K., & Danis, F. (2005). *Ethics forum:* Rural social work practice: Maintaining confidentiality in the face of dual relationships. *Journal of Social Work Values and Ethics*, 2(2). http://www.socialworker.com/ jswve/content/blogcategory/11/37/

Gallagher-Thompson, D., Hanley-Peterson, P., & Thompson, L. W. (1990). Maintenance of gains versus relapse following brief psychotherapy for depression. *Journal of Consulting and Clinical Psychology*, 58(3), 371–374.

Gallo-Lopez, L., & Schaefer, C. E. (Eds.). (2005). *Play therapy with adolescents*. New York: Jason Aronson.

Gambrill, E. (2004). Concepts and methods of behavioral treatment. In D. Granvold (Ed.), *Cognitive and behavioral treatment* (pp. 32–62). Pacific Grove, CA: Brooks/Cole.

Ganzer, C., & Ornstein, E. D. (2004). Regression, self-disclosure, and the teach or treat dilemma: Implications of a relational approach for social work supervision. *Clinical Social Work Journal*, 32(4), 431–449.

Garcia-Petro, N. (1982). Puerto Rican families. In M. McGoldrick, J. Pearce, & J. Girodano (Eds.), *Ethnicity and family therapy*. New York: Guilford.

Gardner, J. R. (1999). Using self psychology in brief psychotherapy. *Psychoanalytic Social Work*, 6(3/4), 43–85.

Garfield, S. L. (1994). Research on client variables in psychotherapy. In A. E. Bergin & S. L. Garfield (Eds.), *Handbook of psychotherapy and behavior change* (4th ed., pp. 190–228). New York: John Wiley & Sons.

Gergen, K. J. (1999). *An invitation to social construction*. London: Sage.

Germer, C. K. (2005). Mindfulness: What is it? What does it matter? In C. K. Germer, R. D. Siegel, & P. R. Fulton (Eds.), *Mindfulness and psychotherapy* (pp. 3–27). New York: Guilford.

Germer, C. K. (2009). *The mindful path to self-compassion: Freeing yourself from destructive thoughts and emotions*. New York: Guilford.

Gil, E. (1991). *The healing power of play: Working with abused children*. New York: Guilford.

Gil, E. (1994). *Play in family therapy*. New York: Guilford.

Gil, E., & Shaw, J. A. (2009). Prescriptive play therapy. In K. J. O'Connor & L. D. Braverman (Eds.), *Play therapy theory and practice: Comparing theories and techniques* (2nd ed., pp. 451–487). New York: John Wiley.

Gilligan, C. (1982). *In a different voice*. Cambridge, MA: Harvard University Press.

Gingerich, W. J., & Wabeke, T. (2001). A solution-focused approach to mental health intervention in school settings. *Children & Schools*, 23, 33–47.

Glaser, B., & Strauss, A. (1967). *The discovery of grounded theory*. Chicago: Aldine.

Godwin, G. (1996). How to keep a journal. *Behavioral Health Treatment*, 2(7), 551–552.

Goldberg, A. (1973). A psychotherapy of narcissistic injuries. *Archives of General Psychiatry*, 28, 722–726.

Goldstein, E. (1995). *Ego psychology and social work practice* (2nd ed.). New York: The Free Press.

Goldstein, E. G. (2007). Social work education and clinical learning: Yesterday, today and tomorrow. *Clinical Social Work Journal*, 35, 15–33.

Gomez-Sanchez, B. (1978). Effective ingredients in psychotherapy: Prediction of outcome from process variables. *Journal of Consulting and Clinical Psychology*, 46, 1023–1035.

Gomory, T. (2001). Critical rationalism (Gomory's blurry theory) or positivism (Thyer's theoretical myopia): Which is the prescription for social work research? *Journal of Education in Social Work*, 37(1), 67–79.

Gonzalez, M. (2002). Mental health intervention with Hispanic immigrants: Understanding the influence of the client's worldview, language, and religion. *Journal of Refugee Services*, 1, 81–92.

Gottlib, I. H., & Hammen, C. L. (2002). *Handbook of depression*. New York: Guilford.

Gray, J. A. (2001). The origin of evidence-based practice. In A. Edwards & G. Elwyn (Eds.), *Evidence informed and client choice* (pp. 19–33). New York: Oxford University Press.

Gray, M., & Fook, J. (2004). The quest for universal social work: Some issues and implications. *Social Work Education*, 23(5), 625–644.

Greenberg, J., & Mitchell, S. (1983). *Object relations in psychoanalytic theory*. Cambridge, MA: Harvard University Press.

Greenberg, R. P., & Dewan, M. J. (2009). Brief psychotherapies: Potent approaches to treatment. *Psychiatric Times*, 26(3), 44–47.

Greene, B. (1993). Psychotherapy with African American women: Integrating feminist and psychodynamic models. *Journal of Training and Practice in Professional Psychology*, 7(1), 49, 65.

Greene, G. J., Lee, M., Trask, R., & Rheinscheld, J. (2000). How to work with clients' strengths in crisis intervention: A solution-focused approach. In A. R. Roberts (Ed.), *Crisis intervention handbook: Assessment, treatment, and research* (pp. 31–55). Oxford: Oxford University Press.

Greenson, R. R. (1967). *The technique and practice of psychoanalysis.* Madison, CT: International Universities Press.

Griffith, J. L., & Griffith, M. E. (2002). *Encountering the sacred in psychotherapy: How to talk with people about their spiritual lives.* New York: Guilford.

Grimm, R. (2003). Narrative therapy with older adults. In J. L. Ronch & J. A. Goldfield (Eds.), *Mental wellness in aging: Strengths-based approaches* (pp. 237–271). Baltimore, MD: Health Professions Press.

Guba, E. G., & Lincoln, Y. S. (1981). *Effective evaluation.* San Francisco: Jossey-Bass.

Guerney, L. (1997). Filial therapy. In K. O'Connor & L. Braverman (Eds.), *Play therapy theory and practice: A comparative presentation* (pp. 131–159). New York: Wiley.

Guntrip, H. (1969). *Schizoid phenomena, object relations and the self.* New York: International Universities Press.

Guntrip, H. (1971). *Psychoanalytic theory, therapy and the self.* New York: Basic Books.

Gusman, F. D., Stewart, J., Young, B. H., Riney, S. J., Abueg, F. R., & Blake, D. D. (1996). A multicultural developmental approach for treating trauma. In A. Marsella, M. Friedman, E. Gerrity, & R. Scurfield (Eds.), *Ethnocultural aspects of posttraumatic stress disorder* (pp. 439–457). Washington, DC: American Psychological Association.

Hanna, F. J., Talley, W. B., & Guindon, M. H. (2000). The power of perception: Toward a model of cultural oppression and liberation. *Journal of Counseling & Development,* 78, 430–446.

Harper, K. V., & Lantz, J. (1996). *Cross-cultural practice: Social work with diverse populations.* Chicago: Lyceum Books.

Harris, D. M., & Parrish, D. E. (2006). The art of online teaching: Online instruction versus in-class instruction.

Harris, R. (2006, August). Embracing your demons: An overview of acceptance and commitment therapy. *Psychotherapy in Australia,* 12(4), 2–8.

Hartley, D. E., & Strupp, H. H. (1983). The therapeutic alliance: Its relationship to outcome in brief psychotherapy. In J. Masling (Ed.), *Empirical studies of psychoanalytic theories* (Vol. 1, pp. 1–37). Hillsdale, NJ: Analytic Press.

Hartling, L., Rosen, W., Walker, M., & Jordan, J. (2000). *Shame and humiliation: From isolation to relational transformation.* Wellesley, MA: Stone Center Working Paper Series, Wellesley College.

Hartman, A. (1978). Diagrammatic assessment of family relationships. *Social Casework,* 59, 465–476.

Hartmann, K., & Levenson (1995). *Case formulation in TLDP.* Paper presented at the annual international meeting of the Society for Psychotherapy Research, Vancouver, British Columbia, Canada.

Hayashi, S., Kuno, T., Osawa, M., & Shimizu, M. (1992). The client-centered and person-centered approach in Japan: Historical development, current status, and perspectives. *Journal of Humanistic Psychology,* 32(2), 115–136.

Hayes, P. (2008). *Addressing cultural complexities in practice: Assessment, diagnosis and therapy* (2nd ed.). Washington, DC: American Psychological Association.

Hayes, S. State of the ACT evidence. *Contextual Psychology.org.* http://www.contextualpsychology .org/state_of_the_act_evidence/

Hayes, S. C., Luoma, J., Bond, F., Masuda, A., & Lillis, J. (2006). Acceptance and commitment therapy: Model, processes, and outcomes. *Behaviour Research and Therapy,* 44(1), 1–25.

Hayes, S. C., & Smith, S. (2005). *Get out of your mind and into your life: The new acceptance and commitment therapy.* New Harbinger Publications.

Hayes, S. C., & Strosahl, K. D. (2004). *A practical guide to acceptance and commitment therapy.* Springer.

Hayes, S. C., Strosahl, K. D., & Wilson, K. G. (2003). *Acceptance and commitment therapy: An experiential approach to behavior change.* New York: Guilford.

Hayward, M. (2003). Critiques of narrative therapy: A personal response. *Australian and New Zealand Journal of Family Therapy,* 24(4), 183–189.

Helms, J. (1984). Toward a theoretical model of the effects of race on counseling: A black and white model. *Counseling Psychologist,* 12, 153–165.

Helms, J., & Cook, D. (1999). *Using race and culture in counseling and psychotherapy.* Boston: Allyn & Bacon.

Herdt, G. (1994). *Third sex, third gender: Beyond sexual dimorphism in culture and history.* New York: Zone Books.

Heron, B. (2005). Self-reflection in critical social work practice: Subjectivity and the possibilities of resistance. *Reflective Practice,* 6, 341–351.

Hick, S. F. (2008). Cultivating therapeutic relationships: The role of mindfulness. In S. F. Hick & T. Bien (Eds.), *Mindfulness and the therapeutic relationship* (pp. 3–18). New York: Guilford.

Hilke, I. (1998). The playing through of selfobject transferences of a nine-year-old boy. In A. Goldberg (Ed.), *The World of Self Psychology: Progress in Self Psychology* (Vol. 14, pp. 71–84). Hillsdale, NJ: Analytic Press.

Hodge, D. R. (2004). Spirituality and people with mental illness: Developing spiritual competency in assessment and intervention.*Families in Society: Journal of Contemporary Human Services,* 85(1), 36–44.

Hoffman, L. (1992). Some practical implications of a social constructivist view of the psychoanalytic situation. *Psychoanalytic Dialogues,* 2(3), 287–304.

Hollifel, M., Geppert, C., Johnson, Y., & Fryer, C. (2002). A Vietnamese man with selective mutism: The relevance of multiple interacting 'cultures' in clinical psychiatry. *Transcultural Psychiatry,* 40(3), 329–341.

Hollon, S. D., & Kriss, M. R. (1983). Cognitive factors in clinical research and practice. *Clinical Psychology Review,* 4, 35–76.

Holmbeck, G. N., Greenley, R. N., & Franks, E. A. (2003). Developmental issues and considerations in research and practice. In A. Kazdin & J. Weisz (Eds.), *Evidence-based psychotherapies for children and adolescents* (pp. 21–41). New York: Guilford.

Horney, K. (1950). *Neurosis and human growth.* New York: Norton.

Howard, K. L., Kopta, S. M., Krause, S. M., & Orlinsky, D. E. (1986). The dose-effect relationship in psychotherapy. *American Psychologist,* 41, 159–164.

Hoyt, M. F. (1995). Single-session solutions. In M. F. Hoyt (Ed.), *Brief therapy and managed care: Readings for contemporary practice.* San Francisco: Jossey-Bass.

Hoyt, M. F., & Berg, I. K. (1998). Solution-focused couple therapy: Helping clients construct self-fulfilling realities. In M. F. Hoyt (Ed.), *The handbook of constructive therapies* (pp. 414–340). San Francisco: Jossey-Bass.

Hudson, W. W. (1990a). *Computer assisted social services.* Tempe, AZ: WALMYR.

Hudson, W. W., & Faul, A. C. (1998). *The clinical measurement packager: A field manual* (2nd ed.). Tallahassee, FL: WALMYR.

Hughes, J. N., & Baker, D. B. (1990). *The clinical child interview.* New York: Guilford.

Hulko, W. (2009). The time-and context-contingent nature of intersectionality and interlocking oppressions. *Affilia: Journal of Women and Social Work,* 24(1), 44–55.

Hunt, L. (2007). *Inventing human rights.* New York: Norton and Company.

Ife, J. (2001). *Human rights and social work.* Cambridge: Cambridge University Press.

Ivey, A. E., Ivey, M. B., & Simek-Morgan, L. (2007). *Counseling and psychotherapy: A multicultural perspective* (6th ed.). Columbus, OH: Merrill.

Jackson, V. (2002). In our own voice African American stories of oppression, survival and recovery in mental health systems. *International Journal of Narrative Therapy and Community Work, 2.*

Jacobs, C. (2010). Spiritual development. In J. G. Lesser & D. S. Pope (Eds.), *Human behavior and the social environment* (2nd ed., pp. 226–242). Boston: Allyn and Bacon.

James, B. (1989). *Treating traumatized children: New insights and creative interventions.* Toronto: Lexington.

James, B. (1994). *Handbook for treatment of attachment-trauma problems in children.* New York: The Free Press.

Jenkins, J. H. (1996). Culture, emotion, and PTSD. In A. J. Marsella, M. J. Friedman, E. T. Gerrity, & R. M. Scurield (Eds.), *Ethnocultural aspects of posttraumatic stress disorder: Issues, research, and clinical applications.* Washington, DC: American Psychological Association.

Jernberg, A. (1979). *Theraplay.* San Francisco: Jossey-Bass.

Johnson, R. B., & Onwuegbuzie, A. J. (2003). Mixed methods research: A research paradigm whose time has come. *Educational Researcher,* 33, 14–26.

Johnston, D. W., Lancashire, M., Matthews, A. M., Munby, M., Shaw, P. M., & Gilder, M. G. (1976, October). Imaginal flooding and exposure to real phobic situations: Charges during treatments. *British Journal of Psychiatry,* 129, 372–377.

Jordan, C., & Franklin, C. (1995). *Clinical assessment for social workers.* Chicago: Lyceum.

Jordan, J. V. (1991). Empathy, mutuality, and therapeutic change: Clinical implications of a relational model. In J. V. Jordan, A. G. Kaplan, J. B. Miller, I. P. Stiver, & J. L. Surrey (Eds.), *Women's growth in connection: Writings from the Stone Center* (pp. 283–290). New York: Guilford.

Jordan, J. V. (1997a). Relational developmental: Therapeutic implications of empathy and shame. In J. V. Jordan (Ed.), *Women's growth in diversity* (pp. 138–161). New York: Guilford.

Jordan, J. V. (1997b). A relational perspective for understanding women's development. In J. V. Jordan (Ed.), *Women's growth in diversity* (pp. 9–24). New York: Guilford.

Jordan, J. V., Kaplan, A. G., Miller, J. B., Stiver, I. P., & Surrey, J. L. (Eds.). (1991). *Women's growth in connection: Writings from the Stone Center.* New York: Guilford.

Joseph, M. V. (1998). Religion and social work practice. *Social Casework: Journal of Contemporary Social Work,* 69, 443–452.

Joshi, P. T. (1998). Guidelines for international trauma work. *International Review of Psychiatry,* 10, 179–185.

Kadushin, A. (1997). *The social work interview.* New York: Columbia University Press.

Kagle, J. D., & Giebelhausen, P. N. (1994). Dual relationships and professional boundaries. *Social Work,* 39(2), 213–220.

Kail, R. (2001). *The development of memory in children.* New York: Freeman.

Kaplan, A., & Klein, R. (1990). *Women and suicide: The cry for connection.* Wellesley, MA: Stone Center Working Paper Series, Wellesley College.

Kaplan, A. G. (1986). The "self-in-relation": Implications for depression in women. *Psychotherapy: Theory, Research, and Practice,* 23, 234–242.

Kaplan, H., Sadock, B., & Grebb, J. (1994). *Synopsis of psychiatry, behavioral science clinical psychiatry* (7th ed.). Baltimore, MD: Williams & Wilkins.

Kaslow, F. W. (1999). The lingering Holocaust legacies in lives of descendants of victims and perpetrators. *Professional Psychology, Research and Practice,* 30(6), 611–616.

Kelly, P. (1996). Narrative theory and social work treatment. In F. Turner (Ed.), *Social work treatment: Interlocking theoretical approaches* (4th ed.). New York: The Free Press.

Kendall, P. (Ed.). (2000). *Child and adolescent therapy: Cognitive-behavioral procedures* (2nd ed.). New York: Guilford.

Kiser, D. J., Piercy, F. P., & Lipchik, E. (1993). The integration of emotion in solution-focused therapy. *Journal of Marital and Family Therapy,* 19, 233–242.

Klee, T. (2000–2005). *Eight stages of object relations.* Retrieved September 17, 2006, from www.objectrelations.org/stages.htm

Klein, M. (1948). *Contributions to psychoanalysis, 1921–1945.* London: Hogarth.

Klein, M. (1964). *Contributions to psychoanalysis, 1921–1945.* New York: McGraw-Hill.

Klosko, J. S., & Sanderson, W. C. (1999). *Cognitive-behavioral treatment of depression.* Northvale, NJ: Jason Aronson.

Knell, S. (1997). Cognitive-behavioral play therapy. In K. O'Connor & L. Braverman (Eds.), *Play therapy theory and practice: A comparative presentation.* New York: John Wiley & Sons.

Knell, S. (1998). Cognitive-behavioral play therapy. *Journal of Clinical Child Psychology,* 27(1), 28–33.

Knell, S. (2009). Cognitive-behavioral play therapy. In K. J. O'Connor & L. S. Braverman (Eds.), *Play therapy theory and practice: Comparing theories and techniques* (pp. 203–236). New York: John Wiley.

Knight, C. (2001). The process of field instruction: BSW and MSW students' views. *Journal of Social Work Education,* 37(2), 357–381.

Ko, S., & Rosen, S. (2001). *Teaching online: A practical guide.* Boston: Houghton Mifflin Company.

Kohut, H. (1971). *The analysis of the self.* New York: International Universities Press.

Kohut, H. (1977). *The restoration of the self.* New York: International Universities Press.

Kohut, H. (1978). Introspection, empathy and psychoanalysis: An examination of the relationship between mode of observation and theory. In P. Ornstein (Ed.), *The search for the self* (Vol. 1, pp. 205–232). New York: International Universities Press. (Original work published 1959)

Kok, C. J., & Leskela, J. (1996). Solution-focused therapy in a psychiatric hospital. *Journal of Marital and Family Therapy,* 22(3), 397–406.

Koss, M. P., & Butcher, J. N. (1986). Research on brief therapy. In A. E. Bergin & S. L. Garfield (Eds.), *Handbook of psychotherapy and behavior change* (4th ed., pp. 664–700). New York: John Wiley & Sons.

Kron, T., & Yerushalmi, H. (2000). The intersubjective approach in supervision. *Clinical Supervisor,* 19(1), 99–121.

Krupnick, J. L., Sotsky, S. M., Simmens, S., Moyer, J., Elkin, I., Watkins, J., & Pilkonis, P. A. (1996). The role of the therapeutic alliance in psychotherapy and pharmacotherapy outcome: Findings in the National Institute of Mental Health Treatment of Depression Collaborative Research Program. *Journal of Consulting and Clinical Psychology,* 64, 532–539.

Kulkin, H. S., Chauvin, E. A., & Percle, G. (2000). Suicide among gay and lesbian adolescents and young adults: A review of the literature. *Journal of Homosexuality,* 40(1), 1–29.

Kvale, S. (1996). *Interviews: An introduction to qualitative research interviewing.* Thousand Oaks, CA: Sage.

Lam, B. T. (2005). An integrative model for the study of psychological distress in Vietnamese-American adolescents. *North American Journal of Psychology, 7*, 89–106.

Lambert, M. (1992). Implications of outcome research for psychotherapy integration. In J. C. Norcross & M. R. Goldfried (Eds.), *Handbook of psychotherapy integration*. New York: Basic Books.

Lambert, M. J., & Simon, W. (2008). The therapeutic relationship: Central and essential in psychotherapy outcome. In S. F. Hick & T. Bien (Eds.), *Mindfulness and the therapeutic relationship* (pp. 19–33). New York: Guilford.

Landreth, G. L. (2002). *The art of the relationship in play therapy*. New York: Brunner-Routledge.

Larner, G. (2004). Family therapy and the politics of evidence. *Journal of Family Therapy, 26*, 17–39.

LaVigna, G. W., & Donnellan, A. M. (1986). *Alternatives to punishment: Solving behavior problems with nonaversive strategies*. New York: Irvington.

Lazarus, L. (1982). Brief psychotherapy of narcissistic disturbances. *Psychotherapy: Theory, Research and Practice, 19*(2), 228–236.

Lazarus, L. (1988). Self psychology: Its application to brief psychotherapy with the elderly. *Journal of Geriatric Psychiatry, 21*, 109–125.

Lazarus, L. (1993). Elderly. In H. Jackson (Ed.), *Using self psychology in psychotherapy* (pp. 135–153). Northvale, NJ: Jason Aronson.

Leary, K. (2000). Racial enactments in dynamic treatment. *Psychoanalytic Dialogues, 10*, 639–653.

Lee, A. C. (2009). Psychoanalytic play therapy. In K. J. O'Connor & L. D. Braverman (Eds.), *Play therapy theory and practice: Comparing theories and techniques* (2nd ed., pp. 83–122). New York: John Wiley & Sons.

Lee, M. (1996). A constructivist approach to the help-seeking process of clients: A response to cultural diversity. *Clinical Social Work Journal, 24*(2), 187–202.

Lee, M., & Greene, G. J. (1999). A social constructivist framework for integrating cross-cultural issues in teaching clinical social work. *Journal of Social Work Education, 35*(1), 21–37.

Lee, M. Y., Greene, G. J., Mentzer, R. A., Pinnell, S., & Niles, N. (2001). Solution-focused brief therapy and the treatment of depression: A pilot study. *Journal of Brief Therapy, 1*(1), 33–49.

Leone, C. (2001). Toward a more optimal selfobject milieu: Family psychotherapy from the perspective of self psychology. *Clinical Social Work Journal, 28*(3), 269–289.

Lesser, J. G. (2000, July). The group as self object: Brief psychotherapy with women. *International Journal of Group Psychotherapy, 50*(5), 363–380.

Lesser, J. G. (2010). Group treatment with children and adolescents. In J. R. Brandell (Ed.), *Theory and practice in clinical social work* (2nd ed., pp. 289–322). Thousand Oaks, CA: Sage Publications.

Lesser, J. G., & Eriksen, H. (2000). Brief treatment with a Vietnamese adolescent: Integrating self psychological and constructionist models. *Crisis Intervention, 6*(2), 29–39.

Lesser, J. G., & Pope, D. S. (2010). *Human behavior and the social environment: Theory and Practice*. Boston: Allyn & Bacon.

Levenson, H. (2003). Time-limited dynamic psychotherapy: An integrationist perspective. *Journal of Psychotherapy Integration, 13*, 300–333.

Levenson, H. (2006). An interpersonal approach: Time-limited dynamic psychotherapy. In A. B. Rochlen (Ed.), *Applying counseling theories: An online, case-based approach* (pp. 75–90).

Levenson, H., & Bein, E. (1993). *VA short-term psychotherapy research project: Outcome*. Paper presented at the annual international meeting of the Society for Psychotherapy Research, Pittsburgh, PA.

Levenson, H., & Strupp, H. (2007). Cyclical maladaptive patterns: Case formulations in time-limited dynamic psychotherapy. In T. D. Eells (Ed.), *Handbook of psychotherapy case formulation* (pp. 164–197). New York: Guilford.

Lifton, R. J. (1979). *The broken connection*. New York: Simon and Schuster.

Lightburn, A., & Sessions, P. (Eds.). (2005). *Handbook of community-based clinical practice*. New York: Oxford University Press.

Lightburn, A., & Sessions, P. (2006). What is community-based clinical practice? In A. Lightburn & P. Sessions (Eds.), *Handbook of community-based clinical practice* (pp. 3–19). New York: Oxford University Press.

Lincoln, Y. S., & Guba, E. G. (1985). *Naturalistic inquiry*. Beverly Hills, CA: Sage.

Lindfross, L., & Magnusson, L. (1997). Solution-focused therapy in prison. *Contemporary Family Therapy, 19*, 89–103.

Linzer, N. (1999). *Resolving ethical dilemmas in social work practice*. Boston: Allyn & Bacon.

Lipchik, E. (2002). *Beyond technique in solution-focused therapy: Working with emotions and the therapeutic relationship*. New York: Guilford.

Lipchik, E., Becker, M., Brasher, B., Derks, J., & Volkmann, J. (2005). Neuroscience: A new direction for solution focused thinkers. *Journal of Systemic Therapies, 24*(3), 49–69.

Locke, D. (1992). *Increasing multicultural understanding*. New York: Sage.

Lofland, J., & Lofland, L. (2006). *Analyzing social settings: A guide to qualitative observation and analysis* (4th ed.). Belmont, CA: Wadsworth.

Lowe, R. (1991). Postmodern themes and therapeutic practices: Notes towards the definition of "family therapy" (Part 2). In *Dulwich Centre Newsletter* (Vol. 3, Publication No. SBG 1093, pp. 41–51). Adelaide, Australia: Dulwich Centre Publications.

Luborsky, L., Crits-Cristoph, P., Mintz, J., & Auerback, R. (1988). *Who will benefit from psychotherapy?* New York: Basic Books.

Luborsky, L., Digiuer, L., Luborsky, E., Singer, B., & Dickter, D. (1993). The efficacy of dynamic psychotherapies: Is it true that everyone has won so all shall have a prize? In N. Miller, L. Luborsky, J. P. Barber, & J. Docherty (Eds.), *Psychodynamic treatment research: A handbook for clinical practice* (pp. 447–514). New York: Basic Books.

Lum, D. (1997). Should programs and service delivery systems be culture-specific in their design? Yes. In D. deAnda et al. (Eds.), *Controversial issues in multiculturalism* (pp. 54–71). Boston: Allyn & Bacon.

Lyubomirsky, S., Sheldon, K. M., & Schkade, D. (2005). Pursuing happiness: The architecture of sustainable change. *Review of General Psychology, 9*(2), 111–131.

Mahoney, M. J. (1988). Constructive meta-theory: Basic features and historical foundations. *International Journal of Personal Construct Psychology, 1*(1), 1–35.

Mahoney, M. J., & Freenab, A. (Eds.). (1985). *Cognition and psychotherapy*. New York: Plenum.

Maki, M. T. (1997). Is a pluralistic multicultural approach to practice preferable to acculturation or assimilation approaches? Yes. In D. deAnda et al. (Eds.), *Controversial issues in multiculturalism* (pp. 1–14). Boston: Allyn & Bacon.

Marcotte, D. (1997). Treating depression in adolescence: A review of effectiveness of cognitive-behavior treatments. *Journal of Youth and Adolescence, 26*, 273–283.

Marshall, C., & Rossman, G. (1989). *Designing qualitative research*. Newbury Park, CA: Sage.

Martin, D. J., Garske, J. P., & Davis, M. K. (2000). Relation of the therapeutic alliance with outcome and other variables: A meta-analytic review. *Journal of Consulting Clinical Psychologist, 68*, 438–450.

Maslach, C., Schaufeli, W. B., & Leiter, M. P. (2001). Job burnout. *Annual Review of Psychology, 52*, 397–422.

Mattei, M. D. (1999). A Latina space: Ethnicity as an intersubjective third. *Smith College Studies in Social Work, 69*(2), 255–267.

McCall, L. (2005). The complexity of intersectionality. *Signs, 30*, 1771–1800.

McCart, M. R., Sawyer, G. K., & Smith, D. W. (2008). Developmental issues in diagnosing PTSD.

McClure, F. H., & Teyber, E. (Eds.). (1996). *Child and adolescent therapy: A multicultural relational approach.* Orlando, FL: Harcourt Brace.

McCollough, J. P. (2003). *Treatment for chronic depression: Cognitive-behavioral analysis system of psychotherapy (CBASP).* New York: Guilford.

McGoldrick, M., & Gerson, R. (1985). *Genograms in family assessment.* New York: Norton.

McGoldrick, M., Gerson, R., & Shellenberger, S. (1999). *Genograms: Assessment and intervention.* New York: Norton.

McKeel, A. J. (1997). A clinician's guide to research on solution-focused brief therapy. In S. D. Miller, M. A. Hubble, & B. L. Duncan (Eds.), *Handbook of solution-focused brief therapy* (pp. 251–271). San Francisco: Jossey-Bass.

McKenzie, W., & Monk, G. (1997). Learning and teaching narrative ideas. In G. Monk, J. Winslade, K. Crocket, & D. Epston (Eds.),*Narrative therapy in practice: The archaeology of hope* (pp. 82–121). San Francisco: Jossey-Bass.

McNamee, S. (1996). Psychotherapy as a social construction. *Family Therapy, 13*, 395–409.

McNeil, T. (2006). Evidence-based practice in an age of relativism: Toward a model for practice. *Social Work, 51*(2), 147–167.

McRae, L. K. (2000). An application of the relational psychotherapy approach to a Mexican-American woman: An exploratory case study using a brief psychotherapy approach. A PsyD. clinical dissertation, California School of Professional Psychology, San Diego, CA.

Meichenbaum, D. (1977). *Cognitive behavior modification: An integrative approach.* New York: Plenum.

Meichenbaum, D. (1994a). *A clinical handbook/practical therapist manual for assessing and treating adults with post-traumatic stress disorder.* Waterloo, Ontario, Canada: Institute Press.

Meichenbaum, D. (1996a). *Mixed anxiety and depression: A cognitive behavioral approach.* New York: Newbridge Communications.

Meichenbaum, D. (2007). Stress inoculation training: A preventive and treatment approach. In P. M. Lehrer, R. L. Woolfolk, & W. S. Sime (Eds.), *Principles and practice of stress management* (3rd ed.). New York: Guilford.

Meichenbaum, D., & Fitzpatrick, D. (1993). A constructionist narrative perspective on stress and coping. Stress inoculation applications. In L. Goldberger & S. Breznitz (Eds.), *Handbook of stress: Theoretical and clinical aspects* (2nd ed.). New York: The Free Press.

Meichenbaum, D., & Goodman, J. (1971). Training impulsive children to talk to themselves: A means of developing self-control. *Journal of Abnormal Psychology, 77*, 115–126.

Meissner, W. W. (1976). Normal psychology of the aging process, revisited-1: Discussion. *Journal of Geriatric Psychiatry, 9*, 151–159.

Meissner, W. W. (1996). The therapeutic alliance and the real relationship in the analytic process. In L. Lifson (Ed.), *Understanding therapeutic action* (pp. 21–41). Hillsdale, NJ: Analytic Press.

Messer, S. B. (2004). Evidence-based practice: Beyond empirically supported treatments. *Professional Psychology: Research and Practice, 35*(6), 580–588.

Meyer, L. H., & Evans, I. M. (1989). *Nonaversive intervention for behavior problems: A manual for home and community.* Baltimore, MD: Paul H. Brookes.

Meyers, S. (1984). Elective mutism in children: A family systems approach. *American Journal of Family Therapy, 12*(4), 39–45.

Miles, M., & Huberman, M. (1984). *Qualitative data analysis: A sourcebook of new methods.* Beverly Hills, CA: Sage.

Miliora, M. T. (2000). Beyond empathic failures: Cultural racism as narcissistic trauma and disenfranchisement of grandiosity. *Clinical Social Work Journal, 28*(1), 43–54.

Miller, J. B. (1986). *What do we mean by relationships?* Wellesley, MA: Stone Center Working Paper Series, Wellesley College.

Miller, J. B. (2002). *How change happens: Controlling images, mutuality, and power.* Wellesley, MA: Stone Center Working Paper Series, Wellesley College.

Miller, J. B. (2003). *Telling the truth about power.* Wellesley, MA: Stone Center Working Paper Series, Wellesley College.

Miller, J. B., & Stiver, I. (1995). *Relational images and their meanings in psychotherapy.* Wellesley, MA: Stone Center Working Paper Series, Wellesley College.

Miller, J. G. (1987). *Toward a new psychology of women* (2nd ed.). Boston: Beacon Press.

Miller, J. P. (1996). *Using self psychology in child psychotherapy.* Northvale, NJ: Jason Aronson.

Mishna, F. (1996). In their own words: Therapeutic factors for adolescents who have learning disabilities. *International Journal of Group Psychotherapy, 46*, 265–273.

Mishna, F., & Muskat, B. (2004). "I'm not the only one!": Group therapy with older children and adolescents who have learning disabilities. *International Journal of Group Psychotherapy, 54*(4), 455–476.

Mitchell, S. A. (1988). *Relational concepts in psychoanalysis: An integration.* New York: Basic Books.

Mittendorf, S. H., & Schroeder, J. (2005). Boundaries in social work: The ethical dilemma of social worker-client sexual relationships. *Journal of Social Work Values and Ethics.* http://www.socialworker.com/jswve/content/view/11/

Moldawsky, S. (1980). Psychoanalytic psychotherapy supervision. In A. K. Hess (Ed.), *Psycho therapy supervision: Theory, research and practice* (pp. 126–135). New York: John Wiley & Sons.

Molnar, A., & de Shazer, S. (1987, October). Solution-focused therapy: Toward the identification of therapeutic tasks. *Journal of Marital and Family Therapy, 13*(4), 349–357.

Monk, G., Winslade, J., Crocket, K., & Epston, D. (1997). *Narrative therapy in practice.* San Francisco, CA: Jossey-Bass.

Morgan, A. (2000). *What is narrative therapy?* Adelaide, Australia: Dulwich Centre Publications.

Morrison, J. (1995). *The first interview.* New York: Guilford.

Morrison, L. L., & L'Heureux, J. (2001, February). Suicide and gay/lesbian/bisexual youth: Implications for clinicians. *Journal of Adolescence, 24*(1), 39–49.

Munro, E. (2002). The role of theory in social work research: A further contribution to the debate. *Journal of Social Work Education, 38*(2), 461–471.

Murphy, Y., Hunt, V., Zajicek, A. M., Norris, A. N., & Hamilton, L. (2009). *Incorporating intersectionality in social work practice, research, policy and education.* Washington, DC: NASW Press.

Murrell, A. R., & Scherbarth, A. J. (2006). State of the research & literature address: ACT with children, adolescents and parents. *IJBCT, 2*(4), 531–543.

Najavits, L. M., & Strupp, H. H. (1994, Spring). Differences in the effectiveness of psychodynamic therapists: A process-oriented outcome study. *Psychotherapy, 31*(1), 114–123.

National Association of Social Workers. (2005). Social work imperatives for the next decade. Retrieved November 14, 2009, from http:// www.naswdc.org/pubs/code/code.asp

National Association of Social Workers. (2008). *Code of ethics.* Washington, DC: Author.

Natterson, J. M., & Friedman, R. J. (1995). *A primer of clinical intersubjectivity.* Northvale, NJ: Jason Aronson.

Neff, K. D. (2003). Self compassion: An alternative conceptualization of a healthy attitude toward oneself. *Self and Identity,* 2, 85–101.

Neff, K. D., Kirkpatrick, K. L., & Rude, S. (2007). Self-compassion and adaptive psychological functioning.

Neimeyer, R. A. (1993). An appraisal of the constructivist psychotherapies. *Journal of Consulting and Clinical Psychology,* 61, 221–234.

Neubauer, P. (2001). Emerging issues: Some observations about changes in technique in child analysis. *Psychoanalytic Study of the Child,* 56, 16–38.

Neville, H. A., Worthington, R. L., & Spanierman, L. B. (2001). Race, power, and multicultural counseling: Understanding white privilege and color-blind racial attitudes. In J. Ponterotto, J. M. Casas, L. A. Suzuki, & C. M. Alexander (Eds.), *Handbook of multicultural counseling* (pp. 257–288). Thousand Oaks, CA: Sage.

Noble, A., & Jones, C. (2005). Benefits of narrative therapy: Holistic interventions at the end of life. *Palliative Care,* 220–225.

Nurius, P., & Hudson, W. W. (1993). *Human services: Practice, evaluation and computers.* Pacific Grove, CA: Brooks/Cole.

Nylund, D. (2000). *Treating Huckleberry Finn: A new narrative approach to working with kids diagnosed with ADD/ADHD.* San Francisco: Jossey-Bass.

O'Connor, K. (2000). *The play therapy primer.* New York: John Wiley & Sons.

O'Connor, K. J., & Braverman, L. D. (2009). Orientation to the text: Cases of Jason L. and Cassie B. In K. J. O'Connor & L. D. Braverman (Eds.) (pp. 1–23). New York: John Wiley & Sons.

O'Hanlon, B. (1999). *Evolving possibilities.* Philadelphia, PA: Brunner/Mazel.

O'Hanlon, W. H. (1987). *Taproots: Underlying principles of Milton Erikson's therapy and hypnosis.* New York: Norton.

O'Malley, S. S., Suh, C. S., & Strupp, H. H. (1983). The Vanderbilt Psychotherapy Process Scale: A report on the scale development and a process-outcome study. *Journal of Consulting and Clinical Psychology,* 51, 581–586.

Oetting, G. R., & Beauvais, L. (1990). Orthogonal cultural identification theory: The cultural identification of minority adolescents. *International Journal of the Addictions,* 25, 655–685.

Ogden, T. (1982). *Projective identification and psychotherapeutic technique.* Northvale, NJ: Jason Aronson.

Ornstein, E. D., & Ganzer, C. (2000). Strengthening the strengths perspective: An integrative relations perspective. *Psychoanalytic Social Work,* 7, 57–78.

Ornstein, P. H., & Ornstein, A. (1972). Focal psychotherapy: Its potential impact on psychotherapeutic practice in medicine.*Journal of Psychiatry in Medicine,* 3, 11–325.

Othmer, E., & Othmer, S. C. (2002). *The clinical interview using DSM-IV-TR. Vol. 1: Fundamentals.* Washington, DC: American Psychiatric Publishing.

Padgett, D. K. (1998). *Qualitative methods in social work research.* Thousand Oaks, CA: Sage.

Padgett, D. K. (2003). *The qualitative research experience* (revised printing). New York: Cengage Learning.

Palombo, J. (1995). Psychodynamic and relational problems of children with nonverbal learning disabilities. In B. S. Mark & J. A. Incorvaia (Eds.), *The handbook of infant, child, and adolescent psychotherapy: A guide to diagnosis and treatment* (Vol. 1, pp. 147–176). Northvale, NJ: Jason Aronson.

Palombo, J. (2001a). *Learning disorders and disorders of the self in children and adolescents.* New York: W. W. Norton.

Palombo, J. (2001b). The therapeutic process with children with learning disorders. *Psychoanalytic Social Work,* 8(3/4), 143–168.

Paniagua, F. A. (2001). *Diagnosis in a multicultural context.* Thousand Oaks, CA: Sage.

Parad, H. J., & Parad, L. G. (1990). *Crisis intervention: Book 2.* Milwaukee, WI: Family Service Association of America.

Patton, M. (1990). *Qualitative evaluation methods.* Newbury Park, CA: Sage.

Patton, M. (2002). Qualitative research and evaluation methods. Sage. Thousand Oaks, CA.

Pekarik, G. (1996). *Psychotherapy abbreviation: A practical guide.* Binghamton, NY: Haworth Press.

Peller, J., & Walter, J. J. (1998). Solution-focused brief therapy. In R. A. Dorfman (Ed.), *Paradigms of clinical social work* (pp. 71–93). New York: Brunner/Mazel.

Perez-Foster, R. (1998). The clinician's cultural countertransference: The psychodynamics of culturally competent practice. *Clinical Social Work Journal,* 26(3), 253–270.

Persons, J. G. (2005). Empiricism, mechanism, and the practice of cognitive-behavior therapy. *Behavior Therapy,* 36, 107–118.

Phelan, T. (1995). *1-2-3-Magic: Effective discipline for children 2–12.* Glen Ellyn, IL: Child Management Press.

Pheterson, G. (1986). Alliances between women: Overcoming internalized oppression and internalized domination. *Signs,* 12, 146–160.

Piaget, J. (1952a). *The language and thought of the child.* London: Routledge & Kegan Paul.

Piaget, J. (1952b). *The origins of intelligence in children.* New York: International Universities Press.

Pieper, M. H. (1999). The privilege of being a therapist: A fresh perspective from intrapsychic humanism on caregiving intimacy and the development of the professional self. *Families in Society,* 80(5), 479–487.

Pinderhuges, E. (1984). Teaching empathy: Ethnicity, race and power at the cross-cultural interface. *American Journal of Social Psychiatry,* 4(1), 5–12.

Pine, F. (1990). *Drive, ego, object and self: A synthesis for clinical work.* New York: Basic Books.

Poindexter, C. P. (2008). *Position paper on human rights and social justice.* Paper presented at the Fordham University Graduate School of Social Service.

Pope, K. S., & Bouhoutsos, J. (1986). *Sexual intimacy between therapists and patients.* New York: Praeger.

Porter, N. (1995). Therapist self care: A proactive ethical approach. In E. J. Rave & C. C. Larsen (Eds.), *Ethical decision making in therapy: Feminist perspectives* (pp. 247–267). New York: Guilford.

Portes, A., & Rumbaut, R. (2001). *Legacies: The story of immigrant second generation.* Berkeley: University of California Press.

Prochaska, J. O., & DiClemente, C. C. (2005). The transtheoretical approach. In J. C. Norcross & M. R. Goldfried (Eds.), *Handbook of psychotherapy integration* (2nd ed., pp. 147–171). New York: Oxford University Press.

Prochaska, J. O., & Norcross, J. C. (2010). *Systems of psychotherapy: A transtheoretical analysis* (7th ed.). Australia: Thomson/Brooks/Cole.

Prochaska, J. O., Norcross, J. C., & DiClemente, C. C. (1994). *Changing for good: The revolutionary program that explains the six stages of change and teaches you how to free yourself from bad habits.* New York: W. Morrow.

Pryor, K. D. (1985). *Don't shoot the dog. The new art of teaching and training.* New York: Bantam.

Puchalsi, C., & Romer, A. L. (2000). Taking a spiritual history allows clinicians to understand patients more fully. *Journal of Palliative Medicine*, 3(1), 129–137.

Rabavilas, A. D., Boulougouris, J. C., & Perissaki, C. (1979). Therapist qualities related to outcome with exposure in vivo in neurotic patients. *Journal of Behavior Therapy and Experimental Psychiatry*, 10, 293–299.

Real, T. (1990). The therapeutic use of self in constructivist/systemic therapy. *Family Process*, 29, 255–272.

Reamer, F. G. (1995). Malpractice claims against social workers: First facts. *Social Work*, 40, 595–601.

Reamer, F. G. (1997). Managing ethics under managed care. *Families in Society: Journal of Contemporary Human Services*, 96–101.

Reamer, F. G. (2001). Update on confidentiality issues in practice with children: Ethics risk management. *Children and Schools*, 27(2), 117–120.

Reamer, F. G. (2003). *Social work malpractice and liability: Strategies for prevention* (2nd ed.). New York: Columbia University Press.

Rehm, L., & Rokke, P. (1988). Self management therapies. In K. D. Dobson (Ed.), *Handbook of cognitive-behavioral therapies* (pp. 136–166). New York: Guilford.

Reichert, E. (2003). *Social work and human rights: A foundation for policy and practice*. New York: Columbia University Press.

Reinecke, M. A., Dattilo, F. M., & Freeman, A. (2003). *Cognitive therapy with children and adolescents: A casebook of clinical practice* (2nd ed.). New York: Guilford.

Ricketts, H. (2000, November). *Parenting in Jamaica: A situation assessment & analysis*. Jamaica: Coalition for Better Parenting, UNICEP.

Rigazio-DiGilio, S. A., Ivey, A. E., Kunkler-Peck, K. P., & Grady, L. T. (2005). *Community genograms: Using individual, family and cultural narratives with clients*. New York: Teachers College Press.

Robinson, D. J. (2001). *Brain calipers: Descriptive psychopathology and the psychiatric mental status examination* (2nd ed.). Port Huron, MI: Rapid Psychler Press.

Rock, B. (2001). Social work under managed care: Will we survive or can we prevail? In B. Rock & R. Perez-Koening (Eds.),*Social worker in the era of devolution: Toward a just practice*. New York: Fordham University Press.

Rock, B., & Congress, E. (1999). The new confidentiality for the 21st century in a managed care environment. *Social Work*, 44(3), 253–262.

Rock, B., & Cooper, M. (2000). Social work in primary care: A demonstration student unit utilizing practice research. *Social Work in Health Care*, 31(1).

Rosen, A., & Proctor, E. K. (2002). Standards for evidence-based social work practice. In A. R. Roberts & G. J. Greene (Eds.),*The social worker's desk reference* (pp. 743–747). New York: Oxford University Press.

Rosen, A., Procter, E. K., & Staudt, M. (1999). Social work research and the quest for effective practice. *Social Work Research*, 23, 4–14.

Rosenberger, J. (1988). Self psychology as a theoretical base for understanding the impact of learning disabilities. *Child and Adolescent Social Work Journal*, 5(1), 269–280.

Rosenberg, J., Gonzalez, M., & Rosenberg, S. (2005). In E. Congress & M. Gonzalez (Eds.), *Multicultural perspectives in working with families* (2nd ed.). New York: Springer.

Rosenthal, B. S. (1991). Social workers' interest in international practice in the developing world: A multivariate analysis. *Social Work*, 36(3), 248–252.

Rowan, T., & O'Hanlon, B. (1999). *Solution-oriented therapy for chronic and severe mental illness*. New York: John Wiley & Sons.

Roy, A., Cooper, M., & Lesser, J. G. (2008). A cross cultural collaborative study of depression and help seeking behavior in two Chinese communities: Boston, U.S. and Guangzhou, China. *International Journal of the Humanities*, 6, 79–84.

Rudd, M. D., Joiner, T., & Rajab, M. H. (2001). *Treating suicidal behavior: An effective, time-limited approach*. New York: Guilford.

Ruiz, P. (1995). Assessing, diagnosing, and treating culturally diverse individuals: A Hispanic perspective. *Psychiatric Quarterly*, 66, 329–341.

Saari, C. (1986). *Clinical social work treatment: How does it work?* New York: Gardner Press.

Sabin, J. E. (1994a). Caring about patients and caring about money. *Behavioral Sciences and the Law*, 12, 317–330.

Sabin, J. E. (1994b). Ethical issues under managed care: The managed care view. In R. K. Schreter, S. S. Sharfsteind, & C. A. Schreter (Eds.), *Allies and adversaries: The impact of managed care on mental health services* (pp. 187–194). Washington, DC: American Psychiatric Press.

Sackett, D. L., Straus, S. E., Richardson, W. C., Rosenberg, W., & Haynes, R. M. (2000). *Evidence based medicine: How to practice and teach EBM* (2nd ed.). New York: Churchill Livingstone.

Safran, J., & Segal, Z. (1996). *Interpersonal process in cognitive therapy*. Northvale, NJ: Jason Aronson.

Safran, J. D., & Reading, R. (2008). Mindfulness, metacommunication, and affect regulation in psychoanalytic treatment. In S. F. Hick & T. Bien (Eds.), *Mindfulness and the therapeutic relationship* (pp. 122–140). New York: Guilford.

Safron, J. D., & Segal, V. (1996). *Interpersonal process in cognitive therapy*. Northvale, NJ: Jason Aronson.

Saville, J. (2003). Historical memories of slavery in the aftermath of reconstruction. *Journal of American Ethnic History*, 22(4), 69–76.

Schamess, G. (1996). Ego psychology. In J. Berzoff, L. Melano Flanagan, & P. Hertz (Eds.), *Inside out and outside in: Psychodynamic clinical theory and practice in contemporary and sociocultural contexts* (pp. 68–103). Northvale, NJ: Jason Aronson.

Scharff, J. S. (1998, May 2). Discussion of Arietta Slade's paper, "Attachment theory and research: Implications for the theory and practice of individual psychotherapy." Conference on the Clinical Implications of Attachment Theory and Research, sponsored by The Center of Adult Development and the International Institute of Object Relations Therapy, Bethesda, MD.

Schiller, I. Y. (1995). Stages of development in women's groups: A relational model. In R. Kurland & K. Salmon (Eds.), *Group work practice in a troubled society*. New York: Haworth.

Schoech, D., & Helton, D. (2003). Qualitative and quantitative analysis of a course taught via classroom and internet chatroom. *Qualitative Social Work*, 1(1), 111–124.

Segal, H. (1974). *Introduction to the work of Melanie Klein*. New York: Basic Books.

Selekman, M. D. (1997). *Solution-focused therapy with children*. New York: Guilford.

Seligman, M., Steen, T., Park, N., & Peterson, C. (2005). Positive psychology progress: Empirical validation of interventions. *American Psychologist*, 60(5), 410–421.

Seligman, M. E. (1990). *Learned optimism*. New York: Alfred A. Knopf.

Seligman, M. E., & Csikszentmihalyi, M. (2000). Positive psychology: An introduction. *American Psychologist*, 55(1), 5–14.

Seruya, B. (1997). *Empathic brief psychotherapy*. Northvale, NJ: Jason Aronson.

Shane, E. (1984). Self-psychology: A new conceptualization for the understanding of learning disabled children. In P. Stepansky & A. Goldberg (Eds.), *Kohut's legacy.* New York: Analytic Press.

Shea, S. C. (1998). *Psychiatric interviewing: The art of understanding.* Philadelphia, PA: W. B. Saunders.

Shea, S. C. (2002). *The practical art of suicide assessment.* Hoboken, NJ: John Wiley & Sons.

Shirk, S. R. (1999). Developmental therapy. In W. K. Silverman & T. H. Ollendick (Eds.), *Developmental issues in the clinical treatment of children* (pp. 63–70). Boston: Allyn & Bacon.

Siegel, A. (1996). *Heinz Kohut and the psychology of the self.* London and New York: Routledge.

Siegel, D. J. (1999). *The developing mind.* New York: Guilford.

Siegel, D. J., & Hartzel, M. (2003). *Parenting from the inside out: How a deeper self understanding can help you raise children who thrive.* New York: Jeremy P. Tarcher/Putnam.

Slade, A. (1996). Attachment theory and research: Implications for the theory and practice of individual psychotherapy with adults. In J. Cassiday & P. R. Shaver (Eds.), *Handbook of attachment: Theory, research, and clinical applications.* New York: Guilford.

Sliep, Y., Weingarten, K., & Gilbert, A. (2004). Narrative theatre as an interactive community approach to mobilizing collective action in Northern Uganda. *Families Systems & Health,* 22(3), 306–320.

Sloane, R. B., Staples, F. R., Cristol, I. H., Yorkston, N. J., & Whipple, K. (1975). *Psychotherapy versus behavior therapy.* Cambridge, MA: Harvard University Press.

Smith, B., Barkley, R. A., & Shapiro, C. (2006). Attention deficit hyperactivity disorder. In E. J. Mash & R. A. Barkley (Eds.), *Treatment of childhood disorders* (3rd ed.). New York: Guilford.

Smith, B., Barkley, R. A., & Shapiro, C. (2007). Attention deficit hyperactivity disorder. In E. J. Mash & R. A. Barkley (Eds.), *Assessment of childhood disorders* (4th ed.). New York: Guilford.

Smith, P. R., & Wingerson, N. W. (2006). Is the centrality of relationship in social work at risk with IVT?

Smyrnios, K. X., & Kirby, R. J. (1993). Long-term comparison of brief versus unlimited psychodynamic treatments with children and their parents. *Journal of Consulting and Clinical Psychology,* 61(6), 1020–1027.

Sommers-Flanagan, J., & Sommers-Flanagan, R. (2009). *Clinical interviewing* (4th ed.). New York: John Wiley & Sons.

Spencer, R. (2000). *A comparison of relational psychologies.* Wellesley, MA: Stone Center Working Paper Series, Wellesley College.

Spivak, G. (2001). The burden of English. In G. Castle (Ed.), *Postcolonial discourses* (pp. 53–72). Oxford: Blackwell.

St. Clair, M. (2004). *Object relations and self psychology* (4th ed.). Pacific Grove, CA: Brooks/Cole.

Steier, F. (1991). Introduction: Research as self-reflexivity, self-reflexivity as social process. In F. Steier (Ed.), *Research and reflexivity* (pp. 1–11). Newbury Park, CA: Sage.

Steinhausen, H., & Juzi, C. (1996). Elective mutism: An analysis of 100 cases. *Journal of the American Academy of Child and Adolescent Psychiatry,* 35(5), 606–615.

Steketee, G. (1987). Behavioral social work with obsessive-compulsive disorders. *Journal of Social Service Research,* 10, 53–73.

Stern, E. N. (1977). *The first relationship: Infant and mother.* Cambridge, MA: Harvard University Press.

Stern, E. N. (1985). *The interpersonal world of the infant.* New York: Basic Books.

Stolorow, R. D., & Atwood, G. E. (1992). *Contexts of being: The intersubjective foundations of psychological life.* Hillsdale, NJ: Analytic Press.

Straker, G. (2004). Race for cover; castrated whiteness: Perverse consequences. *Psychoanalytic Dialogues,* 14(4), 405–422.

Strauss, A. L., & Corbin, J. (1990). *Basics of qualitative research: Grounded theory procedures and techniques.* Newbury Park, CA: Sage.

Strong, T. (2000b). Six orienting ideas for collaborative counselors. *European Journal of Psychotherapy, Counseling, and Health,* 3, 25–42.

Strong, T. (2002a). Collaborative "expertise" after the discursive turn. *Journal of Psychotherapy Integration,* 12(2), 218–232.

Strong, T. (2002b). Dialogue in therapy's "borderzone." *Journal of Constructivist Psychology,* 15, 245–262.

Strupp, H. (1995). The psychotherapist's skills revisited. *Clinical Psychology: Science and Practice,* 2, 70–74.

Strupp, H. H. (2001). Implications of the empirically supported treatment movement for psychoanalysis. *Psychoanalytic Dialogues,* 11, 605–619.

Strupp, H. H., & Binder, J. L. (1984). *Psychotherapy in a new key: A guide to time-limited dynamic psychotherapy.* New York: Basic Books.

Suchet, M. (2004). A relational encounter with race. *Psychoanalytic Dialogues,* 14(4), 423–438.

Sue, D. W. (2004). Whiteness and ethnocentric monoculturalism: Making the "invisible" visible. *American Psychologist,* 761–769.

Sue, W. S., & Sue, D. W. (2003). *Counseling the culturally diverse: Theory and practice* (4th ed.). New York: John Wiley & Sons.

Sullivan, H. S. (1953). *The interpersonal theory of psychiatry.* New York: Norton.

Surrey, J. (1991). The "self-in-relation" theory of women's development. In J. V. Jordan, A. G. Kaplan, J. B. Miller, I. P. Stiver, & J. L. Surrey (Eds.), *Women's growth in connection: Writings from the Stone Center* (pp. 51–67). New York: Guilford.

Surrey, J. L. (1997). What do you mean by mutuality in therapy? In J. V. Jordan, A. G. Kaplan, J. B. Miller, I. P. Stiver, & J. L. Surrey (Eds.), *Women's growth in connection: Writings from the Stone Center.* New York: Guilford.

Surrey, J. L., Kaplan, A., & Jordan, J. (1990). *Empathy revisited.* Wellesley, MA: Stone Center Working Paper Series, Wellesley College.

Sweeney, D. S., & Landreth, G. L. (2009). Child-centered play therapy. In K. J. O'Connor & L. D. Braverman (Eds.), *Play therapy theory and practice: Comparing theories and techniques* (2nd ed., pp. 123–162). New York: John Wiley.

Swinson, R. P., Antony, M. M., Rachman, S., & Richler, M. A. (2001). *Obsessive compulsive disorder: Theory, research, and treatment.* New York: Guilford.

Taffel, R. (2005). *Breaking through to teens: A new psychotherapy for the new adolescence.* New York: Guilford.

Taylor, M. A. (1981). *The neuropsychiatric mental status examinations.* Jamaica, NY: Spectrum.

Taylor, S. E. (1990). *Positive illusions.* New York: Basic Books.

Taylor, S. E., Wood, J., & Lichtman, R. (1983). It could be worse: Selective evaluation as a response to victimization. *Journal of Psychiatry,* 138, 14–19.

Tedeschi, R. G., & Calhoun, L. G. (2004). Posttraumatic growth: A new perspective on psychotraumatology. *Psychiatric Times,* 21, 4.

Thomlison, B. (1984). Phobic disorders. In F. Turner (Ed.), *Adult psychopathology: A social work perspective* (pp. 280–315). New York: The Free Press.

Thomlison, B., & Thomlison, R. (1996). Behavior theory and social work treatment. In F. Turner (Ed.), *Social work treatment: Interlocking theoretical approaches* (4th ed.). New York: The Free Press.

Thyer, B. (2001). What is the role of theory in research on social work practice? *Journal of Social Work Education,* 37(1), 9–26.

Timberlake, E., & Cooke, K. (1984, July). Social work and the Vietnamese refugee. *Social Work, 29*, 109–113.

Tseng, W. S., & Streltzer, J. (1997). *Culture and psychopathology: A guide to clinical assessment.* New York: Burnner/Mazel.

Tu, W. M. (1985). Selfhood and otherness in Confucian thought. In A. J. Marsella, G. K. DeVos, & F. O. K. Hsu (Eds.), *Culture and self: Asian and western perspective.* New York: Tavistock Publications.

Turner, F. (1986). *Social work treatment: Interlocking theoretical approaches* (3rd ed.). New York: The Free Press.

Turner, F. J. (Ed.). (1996). *Social work treatment: Interlocking theoretical approaches* (4th ed.). New York: The Free Press.

United Nations (UN) Universal Declaration of Human Rights. (1948). General Assembly Res. 217A(III) (1948).

Velasquez, J. M. (1997). Puerto Ricans in the counseling process: The dynamics of ethnicity and its societal context. In C. C. Lee (Ed.), *Multicultural issues in counseling* (2nd ed., pp. 315–330). Alexandria, VA: American Counseling Association.

Wachtel, E. (1994). *Treating troubled children and their families.* New York: Guilford.

Wachtel, P. (1982). *Resistance, psychodynamic and behavioral approaches.* New York: Plenum.

Wachtel, P. (1993). *Therapeutic communication.* New York: Guilford.

Wachtel, P. (2009). *Relational theory and the practice of psychotherapy.* New York: Guilford.

Walls, G. B. (2004). Toward a critical global psychoanalysis. *Psychoanalytic Dialogues, 14*, 605–634.

Walsh, R. A. (2008). Mindfulness and empathy: A hermeneutic circle. In S. F. Hick & T. Bien (Eds.), *Mindfulness and the therapeutic relationship* (pp. 72–88). New York: Guilford.

Walter, J. L., & Peller, J. E. (1992). *Becoming solution focused in brief therapy.* New York: Brunner/Mazel.

Webb, N. B. (1996). *Social work practice with children.* New York: Guilford.

Webb, S. (2001). Some considerations on the validity of evidence-based practice in social work. *British Journal of Social Work, 31*, 57–79.

Weiner-Davis, M. (1992). *Divorce busting.* New York: Summit Books.

Weiner-Davis, M. (2001). *The divorce remedy: The proven 7-step program for saving your marriage.* New York: Simon & Schuster.

Weiner-Davis, M., de Shazer, S., & Gingerich, W. J. (1987). Building on pretreatment change to construct the therapeutic solution: An exploratory study. *Journal of Marriage and Family Therapy, 13*, 359–363.

Weingarten, K. (1997). From "cold care" to "warm care": Challenging the discourses of mothers and adolescents. In C. Smith & D. Nylund (Eds.), *Narrative therapies with children and adolescents* (pp. 307–338). New York: Guilford.

White, M. (1986). Negative explanation, restraint, and double description: A template for family therapy. *Family Process*, 25(2), 169–184.

White, M. (1988b, Spring). Saying hello again: The incorporation of the lost relationship in the resolution of grief. *Dulwich Centre Newsletter*, 21–40.

White, M. (1995). *Re-authoring lives: Interviews and essays.* Adelaide, Australia: Dulwich Centre Publications.

White, M. (2000). Reflecting team work as definitional ceremony revisited. In M. White (Ed.), *Reflections on narrative practice: Interviews and essays.* Adelaide, Australia: Dulwich Centre Publications.

White, M. (2001). *Folk psychology and narrative practice.* Adelaide, Australia: Dulwich Centre Publications.

White, M., & Epston, D. (1990). *Narrative means to therapeutic ends.* New York: Norton.

Williams, S. (2001). The mighty influence of long custom and practice. Sexual exploitation of children for cash and goods in Jamaica. In C. Barrow (Ed.), *Children's rights: Caribbean realities* (pp. 330–349). Kingston, Jamaica, West Indies: Ian Randle Publishers.

Windholz, M. J., & Silberschatz, G. (1988). Vanderbilt Psychotherapy Process Scale: A replication with adult outpatients.*Journal of Consulting and Clinical Psychology, 56*, 56–60.

Wingard, B., & Lester, J. (2000). *Telling our stories in ways that make us stronger.* Adelaide, Australia: Dulwich Centre Publications.

Winnicott, D. W. (1965). *The maturational process and the facilitating environment.* New York: International Universities Press.

Witkin, S. L., & Harrison, W. D. (2001). Editorial: Whose evidence and for what purpose? *Social Work, 46*, 293–296.

Wolf, E. S. (1988). *Treating the self: Elements of clinical self psychology.* New York: Guilford.

Wylie, M. S. (1990). Brief therapy on the couch. *Family Therapy Networker, 14*, 26–34, 66.

Yin, R. (2002). *Case study research: Design methods* (3rd ed.). Thousand Oaks, CA: Sage.

Ying, Y.-W. (2009). Contribution of self-compassion to competence and mental health in social work students. *Journal of Social Work Education*, 45(2), 309–323.

Yip, P. S. F., Chi, I., Chiu, H., Wai, K. C., Conwell, Y., & Caine, E. (2003).

Young, J., Beck, A., & Weinberger, A. (1993). Depression. In D. H. Barlow (Ed.), *Clinical handbook of psychological disorders* (2nd ed.). New York: Guilford.

Young, J. E., Klosko, J. S., & Weishaar, M. R. (2003). *Schema therapy: A practitioner's guide.* New York: Guilford.

Young, T. (1993). Children. In H. Jackson (Ed.), *Using self psychology in psychotherapy* (pp. 73–91). Northvale, NJ: Jason Aronson.

Zayas, L. H., Kaplan, C., Turner, S., Romano, K., & Gonzalez-Ramos, G. (2000, January). Understanding suicide attempts by adolescent Hispanic females. *Social Work*, 45(1), 53–63.

Index

Note: page numbers followed by an f indicate figures; page numbers followed by a t indicate tables.

A

Abandonment/instability, dysfunctional thoughts and, 138–139
Abstraction, in mental status exam, 52, 58
Abused children and concept of internal object, 83
Acceptance therapy (commitment therapy), 159–160
  principles, 159–160
Acculturated/assimilated, in multicultural clinical practice, 67
Action, in Transtheoretical Model, 34, 42
Action questions in reauthoring in narrative therapy, 171–172
ACT (acceptance and commitment therapy), 159–160, 164
Address, in religion, 50
Adler, Alfred, 129, 131–132
Adolescents (*see also* Children and adolescents, treatment of)
  advocacy of, 41
  behavioral therapy, case study, 209–213
  introductions, 29
  parents and counseling, 37
  risk management issues, 22
  self-harm, in adolescents, 103–104
  self-psychology treatment, 4, 9–10, 101–104
  suicide and, 20
Affect, in mental status exam, 52, 58
  flat, 52
  blunt, 52
African American clients, 117–121, 168, 208–209
  cultural relational practice, 117
Allness and Neverness, 133
All-or-None Thinking, 133
Alter ego–self-object relationship, 4, 99
American Psychological Association, 164
Amplifying stance in postmodern therapy, 171
Antecedent behaviors, definition of, 154
Appearance, in mental status exam, 52
Approval-Seeking/Recognition-Seeking, 141
Assertiveness training and behavior therapy, 158–159
Assessment, 28–44
  behavioral, 154–155
  in change in the client system, 187–188
  components, 45
  of family, 187–188
  and human rights, 46
  overview, 44
  process of (*see* Clinical interview)
  product of (*see* Psychosocial study, preparation of)
  stages in, 28–31
  in time-limited dynamic psychotherapy, 91
Association of Multicultural Counseling and Development (AMCD), 65
Attachment theory, 98
Attention deficit disorder (ADD), case study, 209–213
Attitude, in mental status exam, 52, 58
Authenticity
  in cultural relational theory, 122
  in therapeutic relationship, 33
Authority-based practice, 214
Automatic thoughts of client, 138, 147–148
  examples of charts, 137f, 146f, 149f, 151f
Aversion therapy, 158
Awareness (being present), 159
Axis, in Multiaxial diagnosis, 54, 61

B

Bandura, Albert, 153, 155
Beck, Aaron, 136–138, 144
Beck's model of cognitive therapy, 136–138, 144–150
Behavior therapy, 152, 165, 208–213
  adolescent, 209–213
  assessment, 154–169
  case studies, 37–38, 40–41, 161–164, 208–213
  with children and adolescents, 41, 154, 155–156, 158, 160, 208–213
  cognitive approach, 33–34, 36, 37, 154–159
  definition of, 152
  empirical evidence, 164–165
  intervention, 41, 154–159
  in obsessive-compulsive disorder case, 161–164
  overview, 165
  research perspectives, 160
  techniques, 41, 152, 155, 158–159, 162–164
  therapeutic relationship in, 29, 33–35, 160
  three generations or waves, 152–153
  traditional, 152–153
Behavioral assessment, 154–169
Beliefs, 49
Bicultural/Multicultural clinical practice, 67
Bipolar disorder, 21
"Bobo" doll study, 160
Boundaries set by professional (*see* Ethics and boundaries of professional)
Boyer, Catherine, 150
Brief Family Therapy Center of Milwaukee, 184
Brief psychotherapy with women, 110–114
Brief treatment, 12–15
  case studies, 104–114
  contraindications for, 15
  first session, 13–14
  models of, 13
  object relations theory and, 88–90

Brief treatment (*Continued*)
research perspectives, 12–13
selection criteria, 13, 15
self-psychology and, 14–15, 104–114
therapeutic relationship, 14–15
trauma in solution-focused brief therapy, 190–191
working relationship, 14
Brooks, Debra, 169
Building the relationship, in Object Relations Theory, 87
Burnout, 26

C
Care
blame and stigma, responding to, 201–202
current acts of, 201
history, 200–201
questions for the child, 202
reflections, 202–203
Case studies
ADAH and, 170
adolescent behavioral therapy, 209–213
adult survivor of physical abuse, 90–97
African American women, 117–121
anxiety, case example, 144–151
attention deficit disorder (ADD), 59, 61, 209–213
beginning phase of treatment, 93, 106–107
behavioral approach of treatment, 161–164
brief treatment, 104–114
child behavioral therapy, 208–209
cognitive processing therapy, (CPT), 144–151f
cognitive treatment for anxiety, 144–151
conduct disorder, 35–38
constructivist framework, 74–77
cross-cultural practice, 74–81
cultural relational framework, 123–127
ending phase of treatment, 44
family, 63, 175–181
family meeting, 192–196
gender change, 105
group treatment, 123–127, 170
middle phase of treatment, 40–42
mixed-methods research, 231–235
narrative therapy framework, 170, 175–181
object relational psychotherapy, 90–97
obsessive-compulsive disorder, 161–164
oppositional defiant disorder (ODD), 208–213
play therapy, 204–208
psychosocial study, 55–64
qualitative research, 224–230
racial identity, 117–121
relational theory, 117–121, 123–127
selective mutism, 206–208
self-psychology, 104–114
single-subject design methodology, 150
solution-focused format, 192–196
stages of change, 35–38
temper tantrums, 209f
time-limited dynamic psychotherapy (TLDP), 90–97
traumatized child, 55–64
violence, 224–230
women with self-esteem problems, 6f, 10, 50t
women's support group, 123–127
CBASP (cognitive behavioral analysis system of psychotherapy), 164
Change
in the client system, assessing, 187–188
client taking credit for, 157
Character Strengths and Virtues: A Handbook and Classification (CSV),142
Child abuse and concept of internal object, 83, 90–97
Child behavioral therapy, case study, 208–209
Child Care and Protection Act, 229
Child Development Center at St. Mary's Hospital, 55, 56
Childhood pathology, 54, 167
Child psychopathology, 199
Children and adolescents, treatment of, 198–213
behavioral therapy, 208
case studies, 206–213
childhood pathology, 199
developmental assessment, 198–199
interviewing, 200–204
learning disturbances, 204
overview, 213
play therapy, 204–208
self-psychology treatment, 4, 9–10, 14–15, 101–104
as suicidal clients, 20
Chronological Assessment of Suicide (C.A.S.E.), 18
Client-centered therapy, 70
Client taking credit for change, 157
Client–worker collaboration, 55, 189
Clinical agenda, 8–10
Clinical interview, 28–44
acts of care, 201
beginning phase, 28
blame and stigma, responses to, 201–202
case studies, 35–38, 40–42
with children and adolescents, 29, 35, 38, 42, 43, 199–204
client's purpose, exploring, 4f, 30–31
client's questions, answering, 30
confidentiality issues, 30, 203–204
first meeting in, 28–29
history of care, 200–201
introductions, 29
middle phase of, 28, 39–40, 44
with parents, 200
questions for the child, 202
reflections, 202–203
self-awareness in, 29
termination phase of, 28, 35, 42–44
therapeutic relationship, 31–34
in Transtheoretical Model, 34–35
treatment planning in, 38
Clinical supervision, 8–10
Coaching, social work and, 22–23
Cognitive behavioral therapy (CBT), 154–155, 159–160
ACT (acceptance and commitment therapy), 159–160
example, 156–157
techniques, 158–159
Cognitive defusion, 159
Cognitive errors, in Beck's model, 136
Cognitive function, in mental status exam, 52, 58
Cognitive processing and social learning theory, 154
Cognitive processing therapy, (CPT), 141–144
case study, 144–151f
interventions, 143–144

positive psychology, 142
strengths of, 143
Cognitive theory, 129–151
ABC of, by Ellis, 131–134
Beck's model of, 136–138
behavior therapy, 154–159
case example, 144–145
client, characteristics of, 130
Cognitive Processing, 142–144
constructive perspective, 134–136
definition of, 129
disturbances in thinking, 132–134
narrative processes, 134
history of, 129
rational emotive therapy, 131–134
schema theory, 138–141
structural approach, 130–131
therapeutic relationship, 129–131
Cognitive treatment
for anxiety, case study, 144–151
interviews, 130–131
Collaborative relationship
between social worker and client, 15–16, 55
treatment plan in solution-focused therapy, 188–189
Commitment therapy (*see* Acceptance therapy)
Community-based practice model, 24, 27, 179
Community, in religion, 50
Compassion fatigue of social worker, 26
Complainants, 188
Complimenting clients, 186
Conceptualization, example of, 37
Confidentiality, 203–204
children and adolescents, 203–204
explaining to client, 30
managed care and, 23
suicidal client and, 19, 20
technology and, 23
Confrontation, in Object Relations Theory, 87–88
Connectedness among group members, 123
Consciousness questions in reauthoring in narrative therapy, 172
Consequences, 135f
definition of, 154
Constructive perspective (CNP), 134–136
and coping, 134
Constructivism, 74–77
in multicultural practice, 72, 74–77
in narrative therapy, 74
Contemplation, in Transtheoretical Model, 34, 40–41
Context, 70–71
Contextualizing stance in postmodern therapy, 171
Conversational narrative, 168 (*see also* Narrative therapy)
Coping skills, 26, 157, 160, 206, 235
self-blame and, 84
Counseling experience of client, 47
Council on Social Work Education (CSWE, 2008), 10
Countertransference, 32–33, 116
definition of, 32
in relational therapy, 32–33, 116
Crain, Connie, 97
Crisis intervention, 196
Cross-cultural counseling, case study, 74–81, 117–121, 174 (*see also* Multicultural practice)
Culture, 6
Culturegrams, 71, 73f
Cultural competence, 66–67
Cultural history of client, 49, 58
Cultural oppression, 67
Cultural relational theory, 122–127
women's groups and, 123–127
Cultural trauma, 68
Culturally specific practice, example of, 72–73f, 75, 78–81
Culture, definition of, 65
Customers, 188
Cyclical maladaptive pattern (CMP), 89

D

Daily Record of Automatic Thoughts, example of, 149f
Daily Record of Dysfunctional Thoughts, 137–138
Data collection and analysis, 157, 222–224
in behavior therapy, 157
in first meeting with client, 28–29
Deconstruction of narrative, definition of, 168–169 (*see also* Narrative therapy)
Defectiveness/shame, dysfunctional thoughts and, 130
Defense mechanisms, 51t
in children and adolescents, 62, 85, 103
Definitional ceremony, 182
Defusion, cognitive, 159
Dependence/Incompetence, 139
Depression of disenfranchisement, 69
Deprivation of Empathy, 138
Deprivation of Nurturance, 138
Deprivation of Protection, 138
Detective club, 169, 170
Developmental assessment of children and adolescents, 198–199
Diagnostic and Statistical Manual of Mental Disorders (DSM-IV), 51–52, 58–60
according to DSM-IV-TR to, 21, 45, 53
positive psychology, 142
rationale for, 60–61
Dialectical behavior therapy (DBT), 159
Dialog, therapeutic, 79, 122, 167
Direct compliment, definition of, 186
Disconnection and Rejection, 138
Discourse sensitivity, 167
Discrimination with clients, 46, 69
Discussion and implications, in research and practice, 230
Disqualifying the Positive, 133
Distancing, definition of, 136
Distortions in thinking, 133
Distressing situations, coping with, 134
Diversity and relational theory, 125
DSM-IV (*see* Diagnostic and Statistical Manual of Mental Disorders (DSM-IV)
DSM-IV-TR (*see* Diagnostic and Statistical Manual of Mental Disorders (DSM-IV)
Documents, therapeutic, 174
Do Something Different strategy, 189, 194
Dream question, 196
Dual relationships, 16–17
Dyslexia, 204

E

Ecomaps, 175
example of, 178f
Editorial reflection, 186

Educational/learning history of client, 48, 58
Ego functions, 50t–51t
Ego weakness, object loss and, 85
Elderly clients and self-psychology, 46, 47, 104
Electronic media and confidentiality, 23
Eliciting stance in postmodern therapy, 171
Ellis, Albert, 131–134
Emotional deprivation, dysfunctional thoughts and, 138
Emotional inhibition, dysfunctional thoughts and, 141
Emotional Reasoning, 133
Empathy, 4f–7f
  biases and, 15
  clinical agendas, 9
  confrontations, 87
  in cultural relational theory, 122
  interpersonal, 93
  relationship, 7t
  in self-psychology, 5t, 6t, 7t, 9, 89, 100, 114
  suicidal clients and, 17
Empirical evidence, 164–165
Empirically supported treatments (ESTs), 215
Empowering the client, 6f, 127, 152, 182, 188–190, 196
Ending phase of treatment, 42–44
Enmeshment/undeveloped self, dysfunctional thoughts and, 139
Entitlement/self-centeredness, dysfunctional thoughts and, 140
Environmental influence, 84–84
Equifinality, definition of, 199
Eriksen, H., 77
Ethics and boundaries, 15–17
  confidentiality, 19, 23
  dual relationships, 16–17
  in managed care, 20–22
  NASW Code of Ethics, 22
  overview, 27
  religion and spirituality, 25
  sexual relationships, 15–16
  suicide threats, 17–20
  therapist self-care, 25–26
  violations, 21
Ethnocentric monoculturalism, 66
Evidence-based social work practice (EBP), 214–217
  recommendations for, 216–217
Evidence, empirical, 164–165
Exception questions in solution-focused therapy, 185
Executive function disorders, 204
Expectations, 91–92
Experience
  subjective, 82–83
Experience questions in reauthoring in narrative therapy, 172, 180, 181
Exploring client's dialog, 4f, 74 (*see also* Skilled dialog)
Expressive arts therapies, 173
Externalizing conversations in narrative therapy, 168
Extinction of behaviors, 153

F

FAP (functional analytic psychotherapy), 164
Faculty field advisor, 10
Failure, 139
Fairbairn, Ronald, 84–85
Faith or beliefs, 49
Family background and history of client, 47–49, 57, 91
Family sessions, 55, 188, 205 (*see also* Solution-focused therapy)
Family story, 175–181
  diagram, 177f
Fee-for-service payment structure, 24
FICA assessment, 49–50
First meeting with client, 28–29
  in brief treatment, 13–14
Focusing on the Negative, 133
Follow-up, of initial interviews, 38–39
Formula First Session Task (FFST), 186
Fortune Telling, 133
Freud, Sigmund, 32, 33, 86, 129, 199
Friends of clients, 16
Functional dependence/incompetence, 139

G

Generations or waves, 152–153, 159–160
Genograms, 175, 176f
  example of, 176f
Global assessment of functioning (GAF) scale, 12, 21, 54, 59, 61
Global economy, social work in, 25
Goaling, 194
Goal setting, 157
  in behavior therapy, 157
  in Psychosocial therapy, 54–55
  in solution-focused therapy, 188
  in time-limited dynamic psychotherapy, 92–93
Guntrip, Harry, 85

H

Health Insurance Portability and Accountability Act (HIPAA), 23
Heterotypic continuity, definition of, 199, 210–212
Holistic approach, 129
Home visit, 179–180
Homework in behavior therapy, 157
Human Rights Commission, 45
  Universal Declaration of, 45
Human rights perspective, 45–46, 47
  principles, 45–46
Hyperactivity, 61

I

IBCT (integrative behavioral couples therapy), 164
Idealizing self-object, 99
Individual, define, 174
Identification, in Object Relations Theory, 87
Imagery, 133–134, 137
Immigrants and refugees as clients, 71–71
Impaired Autonomy and Performance, 139
Impaired Limits, 139–140
Impulsivity, 61
Indirect compliment, definition of, 186
Influence and importance, in religion, 49
Insight, in mental status exam, 52, 58
Insufficient self-control/self-discipline, 140
Integration of research and practice, 214–235
  evidence-based practice, 214–217
  qualitative research, 222–224
  research methods, 217–219
  single-system design methodology, 217–219
Integrative journal, 2–8
  process recording, 3, 8
  example of, 3–7

Integrative model for clinical social work practice, 1–11
  clinical supervision, 8–10
  evaluation and research, 10–11
  evidence-based practice, 1–2
  faculty field advisor, 10
  journaling, 2–8
  overview, 11
  practice class laboratory, 2
  process recording, example of, 4–7f
  Interaction-driven techniques in relational theory, 1, 8
Interdisciplinary collaboration with other professionals, 189
Internal object(s), 82, 83, 84
  child abuse, 83
  internalized oppression, 83
  interpersonal relationships and, 85–86
  oppression and, 83–84
Internalized bad object, 84–85
Internalized good object, 85
International social work agenda, 25
Interpretation, 4f
Intersubjectivity, definition of, 116
Intervention planning, example, 38
Interventions, 143–144, 157
  in behavior therapy, 157
  in positive psychology, 143–144
Interviewing client (*see* Clinical interview)
Intrapsychic relational processes, 4, 70, 82–83, 101, 115
Introductions with client, 29
Introjection and self-blame, 84, 93–94
Irrational beliefs/ideas, 133–135f
  defined, 132
Isolation/alienation, dysfunctional thoughts and, 139

J

Jamaica, West Indies, study of violence in, 224–230
Jamaica Association of Social Workers, 78, 224
Joiner, T., 19
Joining techniques in relational theory, 122, 196
Journaling, 2–8
Judgment, in mental status exam, 52, 58
Jumping to Conclusions and Negative Nonsequitures, 133

K

Klee, T., 87–88
Klein, Melanie, 82–83
Kohut, Heinz, 99–104

L

Labeling and Overgeneralization, 133
Language of narrative, 167
Learning alliance and clinical supervision, 8–10
  agenda for, 8–9
  examples, 9–10
Learning disorders, 204
  in children and adolescents, 38, 48, 52, 54, 102–103, 204
  self-psychology and, 101–104
Lesser, J. G., 70, 72
Letter written by therapist, 175, 177, 179–181
Life story of client, 78, 166, 167, 172, 173
Listening to the client, 4f
"Little Turtle Story, The," 155
Loss, feelings of when terminating treatment, 14, 112

M

Maintenance, in Transtheoretical Model, 35
Major Depression, 21
Maladaptive thought processes, 87
Managed care, 20–22
  choice of provider, 24
  coaching, 22–23
  confidentiality and technology, 23
  ethical dilemmas in, 20–22
  fee-for-service payment structure, 24
  global economy, social work in, 25
  opportunities, 22
  social work, 22–23
  spirituality and religion, 25
Mandated clients, 191
Markens, Jennifer Cass, 97
Marriage diagram, example of, 177f
Matching stance in postmodern therapy, 171
Maturity in self-psychology, definition of, 100
Meaning making, 187, 194
  of client's narrative, 167–169
  in family story, 187
Medical history of client, 48, 58
Memoing, definition of, 224
Mental status and current functioning of client, 50–53, 58–59
  ego function, 50t–51t
  mechanisms of defense, 51t
  exam, 51–52
  categories for, 52
Metaframe, 70
Middle phase of treatment, 14, 107–108
  obstacle to progress, 39, 40–42, 94–95
Mindfulness, 14–15, 117
  -based cognitive theory, 159
  relational, 117
Minimization, 133
Miracle question in solution-focused therapy, 184–185, 190
Mirroring, 5f, 7f
  sought by children, 99, 101–102, 207
Mistrust/abuse, dysfunctional thoughts and, 97, 139
Mixed-eclectic approach to brief treatment, 13, 37
Mood, in mental status exam, 52, 58
Motor activity, in mental status exam, 52, 58
Mixed-methods research, 230–235
Mother–child relationship, 85
Mother–daughter relationship, 122–123
Multiaxial diagnosis, 54
Multicultural practice, 65–81
  case studies, 74–77
  considerations in, 90
  culturally competent case, 66–67
  culturally specific case, 72–73f, 78–81
  cultural trauma, 68–69
  elements of, 67–68
  narrative therapy approach to, 70, 74, 77
  overview, 81
  therapist roles in, 69–70
  transnational immigrants and, 71–72
  treatment models, 70–71
  value system, 65–66
  worldviews of, 67

Multifinality, definition of, 199
Mutual empathy and cultural relational theory, 122
Musturbation, 132

N

Narcissistic needs, 15, 100
Narrative letter written by therapist, 175, 177, 179–181
Narrative Means to Therapeutic Ends, 166
Narrative theater (NT), 182–183
Narrative therapy, 166–183
  case study, 170, 175–181
  collective narrative practice, 182
  constructivism and, 74
  conversations, externalizing, 169
  cross-cultural counseling, 174
  deconstruction of, 168–169
  definitional ceremony in, 173, 182
  framework, 200–204
  language in, 167
  in multicultural case, 70, 74, 77
  narrative theater, 182–183
  overview, 183
  positions, 172–173
  postmodern approach, 166
  reauthoring, 171–172
  relational narrative therapy (*see also* Relational theory)
  research perspectives, 183
  structure of, 167–168
  therapeutic documents, 174
  therapeutic strategies, 171
NASW Code of Ethics, 15, 16, 22, 25
  Committee for the Study and Prevention of Violence Against Social Workers, 27
  Website, 27
National Association of Social Workers (NASW), 15–16
Native Oriented/Traditional, in multicultural clinical practice, 67
Naturalistic inquire (*see* Qualitative research)
Negativity/Pessimism, 141
New meaning, making, 171
Nonverbal learning disabilities, 204

O

Object loss and ego weakness, 85
Object relations theory, 82–98
  brief treatment and, 88–90
  case example, 90–97
  of Fairbairn, Ronald, 84–85
  of Guntrip, Harry, 85
  Interpersonal School, 86–87
  of Klein, Melanie, 82–84
  overview, 98
  research perspectives, 98
  stages in, 87–88
  therapeutic relationship and, 86–87
  of Winnicott, Donald, 85-85
Observational learning and social learning theory, 153
Observation of self, 160
Observational task, 194
Obsessive-compulsive disorder, case study, 161–164
Obstacle to progress in middle stage of treatment, 39, 40–42, 94–95
Oppositional defiant disorder (ODD), case study, 210–213
Oppression, cultural, 67
Orientation, in mental status exam, 52
Other Directedness, 140
Overvigilance and Inhibition, 141

P

Parent involvement in child's therapy, 63, 212–213
Parents and adolescent turmoil, 102, 103
Partnering–self-object relationship, 7f, 46, 99 (*see also* Twinship)
Pavlov, Ivan,
Perfectionism, 133
Perry, Ariel, 208
Personal history of client, 48, 57
Personal questions, answering, 30–31
Person-in-environment perspective, 24
Phonyism, 133
Play therapy, 204–208
  case study, 206–208
Positioning in narrative therapy, 173
Positive consequences, 195
Positive psychology, 142–144
  interventions, 143–144
Positive reinforcement in behavior therapy, 158
Postassessment and self-reflection, 187
Post-traumatic stress, 190–191
Post-traumatic slavery disorder (PTSlaveryD), 68
Preliminary Diagnosis of Relational Pattern, in Object Relations Theory, 87
Preparation, in Transtheoretical Model, 34, 41
Precontemplation, in Transtheoretical Model, 34
Prediction strategy, 18, 174, 189
Prediction Task, 189
Pretend the Miracle Happened strategy, 189
Probing stance in postmodern therapy, 171
Problem of client
  defining and clarifying, 46, 187
  history and presentation of, 47–50, 90
Problematic behaviors and behavior therapy, 156–157
Problem-solving models of brief treatment, 13, 187
Problem-tracking questions in solution-focus therapy, 186
Process recordings, 3–8
Projective identification, definition of, 83
Protection of health information, 23
Psychic reality as relational matrix, 115
Psychodynamic brief treatment, 13, 105–114
Psychological thermometer, 219
Psychosocial study, preparation of, 45–64
  case example, 55–64
  DSM-IV-based diagnosis in, 53
  histories and family backgrounds in, 47–50
  human rights perspective, 45–46, 47
  identification of information, 46
  mental status, functioning, and exam in, 50–53
  model outline, 46–55
  multiaxial diagnosis in, 54
  problem in, presentation and history of, 47
  referral source in, 47
  summary section of report, 55
  treatment recommendations, goals, and evaluation plan in, 54–55
Psychotherapy process research, 215–216
Punishment in behavior therapy, 158
Punitiveness, 141

Q
Qualitative research, 222–224
case study, 224–230
data collection and analysis, 223–224
knowledge construction, 223
researcher as instrument, 223
Questions from client
answering, 30
personal questions, answering, 30–31

R
Rajab, M. H., 19,
Randomized clinical trials (RCTs), 164
Rational, defined, 132
Rational emotive therapy (RET), 131–134
Rational self-statements, 133
Real relationship, 33, 40
definition of, 33
Reason for client's visit, 192, 203
Reassuring the client, 4f, 14, 58, 134
Reauthoring in narrative therapy, 171–172
Reciprocal determinism and social learning theory, 153
Records, 146f, 149f, 151f
Referral of clients, 35
Referral source of client, 35, 47
Reflecting stance in postmodern therapy, 171
Reinforcement for change in behavior therapy, 157
Relapse prevention and behavior therapy, 157
Relational theory, 115–128
case studies, 117–121, 123–127
cultural, 122–123
diversity and, 125
intersubjectivity, 115–117
mindfullness, 117
overview, 128
techniques of, 115–117, 122-123
third space, 116
transference and countertransference, 32–33, 115–117
women and, 117–121, 123–127
Relationship, 122
Relationship authenticity and cultural relational theory, 122
Relationship differentiation and cultural relational theory, 122
Relaxation training, 159
Religion and spirituality, 25, 49–50, 58
of client, 49–50
in social work practice, 25
Research and practice, integrating (*see* Integration of research and practice)
Research methods, for practitioners, 217–219
Research perspectives, 12–13
in behavior therapy, 160
in brief therapy, 12-13
in cognitive therapy, 130, 160
in narrative therapy, 183
in object relations therapy, 98
in solution-focused therapy, 196–197
Research study in Jamaica, West Indies, 230
case study, 224–230
Resistance, 33-34
definition of, 33
to treatment, 33–34
Respondent conditioning, 153
Response, therapists example, 36–37
Retellings of life story of client, 171, 173
Reward systems, 210
Risk assessment, 18 (*see also* Safety)
categories, 19t
Role-plays, 112–113, 137, 189
Rudd, M. D., 18
Ruled out (R/O), diagnosis, 54

S
Safety, 18–20
of social workers, 27
of suicidal clients, 18–20
Saturation, definition of, 224
Scaling questions, 7t, 194
in solution-focused therapy, 185
Schema theory, 138–141
Selection criteria for brief treatment, 13, 15
Self-awareness, in clinical interviews, 29, 159
Self-blame and introjection, 84, 93–94
Self-care of therapist, 25–26
Self-compassion, 25–26
Self-control/self-discipline, dysfunctional thoughts and, 140
Self-determination of client, 25, 196, 215, 217
Self-efficacy, 153
behavior therapy, 153
social learning theory, 153
Self-empathy and cultural relational theory, 122
Self-esteem, 6f
case study, 106, 109, 111
of client, 104
problems associated with children and adolescents, 62, 83, 85, 103
Self-harm, in adolescents, 103–104
Self-help form, in cognitive theory, 136f
Self-in-relation model, 122–123
Self-instructional training, 155
Self-management strategies, 155–156
Self-object, 4f, 6f, 7f, 99–102
definition of, 4, 99
introjection, 92
needs of children and adolescents, 4, 99–100
parental, 102–103
Self observation, 160
Self-psychology, 99–114
brief treatment and, 88
case example, 104–114
children and adolescents, 101–104
elderly clients and, 46, 47, 104
empathy in, 5f, 6f, 7f, 8, 100
learning disorders, 102–103
overview, 114
self-esteem group case, 6f, 10, 62
self-harm, 103–104
sex-change case, 106–109
as theoretical framework, 99–104
therapist role in, 25–27, 100–101
Self-reflection, 187, 195
postassessment and, 187, 195
of students, 4f–7f, 8
of therapist, 25, 186
of worker's, 46
Self-sacrifice, dysfunctional thoughts and, 140
Self-statements, 41, 133, 155, 161
Separating techniques in relational theory, 88

Severe conduct disorder, 35
Sexual relationships with clients, 15–16
Shame and concept of bad object, 84
Single-session solutions, 14
Single-subject design (SSD) methodology, 160, 217–219
SIT (*see* Stress Inoculation Training, (SIT)
Skilled dialog, components and skills, 78–80
Skinner, B. F., 152–153
SMART approach, 169
Social class of client, 49, 58
Social isolation/alienation, dysfunctional thoughts and, 139
Social justice, 47
Social learning theory, 153, 154, 160
Social skills training and behavior therapy, 158
Sociocultural dissonance, 68
Solomon, Helen, 64
Solution-focused therapy, 184–197
  case study, 191–196
  crisis intervention, 196
  brief therapy, 190–191
  editorial reflection, 186
  family assessment in, 187–188
  mandated clients, 191
  origins and framework for, 184–185
  overview, 197
  postassessment and self-reflection, 187
  postmodern approach, 184–186
  research perspectives, 196–197
  strategies of, 189–191
  trauma, 190–191
Solution-oriented family assessment, 187–188
Speech, in mental status exam, 52
Spirituality and religion, 25, 49–50
  of client, 49–50
  FICA assessment, 49–50
  in social work practice, 25
Splitting, process of, 83
Stages, in Object Relations Theory, 87–88
Stages of change, 34–44
  action, 34
  beginning, 28–31
  case examples, 35-38, 40–42
  contemplation, 34, 40–41
  end, 28, 42–43
  maintenance, 35
  middle, 28, 39–40, 44
  precontemplation, 34
  preparation, 34, 41
  termination, 35, 42–44
  in Transtheoretical Model, 34–35
Stress Inoculation Training, (SIT), 156
Structured approach of cognitive theory, 130–131
Student, learning alliance in, 9
Subjugation, dysfunctional thoughts and, 140
  of emotions, 140
  of needs, 140
Suicidal clients, 17–20
  assessment guidelines, 17–18
  children and adolescents, 20
  risk categories, 18–19t
  safety of, 18–20
Suicide risk assessment interview, 18–19 (*see also* Clinical risk assessment)
  guidelines for, 17–18
Sullivan, Henry Stack, 86–87
Summary section of psychosocial study, 62
Supervision, learning alliance in, 9–10
Support, 6f
Symbolic immortality, 69
Systematic, 152

T

Target behaviors, definition of, 154
Technology
  tracking changes, 3
  Microsoft Word, 3
  confidentiality and, 23
  HIPAA and, 23
  Writing process recording, 3
Temper tantrums, case study, 209f
Termination of treatment, 35, 42–44, 88, 181
Theme-specific sociogram, 203
Therapeutic alliance, 14, 15, 87, 98, 215
  authenticity of, 33
  significance of, 33
Therapeutic documents in narrative therapy, 174
Therapeutic relationship in behavior therapy, 160
  obsessive-compulsive disorder, 161–164
  self-management strategies, 154–156
Therapeutic relationship in clinical interview, 31–34
  countertransference, 32–33
  "real" relationship, 33
  resistance, 33–34
  transference, 32
  using in practice, 34
  working alliances, 14, 33
Therapeutic relationship in narrative therapy, 171
Therapeutic relationship in Object Relations Theory, 96–97
Therapeutic strategies in postmodern therapy, 171, 184–186
Therapist
  confrontations, in Object Relations Theory, 87–88
  cross-cultural, roles of, 69
  multicultural role of, 69–70
  role in self-psychology, 25–27, 100–101
  self-care, 25–26
Therapist–family relationship patterns, 187–188
Thinking, disturbances in, 132–134
  examples, 133
Third-party insurers, 21
Third-space, 116
Thought, in mental status exam, 52, 58, 59
Thoughts of client, examples of charts, 146f, 149f, 151f
Time-limited dynamic psychotherapy (TLDP), 88–90
  assumptions, 89
Time-limited therapy (*see also* Brief treatment)
Time out as negative reinforcer, 158
Tokens for good behavior, 158, 210
Traditional behavior therapy, 152–153
Transcription of interviews, 223
Transference, 32–33
  definition of, 32
  in psychoanalytic therapy, 32
  in relational therapy, 32–33, 116
Transactonal/marginal, in multicultural clinical practice, 67
Transitional object, 86
"Transmuting internalization", 99, 101
Transtheoretical, 34

Trauma bonding, 84–85
Trauma
  bonding, 84–85
  cultural, 68–69
  sample study, 60–61, 62, 63
  in solution-focused brief therapy, 190–191
Treatment guidelines
  providers' contributions to developing, 215
  therapy with survivors, 190–191
Treatment, 92–93
  in time-limited dynamic psychotherapy, 92–93
  psychosocial study, 54–55
Trying-on, in self-instructional training, 155
Twinship–self-object relationship, 6f, 7f, 99, 101, 102, 104, 106–109

U
United Nations (UN), 45
Unrelenting/unbalanced standards, 141

V
Validating the client, 7f
Values, 65–66, 160
Violence, case study, 224–230
Visitors, family members as, 188
Vulnerability to harm and illness, dysfunctional thoughts and, 139

W
WALMYR Assessment Scales (WAS), 218
Waves or generations, 152–153, 159–160
Winnicott, Donald, 85–86
Women
  brief psychology and, 110–114
  groups and cultural relational theory, 123–127
  support group, 123–127
Working alliance, 14, 33
Working-through stage, 38
Worldview of client, 66